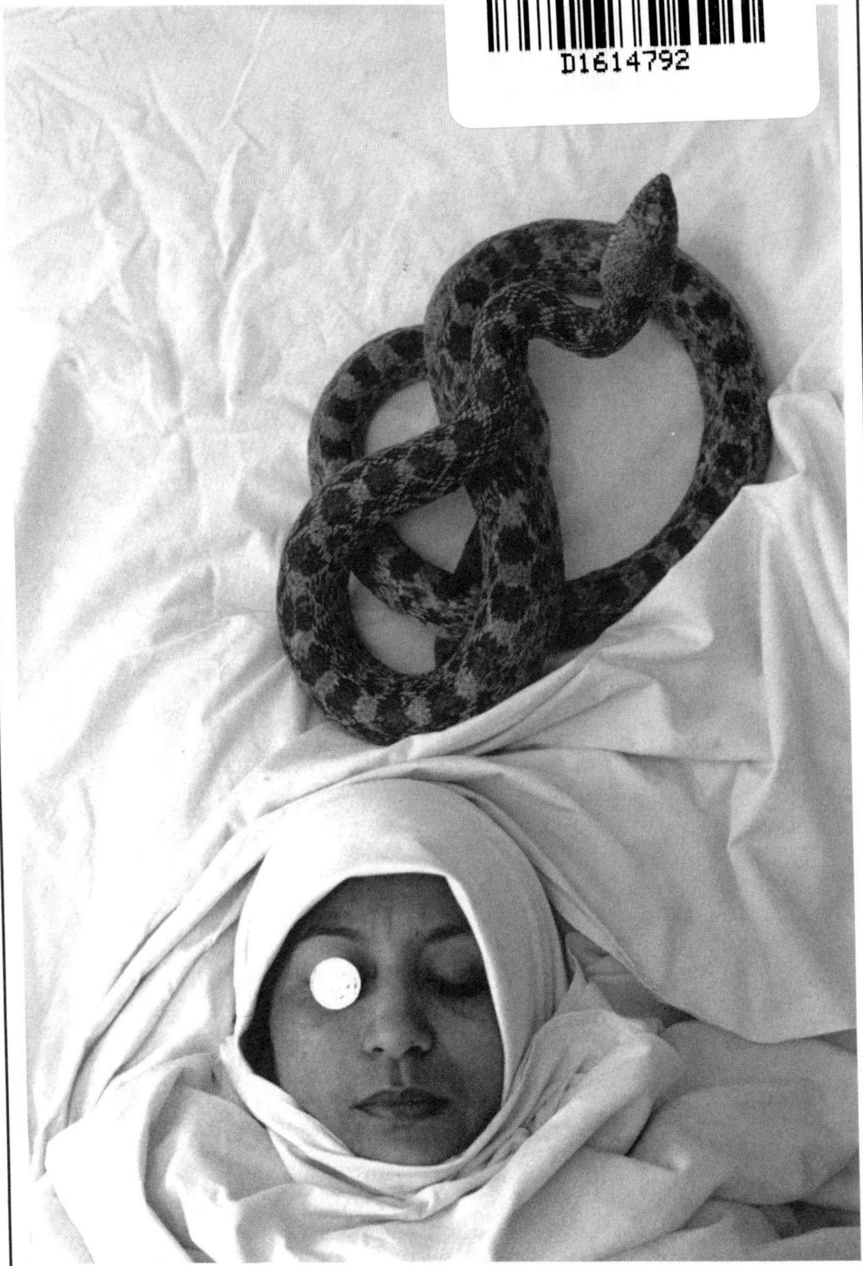

Photograph by George Hallett (p.xxviii) for the cover of the collection of short stories *Wives, Talismans and the Dead* by I.N.C. Aniebo (p. 56)

Photograph by George Hallett for the cover of *Climbié* by Bernard B. Dadié (p.7)

Africa Writes Back

& The African Writers Series the Launch of African Literature

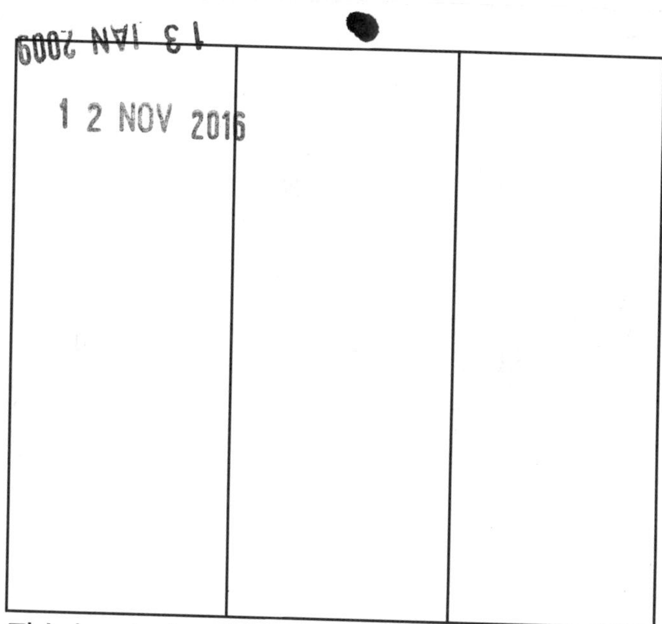

Dedicated to the writers without whom there would have been no African Writers Series

Africa Writes Back

& The African Writers Series the Launch of African Literature

James Currey

Portraits and other photographs
by George Hallett

HEBN
IBADAN

James Currey
OXFORD

EAEP
NAIROBI

Wits University Press
JOHANNESBURG

Weaver Press
HARARE

Ohio University Press
ATHENS

Mkuki na Nyota
DAR ES SALAAM

James Currey Ltd
73 Botley Road
Oxford OX2 0BS
www.jamescurrey.co.uk

Wits University Press
University of the Witwatersrand
1 Jan Smuts Avenue
Johannesburg 2001
www.witspress.wits.ac.za

Ohio University Press
19 Circle Drive, The Ridges
Athens, Ohio 45701
www.ohioswallow.com

Weaver Press
Box A1922
Avondale, Harare
www.weaverpresszimbabwe.com

East African Educational Publishers Ltd
P.O. Box 45314, Nairobi
www.eastafricanpublishers.com

HEBN Ltd
P.M.B. 5205
Ibadan
www.hebnpublishers.com

Mkuki na Nyota
P.O. Box 4246
Dar es Salaam
www.mkukinanyota.com

First published 2008
1 2 3 4 5 12 11 10 09 08

British Library Cataloguing in Publication Data

Currey, James
Africa writes back : the African writers series & the launch of African literature
1. Heinemann Educational Books 2. African writers series - History 3. African literature - Publishing - History - 20th century 4. African literature - 20th century - History and criticism 5. African literature (English) - Publishing - History - 20th century 6. African literature (English) - 20th century - History and criticism 7. Africa - Intellectual life - 20th century
I. Title
070.5'096
ISBN 978-1-84701-503-7 (James Currey cloth)
ISBN 978-1-84701-502-0 (James Currey paper)

Library of Congress Cataloging-in-Publication Data available upon request

ISBN 10: 0-8214-1842-4 (Ohio University Press cloth)
ISBN 13: 978-0-8214-1842-0 (Ohio University Press cloth)
ISBN 10: 0-8214-1843-2 (Ohio University Press paper)
ISBN 13: 978-0-8214-1843-7 (Ohio University Press paper)
ISBN 978-1-77922-075-2 (Weaver Press paper)
ISBN 978-1-86814-472-3 (Wits University Press paper)
ISBN 978-978081-202-7 (HEBN paper)

Preparation for typesetting
Penny Butler
Typesetting
Kate Kirkwood
Cover & Jacket preparation
Glenda Pattenden
Proofreading
Lynn Taylor & Clare Currey
Indexing
Margaret Cornell

Typeset in 10.5/11.5 Monotype Bembo
by Long House, Cumbria
Printed in South Africa

Contents

Foreword

The African Writers Series files are now held in the University of Reading library (RUL MS 8221). The archivist Mike Bott persuaded several of the leading British publishers to lodge their archives with him, creating a key resource on British twentieth-century writing and publishing.

I started by examining the publishing correspondence with some of the most outstanding authors who appeared in the Series; they were also the writers of vivid letters. I have focused in particular on eight writers who have gained international recognition. The correspondence with Bessie Head, Nuruddin Farah and Dambudzo Marechera is singularly rich. The files show something of the way in which Ngũgĩ and Henry Chakava developed publishing in the languages of East Africa as well as in English. The correspondence with Mazisi Kunene, Alex la Guma and Dennis Brutus is interlocked with the liberation struggle in South Africa. Letters, reports and three-line notes from Chinua Achebe are scattered through the files of the many other writers who are part of the extraordinary Series of which he was the Founding Editor.

The intention of the book is to provide a narrative of how the African Writers Series came together. The shape emerged from the writers and the adventurousness of their writing. It is a study of the publishing process working in unprecedented conditions. The book provides evidence of the ways in which estimation by a publisher of the work of writers grows and, sadly on occasion, diminishes. The book gives examples of how the views of publishers and their advisers emerge as they consider a new manuscript, and then coalesce and change as they assess further work by the same author. The initial discussion is literary but then reflects practical and political realities. Decisions can then be affected by the economics of the firm and the publishing industry at the time. Selective quotations are used to reveal what has emerged from the files rather than what the 'conspirators' (p. 24) think they remember. Needless to say, memories do play a lively part.

Acknowledgements

I should like above all to acknowledge the help of Mike Bott, who was the Librarian in charge of the Archive in the University of Reading who built up their renowned publishing collection. The African Writers Series files were the first to be catalogued after Heinemann Educational Books lodged their collection. His help and enthusiasm helped me start on this project. On my visits to Reading Verity Andrews handled my requests with the most helpful and warming good cheer. I am grateful to Robert Sulley, who, when International Director of Heinemann Educational Books, gave authorisation to Mike Bott to allow me access to this historic collection.

It was in 2000 at the conference at Bard College celebrating Chinua Achebe's seventieth birthday that I realised that many people there had little idea of the importance of the vital role he played in pushing Heinemann to the limits in their selection of work for the African Writers Series.

I have shown the detailed sections on Publishing Chinua Achebe, Ngũgĩ, Nuruddin Farah and Dennis Brutus to those authors as I draw heavily on their lively letters and other writing in the Archive. I have had the enthusiastic support of the Bessie Head Foundation in Botswana. Sadly Mazisi Kunene, honoured as the first poet laureate of South Africa, died during work on this book and before I was able to send him a draft of the section on publishing the translations of his work in Zulu. This pioneering generation is passing; Cyprian Ekwensi, Mongo Beti and Sembene Ousmane are among those who have died during the writing of this book. We are all indebted to Flora Veit-Wild for her remarkable work on Dambudzo Marechera.

The section on publishing and selling the African Writers Series (pp. xiii–xxvii) shows the commitment of so many of my colleagues at Heinemann to the co-operative success of the African Writers Series. Keith Sambrook, Aig Higo, Henry Chakava, John Watson and Tom Seavey gave time and exceptional attention to the manuscript as it developed. Working with Penny Butler on the preparation of the manuscript for press has brought back many of the memories of the years when we worked together. For all of us Alan Hill is an enthusiastic presence. The contributions of many other colleagues are recorded in the preliminary section on Publishing and Selling the African Writers Series.

I have known what it is to have understanding publishers in the detailed work by Gill Berchowitz of Ohio University Press, whose publishing apprenticeship was with Oxford University Press and Ravan in South Africa. Veronica Klipp of Wits University Press, and formerly of KwaZulu-Natal University Press has backed this book because she feels that it will show many South Africans what they were missing when cut apart from Africa to their north. My colleague Douglas Johnson used long train journeys to pencil my draft heavily and, with his knowledge of Sudan and North Africa, it was of particular interest to discuss with him the problems of translation which we faced in running Arab Authors. The detailed work Lynn Taylor and I did together on *The Companion to African Literatures* has been of constant value in the preparation of this book. Valuable reports and detailed corrections have come from Clive Wake, Bernth Lindfors, Christopher Heywood and Mike Kirkwood. David and Marie Philip not only gave us repeated hospitality but also had early drafts inflicted on them.

Kate Kirkwood, in typesetting this book, has worked co-operatively with me as I have developed and changed the design of this book in a self-indulgent manner.

The mixed experiences of Clare Currey and our children probably are most vividly revealed in the chapter on Dambudzo Marechera. Airmail letters kept between her and me have been an atmospheric resource in writing this book, especially as she is good at using dates. Much of the demanding labour of preparation and checking of this manuscript and proofs has depended on her ever reliable support.

The Companion to African Literatures

Opinions from G.D. Killam's and Ruth Rowe's *The Companion to African Literatures* (James Currey and Indiana University Press 2000) have been used to give some impression of the way in which the writers selected for the Series have come to be regarded at the turn of the century. The collection and editing of *The Companion* involved many of the people who had been integral to the growth of the Series and to the establishment of African literature. Quite a few of the contributors had been, as publishers' advisers, among the first people to consider the work of those then unknown authors.

The references to *The Companion* in this book will be taken usually from the relevant alphabetical entry by author or book title. A page reference shows that the quotation comes from general entries on 'Topics and Themes'.

Ngũgĩ on a rainy day in 1979 outside Heinemann's three publishing houses in Bedford Square, where the Publishers' Association and many publishers were neighbours. The editorial offices of the African Writers Series were on the second floor

The dining room in the Heinemann basement which was much used to entertain visiting authors from Africa and to have meetings with other publishers such as André Deutsch (p.15).
Kole Omotoso (*right*) from Nigeria in discussion with Meja Mwangi from Kenya.
(*Bottom*) From left to right; Meja Mwangi, Cosmo Pieterse, James Currey, Marguerite Omotoso, unrecognised, Christie Archer

Publishing & Selling the African Writers Series

In references initials are used for Keith Sambrook (KS), Aig Higo (AH), James Currey (JC) and Henry Chakava (HC).
Alan Hill's name is used in full because he shares the same initials with Aig Higo.
When the work of a particular author is discussed in detail initials are used e.g. Chinua Achebe (CA).

Alan Hill

Alan Hill was as proud of setting up the African Writers Series as anything else he did in an outstanding publishing career in which he built up Heinemann Educational Books to be the largest educational publisher in the Commonwealth.

Chinua Achebe said in an interview in the *Paris Review* (p. 28), 'Other publishers thought it was mad, that this was crazy. But that was how the African Writers Series came into existence. In the end, Alan Hill was made a Commander of the British Empire for bringing into existence a body of literature they said was among the biggest developments in British literature of this century.'

Alan Hill was born in 1912 at Barwell in Leicestershire. His father was a schoolteacher who later worked for the National Union of Teachers. He was educated at Wyggeston Grammar School and read English at Jesus College, Cambridge. He joined the nascent education department at William Heinemann in 1936. During the second world war he served as a Squadron Leader in the RAF. After the war he built up the Heinemann education list. In 1959 he was sent by the Publishers' Association on a tour of South Africa and West African countries. West Africa became one of his first overseas targets. In 1960 Heinemann Educational Books was established as a separate company within the Heinemann Group of Publishers. He was later to become managing director of the whole group; he retired in 1979.

He lived in the Hampstead Garden Suburb which was much favoured by the professional left who made the welfare state a reality in Britain. Keith Sambrook not only shared his Leicestershire and Cambridge origins but lived round the corner in 'the Suburb'. Whenever necessary Keith Sambrook would ask Alan Hill for a lift into the office in the morning; over the years Alan Hill's support for quite a few new writers was obtained while waiting in the traffic jams of North London.

Chinua Achebe's 'conspirators' in the launch of African literature. (*Top*) Keith Sambrook, Alan Hill and James Currey with Cyprian Ekwensi, in Ibadan early 1980s. (*Photo Aig Higo*) (*Middle*) Aig Higo at Bob Markham's house on his first morning in East Africa, with James Currey (left) and Bob Markham, February 1973. (*Photo Clare Currey*) (*Bottom*) Henry Chakava in James Currey's office during his training period at 48 Charles Street in 1973; the posters are for the South African meeting at the Africa Centre (p.88). (*Photo Satoru Tsuchiya, the translator of work by Mazisi Kunene and Amos Tutuola into Japanese*)

Alan Hill asked Chinua Achebe to write the preface to his autobiography *In Pursuit of Publishing* (John Murray 1988, p. ix). Chinua Achebe said: 'What makes Alan Hill's counsel so indispensable … is that he actually believes that publishing can be high-minded, adventurous and profitable. And has proved it.'

Keith Sambrook

Keith Sambrook found the final manuscript of Ngũgĩ's *Weep Not, Child* on his desk when, on 1 January 1963, he started work with Alan Hill at Heinemann Educational Books. A month earlier Chinua Achebe had been appointed as Editorial Adviser to the African Writers Series. The first 30 titles they selected were to shape the development of African literature. Keith Sambrook and Chinua Achebe shared two ambitions; they wanted students in African schools and universities to be able to read imaginative work by Africans; and they were determined to introduce African writers to an international literary audience.

Keith Sambrook established companies in Nigeria and East Africa; they contributed to the effective marketing which made the Series profitable enough to experiment with new writing. At the same time he built up companies in Hong Kong, Singapore, Malaysia, India, the Caribbean and the US. HEB Inc, the company he established with John Watson in New Hampshire was, with imaginative marketing by Tom Seavey, to be crucial for new publishing in the Series when the sales within Africa disappeared during the 'African book famine' of the late 1980s and early 1990s. Keith Sambrook took on the first titles in the growth area of English-language teaching; by the time the list was sold it had an annual turnover of over £30 million.

Keith Sambrook was educated at Loughborough Grammar School in Leicestershire. A credit in Higher Certificate Mathematics equipped him to work constructively with generations of corporate accountants as Heinemann Educational Books expanded.

While in the Royal Navy from 1943 to 1947, he was on one of the northern convoys to Russia and also spent 18 months in the Mediterranean. He read English at Jesus College, Cambridge from 1947 to 1950. His first appointment in publishing was with Manchester University Press, where from 1950 he worked on the list of academic titles in the social sciences. The pioneering sociological and anthropological publications of the Rhodes-Livingstone Institute in Northern Rhodesia were among his responsibilities.

In 1954 he joined the renowned Edinburgh publishing and printing company of Thomas Nelson. In the period of high colonialism, before, during and after the second world war, the firm had worked with enterprising educational officers to produce textbooks which were relevant to the needs of the Caribbean and Africa. He worked on all levels of school and student textbooks for use in overseas markets. He spent the year of 1956/7 on the campus at Legon establishing the University College of the Gold Coast Press at the time of the Suez crisis and Ghanaian independence. At that time Nelson published several books by

President Nkrumah. The following year Keith Sambrook moved to Lagos where he set up a local publishing office in Nelson's Nigerian branch. He then worked for Nelson back in Britain.

Aig Higo

It was thanks to the team of Aigboje Higo and Chinua Achebe that writing from West Africa dominated the first decade of the series. They captured, against several longer-established publishing rivals, many of the outstanding authors.

Aig Higo was born in 1932 in the mid-west of Nigeria and educated at St Andrew's College, Oyo. He trained as a teacher and then, after starting his career, won a scholarship to go to University College, Ibadan. A poet himself, he was a fellow student of writers such as Chinua Achebe, J.P. Clark, Christopher Okigbo, John Munonye and Elechi Amadi. His poetry was selected for the first two substantial verse anthologies: *Penguin Modern Poetry from Africa* and John Reed and Clive Wake's *A Book of African Verse* in the African Writers Series. While teaching at St Andrew's, Oyo, he took an active part with Chinua Achebe and others in the pioneering Mbari Club. He went to the University of Leeds to do postgraduate work in literature under the enterprising Professor A. Norman Jeffares. He then became headmaster of the Anglican Grammar School at Otuo in the mid-west. It was Derry Jeffares who, describing him as one of the best of his recent MA students, suggested to Keith Sambrook that Aig Higo might well be interested in becoming a publisher.

Aig Higo became manager and publisher of Heinemann Educational Books (Nigeria) in January 1965. Keith Sambrook's story of his appointment is in the Nigeria chapter (p. 4). In the Heinemann tradition, although an arts graduate, he proved to be an enterprising science publisher with the publication of the Nigerian Integrated Science Project. By 1972 the business had grown so much that he determined that it was essential to make the heavy investment needed to build a warehouse. He took close personal control of the design of the most elegant warehouse in the publishers' enclave in Jericho, Ibadan, alongside Oxford University Press and Evans Brothers. He handled the opportunities of the Nigerian Indigenisation Decree with an imaginative offer of shares to authors, educationists, religious organisations, and university staff. This expansion was just in time to take advantage of the growth of Nigeria's oil industry which enabled the government to spend 25 per cent of Nigeria's GDP on education. There was investment in Universal Primary Education (UPE) and a phenomenal expansion of secondary schools and universities. He brought in Akin Thomas from Cambridge University Press and appointed him as editorial director. Akin Thomas took up a position at the Nigerian apex of the editorial triangle; a great many of the most trenchant reports came from Aig Higo himself.

Aig Higo was chairman of the Nigerian Publishers Association when rivalry between book companies was at its most fierce. This fiercely competitive period of expansion led to over-spending and the closure of the Nigerian foreign exchanges in April 1982. This had the advantage that Heinemann Educational Books (Nigeria) had to print and publish more of its own books in the country, which resulted in the active encouragement of poets, playwrights and novelists. He retired and became chairman in 1994.

Aig Higo gave a job to one particular young man just out of school, let him go off to do a science degree at the University of Ife, and then rehired him. This was Ayo Ojeniyi, who succeeded Aig Higo as managing director. He organised the publication of *Issues in Book Publishing in Nigeria* in 2005 on the occasion of Chief Aig Higo's seventieth birthday. In it he lists among Aig Higo's honours: Honorary Fellow of the Nigerian Academy of Letters, Honorary Life Member of Science Teachers Association of Nigeria, Fellow of the Nigerian Institute of Management and of the Nigerian Institute of Publishers, Knight of St Christopher of the Anglican Church (Nigerian Communion) and *Afimoseso of Ibadanland*.

James Currey

James Currey's publishing apprenticeship proved to be relevant to the running of the African Writers Series from 1967 to 1984. He worked from 1959 to 1964 for Oxford University Press in Cape Town in the period from the Sharpeville massacre to the Rivonia trial. Through his additional work designing the radical monthly *The New African*, he came to first know writers of resistance such as Dennis Brutus, Bessie Head and Alex la Guma. In 1961 he drove all the office equipment for the liberal newspaper *Contact* to safety in Swaziland. The more frustrated he became by South Africa the more excited he became by the writing to the north. In July 1964 he enabled the editor of *The New African* to escape from South Africa by leaving him on a Norwegian sugar ship to Canada and leaping over the side (p. 187). After his own escape, he ran the Three Crowns series and the African academic list for Oxford University Press in London from 1965 to 1967.

James Currey was born in England in 1936. He was educated at Kingswood School, Bath and Wadham College, Oxford. His family connections made him curious about the realities of the regime in South Africa. His poet father and writer mother were both born in South Africa. A forebear, who went to Natal in 1849, started a newspaper and wrote cantankerous articles in *The Natal Witness* about the colonial government's treatment of the Zulus.

He went to work with Keith Sambrook and Alan Hill on 1 April 1967 when the African Writers Series already had a flying start. He was also responsible for the school and university textbook list. Among much other publishing, Keith Sambrook and he also started the Caribbean Writers Series and Arab Authors. Indebtedness, following the closure of the Nigerian foreign exchanges in April 1982, led the new owners of Heinemann to decimate publishing on Africa.

In 1985 James and Clare Currey set up their own imprint. James Currey Publishers has established itself as a leading publisher of academic work on Africa. He has probably published more books on the history of the Africans themselves than existed when he read history at Oxford; these include the eight-volume

UNESCO General History of Africa. The work he has published on African writing includes *The Companion to African Literatures* which has been endlessly valuable in providing detail for this book. The African Studies Associations of both Canada and the US have recognised the contribution of the firm to the publication of African studies. The same recognition was given in 2008 by the African Literature Association in the US. He is a vice-president of the Royal African Society and has been seconded as the publishing specialist to the Council of the African Studies Association of the United Kingdom.

Henry Chakava

Henry Chakava's contribution to the African Writers Series also appears throughout the book with his reports on, objections to, and support for books from all over Africa. The East African chapter (p. 85) shows how Henry Chakava turned it into the Series of first choice in East Africa, as it already was in West Africa. His bravery in the period of the autocratic rule of Moi, in both political and commercial terms, is recorded in the section on Ngũgĩ (p. 113). In particular he made us all engage with the problems of how to use published writing to record the continent's oral literature.

Henry Chakava was born in 1946 in western Kenya. He was educated at the Friends' School, Kamusinga, and went on to the renowned Literature department of the University of Nairobi which was run with great inspiration by Ngũgĩ and Taban lo Liyong. He was awarded a first-class degree in Literature and Philosophy. He had begun postgraduate work when, in 1972, Bob Markham offered him a job as an editor at Heinemann Educational Books in Nairobi. He spent the winter of 1973 in London working with Keith Sambrook and James Currey at the Heinemann Educational Books offices in Mayfair. He lodged with the South African exile publisher Ros de Lanerolle (p.xvii), went to a course at the London College of Printing and learnt the skills of the publisher's party.

At the age of only 30 he took over as managing director from Bob Markham. In 1985, in the period when the Heinemann Group had four owners in five years, he started a process which led in 1992 to the formation of East African Educational Publishers (EAEP) as a company totally owned by Kenyans. It is now one of the largest indigenous publishers on the continent.

He has founded and worked for regional and international book trade organisations to get African governments to appreciate the strategic value of publishing. He was, for ten years between 1982 and 1992, chairman of the Kenya Publishers Association. He led the successful campaign which ended the state monopoly in textbook publishing in Kenya and East Africa.

He has contributed to or written some thirty books. *A Decade of Publishing in Kenya: One Man's Experience* 1977–1987 (ABPR Oxford 1988) has been of particular value in the writing of this book. Among many awards is an honorary doctorate from Oxford Brookes University, which runs the internationally renowned publishing course.

The advisers

In this book it rapidly becomes apparent how the publishers depended on an army of advisers and readers to present formal reports and flesh out the potential in hopeful manuscripts. Many of the advisers also acted as editors in rewriting, editing and preparing manuscripts for typesetting,

Keith Sambrook and I came to depend in particular upon a consistency of voice and a steadying nerve from the South African exile publisher Ros Ainslie, who usually used her married name Ros de Lanerolle to sign reports and letters. She worked in Cape Town at the turn of the 1950s and 1960s on *Africa South,* founded and edited by Ronald Segal who in exile ran the Modern African Library for Penguin; she edited some of the titles in that collection which was a non-fiction parallel to the African Writers Series. She worked for the ANC in London and, as she approached fiction from a political stance, this meant that she favoured work of social consciousness. She became, before her early death, managing director of The Women's Press.

We used the skills of two novelists working in Britain. Richard Lister was a metallurgist who had turned to the writing of travel books and novels and had had stories published in *The New Yorker, Punch* and *Atlantic Monthly*. He could almost always quietly win the confidence of a writer because he showed professional respect for what that writer was trying to achieve. He proved himself the 'chum' whom Bessie Head needed to work on the final draft for *The Question of Power.* John Wyllie was a Canadian who had been in the RAF during the second world war; Doubleday published a sequence of his detective stories in which, unusually for those days, the detective Dr Quarshie was black. I knew I could always call on his skills as a 'plotsmith'; I would ask him to suggest possibilities to the author of a promising manuscript where he could see a story struggling to get out. His part in the Dambudzo Marechera saga is an example of heroic failure.

Consideration of the work from certain countries in Africa came to depend strongly on the advice of key individuals. The academic Robert Fraser, now at the Open University, is author of several books including *West African Poetry* (Cambridge University Press 1986) and *The Novels of Ayi Kwei Armah* (Heinemann 1980). His reports show a firmness of insight which was of importance in handling writers of poetic originality from Ghana, Sierra Leone and The Gambia. Akin Thomas, as editorial director in Ibadan, commissioned and forwarded a flow of distinguished advice from academics in the rapidly expanding Nigerian university system. When one reads reports by Molara Ogundipe-Leslie, Michael Echeruo and many others, one is again and again delighted by the way that their opinions lifted our understanding of new work, as much from other parts of Africa as from Nigeria itself.

Henry Chakava in Nairobi, in sending London and Ibadan a flow of his own reports and assessments, depended very heavily on the skilled advice of the writers Laban Erapu and Richard Ntiru. However, it was the reports from Simon Gikandi which immediately stood out from the time when he first went to work with Henry Chakava as a student; I continued to call on him for opinions while he was working on his doctorate at Edinburgh. After several other North American appointments, he is now a professor at Princeton.

We depended on advisers to help us choose and translate representative work in French, Arabic and Portuguese. The chapter on the writing of negritude in French shows the creative role of Clive Wake, a South African, and of Abiola Irele, a Nigerian, both with doctorates from the Sorbonne. Advice, suggestions and translations also came from John Reed, who taught in Rhodesia and Zambia, and Gerald Moore, who was at both Ibadan and Makerere universities in their formative years. These four were the main translators of work from French in the first ten years. Later Adrian Adams who lived in Senegal worked on Sembene's *Le dernier de l'Empire*. Denys Johnson-Davies got us to appreciate the reasons for developing the Arab Authors series out of the Egyptian and Sudanese titles in the African Writers Series. He is renowned as a translator of singular literary skill and he gave us advice on the cultural, as well as linguistic, ability of other translators from Arabic in portraying work through the medium of English. Michael Wolfers was central to our translation of work from Angola; we also benefited from the enthusiasm of historians of Portuguese Africa and in particular from the knowledge of Tamara Bender.

A network of South African writers, journalists and academics, mostly in Britain, gave opinions on manuscripts and edited scripts from across the whole of Africa. Certain names make repeated appearances in the consideration of manuscripts throughout this book. Randolph Vigne, editor of *The New African*, put us in touch with Bessie Head. Cosmo Pieterse introduced us to numerous playwrights, artists, poets and journalists from all over the continent. Hilary Mutch was a young South African working in the BBC Africa Service, who reliably produced sharp and constructive reports on novels whether about Robben Island or Biafra. Several South African writers – among them C.J. 'Jonty' Driver, Myrna Blumberg and Mary Benson – went out of their way to make sure that the literary editors of the London dailies, Sundays and weeklies reviewed the work coming from the continent. Doris Lessing was central to our work on the publication of Zimbabwean writers. Academics in South Africa such as Guy Butler, Colin Gardner, Stephen Gray and Tim Couzens fed us with ideas. Arthur Ravenscroft was among the teachers in the new Commonwealth literature course at the University of Leeds at which Ngũgĩ, Wole Soyinka and Aig Higo did post-graduate work.

Our connections were very strong with the African literature courses at the new plate-glass universities. Among the academics who helped us were Alastair Niven at Stirling and Lan White at York. At the University of Kent at Canterbury Clive Wake, Lyn Innes and Louis James were enthusiastic builders of this newly popular subject.

Bob Windsor, who taught in a Ugandan school, was commissioned to edit the Heinemann Secondary Readers from shorter scripts originally submitted for the African Writers Series. We got this wrong in design and marketing. Our colleagues in Africa advised us against any reference to the Series itself and after I left a new series was successfully launched as the Junior African Writers Series (JAWS).

The editors

The names of many of Keith Sambrook's and my colleagues who edited and produced books appear in quotations from the correspondence with individual authors throughout the book.

Ann Scorgie joined us in the late 1960s as an editor from William Heinemann and was very well regarded by authors such as Dennis Brutus. She decided that she ought to have a university degree and Clive Wake found her a place at the University of Kent as a mature student. He told me that her interventions lifted the class and she amazed the students just out of school by arguing with her teachers and correcting them about the latest developments in African writing. She had come to university with more up-to-date information on the fast-moving subject of African literature than her teachers.

Penny Butler, as my deputy in the hyperactive period of the late 1970s and early 1980s, made the African and Caribbean department the one in which people sought jobs. She managed the flow of the textbooks, which were technically far more complicated than books in the African Writers Series. As the Zimbabwean chapter (p. 275) shows, she became deeply involved with Zimbabwe Publishing House's plans as well as with textbook publishing for Botswana, Lesotho and Swaziland. I thought so well of Ingrid Crewdson's handling of authors and of her book design that I got her to join us when we started James Currey Publishers. Susie Home kept enormous numbers of new books and covers flowing through the printers and in recent years has joined Keith Sambrook in teaching the history of the book at the University of London. John Myers worked with us until he was head-hunted by Zimbabwe Publishing House and has since worked in Geneva on publishing work for various UN agencies in Geneva.

Our correspondence with the authors was typed, carefully ordered and despatched at one time or another by several secretaries; it was their work which has made the department's files such an asset at the University of Reading archives. The most famous secretary was Lisa Coleman who, over a period of six years, came to be as familiar to the authors as the editors. Visiting authors first turned to her for all sorts of help. The rest of the firm went quiet over the academic and school break of July and August. However that was the season when even more of our authors arrived on the doorstep from all over Africa and America with requests for advances on royalties and problems to be solved over travel, accommodation and shopping. There were many unexpected requests. Penny Butler remembers taking Professor Adu Boahen to a ship's chandlers to buy hurricane lanterns because Ghana had no power. One Monday morning Akin Thomas from Ibadan told us he needed a million packets of crayons for a state order for colouring books.

Vicky Unwin was selected by the directors of Heinemann Educational Books as a trainee. Unlike the rest of us she had passed many of her formative years in Africa where both her parents had lived and worked. She demanded, to the annoyance of Heinemann's top management, that she join the African and Caribbean department, which she took over when I left the firm at the end of 1984.

She worked, as I did, for Heinemann Educational Books for 17 years. To her great credit in the era of debt she managed, with the support of John Watson and Tom Seavey at Heinemann Inc in the US, to keep new work and new translations appearing in the Series in spite of frequent changes of policy by the management of Heinemann Educational Books.

Selling the African Writers Series

The William Heinemann bookshop representatives were responsible for taking orders in the British general bookshops for the hardback novels by African writers and for the African Writers Series paperbacks. We did our best to respond to their requests to spend more on jacket artwork and to increase discounts. An elaborate form of torture was when I had to present the new titles in the Series at the sales conference on a heavy afternoon after the reps had had their final lunch following three days of hearing about Martin Gilbert's latest Churchill volume, the delights of some celebrity biography, or the sweaty Africa in the latest novel by Wilbur Smith. At Heinemann Educational Books, with the arrogance of upstarts, we looked down on the middlebrow books which they were so successful at selling to the conservative bookshops which were their best customers.

In the late 1970s we realised that the bookshop market in Britain for Heinemann academic books had steadily become different and more promising and that was where lay the interest in the African Writers Series. The appointment of Paul Richardson, as marketing director at Heinemann Educational Books in the late seventies, transformed the marketing of African books within Britain. As an editorial director he had built up the leading sociology list and so he knew, and I knew, that our books were being undersold in the British market.

Keith Sambrook and I, with Alan Hill's support and Paul Richardson's advice, had built up a list of academic books on Africa from the new universities in the continent which we were determined would rival the outstanding Longman list. In the 1960s the new generation of plate-glass universities in Britain had joined the ancient and redbrick foundations. Campus bookshops had sprung up and academic books needed different marketing. By this time we had the Caribbean Writers Series and Arab Authors to sell alongside the African Writers Series.

Helen Johns, the enthusiastic marketing manager, arranged window displays and exhibitions in bookshops from the University of Sussex to James Thin's in Edinburgh. For a month nobody could walk downstairs in the elegant new Heffers bookshop, opposite Trinity College in Cambridge, without going through the mezzanine display of enlarged photographs of African authors amid generous numbers of their books. There were racks of multiple copies of all three series downstairs in the Norrington Room at Blackwells in Oxford, from which the buyers drew copies to supply libraries across the English-speaking world and in the oil-rich libraries of the Gulf. Dillons at the top of Gower Street was strategically placed near University College in the University of London and round the corner from the School of Oriental and African Studies and the Institute of

Commonwealth Studies. Birkbeck College across the street was providing further education to many newcomers from the Commonwealth. Dillons found it valuable to have the African Writers Series stocked from floor to ceiling along with the critical series, Studies in African Literature. A whole new generation of radical and alternative bookshops were springing up in cities like Manchester, Bradford and Leicester as well as in parts of London like Balham and Brixton which had never been visited by the William Heinemann reps. The New Beacon bookshop in Finsbury Park, a pioneer of the 1960s, came into its own. The Africa Book Centre Bookshop in Covent Garden was just starting. A new injection of money and enthusiasm had been put into the education system with the appointment of multicultural advisers, especially in the big cities of the north and in the counties round London. The Inner London Educational Authority (ILEA) under Ken Livingstone stood out. Vicky Unwin worked with their advisers to provide help for the start of the Association of the Commonwealth Teachers of English (ATCALS) which mounted a campaign which eventually succeeded in getting books from the new Commonwealth on to British exam syllabuses. All the experience she built up at this time was to be vital in the years of the African book famine in the late 1980s when sales outside Africa in Britain, Europe, the Commonwealth and the US became vitally important to the survival of the Series.

Corinne Gotch in the publicity department of the Bedford Square offices gave a new impetus to publicity in the British market and promotion in the press which was needed to back the efforts of the sales department. The seasonal needs were relentless for catalogues, leaflets and publicity material to promote the African and Caribbean Series in the British, African and world markets; she had to extract copy from all the members of my department against fierce deadlines. (She was later to make such a success of promoting the activities of the Booksellers' Association that her smiling face appeared almost weekly in *The Bookseller.*)

Mailing of this publicity material was the lifeblood of the list. The Series could not have survived without bookshop representation in Britain and Europe. The educational representatives in Nigeria and Kenya first and foremost visited schools. Keith Sambrook and our colleagues used to keep in touch when possible with the main bookshops on African visits. Much the most effective means of keeping in touch was the mailing of Advance Information Sheets (AISs), leaflets and catalogues. Mailing depended on the steady day-to-day additions and changes to mailing lists of accurate details for booksellers, government education departments, secondary schools and university departments in Britain, throughout the Commonwealth and mainland Europe. This was all handled at the Kingswood warehouse by the promotions manager, David Allen. In the days before computers were affordable the mechanics were the much more laborious punched-card systems. There were a lot of countries in Africa which could not be visited regularly. Malawi had in the 1980s almost dropped off the list. I arrived in Lilongwe, the new South African-built capital, and visited the glass-clad education ministry. One of the inspectors asked solicitously about Mr Allen, with whom he conducted a regular correspondence over inspection copies of new textbooks and titles in the African Writers Series.

The large numbers of copies in the Series were sold to secondary schools. Examples from Zambia give some idea of the kind of individuals who were excited by the books and on whom we depended to generate sales. A friend at Munali, the elite boarding school on the edge of Lusaka, before he went to bed, had to go round the lavatories to clear out the boys who were avidly reading books from the African Writers Series. Another teacher in Zambia who ran the school library called it 'the most stolen series'. These people depended on David Allen and his staff to keep them up-to-date with the many new titles which appeared in each mailing. One of the most valuable initiatives worked out by David Allen and Keith Sambrook was the free-copy distribution of something over a hundred copies of new titles to key individuals round the continent and in the Commonwealth who were likely to review, put books on courses or encourage new writers. Particularly influential were the activities of people in further and extramural education. In addition there was wide distribution of review copies to newspapers and journals throughout Africa and the Commonwealth.

The extraordinary sales, especially in Nigeria but also in Kenya and Zambia, disguised the way that the market was shrinking in certain countries like Ghana and Tanzania. When the Nigerian foreign exchanges closed in April 1982 it left Heinemann and the other big British publishers with those container-loads of books unpaid for. This was the beginning of the debt crisis and by 1985 there was, what the historian Michael Crowder so vividly called, 'the African book famine'. Kenya, South Africa, Botswana and newly independent Zimbabwe still had some foreign currency but otherwise the sales for the African Writers Series dropped away. Countries even found it difficult to pay for set books. The situation had become reversed. Imaginative marketing lifted the sales in Britain, Europe and the Commonwealth and it was the recently established company in the US which became vital to the future of new publishing in the Series.

HEB Inc & the American dimension

Alan Hill, at the very beginning in the 1960s, tried to interest a US publisher in co-publishing the whole African Writers Series in North America. The proposal was considered carefully by the renowned paperback imprint Doubleday Anchor; this would have been historically appropriate in that William Heinemann had been owned for a period in the 1920s by Doubleday. Minimal distribution of the Series alongside other Heinemann Educational Books titles was provided in the 1970s by Humanities Press, an importer in New Jersey which gave no discounts and refused desk-copy requests. Distribution of the Series was handled, and continued to be handled, in Canada by Bellhaven House and later by Irwin Publishers.

Heinemann Educational Books Inc (affectionately known in Bedford Square just as 'Inc', pronounced as 'Ink') was established in 1978 initially in Exeter, and then in Portsmouth, New Hampshire. John Watson came from Heinemann Educational Books in Singapore and he was joined by Tom Seavey, who had wide marketing experience in the US with firms such as Holt, Rinehart. They quickly transformed the availability in the US of the books in the Series in which Heinemann had rights. The demand from US universities lifted the sales as titles became used far beyond the literature departments. I met David William Cohen of The Johns Hopkins University in early 1979 and he amazed me by telling how he, a historian, used a dozen African novels with his first-year students who had opted for the course in African history. He said that at the beginning of the year his students saw Africa as a single continent. By the end of the year and some 12 novels later his students understood the variety of Africas and he could begin to teach them. He told me that the establishment in New Hampshire had transformed the access of his students to this rich resource.

In 1978 the African Writers Series was only known in the US as a collection by visiting African students and teachers, and by those American academics who had spent time in Africa. However, not all titles were available, as some fifty titles in the Series had been published in US editions. Some had been originated by American publishers and the rights in some titles had been sold by Heinemann. Sometimes, irritatingly, rights were tied up even if books were not actually in print. The titles which were not free for HEB Inc to sell were often major books such as all Chinua Achebe's works and several of those by Ngũgĩ. Other important African Writers Series authors with American publishers included Nuruddin Farah, Alex la Guma, Steve Biko, Kofi Awoonor, Dennis Brutus, Sembene Ousmane, Mongo Beti and Buchi Emecheta. The tussle over the American rights is central to the account of the publication of Ayi Kwei Armah's *The Beautyful Ones Are Not Yet Born* (p. 74).

HEB Inc's initial strategy was to focus on the educational market in US colleges and universities and – to a lesser extent – in high schools. At that time, exchange rates were favourable and the controlling British African Writers Series prices were still reasonable, so that HEB Inc could list most books in the \$3.50–5.00 range, at which price they could be considered for class adoption. HEB Inc produced its own complete descriptive catalogue for the Series on an annual basis; this was mailed to a comprehensive list of academics with an interest in African literature and world literatures written in English, as well as to specialists in other disciplines such as African history, politics, economics and anthropology. The company set up a fairly liberal examination and desk-copy policy as well as a standing-order plan for libraries (always quite good customers for the Series). A good deal of hand-holding was provided for teachers not familiar with the Series, or indeed with Africa. The country of origin of the writers was of particular interest and readers wanted to know where the writers' countries were in the continent. Sandra and Nick Hudson of the HEB Australian company had encountered the same problem and invented the African Writers Series calendar, which had a bold map with the authors put into country lists (Nigeria and South Africa long; Malawi and Ethiopia tiny). HEB Inc put together introductory packs of key titles at a discount aimed at the high-school market. Lists of titles under key topics were circulated to help teachers experiment with a wider range of titles (for instance, women in African society, the literature of apartheid, the clash of traditional religion and Christianity, the struggle against colonialism and the politics of post-colonial societies). Good use was made of *A Handbook for the Teaching of African Literature* by Elizabeth Gunner (Heinemann 1984), even though this had been designed for use in British schools. HEB Inc also imported and distributed large quantities of special promotional materials from David Allen at Kingswood, such as posters featuring George Hallett's *African Writers Series Portfolio* of African authors. HEB Inc built the series Studies in African Literature into a useful resource for American teachers of African literature; titles on the work of important authors gave teachers confidence to bring new books on to their reading lists. HEB Inc began to add titles by US university teachers to this parallel critical series and joined James Currey Publishers to restart it in 1985. Gradually, John Watson, Tom Seavey and their team built up a large adoption business for the African Writers Series in all sorts of courses right across the humanities, and not just for those in African literature. HEB Inc became a more and more important customer for the Series and during the early 1980s its orders, alongside those from Nigeria and Kenya, became critical to London's build-up of print runs for new titles and for reprints.

There are two major annual national academic meetings about Africa in the US. The African Literature Association meets on different university campuses in the US in most years, and every third year or so in an African city such as Alexandria or Accra. Several times bigger are the meetings of the African Studies Association which take place in downtown US hotels with a local university playing host. The book exhibits are in vast ballrooms and there was always enthusiasm, interest and the active sale of the African Writers Series alongside other African studies books. It was an excitement to work on the HEB Inc stand and see piles of the newly published titles, on which one had laboured for years, being hoovered up into bags by enthusiastic academics. As it was often difficult for teachers to see the books in their local campus textbook depositories, many of them saved their budgets to spend at these meetings once a year.

In the early years HEB Inc did not try to promote the Series heavily to trade bookstores; however, right from the start they did offer an agency plan which provided booksellers with an extra discount if they agreed to stock a range of titles from the Series (the standard discount on African Writers Series then was short, at 20 per cent). This had some small success with specialist stores. I remember being impressed with a bookstore in Greenwich Village, New York which put all its African writers, including a good representation from the Series, in alphabetical order by author with all the other writers of American and world literature. Later on, with encouragement from the British holding company, all the US companies in the group including HEB Inc (by then plain Heinemann) did launch a full-scale joint trade operation under the direction of an experienced trade sales manager, which employed freelance bookstore reps and handled promotion through a specialist trade PR agency. The African Writers Series was an important part of this trade venture, though sales never reached the necessary critical mass to repay the energy and expense. As far as the Series was concerned, only the really major authors – Chinua Achebe, Nuruddin Farah, Ngũgĩ – could obtain ongoing shelf space in the typical American bookstore in one of the national chains. Although many individual African Americans were enthusiastic customers, it was found to be difficult to interest the African-American trade market in the Series. In autumn 1996 Heinemann decided to cut the Series trade terms back to the original short discount from full trade terms, and reinstated an agency plan for stores which agreed to stock a range of titles. From this point on titles from the African Writers Series were rarely to be seen in trade bookstores in America.

John Watson became a bibliographic sleuth as he worked steadily to seek the reversion of rights from American publishers on a title-by-title basis. For instance, by 1985 HEB Inc was at last able to list – for a time – in the US the AWS editions of *Things Fall Apart* and *No Longer at Ease*, and *The Beautyful Ones Are Not Yet Born*. Partly thanks to their annotated editions *Things Fall Apart* became the second most adopted text in US high schools. Ironically, just as the rights situation was beginning to be cleaned up, Heinemann in Britain started to put Series titles out of print as the African debt crisis got worse. (Occasionally the US company had sufficient inventory for it to be able to keep titles in print long after they disappeared from the list in Britain.) By 1986, there were over 20 out-of-print AWS titles in the US, so many in fact, that – to try to cut down on customer service enquiries – HEB Inc started to print a list of OP titles in its catalogues. In 1986, this list included titles by Taban lo Liyong, Lenrie Peters, René Maran, Sembene Ousmane, Alex la Guma and Naguib Mahfouz, as well as several anthologies of poetry and plays. As HEB Inc gained confidence in its marketing ability, and when North American rights were available, the US company itself started to reissue in the Series titles which were out of print in Britain and Africa. Two such were René Maran's *Batouala* and Sembene Ousmane's *Tribal Scars*, and there were others as the years passed. But the list of out-of-print titles continued to grow year by year.

There were on occasion titles for which HEB Inc lost American rights, because of events beyond its control. The most financially notable loss, until Chinua Achebe's books were taken away, was Nuruddin Farah. HEB Inc had originally done well with three of his titles – *From a Crooked Rib, A Naked Needle* and *Sweet and Sour Milk* – but Heinemann in Britain without consulting Inc let rights revert to Nuruddin Farah and the titles were subsequently sold in the late 1980s to other publishers in the US.

HEB Inc began to contribute new books to the Series. *Unwinding Threads: Writing by Women in Africa* (1983 AWS 256), edited by an American academic, Charlotte Bruner, was planned from the start as a teaching anthology. Chinua Achebe and Lyn Innes had both taught in universities in the US and were asked to keep that experience in mind when they made the choice for *African Short Stories* (1985 AWS 270). The US market was a dominating consideration in selection of *The Heinemann Book of Contemporary African Short Stories* (1992) and of *The Heinemann Book of African Women's Writing* (1993), also edited by Charlotte Bruner. During the late 1980s and 1990s sales to the US became crucial, especially in supporting the publication of any new titles in the Series, as is shown in the Conclusion, 'Is there still a role for the African Writers Series?' (p. 296)

& The African Writers Series Portfolio George Hallett's covers

The African Writers Series portfolio of large portraits by George Hallett of 16 outstanding writers was one of the most stylish pieces of publicity produced by Heinemann. All the photographs in this book, with the exception of p. xiv, are by him. He has had an exhibition in the BoKaap Museum in Cape Town of his photographs of his native District Six. He has also exhibited his photographs in England at Spitalfields in London and Edgbaston in Birmingham.

(left) Self-portrait, about 1982

George Hallett wrote in July 2007:

> Shortly after my arrival in London in 1970 I was introduced to James Currey by an old friend, Isaiah Stein, a South African exile then working for the publishers Heinemann in Mayfair. We met in a beautiful traditional pub with ornate mirrors and dark wooden interiors. Some of the other directors from Heinemann were also around enjoying a tankard of bitter. In this pleasant convivial atmosphere James Currey spoke animatedly about the African Writer Series. He wanted to change the look of the covers from a rather academic look using drawings, to a more contemporary style using photographs. Turning his gaze towards me he asked me if I ever had done any covers in South Africa. I replied positively, adding that I did not have any examples to show him. However, if he gave me an opportunity, I would love to show him what I could do. After that liberating lunch I was invited to his office where he presented me with the manuscript of *The Tongue of the Dumb* by Dominic Mulaisho (p. 243).
>
> On my way home on the underground, I started reading the manuscript. By midnight I was thinking about images to put on the cover. I had taken a photograph of a wooden sculpture by Frank Brown, a relative of

the artist Peter Clarke. By cutting the picture into strips and, rearranging them, I created a new image of the work. I delivered the cover the next morning to an astonished James Currey. He was delighted with the image. Many more covers followed and a creative relationship was established with HEB that lasted well over a decade.

Friends from the extensive South African exiled community in London and further afield became my models and accomplices in the creation of new covers. Pallo Jordan danced for *A Dancer of Fortune* (p. 242). Louis Moholo was hung upside down with handcuffs for *Robben Island* (p. 184). Lorna de Smit became a corpse with a silver coin over one eye while a Gabon viper kept vigil nearby (inside front cover). Gavin Jantjes and his wife transformed into characters for Nuruddin Farah's tragic tale of life in his homeland. Jimi Mathews, while studying photography with me in the French Pyrenees, suffered the indignities of a prisoner of war wearing only an old rag around his waist and bleeding from a headwound.

I soon discovered a massive warehouse in Camden Town that had the most incredible collection of props, historical costumes and guns of every description for the film and television industry. This was my Hamley's toy shop! I even found a South African policeman's uniform from the apartheid era to illustrate one of Alex la Guma's novels set in District Six. Nigerian soldier's uniform from the Biafran war? No problem. Our little team of exiles created quite a stir one night in a quiet North London street; I had three guys dressed up as soldiers with automatic weapons at a road block somewhere in Nigeria. Lighting was from the overhead street lights; very effective, with a red Volkswagen beetle contrasting with the green camouflage uniforms (p.37). The British Museum kept me supplied with Gabon vipers and stuffed exotica from the African forests. African masks I found in galleries in Bond Street, where they were fetching very high prices.

I had to create my covers with real people and objects. High-contrast film became a favoured way of creating stark graphic images. Overlaying multiple negatives when printing in the darkroom was a new way of developing designs. Double exposures in the camera was another way of creating images for covers. This was long before computer-generated images became possible.

I was invariably disappointed with the passport photographs that authors sent to put on the back covers of their books. So when I heard that a writer on Heinemann's list was in town, I would set up a meeting to obtain a good portrait. And what a joy it was to attend African writers' conferences in Berlin in 1979 and Frankfurt in 1980. My mission was to corner all the writers individually and convince them to give me a few minutes of their time so I could photograph them. James Currey asked me to select portraits from my collection for the *African Writers Series Portfolio* (Heinemann 1982). Many of them have also appeared in *Portraits of African Writers* (Wits University Press 2006).

Main dates for the African Writers Series

1956 Publication in Paris of Mongo Beti *Le Pauvre Christ de Bomba*, Ferdinand Oyono *Une Vie de Boy*, Sembene Ousmane *Le Docker Noir*, Bernard Dadié *Climbié*, David Diop *Coups de Pilon* (All to appear in translation in the Series).

1958 17 June. Chinua Achebe *Things Fall Apart* (and *No Longer at Ease* 1960) published in hardback by William Heinemann.

1960 Heinemann Educational Books (HEB) set up as a separate company within the Heinemann Group of Publishers. Nigerian independence.

1961 Mbari Club founded. (17 titles published before 1966. Several reprinted in African Writers Series.)

1962 **African Writers Series founded** by Alan Hill and Van Milne.
July. Literature Conference at Makerere, Uganda; Chinua Achebe was offered manuscripts of *The River Between* and *Weep Not, Child* by Ngũgĩ.
December. Chinua Achebe appointed Editorial Adviser.

1963 1 January. Keith Sambrook joined Heinemann Educational Books to develop the list for Africa, Caribbean and South-east Asia.

1964 Heinemann-Cassell Nairobi sales office opened with Bob Markham as manager.

1965 January. Aig Higo became manager of Heinemann Educational Books in Nigeria.

1967 1 April. James Currey joined Keith Sambrook to develop African and Caribbean list, including the African Writers Series and the Caribbean Writers Series.
July. Nigerian/Biafran civil war starts.

1970 Nigerian/Biafran civil war ended.
Henry Chakava became editor at Heinemann Educational Books (East Africa).

1972 **Tenth anniversary** of the African Writers Series celebrated in London. Chinua Achebe stood down as Editorial Adviser of the Series with the publication of his stories *Girls at War* (ALT 100).

Aig Higo and Akin Thomas in Ibadan, Henry Chakava in Nairobi, and Keith Sambrook and James Currey in London formed an international triangle of editorial consultation for the Series.

1970–3 Average 20 titles per year published.

1974 The Nigerian Indigenisation Decree; 60 per cent of shares in Heinemann (Nigeria) had to be owned by Nigerian nationals.

1975 Henry Chakava became managing director of HEB (East Africa).

1976 July. Mwai Kibaki, then Minister of Economic Affairs, launched Ngũgĩ's *Petals of Blood* in the City Hall, Nairobi. On the last day of year Ngũgĩ wa Thiong'o was detained on orders from President Kenyatta.

1977 December. Ngũgĩ released and Henry Chakava gave him a desk in his office.

1978 Heinemann Educational Books (Inc) established in the US under John Watson.

1980 Zimbabwe freedom.
(1982 Zimbabwe International Book Fair established.)

1982 **Twentieth anniversary** of the African Writers Series not marked.
April. Nigerian foreign exchanges closed, leaving Heinemann and British and Nigerian publishers with massive debts. 'The book famine' began.

1983 Heinemann Group taken over for first time (4 owners within 5 years)

1984 James Currey left Heinemann Educational Books because the new management demanded that new book publishing in the Series be reduced to one or two titles per year. 270 titles had been published in the Series and only 15 had been put out of print.

1985 James Currey Publishers founded. Vicky Unwin took over the management of the African Writers Series.

1988 Keith Sambrook joined James Currey Publishers.

1992 Henry Chakava started East African Educational Publishers (EAEP) as fully-owned Kenyan company.

1992/3 **Thirtieth anniversary** celebrated in London at Dillons Bookshop.

2000 To mark the millennium ZIBF backed initiative to select 'Africa's 100 Best Books'. 21 were in the African Writers Series; another 12 of the titles were by authors who had other books in the Series.

2002 **Fortieth anniversary** marked in twelve places around the world.
Only 70, out of some 370 titles, still in print.

2003 Heinemann management announced that no new titles would be added. Heinemann International Division disbanded.

2008 64 titles still in print.
International celebrations of the fiftieth anniversary of the publication by William Heinemann of Chinua Achebe's *Things Fall Apart.*

The Berlin Festival, June 1979. Wole Soyinka giving an evening reading in the Kunstlerhaus-Bethanien. This was the stage for performances by all the writers including, remarkably and unexpectedly, Dambudzo Marechera (p. 290).
(*below*) A daytime session in the conference centre in West Berlin, just across a canal from 'The Wall'. James Currey is in danger of sending to sleep Mongo Beti (*to the left with translation headphones*) and Edouard Maunick from Mauritius (*to the right*). George Hallett was the official photographer.

INTRODUCTION
The Establishment of African Literature

The starting line

Chinua Achebe said in a lecture in 1998 at Harvard:

> The launching of the Heinemann's African Writers Series was like the umpire's signal for which African writers had been waiting on the starting line. In one short generation an immense library of writing had sprung into being from all over the continent and, for the first time in history, Africa's future generations of readers and writers – youngsters in schools and colleges – began to read, not only *David Copperfield* and other English classics that I and my generation had read, but also works by their own writers about their own people. (*Home and Exile* Oxford University Press New York 2000, p.51)

Forty years on, Chinua Achebe still places the emphasis on education in Africa itself. He later came to be concerned also that the writers should be heard across the world.

The African Writers Series was founded in 1962, which was almost exactly 25 years after the start of Penguin Books. The Series was to become to Africans in its first quarter century what Penguin had been to British readers in its first 25 years. It provided good serious reading in paperbacks at accessible prices for the rapidly emerging professional classes, as the countries became independent. The colour orange for novels was shamelessly copied from Penguin. By the time of the tenth anniversary in 1972 it had come to be called in Africa the 'orange series' and was stacked high in the key positions inside the entrances of the university campus bookshops from one side of Africa to the other. The writer and critic Edward Blishen said at the time of the tenth anniversary in 1972:

> I shall tell my grandchildren that I owe most of what education I have to Penguins and that through the African Writers Series I saw a new, potentially great, world literature coming into being. (quoted in Alan Hill, *In Pursuit of Publishing*, p.123)

English was the lubricant of the English-speaking world. It was not only how authority was imposed but it was also the way in which the subject peoples reacted to that imposition of power. Writers in India, the Caribbean and Africa came to take advantage of the language that they shared, but they had to have publishing opportunities. And to begin with those opportunities were almost all in London. By 1962 quite a lot of work by Caribbean writers had been published in London. Some Indian writers were well-established on London lists. But practically no creative work by Africans had appeared. The African Writers Series, with its photos of the authors on the back cover, gave the idea to Africans that they might get published. This book is called *Africa Writes Back* because, over the last 50 years, it shows how Africans achieved the confidence to write back in novels, plays and poetry about what was happening to them.

The hardback publication of Chinua Achebe's novel *Things Fall Apart* on 17 June 1958, by the well-known London publishing house William Heinemann, is now seen as a landmark in the establishment of African literature (p. 28). When Alan Hill, as a director, went for a first visit to Nigeria in 1959 he expected to be praised for the firm's enterprise. However, at the elite University College in Ibadan most of the expatriate staff refused to believe that a recent graduate could have had a novel published by a prestigious London publishing house. Alan Hill was described to me as 'an inspired madman' by Julian Rea, head of the outstanding Longman Africa division. He made a success of the things that other British publishers thought were a waste of time. A grandson of missionaries, he grew up knowing where Africa was. To him it was a matter of faith that what Chinua Achebe had done could be achieved by other writers in Africa.

Alan Hill, in the heady atmosphere of the independence years (Ghana 1957, Nigeria 1960), saw the need to make serious general books by Africans available in a paperback series like Penguin. Van Milne, who worked at Heinemann Educational Books for almost three years before returning to the Scottish publisher Nelson, planned the Series with him. The first titles in 1962 included Chinua Achebe's *Things Fall Apart* and, in 1963, its sequel *No Longer at Ease*. Cyprian Ekwensi, who had been publishing in Nigeria and Britain since 1947, found among his manuscripts a novel set among the Fulani of northern Nigeria called *Burning Grass*; this new work was revised by Van Milne with the aim of making it suitable for the educational market. Van Milne managed to secure the autobiography of Kenneth Kaunda. It was called *Zambia Shall be Free*, as the country did not achieve independence until 1964. First printings of each title were about 2,500. It was a cautious start.

It was the received wisdom in much of British publishing in the early 1960s that the only books that could be sold in Africa were school textbooks. The colonial authorities thought of books for a purpose – the education of a new elite. Books for enjoyment which enhance understanding of other Africans' ways of love and death were not on their agenda.

First-time publication of new fiction

There was a big problem. Paperbacks are mostly reprint series. But what to reprint when so few novels by Africans had been published in hardback by British or American publishers? In that very year of the start of the Series, 1962, there was a conference on African writing at Makerere University College in Uganda in July. Chinua Achebe heard a knock at the door of his guest house in the evening and found a student standing there who offered him the manuscripts of two novels. The name of the Kenyan student was Ngũgĩ.

Alan Hill tells what happened next. It must be remembered that at that time telephoning from Africa was difficult and expensive and also Van Milne would have had to be very insistent to have managed to get Alan Hill out of a board meeting:

> I was at a board meeting at our offices in Kingswood in Surrey and I had a telephone call from Van Milne … he said that a young student at Makerere had shown to Achebe an almost finished manuscript of a novel he'd written. Achebe was very impressed with it and he'd shown it at once to Van Milne. Van Milne read it and told me over the phone 'I think it is terrific, and I want your agreement to take on this book sight unseen.' And I said, 'You've got it,' and went back to the meeting. The book was Ngũgĩ's *Weep Not, Child*. Now it would never have come to us in that way if the author hadn't taken it and shown it to Achebe. ('Working with Chinua Achebe: James Currey, Alan Hill and Keith Sambrook in conversation with Kirsten Holst Petersen', in Kirsten Holst Petersen, *Chinua Achebe: A Celebration*, Dangaroo Press 1990 and Heinemann 1991 p. 153; henceforth Petersen)

This gave Alan Hill and Van Milne the idea that Chinua Achebe could be a magnet for young writers. Alan Hill got his deputy Tony Beal, when he was visiting Nigeria in November 1962, to ask Chinua Achebe to be Editorial Adviser to the African Writers Series. He immediately agreed. The combination of this editor and his publishers was to prove exceptional.

Keith Sambrook found Ngũgĩ's manuscript on his desk when he arrived from Nelson in January 1963 to take over Van Milne's job. *Weep Not, Child* was to be the first new novel for the Series which was also to be published in hardback for the international literary market as well as in paperback. That was the moment of take-off, when Heinemann Educational Books made a total commitment to the role which was at that time almost exclusively performed in London by general literary publishers, which was the first-time publishing of novels in hardback.

The team comes together

Alan Hill had put Keith Sambrook in charge of the rapid expansion of offices in what we were then starting to call the third world. Early in 1964 during a visit to Nigeria they gave a party at the Hotel Bristol in Lagos to celebrate the publication of Chinua Achebe's third novel, *Arrow of God*. Their major reasons for being in Nigeria were to interview candidates and appoint a successor to Chief Fagunwa, the famous Yoruba author who was the first manager of Heinemann Educational Books in Nigeria. He had tragically been drowned in October 1963 on a Niger ferry crossing, when travelling back to Ibadan after a visit to the north with Keith Sambrook.

Keith Sambrook gives an account of the appointment of Aig Higo:

> We wanted to offer him the post at once and let him know before we left Nigeria. Alan told me, 'Get him on the blower.' When that didn't work, Alan suggested we cable him. Past experience told me that might not work either so I persuaded Alan, to be certain of making the offer clearly, we had to go to Otuo and back within 48 hours. Once convinced, Alan was enthusiastic and we set off in the HEB Peugeot …
>
> We arrived at Otuo around the middle of the second day, found the school [where Aig Higo was headmaster] and immediately sighted Aig walking across the compound. In a fair imitation of H.M. Stanley, Alan advanced with outstretched hand and greeted Aig, 'Mr Higo, we meet again; I'm sure I needn't tell you we haven't come all this way to say that we are offering the job to somebody else.' (F.A. Adesanoye & A. Ojeniyi *Issues in Book Publishing in Nigeria* HEB Nigeria 2005 p. 4)

This was another significant moment in the establishment of the Series. Aig Higo had been at the University College, Ibadan with Chinua Achebe and they had both been actively involved in the Mbari Club with its pioneering publishing list. The Heinemann Educational Books office was in Ibadan and Chinua Achebe was working just down the road at Federal Broadcasting in Lagos. Their work in bringing in writers from Nigeria, Ghana and Gambia quickly made it, despite many rivals, the Series of first choice in West Africa (p. 39). Keith Sambrook and Chinua Achebe built on the success of the initial four titles with a canny selection of titles. There were anthologies of poetry, prose, short stories and plays. There were some translations from African languages. However, it was the writers in French who had already shown originality and elegance. In 1956, two years before Chinua Achebe's first novel was published in London, first novels by Mongo Beti, Ferdinand Oyono and Sembene Ousmane were all published in Paris. Translations into English of books by these authors helped enhance the overall quality of the Series.

How could the Series fail after such a start? It might well have done. It was a literary series of original contemporary work, but it was published by an educational company. Heinemann Educational Books was publishing texts for an educational system which did not yet have a place for African writers. The cynical commercial logic was that publishing new creative writers of unestablished standards was not the job of an educational publisher. When the Series was started it could not be foreseen that the secondary-school examination boards would prescribe books by young living Africans. The exam boards were still based in Cambridge, London and Durham. Like Oxford University Press, they preferred their authors dead. However, in the heady years of independence, new examination boards were set up in Africa. WAEC – 'Wayec' as everybody came to call it – was the West African Examinations Council for Nigeria, Ghana, Gambia and Sierra Leone. EAEC was the East African Examinations Council for Kenya, Uganda and Tanzania. We did not know that the examiners would so delight in raiding the African Writers Series to prescribe texts. In this they were far more adventurous than the English boards, where Gerard Manley Hopkins was as close as they got to a modern poet. Chinua Achebe's encouragement of Heinemann to experiment paid off in a way that we London publishers, who had grown up among the dead poets of the English educational system, had never imagined it could. The enrichment of education for Africans was central to Chinua Achebe's philosophy and school and university sales of set books made viable the whole adventure of trying out a range of new writers.

Alan Hill said in Kirsten Holst Petersen's book:

> By 1967 it was clear we were on to something big and that we could no longer run the African Writers Series as an 'add-on' to our educational publishing. So I invited James Currey of the Oxford University Press to join us and to run the African Writers Series as his specialism. (Petersen p. 154)

When Alan Hill interviewed me we talked about educational and textbook publishing for Africa. Only when the interview seemed to be coming to an end did he ask me whether I would be interested in working on the African Writers Series. The interview, which had gone well, then took off. I could hardly believe the enthusiasm of this managing director for a marginal literary and political series. At the Oxford University Press, after Rex Collings had left, there was nobody in management in London who was really interested in the Three Crowns series that he had started. It was seen as a worthy obligation to the branches in Africa, which might help correct the impression that Oxford University Press was only interested in making money out of textbooks (p. 14).

In February 1967, while still working out my notice at Oxford University Press, Keith Sambrook invited me round to meet Chinua Achebe, who was visiting London on diplomatic business for the eastern part of Nigeria which was about to declare itself Biafra. I left the cloistered corridors of Oxford University Press on a sombre February morning. During the meeting I produced, with some diffidence because I had failed to get the book accepted at Oxford University Press, the translations from Arabic of short stories by the Sudanese writer Tayeb Salih under the title *The Wedding of Zein* (p. 175). The two men looked carefully at the work and within minutes they had both agreed with enthusiasm that it ought to go into the new Series. It was transforming for me to find such self-confident acceptance of worth.

Sex, religion & politics

Ferdinand Oyono's *Houseboy* (p. 60) was also among the first titles which presented questions about what was appropriate for a school textbook publisher. One must remember that in 1966 it was relatively soon after the permissive breakthrough provided by the Lady Chatterley trial in 1961. Penguin's printer Cox and Wyman had been hauled into court. Their proofreader went through the proofs of Oyono's *Houseboy* to search for four-letter words.

Our more cautious colleagues in the London office were concerned that sex, religion and politics might keep such books out of schools. Denys Johnson-Davies, Tayeb Salih's translator and friend, after the quick success with getting

Wedding of Zein into the African Writers Series, brought round his translation of Tayeb Salih's novel *Season of Migration to the North* (p. 175). Keith Sambrook and I were worried whether we could get this book accepted because it finishes with a sexually violent death in London 'in the land of jig jig'. Our colleagues reluctantly agreed to the acceptance of Ayi Kwei Armah's *The Beautyful Ones Are Not Yet Born*, in spite of the carefully developed image of shit for corruption (p.73). We had a touch-and-go battle over Sembene Ousmane's *God's Bits of Wood*, the heroic epic of labour resistance on the Dakar–Niger railway line, since one of our colleagues maintained that it would be too long and therefore too expensive to be used in schools; with sales of over 50,000 copies, the English translation outsold the French original (p. 62).

The inhibitions which concerned an educational publisher did not worry Chinua Achebe. He wanted the Series to reflect all the richness and variety of an emerging Africa. He was concerned with the widest literary criteria. All these books had to be approved for publication by a formal committee of directors and editors sitting every Wednesday round a table beneath the chandeliers of the ballroom of a house in Charles Street, Mayfair which had belonged to Lord Randolph Churchill and his wife Jenny. After the discussion had gone on for some time about whether certain subjects would cut out the book from schools, Alan Hill in the chair would say, 'Well, James, what did the old Chinua say?' He knew, everyone knew, that if I had brought the proposal to the meeting then young Chinua Achebe would already have said 'yes' (even if it was on the telephone while passing through London from the Uli airstrip in Biafra to raise funds in America). So Alan Hill would say, 'Right James. You want to do it? Go ahead and do it!' With the imaginative support of Chinua Achebe for the first 100 titles in the series, Heinemann established that there was a general as well as an educational market in Africa. The big sales of the adopted titles prescribed for exams allowed us to experiment. Alan Hill pointed out that in 1984 approximately one-third of the total revenue for some 250 titles in the Series came from sales of Chinua Achebe's books.

Alan Hill explained in an interview that this take-off needed an educational publisher:

> Then why Heinemann Educational Books? The reason is simple. We were the only firm with the faith – the passion almost – and the will to do the job; and we had Chinua Achebe's first two novels to give us a flying start. Also – and this was essential – we had the necessary business set-up to sell books within Africa itself. The big fiction houses were useless; they didn't reach black Africa; for the book trade in the continent was almost entirely educational. William Heinemann, our fiction and general company, had never sold books in Africa outside the European communities. Only the educational company had the know-how and the marketing organisation to bring the African Writers Series to the ordinary African. (Petersen p. 152)

Jenny Uglow, in an article in the *Independent on Sunday* (3 January 1993) at the time of the 30th anniversary of the Series, described the Heinemann people who shaped the Series as 'idealists'. I think it is better to call us enthusiasts. We were certainly realists. The success of the Series – and the survival of our jobs – depended on making it work within the terms of London publishing. The Heinemann Group was owned by a conglomerate called Thomas Tilling which was traded on the London stock exchange. Alan Hill told me, on a long car journey to the Heinemann walking weekend in the Lake District soon after I started to work with him, that as long as Heinemann handed over the prescribed percentage to Tilling we would have the financial room to experiment in the Series. As he told Kirsten Horst Petersen:

> ... you have to remember that we were not dominated by a money-grabbing ideology in those days. Publishing has changed a lot since then, and I don't really care for the accountancy-ridden profit-making of present-day publishing firms which are now in the grip of the big corporations who are only interested in the profits which the products make ... Whether it was profitable or not wasn't a really major consideration. The fact that the overall series was profitable, of course, meant that nobody interfered with us. We later published a whole lot of books which were not profitable. But these were carried by the profits generated by some 'big-selling' authors ... (Petersen p. 157)

I would have put it another way. Almost all the later titles, many books by new writers, were to be reprinted. They were carried to profitability by the Series. Although their sales were occasionally modest, rarely did stocks of overprinted books lie heavy on the shelves for very long, as they too became more widely acclaimed. Chinua Achebe and our colleagues in Africa urged us on to this reinvestment in new writers. Success fed on success. Many of our experiments worked for us, for the authors and for Tilling.

Books were kept in print, which did not happen under other British and American trade paperback imprints. Teachers and exam authorities could be sure that when they prescribed a book it would be available from Heinemann. For the first time in the late 1970s I was asked by the accountants to enquire whether four slow-selling titles should be put out of print. There was a scream of outrage from Ibadan and Nairobi and their reaction was justified when the following year there was a single order for 4,000 copies from Lesotho for *Climbié*, Bernard Dadié's novel of childhood in the Ivory Coast. It cost very little to keep sleepers in the catalogue; just some rack space, some computer space, a royalty statement and a modest amount of optimism.

An international triangle of choice

I visited Chinua and Christie Achebe at the University of Nigeria at Nsukka in 1971 after the end of the civil war. The house was a shell. The walls were black. There was no power. Chinua Achebe gave me the manuscript of his short stories called *Girls at War*, which was to become AWS 100 when published on the tenth anniversary of the Series in 1972. He said that the time had come to hand over his role as Editorial Adviser to another African writer and he and I agreed that nobody could be more appropriate than Ngũgĩ, especially as there needed to be more books from East Africa. Ngũgĩ immediately accepted but then decided, after some six weeks, that the duties would interfere with his own writing.

Our initial reaction was disappointment. However Aig Higo, Alan Hill, Keith Sambrook and I, after discussing other possible candidates, took a positive decision to widen the African input into the Series. With the appointment of Henry Chakava, Heinemann now had an active editorial office in Nairobi as well as in Ibadan. So we decided that we would replace the Editorial Adviser to the Series with a triangular system of consultation between the publishing editors in Ibadan, Nairobi and London. In Nairobi Simon Gikandi and Laban Erapu all stand out. Aig Higo kept us in touch with the active Nigerian literary scene with the help of Akin Thomas, his editorial director. Chinua Achebe, now called the Founding Editor, continued to give us advice on individual manuscripts and to put interesting new work our way.

These colleagues in Africa found new writers. They assessed scripts. They got readers' reports. They criticised the reports I sent from our advisers in Britain. What we learnt to avoid were committee choices. Nobody had a veto. If somebody supported a book strongly enough then it got published. What were needed were enthusiastic and considered voices. The rich outpouring of new writing fed on itself and gave people all over Africa the hope of publication. Manuscripts in various stages of clarity, even in handwriting, poured into the offices in Ibadan, Nairobi and London. A substantial proportion was sent out for report by readers who were often novelists, playwrights and poets in their own right. If the reports were modestly encouraging, copies of the manuscripts were circulated to the other offices in the triangle. Of course most of the manuscripts had to be turned down, but there was an active policy of letting writers see reports; writing is a lonely business and the plain rejection slip is dispiriting. It is now impossible to say what proportion of manuscripts were rejected compared with those which were accepted; it was probably of the order of 40 or 50 to 1. There was in this policy a heavy investment of time, administration, money and concern.

There was almost total agreement between the triangle of Nairobi, Ibadan and London over choosing novels and collections of short stories. Selection of poetry depended upon the support of the poet by individual editors and advisers. Plays depended upon the few active producers who could visualise the scripts in production, not just under the proscenium arch but in open-air theatres built of earth and off the back of trucks in the besieged townships of South Africa.

Heinemann had built an active international network of choice in Africa. Consultation was not without considerable effort and expense. Again and again one is reminded that telephoning was expensive and unreliable. Cables, and then telexes, were the text messages of the time and even more likely to be ambiguous. Photocopying the wide range of hopeful manuscripts to share between three offices was still relatively expensive. Air fares were still high (in 1959 it had cost Oxford University Press as much as my annual salary to fly me to South Africa). On my visits to Africa I was only able to justify the heavy costs of travel by going to see the educational authorities about textbook adoptions during the working day; in the evenings my African colleagues and I could drink and eat with the writers or go to see their plays. It would never have been cost-effective to go round Africa just to see the writers. We invested all this effort to bring on new writers. Increasingly there were publishers in the larger African countries encouraged by the market which had grown for creative writing. However, the African Writers Series was so dominant that most of the writers offered their work to us first.

The most ambitious authors wanted, as Dennis Brutus put it, to be considered as 'a writer' and not just 'an African writer' (p. 210). With Heinemann they could usually have it both ways. In Britain and in America we take it for granted that there are many outlets – books, journals, newspapers, radio and television – which accept creative writing all the time. And we take it for granted that there are literary agents to place work. And we know that once a book is published there is a whole reviewing, promotions and feature-writing industry. We set out to provide the links to get the best of the authors noticed outside Africa. We wanted to persuade that industry to take writing by Africans seriously.

William Heinemann & Heinemann Educational Books

A problem was that in the 1960s paperbacks were not reviewed in newspapers. Novels had to be published in hardback to be noticed. We needed African writers to be considered in the reviewing columns along with the regular output from the hardback literary publishers. Literary editors were snobbish about books coming from an educational publisher. The public libraries closely followed the recommendations of reviewers and bought hardbacks in liberal quantities from the well-established general publishers; they were in effect the major patron of the publishing of new novels and poetry. The sales to the public-library system enabled publishers to go on publishing a book a year by promising writers.

Alan Hill and Keith Sambrook were confident that, as Heinemann Educational Books was active in Africa, we would find new writing of quality which would also be of interest to readers in Britain and around the world. They took it for granted that William Heinemann would, with the precedent of Chinua Achebe, be enthusiastic about publishing hardback editions and getting them reviewed and sold in British bookshops and libraries. However, with one or two exceptions, they found that people at William Heinemann were at best patronising about the well-intentioned efforts of the junior company.

William Heinemann was founded in 1890 by an adventurous young man, whose banker father came from Austria. It became an outstanding imprint. He made a success of publishing work by authors such as Conrad, Maugham, Galsworthy and D.H. Lawrence. When he died in 1920 the firm was taken over for a time by Doubleday, and after the 1929 Wall Street crash by the Evans family who in the 1930s were brilliant salesmen for a list which included J.B. Priestley and Graham Greene.

After the second world war in the 1950s there were few publishing houses in London with general literary lists which made enough money to sustain themselves by the sale of hardbacks, even with the library sales. The managers of subsidiary rights departments were central to the survival of hardback publishers. The sale of rights to separate paperback publishers was just beginning to take off. Sales for translations into a foreign language, often negotiated at the Frankfurt Book Fair, were becoming more important. There might be the occasional sale of film rights, but broadcasting and television were growing.

The sale of US rights was essential. Very few publishers had offices on both sides of the Atlantic. The style of the clauses on market rights was imperial. The British contracts would read along the lines: 'World rights in the English language excluding the United States of America and its dependencies'. The American Memoranda of Agreement would be a matching 'World Rights in the English language excluding the traditional British Commonwealth market'.

Many general publishers were kept afloat by the publication of technical and educational books. It was said that a vital support for the distinguished Faber list was its books on nursing. Longman, founded in 1724, became so successful as an educational publisher that its general list was disposed of by new owners.

Alan Hill was hired by Charlie Evans in 1936 to help expand an educational list for William Heinemann in the hope that its income would come to support the general list. In the postwar period Alan Hill built up the textbook list, particularly in science and in English. This growth could not disguise the fact that in the late 1950s the Heinemann Group of Publishers, including such distinguished literary imprints as Secker and Warburg and Rupert Hart-Davis, was ailing. The British industrial conglomerate Thomas Tilling had a substantial shareholding. (In 1947 the Labour government had nationalised all the Tilling buses; cash rich, Tilling decided to invest in a range of industries and family companies. The Heinemann shares were only a tiny percentage of their holdings across British industry.) After Tilling had taken a controlling share to save the group, a secret deal was negotiated to sell the Group to the New York publishing giant, McGraw Hill. The story goes that the front page of the offer document was accidentally imprinted on the rubber blanket of the Gestetner duplicating machine at William Heinemann and was read with horror by a young executive. An anti-American revolt by young directors made McGraw Hill withdraw their offer. As a reward for his support Alan Hill was able to get Heinemann Educational Books established in 1960 as a separate company; it grew with such speed that this upstart junior came to dominate the Group. This helped keep the Tilling accountants off the backs of the prestigious general publishers, but there was resentment at the success of Heinemann Educational Books.

The excitement about paperbacks

Alan Hill says of the African Writers Series in his autobiography, 'The plan was to start a paperback series … sold at very cheap prices – as low as 25p at the outset'

(Alan Hill p. 123). The African Writers Series was started at a time when paperback publishing was still a new and exciting concept. A revolution in printing technology had taken place in the postwar period as mass-production techniques from America were taken over from newspapers to books; prices tumbled as printers offered space on their new machines. Paperback marketing techniques were revolutionised in order to shift substantial numbers of copies in bookshops; the fight for shelf space began. In 1958, when I joined Oxford University Press, it published every academic textbook and general book in hardback alone. I remember Hugo Brunner, later to be managing director of Chatto and Windus, saying on our first days in publishing almost as a statement of revolutionary ideology: 'Oxford University Press must do paperbacks.'

Penguin was the renowned pioneer and, since 1937, had virtually stood on its own as a paperback publisher subcontracting rights from hardback publishers. Fontana was a subsidiary of the Glasgow printer and publisher William Collins. Pan was set up by the hardback publishers William Collins, Macmillan and William Heinemann, but it subcontracted books from across the whole of British publishing. In 1957 A.S. Frere, the chairman of William Heinemann, commissioned a report on the feasibility of William Heinemann setting up its own paperback imprint by subcontracting books from other publishers with only a small proportion of titles from their own list. This plan was presented to the directors in the board room at the printing house/warehouse among the trees at Kingswood by a young man called James Chesterman (J. St John, *William Heinemann 1890–1990*, p. 368). The meeting went against his proposal because it clashed with William Heinemann's shareholding in Pan and he told me: 'I walked out of the meeting and I walked out of publishing!'

The William Heinemann directors had gone for a compromise which was becoming used more frequently by hardback houses, including Oxford University Press. This was for the originating publisher to produce 'paper-covered' editions of their own titles which they marketed themselves. They were printed on good paper with sewn binding and differed only from the hardbacks in that they had printed card covers wrapped round. Paper-covered editions allowed for sheets to be printed at the same time as the hardbacks, held in sheets and then bound in these covers for publication 18 months later. Also the newly available offset technology meant that the typesetting of an original hardback edition could be photographed and reduced to a smaller format without the cost of resetting and proofreading. To Alan Hill and Keith Sambrook these new concepts seemed to be ideal for William Heinemann to publish hardbacks of new authors and for Heinemann Educational Books to put them in paperback. Paper-covered editions could be made economic at higher prices on smaller runs than paperbacks. So this process was valuable for small print runs in the Series to try out books by new authors.

However, it was the big new printing presses which enabled Heinemann Educational Books to supply the demand as the sales took off in Africa. Mass-market paperbacks are printed like newspapers off rolls of cheap chemical paper with integrated unsewn binding at the end of the production line. Tilling, the owners of the Heinemann Publishing Group, were at a later date to buy Cox and Wyman, which was one of the biggest paperback printers in Britain. The magic number for getting on to these big machines was 10,000 copies and by the mid-1970s most new novels in the African Writers Series were being printed this way, as long as we felt sure that we could sell within three years. We even printed 9,000 copies of Dennis Brutus's poetry. Heinemann Educational Books could build up the print runs and keep the prices down by selling to the only sizeable market there was in Africa at the time, the educational market. Out of this grew a new general market for a wide range of books in the Series.

The dual mandate

Alan Hill and Keith Sambrook proposed that William Heinemann publish hardbacks of books by the outstanding African writers so that the books could get reviews and library sales. A tussle ensued between Heinemann Educational Books and William Heinemann about the details of how this would work. Heinemann Educational Books was confident that it would be bringing interesting work to William Heinemann, which would help refresh their reputation. William Heinemann almost certainly doubted that Heinemann Educational Books would bring publishable work their way.

There is a centrally significant undated memo sent during 1963 by Keith Sambrook to William Heinemann about the relationship between the companies over the publication of Ngũgĩ's *Weep Not, Child*. Keith Sambrook remembers that he was dealing with the editorial director, David Machin, who was serious about the potential for new authors from Africa; soon afterwards, he became a literary agent and took on the representation of Ngũgĩ's work. Keith Sambrook apologises to him:

> I expect you will think we are being very particular about this book but I can foresee difficulties with original work that we want to add to the African Writers Series. The Series is getting widely known in Africa and a considerable amount of writing is coming in direct to H.E.B. All being well some really good work will reach us through our contacts there, particularly Chinua Achebe who is, as you know, editorial adviser to the series.
>
> Now, the most one can offer a writer through the A.W.S. is a paperback market in Africa and 7 1/2% royalty. We want to be able to offer a hard-covered edition, world sales, full promotion and royalty on the hard-cover of at least 10%. We need to be able do this to get and keep the best writers.

William Heinemann wanted to have the conventional delay of 18 months between the publication of the hardback and the paperback. Heinemann Educational Books felt that, as most of the sales would be in Africa, there should be no delay between the two editions. Heinemann Educational Books did give way on this delay and it proved repeatedly to be a nuisance in launching new writers in Africa.

Keith Sambrook pointed out that by using the new paper-covered system

William Heinemann would have the financial advantage of getting sewn sheets for hardback binding and jacketing at a fraction of their usual cost. The origination costs of editorial work and typesetting would be spread over a print run of four or four times the usual hardback run. He stated very firmly:

> In return for this, and for our overhead (Ibadan office, travel in Africa etc) we are looking for terms which will meet our conditions. We are not anxious to cede 'first published' notices or first reviews (which means simultaneous publications) and we want as a matter of course, to be able to offer a higher royalty.

He also said in this memo that Heinemann Educational Books might bring out the hardback edition under the Heinemann imprint rather than under the Heinemann Educational Books imprint. This imprint was already widely used by Heinemann Educational Books for its paper-covered editions of its academic and serious general-market books which needed bookshop distribution which was, in any case, handled in Britain by the William Heinemann bookshop reps (p. xxii). Keith Sambrook goes on to say that they did not think that this was best for the titles by African writers:

> If we were to keep the hard back rights ourselves we should run into marketing difficulties and possible confusion over imprints but our view is that it might nevertheless be better for us to undertake both editions.
>
> If, of course, we can come to an agreement with you on Ngũgĩ, with future titles in mind (and I am sure that there will be A.W.S. which will interest you if you want to take on the best African Writers) then, so much the better all round. (KS to William Heinemann 1963 undated)

In the early days of the Series Alan Hill and Keith Sambrook persuaded William Heinemann to publish selected novels in hardback. Keith Sambrook points out that William Heinemann had very little financial interest in publishing hardbacks of the titles found and accepted for the African Writers Series by Heinemann Educational Books. William Heinemann was the originating publisher for all of Chinua Achebe's five novels and controlled all the subsidiary rights. They thus retained a percentage of the royalties paid by Heinemann Educational Books on their enormous sales. William Heinemann only originated two other titles in hardback which then appeared in the Series.

Martin Secker and Warburg was also in the Heinemann group and they had a reputation for books of intellectual distinction, such as George Orwell's *Animal Farm*. There were collaborations with them, especially after Tom Rosenthal took over as managing director, though he was only interested in subleasing rights to us in their books and not in trying out any of our discoveries on the general bookshop market in hardback, as his response to Ngũgĩ's *Petals of Blood* shows (p. 127). We were glad in 1971 to take paperback rights for the translation of Yambo Ouologuem's *Bound to Violence* (p. 67), a cinematic patchwork of a novel which achieved notoriety for the author's use of cuttings from Graham Greene. After 1979 we gave a substantial new market to Jomo Kenyatta's *Facing Mount Kenya*, which Secker and Warburg had first published in 1937. Secker and Warburg also commissioned and published in 1975 Wole Soyinka's substantial anthology *Poems of Black Africa* (p. 95). Tom Rosenthal knew that, even after the libraries had bought the hardback, Seckers needed the income from the African Writers Series paperback. Although Wole Soyinka had reservations about the 'orange ghetto', it was only through the African Writers Series paperback that Africans could delight in the richness of their continent's poetry.

Heinemann Educational Books, as an academic publisher, did in the late 1960s start issuing hardback editions of selected titles under the Heinemann imprint. Keith Sambrook and I, soon after the publication of *A Grain of Wheat* by Ngũgĩ, discreetly dropped the reference to the educational company on the title pages of the African Writers Series, though on the verso the full legal name of the company was recorded. This disguise did not really work and in any case became less and less important in the 1970s as enterprising reviewers began to realise that there was a new vitality in the writing from Africa and looked for the orange paperbacks for something special. C.J. Driver in *The Guardian* (29 July 1976) contrasted the rewards of reading Nuruddin Farah's African Writers Series paperback of *A Naked Needle* with 'the insipidities' of the other books from British publishers which he had been sent to review (p. 161).

Were there rivals?

Alan Hill in his autobiography tends to present the African Writers Series as carrying all before it. However, there were substantial rivals that also set out to publish African writers. Oxford University Press started the Three Crowns series in 1963, almost at the same time as Heinemann started the African Writers Series. It should have been a major rival, but Oxford University Press had an extraordinary self-denying ordinance that it would not publish novels by contemporary writers. Curiously it would allow the publication of short stories by modern writers, even though these collections have always sold less well than novels.

Rex Collings was the publisher at Oxford University Press who drove the concept of this new paperback series through against doubting colleagues. It was significant that he had had his publishing apprenticeship at Penguin. He conceived of Three Crowns as a 'Penguin' series of African and third-world writing which would include 'Pelican'-type titles, such as *Seven African Writers* by Gerald Moore. The series became best known for its playscripts by Wole Soyinka, J.P. Clark and Athol Fugard.

Rex Collings went off to work for Methuen in 1965, which had the most distinguished list of playscripts and appreciated the importance of Wole Soyinka, who had agreed to offer his future work to them. Rex Collings was, under his own imprint, still publishing Wole Soyinka in 1986 when he became the first writer from Africa to be awarded the Nobel Prize for Literature. Rex Collings was a crucial influence in my own publishing apprenticeship. He arranged that I should, while travelling back through Africa in 1962 on leave from Oxford University Press in Cape Town, meet the writers in heady Lagos and Ibadan.

When he went to Methuen he managed to make sure that I could take over Three Crowns and all his other pioneering general academic publishing on Africa.

Collins was a Scottish printer turned publisher with a big textbook list. Its Fontana paperback series was well established in British bookshops. There were about 20 African titles in the series, several of which sold well in Nigeria and West Africa. Sales of the translation from French of Camara Laye's *The African Child* (1954) rivalled the early sales of Chinua Achebe's novels because of textbook adoption by WAEC. Fontana used full-colour photographic covers, whereas in the 1960s the Heinemann AWS covers for novels were mostly in the classic Penguin orange and black. Hans Zell, when manager of the Fourah Bay University College Bookshop in Sierra Leone, gave me an example of the popularity of the Fontana books in 1968. One evening after dark, with the store packed with students, the lights failed. Hans Zell leapt across the counter and bolted the door as quickly as he could. When the lights came on again, he told me, it was the Fontana books which had been nicked and not the African Writers Series. Kole Omotoso's uncle was a representative for Collins and he produced figures which showed how well their Fontana titles were selling in Nigeria; just as well but no better than the bestselling Heinemann titles. The thriller writer Eddie Iroh was to belabour Heinemann for not selling his thrillers like Fontana. However Fontana kept only about twenty African titles in print in total while Heinemann published some twenty new titles in the Series a year and sales of new authors indeed were lower.

Buchi Emecheta's first two autobiographical novels of an Igbo woman's response to life in Britain, *In the Ditch* and *Second-Class Citizen*, were published by Fontana. Her reputation was well-established with four books by 1979, when she approached us with *The Joys of Motherhood* (AWS 227), which we put in the African Writers Series with a full-colour cover. In 1994, when it had become difficult to sell books to Africa, Heinemann bought in six of the previously published titles and gave heavy promotion to them because her work went down well in British schools and she was available for personal promotion. They also appealed to the market in the US.

Longman tried several times to start series which would rival the African Writers Series. Drumbeats included both Caribbean and African writers. Longman published a collection of promising short stories by a 19-year-old called Ben Okri, who was in 1981 to be the second African winner, after Nadine Gordimer, of the Booker prize, with his novel, *A Famished Road*, published by Jonathan Cape.

André Deutsch was the London hardback publisher who was most seriously engaged with the exceptional work which was coming from Africa and the Caribbean. In the 1950s the firm had taken on a range of writers from the Caribbean, such as V.S. Naipaul, Michael Anthony, Earl Lovelace and Eric Williams, the historian prime minister of Trinidad. Writing from the Caribbean was a particular interest of his colleague Diana Athill, who wrote a revealing and engaging account of the author–publisher relationship called *Stet*. André Deutsch was the only British publisher without an educational list to make a substantial effort to do something new about publishing writers from West and East Africa.

He started both the African Universities Press in Lagos and the East African Publishing House in Nairobi. In the 1960s this Kenyan company's Modern African Library was the dominant series in East Africa in the way that the African Writers Series had become in West Africa. The contacts André Deutsch made through these experiments meant that during the 1960s his firm enthusiastically tried out new writers, most of whom we reprinted in the African or Caribbean Writers Series.

During the 1970s and early 1980s, André Deutsch and Piers Burnett would show us hopeful new manuscripts which they would only take on for hardback publication if they could subcontract to Heinemann for the African or Caribbean market. One of these was the delightfully titled *My Mercedes is Bigger than Yours* by Nkem Nwankwo (1975 AWS 173). When Heinemann Educational Books was in Bedford Square and André Deutsch was round the corner in Great Russell Street, the dining rooms of the two publishing houses were useful places to spread out manuscripts, reports and copies of books. It was an informal but continuing and serious series of meetings. We never established as productive a relationship with William Heinemann and Secker and Warburg, even though they were in the same group of publishers as Heinemann Educational Books.

Broadcasting as a patron of writers

Partly thanks to André Deutsch, publication of writers in English from the Caribbean was a decade ahead of those from Africa. There had been many chances for publication in journals in the Caribbean and in books from well-established and adventurous publishers in Paris and London. But the writers had, in particular, been given the confidence that they could write by Henry Swanzy, who ran the weekly programme 'Caribbean Voices' for the BBC. Austin Clarke, the Barbadian writer whose first novel was published by William Heinemann in 1964, at a meeting in 2004 told of how important it was to get a contribution broadcast on 'Caribbean Voices'. He said that the fact that your work was taken seriously in London was an amazing encouragement to a young writer. The BBC Colonial Service, as it was still called, went out from 101 Oxford Street which became the centre of patronage for Caribbean writers who were trying to make a living in the literary world of London. Henry Swanzy won their laughter by clowning impromptu performances in the BBC canteen. One of his scripts unhesitatingly introduces a review of a very slim volume published in Port of Spain by saying these poems are the work of 'genius'. This time he was right; it was the first book of poems by a poet from St Lucia called Derek Walcott, who was to be the first writer from the Caribbean to win the Nobel Prize for Literature. My novelist mother told me with great admiration of George Lamming, who had been brought to lunch by Henry Swanzy. Thanks to Henry Swanzy and my South African poet father I grew up assuming that there was writing of interest across the world and not just in Fitzrovia, those pubs from Fitzroy Square to Soho where the literary and broadcasting business of the time was drunkenly done.

Broadcasting might have taken as influential a part in the encouragement of writing in Africa as the BBC's 'Caribbean Voices' had done in the West Indies. 'West African Voices' did try to follow the West Indian model. Henry Swanzy spent a year in Accra at about the time of Ghana's independence in 1957 launching a programme called 'Voices of Ghana'. Nkrumah had ambitions to rival Nasser in his outreach in the period just after the Suez crisis when 'The Voice of Cairo' was considered by many British to be the voice of the devil. If Henry Swanzy had been given an African programme from London, perhaps the BBC would have played an equally important role in the establishment of African literature.

The emergence of African literature was reflected rather than created by the broadcasters. A crucially important facilitator of this period was Dennis Duerden, the art critic and artist, who had worked for the BBC Hausa Service in London. Zeke Mphahlele persuaded the Congress for Cultural Freedom to back the setting up of the Transcription Centre in London. The plan was to record programmes by writers, artists and critics which would then be syndicated at a token cost to radio stations in Africa in the period as the countries became independent. They circulated an informative newsletter, *Cultural Events in Africa*. By extraordinary serendipity, when Oxford University Press moved in 1966 from near St Paul's to the Bishop of Ely's House in Dover Street in the West End of London, the Transcription Centre had its offices and studios next door. It was easy to drop in and keep in touch with whoever was visiting London. It became an important source of jobs and was a meeting place for African poets, writers and artists; the BBC canteen had provided the same kind of rendezvous for writers recording for 'Caribbean Voices' in the 1950s.

Dennis Duerden wanted to expand the role of the Transcription Centre so that it would become an Mbari Club in London. He even negotiated a lease for suitable premises, but was stopped. The archives, which have been bought by the Harry Ransom Research Center in Austin, Texas, show that the funders at the Congress for Cultural Freedom were determined to restrict Dennis Duerden to broadcasting. However in an informal way the Transcription Centre did become a club. The administrator, Maxine Lautré, wife of Chris MacGregor, leader of the South African jazz group Brotherhood of Breath (p. 205), managed to keep the business of the Centre going in spite of demands from poverty-stricken artists. Cosmo Pieterse and Dennis Duerden have edited a selection of the Transcription Centre's broadcasts under the title *African Writers Talking* (Heinemann 1972). Dennis Duerden, like Rex Collings, provided practical help for Wole Soyinka when he was imprisoned and tried for holding up a radio station in western Nigeria and broadcasting a message against the war.

Ezekiel Mphahlele, the South African exile writer, had been the first chairman of Mbari in Ibadan. He went to work for the Congress for Cultural Freedom which operated from Boulevard Haussmann in Paris. They sponsored the influential Makerere meeting of writers in July 1962 where Ngũgĩ brought his manuscripts to Chinua Achebe (p.3). Their backing for the Transcription Centre was vital. They also supported African journals which had a key role in the establishment of African literature: *Black Orpheus* in Ibadan, *Transition* in Kampala,

The Classic in Johannesburg and *The New African* in Cape Town (p. 186) and, in exile, in London. The most famous journal the Congress backed was *Encounter* in London. It later emerged that the funds for the Congress came from the CIA and were laundered through various well-known funds as well as by their own Farfield Foundation. The Cold War logic was that publishing in Russia was backed by the state and this covert CIA operation was a way of giving cultural journals and organisations a chance to survive. The African Writers Series never needed such support and survived in the marketplace by exploiting the laws of Western capitalism.

Plays for playing

The BBC Africa Service, openly funded by the British taxpayer through the Foreign Office budget, was to become an important patron of one-act plays, of poetry and of short stories. Several anthologies were to appear in the African Writers Series of work chosen from broadcasts. But the BBC never provided in Africa the degree of early encouragement that, with an inspired producer and active local agents, it had done in the Caribbean.

This book focuses on fiction, poetry and oral literature in the African Writers Series. It was much more difficult to publish drama. None of the publishing editors in Africa or Britain closely associated with the African Writers Series had had the experience of producing plays. I certainly could not judge on the page what might work in performance. So we heavily depended on a few people with a wealth of practical experience of producing plays.

In the spring of 1965 Rex Collings bequeathed me a whole cupboard of manuscripts and proofs at the Oxford University Press. Among them were several plays which were already contracted for Three Crowns. In 1962 Rex Collings had managed to persuade his colleagues to start the series with two plays by Wole Soyinka which had been first published by Mbari in Ibadan. They were *A Dance of the Forests* and *The Lion and the Jewel,* which he had worked on while a playscript reader at the Royal Court in London after postgraduate study at the University of Leeds. In the cupboard were proofs of Wole Soyinka's *The Road* and a script for his *Kongi's Harvest*. J. P. Clark had turned an Ijaw epic into a play called *Ozidi*; this was my first encounter with a writer making use of the oral tradition in a written form. Three Crowns became best known for the publication of single playscripts particularly from Africa. Caroline Davies in her interesting article on the Three Crowns ('The politics of postcolonial publishing' *Book Publishing*) has detailed how hard Oxford University Press found it to sell books in this tiny format with spines that could hardly be read on the shelves of university bookshops. She says that even a renowned play like Wole Soyinka's *The Road* sold only about 12,000 copies. I felt that the playscripts Rex Collings had collected often tended to be constricted by the proscenium arches of the national theatres in Africa which had been Cold War gifts at the time of independence.

Based on my experience at Oxford University Press of how difficult it was to sell individual playscripts, Keith Sambrook and I decided that we could give better value for money by including anthologies and collections of plays within the African Writers Series. These would aim to give a range of examples of how playwrights were writing for new audiences. At least you could read the spines on the shelves of bookshops. Henry Chakava, partly because there was a very successful schools drama competition in Kenya, met the demand with an East African series. Some of the individual scripts which originated in Nairobi, such as the plays by the Ngũgĩs and Mĩcere Mũgo (p. 119), were also, however, included as individual titles in the African Writers Series. There were two main sources for the anthologies which we published fairly regularly over the years: radio broadcasting and the travelling theatres attached to universities in Africa.

The broadcast plays produced for the Transcription Centre and for the BBC African Service were a rich source. Five of the early anthologies were assembled between 1968 and 1972 by Cosmo Pieterse, the South African exiled writer. I first met him at the Transcription Centre where he produced plays for syndication. He used to drift over to the Heinemann offices, two streets and Berkeley Square away, with a ragged pile of scripts and, after an amiable set of casual meetings, an anthology would be assembled. He was found equally useful by Gwynneth Henderson, an adventurous producer on the BBC African Service, and he edited a collection with her from broadcast plays on which they had worked together. They both believed that the dramatic form was closest to the African oral tradition. Cosmo Pieterse was so imbued in that tradition that he disappeared. We had addresses first in the US and then in Rhodesia but he did not find writing letters fitted in with the way he worked.

The travelling theatres were usually based at universities which often produced plays in African languages. *The Imprisonment of Obatala* by Obotunde Ijimere (1966 AWS 18) gives English adaptations of the work from the renowned Yoruba travelling theatre in Nigeria. David Cook and Miles Lee edited a collection from the Makerere Travelling Theatre in Uganda under the title *Short East African Plays in English* (1970 AWS 28). *South African People's Plays* (1981 AWS 224) by Gibson Kente and others gave examples of experimental workshop plays which were being clandestinely performed in the period after the Soweto risings of 1976. The actors would arrive in a township, spread news of their performance by word of mouth and be on their way by the time that the police heard that a performance had taken place.

Michael Etherton was immersed in the travelling theatre tradition but he took a dramatic step in that he created theatres. At the University of Zambia he organised students to build their own outdoor theatre. This had the backdrop of an old tobacco barn and was faced by a half-moon of banked earth seats. Needlessly, he was expelled from Zambia and went on to the University of Kaduna in northern Nigeria, where he worked with a local builder who was skilled in the ancient techniques of earth architecture which stretch all the way to beyond Timbuktu. He and I worked on a pair of anthologies with the titles

African Plays for Playing (1975 AWS 165, 1976 AWS 179). We saw no point in publishing plays which had not been tried and developed under the pressure of actual performance. I had a tense exchange with Nuruddin Farah (p. 161) because our readers did not feel that his written scripts had been produced on stage. As the son of a playwright I understood the way a script is taken out of the author's possession by a producer and actors who can make the words come alive and, when they do not, get the author to rewrite. So the African Writers Series far outpaced Three Crowns even in the publishing of plays.

The challenge of politics

Blue was used by Van Milne in the African Writers Series for titles by politicians and for autobiographies. This colour for non-fiction was just as shamelessly copied from the Pelican imprint as orange for fiction had been copied from Penguin; the adoption of these colours is a reflection of how the Penguin company imprints dominated British paperback publishing at the beginning of the sixties. Blue covers were first used by Van Milne for Kenneth Kaunda's *Zambia Shall be Free*, which was the fourth title in the Series. If Van Milne had stayed at Heinemann after publishing the first four titles there might have been more titles by politicians. The Kwame Nkrumah titles he brought out in hardback at Heinemann never appeared in the Series. *Neo-colonialism* AWS 49 was announced but not published. His wife June Milne was later to establish the Panaf imprint which made editions of all Nkrumah's work available in paperback.

Keith Sambrook told me that Ruth First walked into the office one day soon after the Rivonia verdict with the suggestion that Nelson Mandela's speeches be collected under the title *No Easy Walk to Freedom*, originally published in 1965; this book only really took off after it was reprinted in the African Writers Series (1973 AWS 123) on the tenth anniversary of his first imprisonment on Robben Island (p. 118). Steve Biko's black consciousness movement reflected the next long dark phase of the struggle in South Africa and his writings were published in 1980 under the title *I Write What I Like* (1979 AWS 217) after his death in police custody.

There was an important quartet of non-fiction texts from Kenya. We subcontracted from André Deutsch *The Challenge of Nationhood* (1970 AWS 81) which were the speeches of the charismatic young Tom Mboya, from the time just before he was assassinated. Ruth First worked on the autobiography of Oginga Odinga which had the all too prophetic title of *Not Yet Uhuru* (1968 AWS 38). His connections with the Chinese had frightened the new Kenyatta government. In 1967 Keith Sambrook took his page proofs to Kisumu where he was under house arrest. His son Raila Odinga may or may not have won the Kenyan presidential election of December 2007 in contest with Ngũgĩ's old economics teacher Mwai Kibaki. In 1979, soon after Jomo Kenyatta's death, we subcontracted from Secker and Warburg the book *Facing Mount Kenya* (1979 AWS 219), which was based on the thesis Kenyatta had written in the 1930s under the famous anthropologist Bronislaw Malinowski at the London School of Economics. And of course Ngũgĩ's *Detained*, again in blue covers, was one of the most significant texts about the reality of the way that Kenyatta's KANU government came to run Kenya (p. 119).

A long tradition of writing by Africans

The Series set out, again in Pelican blue covers, to represent the long history of publication in English of work by Africans. Chinua Achebe suggested in 1964 to Keith Sambrook the inclusion *of The Interesting Narrative of the Life of Olaudah Equiano or Gustavus Vassa the African*. This racily written, and somewhat imaginative, travelogue played a key part in the campaign which achieved the parliamentary abolition of the North Atlantic slave trade in 1807. Keith Sambrook, while at Nelsons, had worked on a path-breaking anthology on West African writing with Paul Edwards of the University of Edinburgh. The latter had taught in the free slave colony of Sierra Leone and so was equipped to edit the book which was published under the title *Equiano's Travels* (1967 AWS 10). One hot summer afternoon Paul Edwards appeared in a lather of excitement at the Heinemann offices at 48 Charles Street in Mayfair having just found out that another freed slave, Ignatius Sancho, had lived and established a business in the very same street in the late eighteenth century; sadly he never got round to a book for the Series from Ignatius Sancho's writings to follow his success at introducing Olaudah Equiano in the 1960s to a new audience at the time when the countries of Africa were being freed from a later form of oppression. In the period of independence the African Writers Series set out to give Africans the freedom to write back.

Three books were published close together in 1973/4 which represented this long tradition of writing, in both English and French. Lalage Bown's anthology, *Two Centuries of African English* (1973 AWS 132), made a cultural and political statement in its very title; most of its earliest examples came from West Africa. The satire, *The Blinkards*, by Kobina Sekyi (1974 AWS 136) was first performed in the Gold Coast in 1915. René Maran was a founder in 1924 of one of the earliest journals of negritude in Paris; his novel *Batouala* (1973 AWS 135) was the first title by a black writer to win the eminent Prix Renaudot.

Emmanuel N. Obiechina in *Onitsha Market Literature* (1972 AWS 109) gave examples of an outburst of popular writing and publishing. This extraordinary example of Nigerian enterprise grew at Onitsha, where the great river and land routes crossed at the Niger ferry. At the end of the second world war the government and the West African Frontier Force disposed of surplus printing presses. There was more than enough capacity to supply the stationery needs, and so the printers began to print popular novels, aids to marriage and money-making, and books on religion. Cyprian Ekwensi's first novel for adults, *When Love Whispers*, was published in Lagos and then in Onitsha in 1947. Less well-known, but equally active, were the small presses of Ghana (p. 72).

A range of standards?

The African Writers Series so dominated the field that understandably there have been criticisms of aspects of the way it developed. It has always been fashionable to attack the Series for a range of standards. Heinemann, under the enthusiastic chairmanship of Alan Hill, allowed the Series to grow as talent was found and nurtured. A total of 270 numbered titles appeared during the years from 1962 to 1984. Some one hundred new titles, without the convenience of numbers, were added from 1985 to 2003 (Appendix p. 301).

Were too many books published? Chinua Achebe's reply to this last question by an interviewer for the London *Independent on Sunday* (3 January 1993) at the time of the thirtieth anniversary at the end of 1992 was, 'All I can say is, better too many than too few.' Our aim was to publish as many good books as possible. In the four years from 1970 to 1973 we published an average of twenty books a year. A lot for a single publisher. Not many for a continent. The accountants wanted winners every time. Our colleagues in Africa and we in London wanted as wide a choice as possible. Some became winners to our surprise. The overall success of the Series gave us the freedom to experiment.

There have been accusations that the Series is an 'orange ghetto' where people are treated as 'African writers' rather than just as 'writers'. This introduction has many examples of how we managed to get outstanding writers from Africa recognised in the British and American publishing industry. However, to be included in the Series could also be an enormous advantage not just in the continent itself but in making original work available to people across the world who have a particular interest in Africa. Wole Soyinka's novel, *The Interpreters*, had been published in hardback in 1965 by the great and imaginative André Deutsch. Wole Soyinka did not want it in the African Writers Series. However, his stance took little account of the realities of British bookselling. It was subleased to Panther paperback, who put it out of print six weeks after publication because of the high returns from paperback booksellers in the UK: more space had to be made on the shelves for fast-selling titles by authors like Wilbur Smith. It did eventually appear in the African Writers Series (1970 AWS 76); although an intellectually challenging novel it has sold over 100,000 copies and, like Heineken lager, has reached parts of the world that other paperbacks could not reach. (Heinemann has always benefited in Africa from this confusion of brand names.)

Gareth Griffiths in his book *African Literatures in English* (Longman 2000 p. 79) credits Heinemann with far greater ability to 'control' African literature than was the day-to-day reality. He writes: 'It is arguable that … the aim of a series like the African Writers Series was not so much to publish existing contemporary African English writing as to create it.' It was much more fun than that. All of us in Ibadan, Nairobi or London could only respond to what work was available either from other publishers or in manuscript. It was a long way from carefully constructed textbook publishing. As individuals we were all concerned with the provision of a range of worthwhile books for people to read, not just for education, but to buy for pleasure and entertainment – to help create in Africa what is known elsewhere as 'a general market'.

It has often been alleged that the African Writers Series creamed off the most publishable manuscripts and so made local publishing less viable. Heinemann's demonstrable ability to get an international market both within Africa and across the world did tend to make it the publisher of first resort for authors. But national publishers often had the initial advantage over Heinemann and could do better in their home market, especially as people are interested in local authors. A national publisher is best placed to stimulate demand, keep prices down and reprint fast sellers. The East African Publishing House in Nairobi started the Modern African Library in the 1960s at about the same time as the African Writers Series. Okot p'Bitek's *Song of Lawino* and *Song of Ocol*, two of the most influential works from Africa, first appeared in that series and, only when the company got into financial difficulties in the 1980s, were they sublicensed to Heinemann (p. 98). For the first time Okot p'Bitek's work became available easily in West Africa, in southern Africa and in Britain. The strength of Ravan, Ad Donker, David Philip and other South African publishers meant that, in spite of censorship, many of the writers, such as Mongane Wally Serote, were first published in South Africa before the titles were reprinted in the African Writers Series. In the years after belated Zimbabwean independence a whole cluster of authors were developed by local publishers, above all by Baobab, but also in rivalry by Mambo, College and Zimbabwe Publishing House. Irene Staunton at Baobab not only had the editorial skills of nursing good books out of promising manuscripts but also appreciated the need to support authors by selling international rights (p. 275).

There have also been questions about whether cultural values intrinsic to the process of selecting material for a metropolitan publisher reinforced colonial ideologies. It was rather the other way round. Writers who were initially recognised in Africa later gained international recognition. I was not allowed, did not want, to take on books in London without the support of my colleagues in Ibadan or Nairobi. The Somali writer Nuruddin Farah (p. 154) is an example. It was critics such as Molara Ogundipe-Leslie in Ibadan and Simon Gikandi in Nairobi who identified the qualities which reviewers in London and New York now recognise.

Conspirators in the launch of African literature

On the occasion of his seventieth birthday in 2000 at a conference at Bard College, where he teaches in New York State, there was a distinguished attendance by academics and writers – there were three Nobel prize-winners for literature listed. However, few people there knew of the vital importance of his work on the African Writers Series in encouraging people to write in Africa. Maya Jaggi in an interview on that occasion for *The Guardian* (18 November 2000) quoted Ngũgĩ as saying that Chinua Achebe 'made a whole generation of African people believe in themselves and in the possibility of their being writers'. Maya Jaggi asked Chinua Achebe in the same interview about the fact that he was not paid a fee as Editorial Adviser to the African Writers Series. He replied:

> I thought that it was of the utmost importance. People in England were sceptical. so I knew that I was a conspirator. I was naïve enough to think that if you do good work, you'll get your reward in heaven.

In October 2005 at a meeting at Queen Mary College in the University of London Chinua Achebe again used the phrase 'conspirator in the launch of African literature'. This book will show the 'conspirators' as Alan Hill, Aig Higo, Henry Chakava, Keith Sambrook and myself. We all took advantage of English to provide an international network. We used the links between London and Africa to stimulate an explosion of creative writing in Africa. In these days of so much Afro-pessimism one can say that African writing, as with African music, has reached out across the world. Chinua Achebe in *Home and Exile* (p. 75) acknowledges a debt to Salman Rushdie for his description of the postcolonial in just four words: *The Empire Writes Back*. In this book *Africa Writes Back*.

A Postscript

> 'Like this dispute over your father's inheritance ... the lawyers are eating very well off this case, I believe. How does the saying go? When two locusts fight, it is always the crow who feasts.'
>
> 'Is that a a Luo expression?' I asked. Sayid's face broke into a bashful smile.
>
> 'We have similar expressions in Luo,' he said, 'but actually I must admit that I read this particular expression in a book by Chinua Achebe....' (p. 382)
>
> – Barack Obama *Dreams from My Father*, Crown 2004 Canongate 2007

Works cited apart from titles in the African Writers Series

Chinua Achebe *Home and Exile* Oxford University Press New York 2000 and Canongate, Edinburgh 2003

Festus A. Adesanoye & Ayo Ojeniyi *Issues in Book Publishing in Nigeria* HEB Nigeria 2005

Caroline Davies 'The politics of postcolonial publishing: Oxford University Press's Three Crowns Series 1962–1976', *Book Publishing* Penn State University Press

Ezenwa-Ohaeto *Chinua Achebe: A Biography* James Currey, HEB Nigeria and Indiana University Press 1997

Gareth Griffiths *African Literatures in English – East and West* Longman 2000

Alan Hill *In Pursuit of Publishing* John Murray 1998

Kirsten Holst Petersen 'Working with Chinua Achebe: James Currey, Alan Hill and Keith Sambrook in conversation with Kirsten Holst Petersen', in *Chinua Achebe: A Celebration* Dangaroo Press 1990 and Heinemann 1991

Douglas Killam & Ruth Rowe *The Companion to African Literatures* James Currey and Indiana University Press 2000

J. St John *William Heinemann 1890–1990* William Heinemann 1990

Cosmo Pieterse and Denis Duerden *African Writers Talking* Heinemann 1972

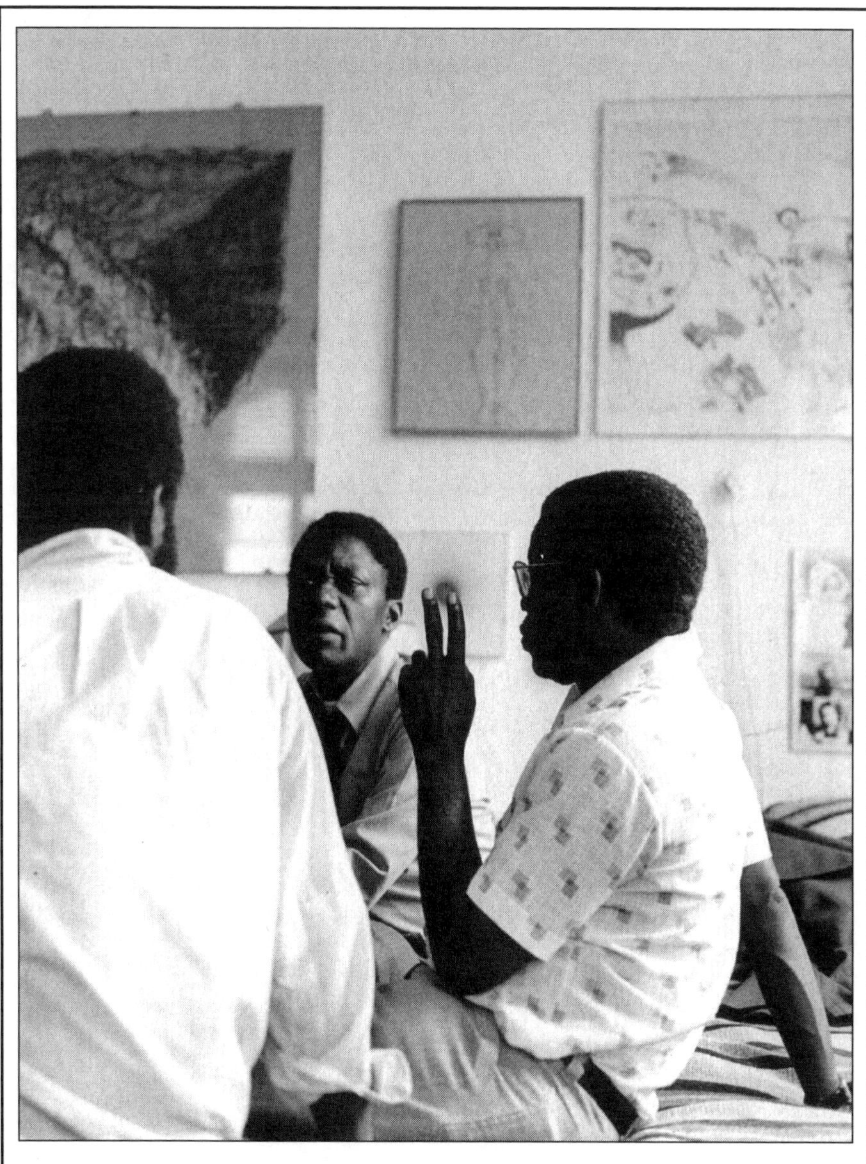

Chinua Achebe in conversation with Mongo Beti at the Berlin Festival June 1979

PUBLISHING Chinua Achebe

'Achebe is the man who invented African literature because he was able to show, in the structure and language of *Things Fall Apart*, that the future of African writing did not lie in simple imitation of European forms but in the fusion of such forms with the oral traditions.' Simon Gikandi, who worked on the African Writers Series as a postgraduate in Kenya and is now a Professor at Princeton University, thus explained the fundamental importance of Chinua Achebe's achievement (quoted from HEB Inc US edition 1996, in Ezenwa-Ohaeto's biography *Chinua Achebe* James Currey, HEB Nigeria and Indiana University Press 1997).

Chinua Achebe was born in Ogidi in the east of Nigeria. His father worked for missionaries as a catechist. Chinua Achebe was educated at the Church Missionary Society primary school, and then was chosen for Government College at Umuahia where, with firm encouragement by the headmaster to use the library, he found books from across the world but not from Africa. When he entered the elite University College, Ibadan, only some one hundred students before him had taken the University of London graduation exams. In 1954 he became a talks producer for the Nigerian Broadcasting Corporation and in 1961 he was appointed Director of External Broadcasting. His first novel, *Things Fall Apart*, was published in hardback by William Heinemann in 1958 (1962 AWS 1) and *No Longer at Ease* followed in hardback in 1960 (1963 AWS 3). In December 1962 he agreed to become Editorial Adviser to the African Writers Series. Two more novels, *Arrow of God* (1964 AWS 16 2nd edn 1974) and *A Man of the People* (1966 AWS 31), were published before he went east after the first Nigerian coup and worked in the diplomatic service of the Republic of Biafra. After the war he collected his stories under the title *Girls at War* (1972 AWS 100) and its publication marked his standing down as Editorial Adviser to the African Writers Series; after this he was called Founding Editor. He has published several stories for the young as he shares with Ngugi a commitment to providing books for children which are set in Africa. His poetry in English, *Beware, Soul Brother* (1972 AWS 120), won the 1972 Commonwealth Poetry Prize, although he has said that he is happier with writing poetry in Igbo. *The Trouble with Nigeria* (1983) was published in the year after the collapse of the oil-rich economy. He supported the growth of publishing in Nigeria by giving the originating rights in these last two and in other titles to Nwamife/Fourth Dimension in Enugu. Many of his essays – especially one on Conrad's *The Heart of Darkness* – have been influential and Heinemann published collections under the titles *Morning Yet on Creation Day* (1975) and *Hopes and Impediments* (1988). His fifth novel, *Anthills of the Savannah*, was published in 1987 (1998 AWS). Since 1970 he has taught at the University of Nsukka and various universities in the US; he has been given over 20 honorary degrees. He is now Professor of Literature at Bard College in New York State. A series of lectures given at Harvard was published under the title *Home and Exile* (OUP New York 2000). In 2007 he was awarded the Man Booker International Prize which recognised his achievement as a whole; he was pleased by the fact that this prize considers the life work of outstanding writers in all the languages in the world.

This section, called 'Publishing Chinua Achebe', focuses on his relationship as author with the conspirators at Heinemann Educational Books. Of course his correspondence as Editorial Adviser to the African Writers Series appears throughout the book.

The mythology over Things Fall Apart

If people have read one novel from Africa it is most likely that it will have been *Things Fall Apart*. Sales in English may well have passed 10 million. There have been translations into almost 50 other languages. It now appears in Penguin Modern Classics. This has happened because it was published in paperback in the African Writers Series. First and foremost Chinua Achebe addressed the book, through the medium of English, to his fellow Africans. But how could they read it? The African Writers Series provided the chance for Africans to do so. The Series also carried the book round the world to a whole new audience interested in independent Africa.

The New York Herald Tribune described *Things Fall Apart* in 1958 as: 'an authentic native document, guileless and unsophisticated'. British reviews were a little more intelligent. *The Times Literary Supplement* said: 'The great interest of this novel is that it genuinely succeeds in presenting tribal life from the inside. Patterns of feeling and attitudes of mind appear clothed in a distinctive imagery, written neither up nor down…His literary method is apparently simple, but a vivid imagination illuminates every page, and his style is a model of clarity' (quoted in Alan Hill *In Pursuit of Publishing* p. 121). The reviews were not good enough for William Heinemann to be able to place the paperback rights with Penguin, Pan, Fontana or with any other of the mass-market paperback publishers in Britain. In 1962 William Heinemann subcontracted the paperback rights to Heinemann Educational Books for the Commonwealth market and eventually sold the US paperback rights to Fawcett.

The mythology about the publication of *Things Fall Apart* is substantial. A calm and amusing account by Chinua Achebe himself appeared in 1995 in that remarkable sequence of interviews with writers from across the world in *The Paris Review* ('The Art of Fiction' CXXXVIV Interviews by Jerome Brookes 1994). Chinua Achebe told how, when he was working for Federal Broadcasting in Lagos, he was in 1957 given a scholarship to study for some months at the BBC. In London he nervously ventured to give his manuscript to Gilbert Phelps, one of the instructors at the BBC, who was himself a novelist:

> He was not really enthusiastic. Why should he be? He took it away, very politely. He was the first person outside of myself, to say, 'I think this is interesting.' In fact he felt so strongly that one Saturday he was compelled to look for me and tell me. I had traveled out of London; he found out where I was, phoned the hotel and asked me to call him back. When I was given this message, I was completely floored. I said, maybe he doesn't like it. But then why would he call me if he doesn't like it. So it must be that he *likes* it. Anyway, I was very excited. When I got back to London, he said, 'This is wonderful. Do you want me to show it to my publishers?' I said, 'Yes, but not yet.' Because I had decided that the form wasn't right. Attempting to do a saga of three families, I was trying to cover too much ground in this first draft. So I realised that I needed to do something drastic, really give it more body. So I said to Mr. Phelps, 'Okay, I am very grateful, but I'd like to take it back to Nigeria and look at it again.' Which is what I did. (*Paris Review* pp. 150–1)

He had been told that to make a good impression he ought to have the manuscript well typed. So he found an agency through *The Spectator* and sent the manuscript with a postal order to pay for two typed copies:

> Weeks passed, and months. I wrote and wrote and wrote. No answer. Not a word. I was getting thinner and thinner and thinner. Finally, I was very lucky. My boss at broadcasting house was going home to London on leave. A very stubborn Englishwoman. I told her about this. She said, 'Give me their name and address.' When she got to London she went there! She said, 'What's this nonsense?' They must have been shocked, because I think their notion was that a manuscript sent from *Africa* – well there's really nobody to follow it up. The British don't normally behave like that. It's not done, you see. But something from Africa was treated differently. So when this woman, Mrs. Beattie, turned up in their office, and said 'What's going on?' they were confused. They said, 'The manuscript was sent but customs returned it.' Mrs. Beattie said, 'Can I see your dispatch book?' They had no dispatch book. So she said, 'Well, send this thing, typed up, back to him in the next week, or otherwise you'll hear about it.' So soon after that, I received the typed manuscript of *Things Fall Apart*. One copy, not two. No letter at all to say what happened. My publisher, Alan Hill, rather believed that the thing was simply neglected, left in a corner gathering dust. That's not what happened. These people did not want to return it to me and had no intention of doing so. (*Paris Review* p. 151)

Alan Hill said in an interview with Kirsten Holst Petersen that he had once asked Chinua Achebe whether he would ever have rewritten the manuscript. His reply was: 'I would have been so discouraged that I would probably have given up writing altogether … and if I had rewritten it, it would have been a different book.' (Petersen p.149)

Chinua Achebe's entertaining account of reactions at William Heinemann owes much to Alan Hill:

> Anyway, when I got it I sent it back up to Heinemann. They had never seen an African novel. They didn't know what to do with it. Someone told them, 'Oh, there's a professor of economics at London School of Economics and Political Science who just came back from those places. He might be able to advise you.' Fortunately, Don Macrae was a very literate professor. A wonderful man. I got to know him later. He wrote what they said was the shortest report they ever had on any novel – seven words: *The best first novel since the war.* So that's how I got launched. (*Paris Review* pp. 151–2)

Like all good stories it is an improvement on the files. Gilbert Phelps, as he had promised, contacted James Michie who was his editor at William Heinemann. There is a whole page report from Gilbert Phelps typed single-spaced in which the opening paragraph says:

> This is a very exciting discovery: a well-written novel about the break-up of tribal life in one part of Nigeria. It is full of characters who really live, and, once begun, it is difficult to put down. It is the first novel, I think, on this fascinating theme. (Report by Gilbert Phelps for William Heinemann 23 September 1957)

There is an additional handwritten paragraph at the foot of the page which was probably added by the William Heinemann editor, Moira Lynd:

> The writing is simple (I wish that all the names were as simple) and extremely effective. There is a slight shortage of commas and a few tiny slips … But in general this is the best sort of plain English. Likeable, exciting, new, strongly recommend.

The novel which forecast a coup

William Heinemann published all Chinua Achebe's five novels in hardback. They were all subcontracted to Heinemann Educational Books for paperback publication in the African Writers Series. As reprints of previously published work, there is little about them in the African Writers Series files.

It was Alan Hill who built up a close publishing relationship with Chinua Achebe. With the quick success of his titles in the African Writers

Series the royalties began to grow. Alan Hill told Kirsten Holst Petersen:

> In those early days I used to go out to see Achebe in Nigeria, in Lagos. He was the very image of a modern Nigerian 'yuppie' in those days. He had a very handsome British colonial-type house, he used to wear a sharp suit, dark glasses and he had a Jaguar car. (Petersen p. 153)

Keith Sambrook, when he first arrived at Heinemann Educational Books in 1963, found David Machin, the editorial director at William Heinemann, sympathetic. Keith Sambrook remembers working with Chinua Achebe in 1963 on the manuscript of *Arrow of God*. It is always paired with *Things Fall Apart* as a novel about traditional life. *The Times Literary Supplement* said that it was: 'primarily a story of village life, centring on the struggle for authority of Ezeulu, chief priest of Ulu, the traditional god of his Umuaro people against both rivals in his own tribe and also district officers and Christian missionaries. And through this combination of concentration and authenticity the novel gets its power'. Somewhat unusually Chinua Achebe said in 1974 that he would like there to be a new edition and he gave the reason in the Preface with his usual charming elegance:

> Whenever people have asked me which among my novels is my favourite I have always evaded a direct answer, being strongly of the mind that in sheer invidiousness that question is fully comparable to asking a man to list his children in the order in which he loves them. A paterfamilias worth his salt will, if he must, speak about the peculiar attractiveness of each child.
>
> For *Arrow of God* that peculiar quality may lie in the fact that it is the novel which I am most likely to be caught sitting down to read again. On account of that I have also become aware of certain structural weaknesses in it which I now take the opportunity of a new edition to remove … (*Arrow of God* 2nd edn p. ix)

His other three novels reveal three stages of a tragic progression in modern Africa: *No Longer at Ease* about corruption in pre-independent Nigeria, *A Man of the People* about the corruption of politicians leading to a coup and *Anthills of the Savannah* on the realities of military rule. I remember in 1960, during my first year living in Africa, finding a copy of *No Longer at Ease* on the bookshelves of Randolph Vigne in Cape Town. The man in the white suit striding across the jacket gave one's liberal soul a lift (p. 37). Then one read the tragedy of this 'been-to' with his overseas education coming back to Nigeria just before independence. When I found this book I had not heard of *Things Fall Apart*. The sweaty grime of Chinua Achebe's Lagos was as important to me as the grittiness of Nadine Gordimer's Johannesburg in *The Lying Days*, which was also published in 1958.

His fourth novel, *A Man of the People*, became part of Nigerian history. Chief Nanga is the charismatic man of the title. The regime in this newly independent African country, which certainly resembled Nigeria, has become so corrupt that military intervention is seen as the only possible redemption for a society in which traditional and imported ways of government have failed to work. A week after the book was published in January 1966 there was the first military coup d'etat in Nigeria. Coups were beginning to become a common event in Africa. Immediately it was rumoured that the broadcaster Chinua Achebe must have known about the coup. Such accusations did not take into account that the publishing process for a book rarely takes less than nine months. It swiftly became clear to Chinua Achebe that he must slip away to the east.

Divided loyalties

It was appropriate that the civil war between Federal Nigeria and Biafra, which started in July 1967 and ended in January 1970, came to be called the Biafran war, especially in the case of novels where some three-quarters of the writers came from eastern Nigeria. It was the event which was to dominate the new work which was published in the 1970s.

Chinua Achebe, as Editorial Adviser to the African Writers Series, kept in touch with us as much as he could during the war; he was anxious to continue to encourage the new writing which was now coming into our offices from all over Africa. His role was diplomatic, so he often travelled to the US to canvass support for Biafra. He increasingly found London a waste of time as Wilson's government had come out in favour of the Federal Nigerian government. Trenchant notes reached us by mysterious means through the Biafran network. Sometimes a telephone call would come from Heathrow after he had landed in London. Alan Hill explained the complexity of his journeys:

> He used to get into a clapped out Super Constellation aircraft at the Uli-Ihiala airstrip and he'd fly to Lisbon, then he'd transfer to an ordinary commercial aircraft and come to London. Then he'd come strolling into the office as cool and humorous as if he'd just come from Chelsea or Kensington. (Petersen p. 155)

Just after the end of the war there is a key letter from Chinua Achebe to Alan Hill dated 21 June 1970 in which he accepted an invitation to join the board of Heinemann Educational Books (Nig.) Ltd, as the letterhead had it:

> Each of your letters was a tonic. Christie and I are most grateful for the real friendship which you have always shown to us but especially for your kind thoughts in our recent troubles …
>
> Aig has just visited us again bringing as usual much material – and spiritual – comfort. I am sure my children think of him by now as a kind of fabulous god-father.

> I notice the great strides which AWS has taken in the last three or four years. I do congratulate you. I look forward to playing an active role once more in its development. I told Aig I would need to engage a part-time typist and purchase a type-writer.

He switched to his publishing plans:

> I have returned the signed agreement for my short stories to [my agent] Higham. Before we go further could I have a set of the stories for revision? I might even be able to add a new story to the list but that depends how quickly I am able to get back into form. I am also thinking of doing a couple of essays which could go out with some of the earlier ones. Somehow I have to get these things out of my way to see another novel.
>
> So Wilson has lost you the elections. I can't say I'm surprised or even sorry! (CA to Alan Hill 21 June 1970)

He of course knew that Alan Hill was a lifelong member of the Labour Party.

Poetry & other portable publishing

He told me at that time that he had found that during the war it was writing poetry, especially in Igbo, which suited his mood. It was portable and could be worked on in an unsettled life. His first book after the war was his collection of poetry *Beware, Soul Brother.*

There was a conflict in Chinua Achebe's loyalties over who should now be the originating publisher for his work. In 1966 just before the war he had tried to start a publishing house called Citadel Press with the poet Christopher Okigbo, who had been the famous representative for Cambridge University Press. After the war Chinua Achebe supported Arthur and Victor Nwankwo in their establishment of Nwamife Publishers in Enugu, which later re-emerged as Fourth Dimension. This was part of a phoenix-like rising of Igbo culture from the ashes of Biafra. He was clear that, however well he had been treated by Alan Hill, Aig Higo and Heinemann, indigenous publishing must develop in Nigeria and Africa.

In 1973 he gave a paper on 'Publishing in Africa' to a conference on that subject at the University of Ife which only appeared in the US edition of his essays. He maintained:

> But we have got to the point where our literature must grow out of the social dynamics of Africa. The role of the publisher as catalyst is no longer adequate – that of initiating and watching over a chemical reaction from a position of inviolability and emerging at the end of it all totally unchanged. What we need is an organic interaction of all three elements – writer, publisher, and reader –

> in a continuing state of creative energy in which all three respond to the possibilities and the risks of change....[An indigeneous publisher] will learn what he needs but will make his own way in the world. This does not mean that he will lack method and organization. On the contrary, his bookkeeping should be so scrupulous that writers will not hesitate to place their manuscripts in his care, or book-sellers to do business with him. Literary gossip travels very far and fast, and a publisher who is a shoddy businessman will soon find no worthwhile manuscripts coming to him. (*Morning Yet on Creation Day* Doubleday 1975 pp. 110–11)

Chinua Achebe dashed off a five-point letter to Aig Higo on all that was available postwar, a narrow strip of scrap paper. As he wrote, 'The driver taking this away is hovering at the window.'

> I have given a copy of the poems to Arthur for the printers. I have asked him to let you have them first to make a copy for yourself.
>
> Whatever you decide with Nwankwo I'd like to have your opinion of them and suggestions. But I do hope that you can work something out. (CA to AH 28 February 1971)

Aig Higo understood how important it would be for this new publisher in eastern Nigeria to have a book by Chinua Achebe in this grim postwar period. Nwamife first published the collection of Chinua Achebe's poetry under the title *Beware, Soul Brother* in 1971 and Aig Higo, although he would not himself be able to sell copies in Nigeria, arranged for it to be subcontracted for the rest of the Commonwealth to Heinemann in London for the African Writers Series. Chi Ude, an exciting editor at Doubleday in New York, published it under the title *Christmas in Biafra*. (He was later to set up his own imprint in New York called Nok, after the ancient culture of the east of Nigeria.)

Point 4 in this long thin letter to Aig Higo was of special importance: 'I heard from Alan's secretary that my spares have been airfreighted to you ... would Arthur Nwankwo bring them?' Chinua Achebe's Jaguar was one of the smaller, slimmer, lower and sportily elegant Jaguars, which had cut a dash in 1960s Lagos. But when he took it east after the coup it was too low-slung for country roads and he left it in his village throughout the war. He told me that, to his amazement, he found that it had not been commandeered.

Other subjects were packed into this letter. One was the possibility of publishing the film script of *Things Fall Apart* after the film appeared. However, he was later to tell Alan Hill:

> The world premiere of the film of *Things Fall Apart* is on May 16 in Atlanta, Georgia. I plan to go down for it. The makers of the film assure me that I will change my mind and like it. I will certainly give it another trial. (The preview which I had last summer was apparently ruined by faulty projection. But I wasn't

> talking of projection or anything of that sort.) (CA to Alan Hill 27 April 1974)

Chinua Achebe's collection of short stories, *Girls at War*, was published in 1972 as AWS 100 and marked his stepping down as Editorial Adviser to the African Writers Series. The collection was drawn from a wider time-span than the war itself. When Chi Ude published it at Doubleday, Chinua Achebe wrote to me from Amherst in Massachusetts:

> Incidentally I should like you to have it on your files that when you come to reprint *Girls at War* you should use the stories in the Doubleday edition. As you probably know I dropped two early stories and put in one new one. I think it is a better book. It is having excellent reviews and was recommended by *Esquire*(!) … (CA to JC 1 July 1973)

We could not do anything about this at the time because, though we had sold 10,000 in the first year, we had 25,000 left in stock. It was not proving easy to sell short stories even by a writer as well known as Chinua Achebe. Keith Sambrook and I felt that he might have written some more stories by the time a reprint was needed of the slim volume and an enlarged edition would give people a bit more value for their money. We continued with the slim edition and by the tenth anniversary it had sold 90,000 copies.

One of the most influential pieces of collecting which he did in this postwar period were the papers, articles and essays in *Morning Yet on Creation Day* which was published in 1975. This inspired title came at the end of a string of working titles: *The Old and the Novel* (1 July 1973), *Three Bags Full* (27 April 1974), *Black and to Stay, Morning Yet and to Stay* and finally *Morning Yet on Creation Day* (4 May 1974). His gentle authoritative firmness is captured in the photograph on the cover taken for *The Observer* during the whirl of publicity for the hundredth title in the African Writers Series: in profile with his arm raised, he is seated in front of billowing filmy white curtains in his room at The Inn on the Park. It is one of my favourite photographs of an author and the base of the cover design of Ezenwa-Ohaeto's biography of *Chinua Achebe*.

International recognition

Much effort was put into celebrating Chinua Achebe's achievement as Editorial Adviser for the first hundred titles in the African Writers Series. Alan Hill gave a party at the Athenaeum which was attended by literary editors of the newspapers and several established British and African authors. As Keith Sambrook said when inviting Chinua Achebe to another Heinemann gathering: 'There will be all sorts of literary gents in attendance, many of whom you will already know, and others who will no doubt be glad of the opportunity to get to know you.' (KS to CA 27 February 1975)

This was the time when he was becoming recognised internationally. In 1973 two of Britain's new plate-glass universities gave him honorary doctorates. There was an elegant gathering in June by the lakes of Stirling University. On 23 May 1974 he was offered the Scottish Arts Council Neil Gunn Fellowship for 1975. He was told that the first holder of the fellowship had been Heinrich Böll, the Nobel Prize Winner. On 5 June 1974 he was offered a Fellowship of the Modern Language Association of America:

> Our role of Honorary Fellows, limited to forty persons, includes such distinguished men and women of letters as Simone de Beauvoir, Samuel Beckett, Heinrich Böll, Jorge Luis Borges … (MLA to CA 5 June 1974)

Chinua Achebe gave his acceptance speech for his honorary doctorate at the University of Kent in Canterbury's borrowed chapel, Canterbury Cathedral. This was in part due to Lyn Innes who was now at Canterbury University, having worked with Chinua Achebe on his journal *Okike* at Amherst College, Massachusetts. Out of this strong association emerged an anthology edited by Chinua Achebe and C.L. Innes called *Modern African Stories* (1985 AWS 270 and the last title to be given a Series number). These two editors were selected for the 1992 thirtieth anniversary collection, a *Book of Contemporary Short Stories*.

Soon after the collapse of the Nigerian currency in April 1982, I borrowed Chinua Achebe's understanding ear to talk to him about the pressures on the new publishing for the African Writers Series and, as we walked round under the plane trees of Bedford Square, I told him of all the trouble I was having with the accountants wishing to cut back the numbers of books published in the Series. Nevertheless, the African Writers Series catalogue for 1984 listed 17 new titles. Chinua Achebe had far more serious worries, as can be told from the title of another book we subcontracted from Nwamife in 1983 called *The Trouble with Nigeria*. The opening sentence reads: 'The trouble with Nigeria is simply and squarely a failure of leadership' (p. 1).

Alan Hill expressed a typical publisher's feelings when he said on 9 May 1974 to Chinua Achebe's agent, that we all hoped he would produce another novel before long. The problem was not the usual problem of the second novel but that of the second period of his life after the war. Ngugi, for example, did not publish a novel between 1964 and 1977; he then moved into a second phase when he wrote in Gikuyu. It was not until 1987 that Chinua Achebe's fifth novel, *Anthills of the Savannah*, was published in hardback by William Heinemann before appearing in the African Writers Series.

PART

1 Writers from WEST AFRICA

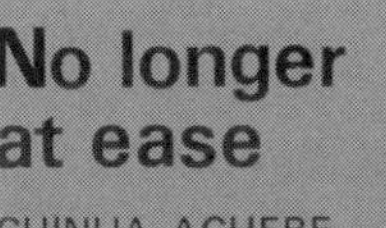

Peter Edwards

George Hallett

George Hallett

George Hallett

Cyprian Ekwensi
Frankfurt 1980

Buchi Emecheta
London 1979

Wole Soyinka
Berlin 1979

1 NIGERIA
The Country where so Much Started

Writing from Nigeria dominated the start of the African Writers Series. When William Heinemann published hardbacks of Chinua Achebe's *Things Fall Apart* in 1958, and of its sequel *No Longer at Ease* in 1960, hardly anybody knew about his achievement in his own country, Nigeria. The appointment in 1962 of Chinua Achebe as Editorial Adviser to the Series did mean that many of the early titles were from Nigeria. His example had set a trend and it was in Nigeria that the novel first took off in Africa. According to *The Companion*, by the end of the twentieth century there were some 500 novels by Nigerians in print, although only a tiny fraction of those appeared in the African Writers Series. The themes which emerged in the work of writers in Nigeria were formative and gave ideas to Africans across the continent of what they might write about.

West Africa the major target

Heinemann Educational Books was granted its independence as a separate company from William Heinemann in 1960, the same year as the freedom of Nigeria from Britain. Alan Hill decided that the two major targets for expansion by the firm were South-east Asia and West Africa. Chief Fagunwa, the famous Yoruba novelist, was appointed as the representative in Nigeria, but died soon afterwards in an accident on a Niger ferry crossing. Keith Sambrook tells of how in 1964 he and Alan Hill were giving a party at the Hotel Bristol in Lagos to launch Chinua Achebe's *Arrow of God*. The tragedy seemed to be seen by Cyprian Ekwensi to have potential for a plot for a novel. Above the drink-fuelled hubbub Keith Sambrook heard his stentorian voice booming, 'I tell you! Daniel Fagunwa was murdered!'

It was not a propitious start. As it worked out, the appointment in 1965 of Aigboje Higo to run the Nigerian office was of key importance in the take-off of the African Writers Series (p. 4). The quick establishment of the dominance of the African Writers Series in Nigeria and West Africa grew out of the close working relationship between Aig Higo in Ibadan and Chinua Achebe in Federal Broadcasting down the road at Lagos.

Initially Heinemann books were stocked and distributed by Longman, but in 1972 Aig Higo, just after the end of the civil war, built a substantial Heinemann warehouse at Jericho in Ibadan in time to be able to handle the African Writers Series by the container load during the oil boom in the middle 1970s. A vivid memory of that period is of seeing the doors of a container being opened in the yard at the warehouse and of a raft of copies of Kenneth Kaunda's *Zambia Shall be Free* flooding out on a wave of sea-water. In a drive to clear the congestion in Apapa docks the container had been pushed off a wharf by an armoured car under the command of a general nicknamed 'The Scorpion'.

There was an important change in 1974 when, under the terms of the Indigenisation Decree, 60 per cent of the shareholding of the Nigerian company had to be sold to Nigerians. Alan Hill and Aig Higo took advantage of this to give authors options to invest, often as advances on their own work. This was in contrast with other British publishing companies which just tended to go for investment with business partners. This policy enabled authors to have a chance to share in the enormous income from the expansion of education with such oil-funded schemes as UPE (Universal Primary Education). Elechi Amadi decided, after initially accepting the offer, that he could not afford it. Chinua Achebe wrote from Amherst College, Massachusetts:

> I understand that the changeover procedures in Nigeria went quite smoothly. I am really glad to be part of another HEB venture of faith. With you and Aig in it I have no doubt that it will be as successful as AWS. (Chinua Achebe to Alan Hill 27 April 1974)

Alan Hill tended to give the impression that Heinemann was alone in its literary initiative in the early 1960s. There were serious rivals such as the African titles included in the Collins Fontana paperback imprint and those published by Longman (p. 14). Textbooks in fact provided the critical mass which enabled several British publishers to distribute new African writing at little risk and with increasing hopes of school sales. The educational publishers also had the means of distributing elsewhere in Africa, even though it was from warehouses in Britain.

Mbari, the pioneers

The brilliant but short history of Mbari Publications in Nigeria in the 1960s shows the difficulties for a general publisher in Africa which did not have an educational list to pay for the costs of effective representation and distribution. From 1957 the magazine *Black Orpheus* introduced a range of new voices including, in translation, the writers of negritude. Mbari provided imaginative patronage of the sort that African writers in French had obtained from Présence Africaine in Paris and Dakar.

The Mbari Club was founded in March 1961 in a converted Lebanese nightclub in Ibadan; food could be ordered in from the restaurant next door. It provided exhibition space for artists. There were premieres of plays by Wole Soyinka and J.P. Clark and the Yoruba travelling theatre gave performances.

Poets such as Christopher Okigbo, Wole Soyinka and J.P. Clark gave readings. Chinua Achebe and Aig Higo were active members. Ulli Beier, a German refugee who had trained in linguistics in London, had joined the extramural department at University College, Ibadan. He and Wole Soyinka were described as the convenors of the Club. Ulli Beier, with his ceaseless energy, facilitated further Mbaris in Oshogbo, Benin City and elsewhere. Never has 'creative outreach' in Africa reached further.

In addition to all this, Mbari started the most significant publishing list of fiction, plays and poetry by Africans in English in the 1960s; 17 titles were published in three years. Lalage Bown, also from the extramural department in the University College, Ibadan, kept the manuscripts flowing to the printers. Sales of Mbari's publications all over the continent showed that there were people who wanted to read writing by Africans; Alex la Guma and Dennis Brutus could not be published in South Africa, but appeared first in the Mbari list in Nigeria.

Certain individuals in British publishing did realise that something special was happening at Mbari. Julian Rea at Longman managed to persuade his colleagues in England to distribute *Black Orpheus* internationally. Keith Sambrook, at Chinua Achebe's suggestion, started negotiating with Ulli Beier for Alex la Guma's *A Walk in the Night* both as a hardback and in the African Writers Series. Rex Collings bought rights in plays by Wole Soyinka and J.P. Clark to appear as founding titles in Oxford University Press's Three Crowns series. Christopher Okigbo agreed with Chinua Achebe and Aig Higo that there should be a collection of his poems in the African Writers Series.

There were other outstanding individuals in this labyrinth of connections spreading out from Ibadan. In the 1950s and until 1966 all roads led to Ibadan, which boasts that it is the largest African town in the continent. Zeke Mphahlele had been one of the *Drum* writers in Johannesburg and his classic autobiographical book *Down Second Avenue* had been published by Faber in 1959. In 1962 he persuaded the Congress for Cultural Freedom in Paris to fund the seminal Mbari meeting of African writers at Makerere University College. They also funded the magazine *Transition* which had been started in 1961 by Rajat Neogy in admiration, though not in imitation, of *Black Orpheus*; Kampala in this period was a cultural centre like Ibadan. Zeke Mphahlele was later to start the Chemchemi Centre in Nairobi in an attempt to replicate the Mbari idea outside Nigeria.

The Biafran war, which started in July 1967, split the nation and the Mbari Club. Chinua Achebe, Christopher Okigbo, Gabriel Okara, John Munonye and others took up positions in the new Republic of Biafra (p. 54). Wole Soyinka was imprisoned for 27 months by the military regime in the west of the country for trying to keep contacts open with friends and writers in the east.

What is West African English?

Nelson, the renowned Scottish publisher and printer, were pioneers in textbook publishing in the West Indies and Africa. They published several novels in Yoruba by D.O. Fagunwa. The first one was published in 1938 and Wole Soyinka translated it into English 30 years later as *Forest of a Thousand Daemons*. Chief Fagunwa was well-known as a writer when he was appointed Heinemann Educational Books' representative in Nigeria.

Amos Tutuola got the idea from D.O. Fagunwa of using Yoruba mythology and wrote several Englished novels. His first manuscript, *The Wild Hunter in the Bush of the Ghosts*, reached Faber, as Bernth Lindfors has shown in his edition, via the Hungarian director of Focal Press who was selling photographic materials to Amos Tutuola to photograph ghosts; the manuscript was in fact decorated with photographs of hand-drawn sketches of the ghosts. Geoffrey Faber read the manuscript of *The Palmwine Drinkard* on a train on the way to dinner at All Souls College in Oxford and insisted that not a word should be changed. Dylan Thomas's excited review in *The Observer* (6 July 1952) drew attention to the extraordinary originality of Amos Tutuola's writing. Unfortunately this made Europeans patronisingly assume that all that could be expected from African writers was quaint and folksy. Alan Hill in his autobiography tells how he was offended by the publisher Fred Warburg telling him that he would have been prouder to publish Tutuola than Achebe. Most literate Nigerians thought Amos Tutuola let them down by his bad English, and it took Chinua Achebe's Equiano memorial lecture at the University of Ibadan in 1977 to make people look again at his originality.

It has been a continuous challenge for writers in Africa to reflect their native languages in their written English. Bernth Lindfors in his seminal article 'The palm oil with which Achebe's words are eaten' in the very first issue of Heinemann's journal *African Literature Today* in 1968 showed how Chinua Achebe seamlessly uses Igbo phrases in his apparently English English. In South Africa R.L. Peteni was given this idea by an article by Bernth Lindfors and set out to reflect his own Xhosa sayings in his novel *Hill of Fools* (p. 194). Gabriel Okara's poetic novel *The Voice* stands out as a knowing linguistic experiment. He informs the English of his main character Okolo with the word order of his own 'straight' Ijo language. This is in contrast to what *The Companion* vividly described as the 'crooked' English of political propaganda. Gabriel Okara's novel was first published by André Deutsch in hardback in 1964, and then in the African Writers Series in 1970 (AWS 68). In 1964 the Ivorian writer Ahmadou Kourouma failed to place *Les Soleils des Indépendances* with a Parisian publisher because of its Malinke-inflected French; it had to be published in Québec where they took a less conservative view of the language.

Themes & periods in Nigerian writing as reflected in the African Writers Series

The three novels in Elechi Amadi's trilogy, starting with *The Concubine*, give a singularly pure picture of life before the arrival of the colonising white man (p.47). Several Nigerian novels of the time also re-create life in the past. Sometimes the personal penalties that characters suffered from religion and other traditions were portrayed. Sometimes there was retreat into the serenity of rural life. Writers were much influenced by Chinua Achebe's *Things Fall Apart* and *Arrow of God*. Flora Nwapa was a skilled story-teller who, in *Efuru* (1966 AWS 26) and *Idu* (1970 AWS 56), became the first writer to put women at the centre, although her early heroines tend to emerge as 'worshipful servant-wives to erring husbands', as *The Companion* put it.

In fact several other publishers, in Nigeria as well as in Britain, issued work by West African writers. There was also work to reprint and some of these titles were later incorporated in the African Writers Series. T.M. Aluko's humorous *One Man, One Wife* (1967 AWS 30) had been published by the Nigerian Printing and Publishing Company in 1959. But there had been no contract and no royalties. Heinemann's interest in reprinting meant that the company belatedly paid Tim Aluko what he described as 'a Christmas present' of overdue royalties (TA to KS 21 December 1965), so that they could maintain their hold on the book.

After independence in 1960, Nigerian writers were all too soon able to find rich material in their own society. In *Kinsman and Foreman* (1967 AWS 32) Tim Aluko wittily satirises the corruption which was already well established in the colonial Public Works Department. The story-teller Cyprian Ekwensi entertainingly portrays efforts at 'African unity' in *Beautiful Feathers* (1971 AWS 84), even though he was working as Head of Information for the new Nigerian state. Wole Soyinka's *The Interpreters* (1970 AWS 76) reflects the disenchantment of young Nigerians with the new political class. Chinua Achebe's *A Man of the People* (1966) was percipient in its forecast of military rule (p. 31). Within six months of its publication the Republic of Biafra had been declared and the Nigerian civil war began, which was to have a deep effect on what went into the African Writers Series.

In the 1970s there was a whole new generation of writers who had been born in the 1940s and who began to bring out new work. Kole Omotoso (p. 52) was among a group who felt that writers should be more concerned with contemporary political and social problems. The Biafran war dominated Nigerian work by new writers which was selected in Ibadan, Nairobi and London for the African Writers Series during the mid-1970s and early 1980s. Books on the theme proved saleable in the general market both in Nigeria and elsewhere in Africa. Some of the established writers also wrote books about the war. Cyprian Ekwensi based his novel *Survive the Peace* on the experiences of people trying to find one another after the end of the war. John Munonye and Elechi Amadi wrote novels about the Biafran war, but both showed themselves more at home in their usual settings. The two most successful books about the war in the Series were both non-fiction and both by military men (p. 58).

Cyprian Ekwensi

The question of popular literature

Many mythologies have grown up about the start of the African Writers Series; there were all sorts of descriptions such as a 'bold venture' or 'a great risk'. It was nothing compared with the investment of time and money needed for a new textbook. The demand for the first four titles did surprise Heinemann. At the time of the first school buying season after the foundation of the African Writers Series Keith Sambrook wrote about Cyprian Ekwensi's *Burning Grass* (1962 AWS 2) to the book exporters for the Church Missionary Society:

> Orders, however, have been far in excess of our most optimistic hopes, and this has caused difficulties in supplying back orders and ensuring that Longmans have sufficient stock under the new arrangements at Ikeja. (KS to Gordon Dawes, CMS, 2 October 1963)

The sales potential for this well-established author was underestimated. The book had, according to Van Milne's presentation to his colleagues in 1962, been 'revised for school reading'. During the 1960s the sale was to build up to average about 12,500 a year, although his books were rarely adopted for exams.

Cyprian Ekwensi, the first writer to make a mark in both Nigeria and Britain, was already well established before the start of the African Writers Series. Born in 1921 in northern Nigeria, he went to Government College in Ibadan, to Achimota College in the Gold Coast and then to study for a degree at the Chelsea School of Pharmacy in the University of London. He died on 4 November 2007.

His first book was *When Love Whispers*, which was published in Lagos and then in Onitsha in 1947. He was soon producing children's stories for Nelson, Longman and Cambridge University Press. His first full-length novel, *People of the City*, was published in Britain by Andrew Dakers in 1954 and then quickly brought out as AWS 5 in 1963 when the sales of *Burning Grass* were so good. His attitude to writing came across in two letters to Van Milne in 1962. He objected to an article in the weekly magazine *West Africa*:

> When I was writing *People of the City* I did not mean it to be 'a proletarian diatribe against the evils of urban culture.' I just wrote, as I always do, for my own pleasure and because I enjoy life and feel like expressing it. (CE to Van Milne 6 August 1962)
>
> ... knowing my philosophy of writing you understand that I am not going to fold my hands while the Ekwensi Admiration Society troops its colours outside the windows on a moonlit night. (CE to Van Milne 24 September 1962)

In Britain or the US at that period a writer with his facility and vital personality would probably have made a fortune. The market in West Africa was so education-based that he felt less secure. When *Lokotown and Other Stories* was published in 1966 as AWS 19, only he and Chinua Achebe had three titles in the Series. There was a tense exchange with Keith Sambrook when Cyprian Ekwensi discovered that Chinua Achebe's name was to appear as Editorial Adviser on *People of the City* when it was reprinted in the African Writers Series. He exploded:

> I absolutely refuse to have his name tagged on to *People of the City*. My name can stand on its own in any market ... If you are terrified about 'literary quality', then drop the whole project. (CE to KS 29 May 1963)

Chinua Achebe and Keith Sambrook took Cyprian Ekwensi's point.

Cyprian Ekwensi was Director of Information at the Federal Ministry of Information from 1961 to 1966. In a letter to Van Milne 1963 he reported how busy he was on the diplomatic and media round presenting propaganda for the new Nigerian state. The years from Nigerian independence in 1960 until the military coup and the Biafran war in 1967 were probably his most productive publishing period.

Hutchinson published *Jagua Nana* in 1961. This introduced one of the most memorable characters in African fiction. Jagua is a prostitute who finances a teacher through law school in England on condition that he marries her on his return. In the 1960s this subject would not have been considered suitable for school reading, and the novel only appeared in the African Writers Series in 1975 (AWS 146) when it was clear that there was a general market in Africa.

Arthur Ravenscroft in an article in *Contemporary Novelists* says:

> *Beautiful Feathers* [1971 AWS 84] is the most successfully satirical of Ekwensi's books, with its wry treatment of politicians and civil servants. Its symbolic big-game hunt, when white observers get away with the quarry while the African delegates to a Conference on African Solidarity squabble among themselves, points to one of Ekwensi's genuine strengths – his sensitiveness to the larger though sometimes obscured political issues of the day.

An ominous paragraph concludes a letter in September 1966 from Cyprian Ekwensi to Keith Sambrook:

> Here in Nigeria, we live in very troubled times. There is a continuous expectation of disaster which somehow seems to be postponed from minute to minute by some unseen forces. There are prayers that the disaster never comes and there is the fear that it is pre-ordained to come somehow and that if it does not come the purification process necessary for the building of a permanent Nigeria will not be commenced. (CE to KS 7 September 1966)

He managed to survive the war, which he was personally against, by falling back on his training as a chemist and importing pharmaceuticals to Enugu in Biafra. He conceived his next novel *Survive the Peace* (1976 AWS 185) at the end of the war in 1970, when he watched scattered families trying to unite. He finished it on the famous University of Iowa Writing Program and delivered the manuscript to Heinemann in 1975. It was serious novel on a world event by a known writer. We felt that it had sales potential in Britain as well as in Nigeria. Moira Lynd, an understanding reader, could not recommend it to William Heinemann, so we decided we would go ahead with the hardback. Ros de

Lanerolle, with her taste for political actuality, in a report dated 5 May 1975 found it 'moving and mature, well controlled and a pleasure to read'. Aig Higo was firmly frank:

> I think we ought to publish. It is a different type of Biafran novel – frank, detailed, down to earth and painful … it is heavy going. Perhaps the typical Ekwensi style suits the mood of 30 agonising months. The second fault can also be sorted out in the House. It is that the English needs to be made a little more international. (AH to JC 13 May 1975)

When I wrote to Cyprian Ekwensi to accept he replied:

> It seems at last my original intention of having Heineman as total Publisher will be realised. As I said, I had Heineman in mind when the book was being written in Iowa. Hutchinson have been publishing for me, but they are not as involved in Africa as your House is. (CE to JC 17 May 1975)

In my publishing proposal in May 1975 I finished with rather too prophetic a recommendation: 'This novel is on offer to Hutchinson for hardback. We should make an immediate bid for the paperback – and, I should suggest, for hardback if Hutchinson are as slow as we usually are over AWS titles nowadays.'

Cyprian Ekwensi became furious that the work on the manuscript was taking so long that the publication was pushed back to the middle of 1976. In an explosive letter he sums up the frustrations of an author's feelings about the extended time it was taking to publish a book by an established author:

> Sometimes I wonder why I ever devoted so much of my life to WRITING … the work put into one book is 6 years and all I have earned so far is the miserable advance of £400 which my agent squeezed out of you. You were crying as you wrote the cheque.
>
> Forgive me, but the long and the short of it – from the Author's point of view – is that Publishers as a class of people are striving to perpetuate the myth and magic of publishing. UNLESS the Writer is out through this tyranny he will not feel that publishing is so difficult. I just can't believe it. AND it has to happen to an established author EACH TIME he writes a new book.
>
> In short, the impression we must all take to our graves is that WRITING is the one profession in which you are an APPRENTICE ALL YOUR LIFE. There is no retirment. You just have to go on struggling in the queue until you die!
>
> Fortunately for me I have now become a Publisher. We recently printed 50,000 copies of a publication on DIMKA called THE WAGES OF TREASON. It sold out THE SAME DAY. We printed a further 30,000 copies within 3 days, and all sold out within 5 days. Maybe because Dimka the Assassin was hot news, but there you are. That's one type of publishing, and you may sneer at it, but it keeps 1000 employees in bread and bacon which is what any PROFESSION is about.
>
> I have written this letter to you because you know already my views on the snobbery which HEINEMAN treats me and my work. Which is one reason why you should strive to prove that my impression is unfounded …

I am one of you now. (CE to JC 10 May 1976)

Aig Higo immediately sent him a letter assuring him of the high esteem in which everybody at Heinemann held him. He reflected:

> You made a point which struck me forcibly; which is the tendency to regard writing or authorship as a profession in which the writer or author remains an apprentice all his life ... Shakespeare, Dickens, Okigbo etc. all died apprentices while the Ekwensis, Achebes, Senghors etc. are the living apprentices! (AH to CE 28 May 1976)

I sent a typical publisher's reply to this onslaught:

> I do understand your frustration. Nevertheless, you put completely the wrong interpretation upon it. As I said in my cable, yours is the only book from the African Writers Series we have the honour to be putting out in hardback this year. We have to make sure we have enough time to build up the publicity. Only yesterday I was having lunch with the literary editor of the *Sunday Times* which is just about the most prestigious reviewing vehicle in London, and telling him about your novel. We are proud to be publishing it. We intend to give it the treatment it fully deserves. (JC to CE 19 May 1976)

The trouble was that Aig Higo and I did feel that the book needed nursing. Heinemann, with its market in the university bookshops, was demanding a sophistication which its editors in Africa and Britain were now finding in the manuscripts of a whole new generation of new writers from Africa.

We were not the only people to be confronted by Cyprian Ekwensi. He told us one day in Aig Higo's office soon after the war about his efforts to get the substantial Russian royalties which had been building up in blocked roubles. He told us, 'I went to the Russian embassy in Lagos and said "Where is my money?" The Russian smiled. I said "I have no money. I have been in a war. You tell me my books are selling millions! You must pay me my money!" The Russian took me downstairs to a room without windows. The Russian sat on the other side of the table. I asked for my money. The Russian smiled and smiled and smiled. The Russians! They are not people!'

Elechi Amadi

Life before the Europeans

A letter dated 8 November 1963 arrived from a Captain Elechi Amadi of the Military School, Zaria with a manuscript called *The Concubine* and a postal order for 5 shillings in case it was rejected. He said:

> The title of this book and a few passages in it will probably make it unsuitable material for your African Writers Series which is educational. However if the material is worth publishing at all I don't mind in what series you put it. (EA to HEB 8 November 1963)

Heinemann was to publish almost all of Elechi Amadi's work. He was a writer whose assured style came to be highly regarded by academics in a secret and private way. 'It is perhaps easy to mistake Amadi's elegant restraint as lack of profound and passionate concern', says the contributor to *The Companion.*

Keith Sambrook went to Nigeria in April 1964 for the launch of *Arrow of God* which develops the theme, initiated in *Things Fall Apart*, of the impact of British imperial rule on Igbo traditional life. Chinua Achebe and he decided to publish Elechi Amadi's novel, which was set in an earlier period before the arrival of white men; its concerns overlapped with those of Chinua Achebe. It made an interesting comparison, not least in the confidence of its writing.

This was the first of a carefully constructed trilogy *The Concubine* (1966 AWS 25), *The Great Ponds* (1969 AWS 44) and *The Slave* (1978 AWS 210). The novels drew on the history of Elechi Amadi's Ikwerre people in eastern Nigeria before the coming of Europeans. On the last page of *The Great Ponds* it is revealed that the plague called *wonjo,* which is overwhelming the villagers even though they have never seen a white man, is the Spanish influenza of 1919. His stories show how the relationships of individuals suffer because of the ances tral tradition. Recognition outside Africa only came slowly. We were not able to place his first two books with any American publisher, although sales were building up through the importer Humanities Press. I wrote in 1972:

> There is no doubt that your public is steadily growing. I find again and again that people who 'discover' your books think that they are the only people who appreciate them and are surprised to hear about how many others there are. For instance, when Dr Eustace Palmer of the University of Sierra Leone sent us his manuscript for *An Introduction to the African Novel*, he headed his chapter on your work, 'In Defence of *The Concubine*'. Fortunately we were able to persuade him that was not necessary, but there is no doubt that people are still discovering your work. (JC to EA 28 November 1972)

Elechi Amadi, with military determination and with the experience of a civil war between the second and third volumes of the trilogy, delivered *The Slave* in 1977. Henry Chakava and Laban Erapu in Nairobi were reserved:

> ... the East African reader will feel quite disappointed that after 200 titles in the AWS, we are taking him back to the period before *Things Fall Apart.* But strictly as a novel it reads well. (HC to JC 7 October 1977)

We did try to persuade him to rewrite the concluding chapters but I made it clear in sending the reports that we would publish it whether he changed it not. Aig cabled:

> FOUND SLAVE OWNER IN PORT-HARCOURT LAST WEEK TO MY SURPRISE ... HE WILL NOT (REPEAT NOT) RE-WRITE THE SLAVE. I FEAR WE SAW HIS POINTS AND AGREED. (AH to JC 31 October 1977)

The Biafran war deeply affected his personal and writing life and he was to write one of the very best books about the war called *Sunset in Biafra* (1973 AWS 140) (p. 58). Distribution of his first two books was badly hit. A hardback edition of *The Concubine* was published first in 1966, so publication of the AWS edition was held back for 18 months and reached Nigeria in the period leading to the war. Elechi Amadi had left the army and was teaching at Igrita Grammar School in Port Harcourt, which was to become the oil capital of Nigeria. Keith Sambrook wrote to him in February 1967 a month after the coup and six months before the outbreak of war:

> I think that one of the reasons that the book is not on sale in the East is that very few Eastern Bookshops have been ordering from Lagos recently. In previous years they visited the warehouse to collect their books and benefit from the extra discount on 'collected' sales. This has not been easy for them this year. The best chance is CMS and they have recently taken extra stocks of some of our titles in Onitsha and Port Harcourt. (KS to EA 8 February 1967)

This annual migration of booksellers reflected the enormous demand for books and learning in the east.

Nothing was heard of Elechi Amadi for over a year and half until one day he appeared at the Ibadan office, as Aig Higo reported to us:

> Elechi lost his job and was detained by Ojukwu in July last year. He escaped only on the liberation of Port-Harcourt by Federal Forces. Between July last year and now, he has not received any salary so he really was desperate when he came in. He had practically nothing except for a handbag containing a new manuscript which he submitted to me. (AH to KS 5 November 1968)

This manuscript was of a rather stylised Shakespearean verse drama *Isiburu* which was being put on as a Christmas production under wartime conditions. Aig Higo gave him a loan and wrote on 5 November 1968 asking that London turn this into an advance on royalties. (It was published in a school series rather than in the AWS.)

Henry Chakava lamented in 1977 on reading *The Slave* that Elechi Amadi had not written about contemporary Africa. In the 1980s he did use the Biafran war as the setting for his fourth novel which turned out, in terms of relations with his publisher, to have the rather too appropriate title of *Estrangement* (1986). David Cook, formerly the adventurous professor of English at Makerere and in the early 1980s at Lagos, had a deep admiration of Elechi Amadi as 'such an assured stylist'. Although his report was reserved he wrote:

> This is an ambitious work which juxtaposes many of the contrasted basic ingredients of contemporary Nigerian life with a new urgency. The strong pull of the umbilical cord of tradition provides the central tension of the novel. (Report by David Cook undated)

The manuscript arrived at just about the time that the foreign exchanges closed in April 1982, leaving Heinemann in a position where it would take years of negotiation to get foreign currency to meet a percentage of the debts for the container loads of *The Concubine* and other books which had flooded into Nigeria in the oil-boom years. Elechi Amadi had come to expect substantial advances for his new titles. By 1982 sales of *The Concubine* approached 300,000. Sales of *The Great Ponds* and his autobiographical *Sunset in Biafra* were each round a healthy 50,000. *The Slave*, the third volume in the carefully planned trilogy, had reached only 10,000 five years after its publication. This pattern of declining sales for later titles by a successful writer was not uncommon in the African Writers Series and the enormous sales of *The Concubine* reflected its early adoption as a set book. A new canon had been established among the early titles. As John Watson at Heinemann Inc found, the company's accountants had come to expect the enormous set-book sales; they undervalued the steady sale of a wide range of titles in the Series and dismissed 10,000 sales for a novel as a failure.

I wrote to Elechi Amadi on 12 January 1984 to accept *Estrangement.* He objected that the £2,500 advance on all his work was scarcely more than what we had offered for *Sunset in Biafra* in 1972. He demanded £10,000 but, in the situation of economic collapse in Nigeria, we stuck to our original offer. He asked for the return of the novel in March, but on 6 July 1984 wrote:

> Since you are still holding on to *Estrangement* in spite of my letter of 23rd Mar., you might as well get on with the publication. Moreover my wife Hilary is expecting our baby in August and I need sterling. Please instruct your bankers to pay the royalty advance of £2,500 (plus a wedding present?) into my accounts. I hope you will stretch a bit or I shall blame Heinemann if the baby suffers from malnutrition. Besides, Heinemann may well have a stake in the child because a prenatal divination here strongly indicates that it will write better than the father. You may be pleased to know that a publishing house I contacted could not offer me better terms. (Is there an OPEC-like cartel of UK publishers?) (EA to JC 6 July 1984)

I wrote to him in September 1984 at the time when I was told by the new management at Heinemann that I would have to reduce publishing in the Series to a couple of titles a year. I told him that we only planned to print 3,000 copies and said:

> I know that these negotiations have been a disappointment for you. They have been for me also. But the international debt crisis has led to all sorts of estrangements which are the more painful because of the past relationships. (JC to EA 10 September 1984)

In writing to Vicky Unwin in 1985 he said:

> Thanks for your circular letter announcing the departure of Mr. James Currey and reaffirming your commitment to the continuing growth of the AWS. James Currey is a personal friend and his departure makes [me] sad. However I hope HEB will fill the gap and pursue its noble objectives. (EA to VU 2 May 1985)

John Munonye

Making the ordinary extraordinary

Of John Munonye *The Companion* maintained: 'Not even Chinua Achebe, a contemporary with the same background and a similar folkloric imagination, paints rural characters with as much sympathy.' The two writers were contemporaries at the new University College at Ibadan. Like Elechi Amadi he set out, in a highly organised way, to write a trilogy. *The Only Son* (1966 AWS 21) and

Obi (1969 AWS 45) were written before the war and the project was only completed a decade later with *Bridge to a Wedding* (1978 AWS 195). The theme of these three novels is *ahamefule* (may my ancestral identity be preserved) which is fulfilled in children and a family house; the setting is among the Igbo of eastern Nigeria, but the elegance of his English enabled readers throughout Africa to respond to this universal theme within the context of their own societies. The hero of *The Oil Man of Obange* (1971 AWS 94) tries to find school fees for his outstandingly clever children. Mishaps feed on mishaps. The loss of his one economic asset, a bike, brings one to understand the mechanics of destitution; for him suicide is the only way out. *The Companion* described it as a 'classic in the vivid depiction of the common person'. *A Dancer of Fortune* (1970/1974 AWS 153) is a picaresque novel about Ayasko the dancer, who uses his talents to advertise the wares of the patent-medicine vendor Avarido. They are all engaged, as the reader Richard Lister pointed out, in making a fast buck, doing one another down, horse-trading, infighting, stabbing one another in the back and battening on a credulous public.

There is a letter from John Munonye headed Ministry of Education, Republic of Biafra, no town no address:

> Nothing terribly exciting from this end. The guns boom and the planes roar, and citizens die in hundreds; but the cause is far from being lost. It is all one tremendous experience …
>
> A manuscript lies somewhere in my village residence and I would be glad to send it on to you. Please confirm that I could. I would then start exploring the means. I have asked my 'postal agent' to let you know the address through which to reply. (JM to KS 8 February 1969)

Unfortunately his attempt in *A Wreath for the Maidens* (1973 AWS 121) to write a novel about the war was not an altogether successful move. Hilary Mutch, a South African who worked on the BBC Africa Service, wrote:

> Munonye's story is about confusion. But like a political history of post-war France, one easily gets bogged down in names, titles, ever-changing power groupings. Now the chaos of war, the corruption and double dealing of the politicians is essential to the book, but there is no need for this disorder to be mirrored in the writing. I feel that a very stark, tight, language would give the story greater impact; at present it is obscured by padding.
>
> The war scenes themselves are handled with simplicity and lack of melodrama which makes the casual deaths of the people one has come to know, more poignant. (Report by Hilary Mutch 20 October 1971)

He rewrote this first draft of this war novel with his usual craftsmanship. However, his next two novels returned to the lives of ordinary people trying to hold their lives together in the chaos of daily life.

John Munonye had been brought up in the imperial tradition of the Greek and Roman classics. After the war he became principal of a leading teacher training college at Owerri. Above the town rose the gaunt girders of the dome of the new basilica which had been started before the war by the Roman Catholic church; the great walls were pockmarked with bullet holes. Opposite the college was the

Nigerian Federal Garrison of occupation where the bugler blew *reveille* as the sun went down. John Munonye had assembled a group of his teachers to meet me at dinner in his house. The excited brilliance of these young men's conversation reminded one of the hopes they had all had for Biafra as a country which would show Africa how things ought to be done.

Kole Omotoso & T. Obinkaram Echewa

Contrasting novels from the 40s generation

Three 'O's – Kole Omotoso, Niyi Osundare and Femi Osofisan – were part of a group of Nigerian writers who had been born in the 1940s and who were beginning to publish novels, plays and poetry in the 1970s in the period after the civil war. They felt that African literature should be about contemporary social and political reality and must explain Africa to the Africans. They maintained that the first generation of African writers had been too concerned with explaining Africa to Europeans. These young writers were now faced with a new literary canon in the universities, examination boards and schools. They felt that this new establishment was focused on the 1960s and was not looking at new writers. They were keen to reach the emerging general and popular book trade and they wrote for the experimental theatre. Aig Higo, Keith Sambrook and I sympathised with their aspirations and were anxious to provide publishing space for a new generation of writers after the war.

The ever alert Paul Edwards at the University of Edinburgh sent part of a novel by Kole Omotoso to us in May 1970. He told us that the author had studied French, English and Arabic at the University of Ibadan. His writing had style and elegance and gave one hopes that here was a new voice from Nigeria. The story of *The Edifice* (1971 AWS 102) was neat and fast-moving. It was the story of a black student in a white man's country and a white woman in a black man's country. Kole Omotoso responded speedily to Keith Sambrook's suggestions about restructuring. Aig Higo enjoyed reading the manuscript and said that he thought that 'Omotoso has nearly arrived,' (AH to JC 13 October 1970) and Chinua Achebe in a letter to Aig Higo of 2 January 1971 made some detailed structural suggestions.

The published book was well reviewed in the London *Sunday Times* and the Scottish press. Angus Calder featured him in *The New Edinburgh Review.* Kole Omotoso's Edinburgh flatmate, Dennis Walder, got an interview with him into *Transition* in Kampala in 1972. He experimented with different literary styles and techniques. He tried his hand at a fast-moving allegory on wartorn Nigeria in a novel called *The Combat* (1972 AWS 122), which was reissued in 2006 by Penguin in South Africa.

Kole Omotoso told me around this time that he was writing 'an African James Bond' aimed at the popular African market. The idea intrigued me and we hoped that this might lead the African Writers Series in a new more popular direction. One time I arranged that we would meet to discuss the manuscript in his carrel in the Edinburgh University Library. A green-suited grey-haired servitor took me up in a lift, through bookstacks and knocked on a door in a dark corridor. Kole Omotoso called 'Come in!' The servitor opened the door. There was the bearded Kole Omotoso with an enormous poster of guns spread all over his sunlit desk. The servitor clearly expected such things from foreign students, looked disapproving and discreetly closed the door behind me. Kole Omotoso was in the middle of choosing an authentic weapon for his detective hero in *Fella's Choice*. Nowadays the Edinburgh police would have had him in as a suspected terrorist.

Kole Omotoso sensibly sent it for consideration for the Collins Crime Club, via his uncle who worked for that publisher. In the end it was published by the new Ethiope Publishing Corporation in Benin, one of a postwar outburst of new Nigerian publishers. Kole Omotoso's talents flowered in serious journalism. In the 1980s his column in the weekly magazine *West Africa* was to be an influential forum for floating new ideas. His dramatic face has been in recent years looking down from billboards in South Africa as he advertises a trendy cell-phone

The Land's Lord (AWS 168) by T. Obinkaram Echewa, published in 1976, was a novel which, in the old-fashioned way, explained Africa to people in America and Britain and reminded everybody of Achebe, Amadi and Munonye. It was just the kind of work of which Kole Omotoso disapproved. The author was teaching in the US and succeeded in placing work in *The New York Times, Newsweek, Time* and *The New Yorker*. Richard Lister, who read the script in London, said:

> I'm surprised not to find the author's name in *The [New Reader's] Guide to African Literature* or your lists, because from the first page it doesn't read like a first novel, but like the work of an extremely intelligent and capable novelist who knows just what he's out to do and how best to do it. (R.P. Lister to JC 27 February 1974)

He likewise impressed readers in Africa. Molara Ogundipe-Leslie at the University of Ibadan was fascinated by what it told her about the background of Chinua Achebe's novels:

> This novel gives flesh, so to speak, to issues previously sketched in Achebe's novels; for one, the doctrinal debates between the missionaries and the Umofians; for another, Ezeulu's questionings of his own role and his own god in *Arrow of God*. It is as if one was in the inner areas of *Things Fall Apart*, and given the opportunity to see the mental wrestlings of the missionaries or to know Ezeulu's philosophical reactions to Christian doctrine ... The novel is structurally beautiful; as poetic in form as it is in language. My verdict is obvious. (M. Ogundipe-Leslie to Akin Thomas April 1974)

Henry Chakava wrote:

> The author's strength of description, his mastery over the use of imagery, and his narrative, against a vividly illuminated background is unquestionably outstanding. This is the first original novel in the series to remind me of Graham Greene – in this case *The Power and the Glory*. (HC to JC 18 June 1974)

T. Obinkaram Echewa was particularly pleased that Chinua Achebe wanted to use an extract in his newly founded journal *Okike*. In 1976 *The Land's Lord* won the substantial English-Speaking Union Award for writers from Africa and Asia. The previous winner had been the renowned Indian writer, R.K. Narayan. *The Crippled Dancer* (1986 AWS 245) was later added to the Series.

Christopher Okigbo & Gabriel Okara

Casualties of the Biafran war

The civil war between Federal Nigeria and Biafra, which started in July 1967 and ended in January 1970, divided publishers and writers. Our contacts with Chinua Achebe as Editorial Adviser became unpredictable (p. 6). In literary terms it was appropriate that it came to be called the Biafran war, especially in the case of novels where some three-quarters of the writers came from eastern Nigeria. It was the event which dominated the new work which was published in the 1970s. Forty years after the start of the war Chimamanda Ngozie Adichie's novel *Half a Yellow Sun* won the Orange Prize for Fiction in 2007; the novel is set in the Biafran war and draws with extraordinary imagination on the experiences of her parents' generation.

Christopher Okigbo, commissioned as a major in the Biafran army, went off and got himself killed in Byronic style at a road junction between Enugu and Nsukka in 1967. Before he had rushed east he had been working on the manuscript of his collected poetry with Aig Higo and Chinua Achebe. He had handed over manuscripts of new work which was to be added to the three books already published by Mbari: *Heavensgate* (1962), *Limits* (1964) and *Silences* (1965). The resulting book *Labyrinths* with *Path of Thunder* (1971 AWS 62) could only be published by Heinemann in 1971 when the east and west had come together again after the war. This was because, although everybody agreed that the royalties should go to Christopher Okigbo's infant daughter, the Mbari Club insisted that the payment be made via them in the west and the family insisted that the payment should be made via them in the east. Heinemann was, as always in hidden circumstances, blamed for the delay in publication, but we were delighted at last to add such a significant collection to our list. His importance has continued to be recognised. As *The Companion* puts it: 'Although his life was brief, he exerted a profound influence on the African literary canon.' When the African Writers Series was under threat David Godwin, Editorial Director at William Heinemann, issued a *Collected Poems* in hardback in 1986 (p. 298). In 2007 the 40th anniversary of Christopher Okigbo's death was marked in London and Boston by a highly individual exhibition of his daughter's dramatic painting combined with a celebration of her father's work. There were poignant worm-eaten remnants of his notebooks and worked manuscripts of his poems. He saw his work in a remarkable succession; he had scribbled, in pencil diagonally down a now yellowed piece of paper, a list of writers over history which started with Homer and Ovid, included Dante, Chaucer and Shakespeare and finished with

Tchicaya U'Tamsi and Christopher Okigbo. He had read Classics at the University of Ibadan and drew upon Greek and Roman poets, on the classics of modern poetry and on his own Igbo literature.

Gabriel Okara, whose experiments with English in *The Voice* (1970 AWS 68) has already been recorded (p. 42), was head of information services for the Eastern Region and gave poetry recital tours in the US to get support for the Biafran cause. He was born in 1921, the same year as Cyprian Ekwensi, and became a bookbinder in the government press in Lagos in 1946. His poetry first appeared in *Black Orpheus*. He wrote prolifically but when, after the war, various people came to press him for a collection, it became clear how little of his work had survived. Abiola Irele was at that time head of Ethiope. He told Akin Thomas in August 1973 that so far he had only been able to lay his hands on 15 of Okara's poems. Eventually in 1976, Ethiope published *The Fisherman's Invocation*. In London it was published in a hardback edition by Rex Collings, and then in the African Writers Series (1978 AWS 183). Theo Vincent, of the University of Lagos, records in his introduction to the collection:

> This volume represents what has been salvaged of Okara's published poetry from anthologies, periodicals and journals, particularly *Black Orpheus* and his latest previously unpublished poems made up of 'Franvenkirche' which was written before the Nigerian civil war and of nine written during and after the war. The consolation is that within these covers we have most of what the poet himself considers his best poems including the prize-winning poem 'The call of the River Nun' that launched him on his poetic career (though he constantly laments the loss of 'The Gambler', 'I've killed the year that killed me' and 'Leave us alone to heal our wounds' – a war poem that was set to music and performed).
>
> Okara is partly responsible for this unfortunate situation. Content for many years to create his poems, read them to audiences and live a life committed to art, he is generally careless with his manuscripts; it did not occur to him, until the civil war broke out, to put his manuscripts together. He assembled what he had of his later manuscripts and survived the war with them only to lose them in Port Harcourt in the uncertain period which immediately followed the formal cessation of hostilities. At this time there were large movements of people and life was still precarious. The loss of these manuscripts is certainly one of the less dramatic tragedies of the Nigerian Civil War. (*The Fisherman's Invocation* p. ix)

S.O. Mezu, I.N.C. Aniebo & Eddie Iroh
The sun rises after the war

Three new novelists born in the 1940s who wrote about the war were included in the Series. S.O. Mezu's novel, *Behind the Rising Sun* (AWS 113), published in hardback in 1971 by William Heinemann, was the first novel about the war by a new writer to go into the Series in 1972. It starts as a classy thriller set among Biafrans living luxuriously in Paris. Charter aircraft are needed to fly supplies into the Uli airstrip. Large deposits are paid to European dealers who do not in fact have any aircraft.

I.N.C. Aniebo had, like Elechi Amadi, started life as a professional soldier in the Nigerian army. He had a spell of duty for the UN in the Congo. During the war he became a lieutenant-colonel in the Biafran army. Aig Higo sent me the manuscript of *The Anonymity of Sacrifice* (1974 AWS 148) on 28 June 1971 with a strong recommendation to publish. It was sent back to the author on the assumption that we were going to publish after revision. On 11 April 1973 I.N.C. Aniebo was writing from the University of California, Los Angeles, complaining to Aig Higo: 'Only God knows when Mr Currey will complete this exercise and come round to taking me off the hook by confirming acceptance or otherwise.' I.N.C. Aniebo understandably complained that he was 'stricken with inactivity' about working on his second novel. A revised script was sent to Henry Chakava, who had only recently joined the Nairobi office. He wrote on 7 May 1973 that he was reluctant to recommend publication as:

> Although the author has adequately described the people involved in this war, he has not painted them against a landscape of war. The reader yearns to know in detail about the trenches, the general terrain, the rain, the mud, the forests, the swamps, mist, fog, etc ...
>
> This also strikes me as a novel for the soldiers who went to war. Consequently it has limited vision. There is little reference to civilian attitudes to this war ...
>
> I am quite certain a better novel will come from the Biafran war. I understand the problem of having to reject a novel with such a long history, but it is a question of deciding between topicality and artistic success. (HC to JC 7 May 1973)

However, on 29 May 1973 Henry Chakava was bowing to 'the enthusiasm of Chinua, Aig and Keith because they know Nigeria well and were more or less physically involved in the Biafran war'. Here is an example of the way our triangular editorial policy worked (p. 8) – strong support rather than a veto.

I.N.C. Aniebo's second novel, *The Journey Within* (1978 AWS 206), was about two couples living in Port Harcourt at the time of another war in faraway Europe, the second world war. In a letter Laban Erapu in Nairobi somewhat bizarrely felt this setting 'out of date'. Another reader, W. Gathoga, appreciates the way that the author, like Chinua Achebe, puts 'in English, African thoughts'. In accepting the book on 25 July 1977 I said we had pleasure in that 'you have fulfilled a great deal of the promise that was shown in *The Anonymity of Sacrifice*.'

While I.N.C. Aniebo was far off in California, Eddie Iroh was always popping into the Heinemann offices, first in Mayfair and then in Bloomsbury. He had also served in the Nigerian army before joining the Biafran War Information Bureau and Reuters news service. In the mid-1970s he was working as an eastern representative for Evans, the London educational publishers, and he was later to push Heinemann hard over sales. His 473-page manuscript of a novel about foreign mercenaries in the Biafran war, *Forty-Eight Guns for a General* (1976 AWS 189), was sent to London on 13 June 1974. The readers in Nairobi, Ibadan and London all lashed out the superlatives. David Mwangi, a Kenyan novelist, admired the way he held the reader's interest. Richard Lister said:

> It really is difficult to speak too highly of this as a superb specimen of its own particular genre, the action-packed thriller. It has a highly complex plot, worked out with immense skill; large numbers of well-drawn, identifiable and not too unsubtle characters. (Report by R.P. Lister 26 July 1974)

The length of the book made it too expensive. On 28 October 1974 I told Aig Higo of how we had costed it using new photo-composition, the cheapest paper, printing on a rotary press together with an Achebe reprint and, for the first time, using unsewn binding (hoping that things would not fall apart). I asked Aig Higo to get Eddie Iroh to cut 100 pages. As he was a journalist, he got down to what Dan Agbese, in an undated follow-up report, called, 'a non-too-careful revision'. Richard Lister wrote on 24 January 1976 'It isn't such a good book as it was, but it's still a good book and eminently worth publishing.'

Eddie Iroh, following Elechi Amadi and John Munonye in proposing a trilogy, had made it clear that there were going to be two other novels to cover the Biafran war. *Toads of War* (1979 AWS 213) switched from the battlefront to Owerri town where a bizarre elite ranging from bureaucrats to clergymen was growing fat on blood money and the black market in the final days of Biafra. *The Siren in the Night* (1982 AWS 255) focused on the aftermath of the war and detailed Eddie Iroh's own experience of intimidation and ethnic loyalties. They were saleable general market thrillers, but were Heinemann the right publishers?

Eddie Iroh was now with Channel 8 television in Enugu and certainly knew about getting publicity, though all too often it was put in hand before books had reached the shops. He repeatedly maintained that Heinemann in Ibadan had not imported enough copies to supply the demand in Nigeria where he was sure that it would sell like 'hot cake'. During the publication of these three books Eddie Iroh kept up a barrage of demanding letters and cables and visits to our offices in London and Ibadan; he also bombarded his literary agent, Bruce Hunter, with complaints. He told us that he operated on the philosophy expressed by the British Labour politician, James Callaghan, when in opposition: 'Modern questions are answered not so much by consistently seeking the answers as by constantly elaborating the question.' He was a sharp dresser. Panels of his elegant brogues were picked out in white. At the launch party given by the British Council in Enugu for *Forty-Eight Guns for a General* he told how:

> The other day, I ran into this very elegant lady in Kingsway shop, who said to me in a properly matronly sort of voice. 'Hello, Eddie. My husband tells me you have just written a terrific book. Congratulations. My God, I thought you were a playboy!' (Speech by Eddie Iroh 1 June 1977)

Olusegun Obasanjo
Military command

Certainly when Heinemann in Nigeria had a saleable book they were able to shift large numbers of copies, and not just to schools. They did best with two autobiographical accounts of the Biafran war by trained military men.

Elechi Amadi's *Sunset in Biafra* (1973 AWS 140) is his account of what it was like to be in the war. It is all the more powerful for being so understated. He uses his writing skill to make you feel the reality. One section of great vividness is about the three days when he was holed up with other civilians in a church in Port Harcourt while the battle swirled around. As a trained soldier his skill and discipline were undoubtedly useful. He understood the power of carrying a gun (p. 47).

Olusegun Obasanjo's book about the Nigerian civil war, *My Command* (1981 AWS 249), was the first to be written by one of the top commanders. On the African Writers Series cover there was a photograph of his solid figure, in a military uniform with his swagger stick, standing astride the centre of the conquered Uli airstrip from which Chinua Achebe had taken off so many times. The Biafran military, with amazing improvisation, had taken a straight piece of road, cut back the rainforest on both sides and landed aircraft at night with essential supplies and personnel right up until the collapse of Biafra. It was still impressive when driving along it a year after the war, although the bush was beginning to grow over the wrecks of aircraft. Olusegun Obasanjo was military head of state of Nigeria from 1976 to 1979. He was to become influential in African diplomacy; in 1986 he led the Eminent Persons Group whose report on South Africa triggered a state of emergency. He then was elected as head of state as a civilian. The book was certainly a coup for Heinemann Nigeria.

The first time round Heinemann Nigeria had ordered 10,000 copies of the hardback edition. It had a sober brown cover based, at Aig Higo's command, on the same style as the Jonathan Cape edition of Richard Crossman's diaries. In London we did not believe that they could sell that number of hardbacks. After copies had been airfreighted in, the sales took off. One morning in 1981 Cyprian Ekwensi entered Aig Higo's office booming in a great voice: 'Why are you not selling my books in the go-slow?' He then reported how the Lagos newspaper vendors had found a ready market for the Obasanjo hardback as the Nigerian elite were at a standstill in their cars in the Lagos traffic jam. The books were being bought at full price for cash in the Lagos bookshops and sold on at twice the price as the boys scampered among the fuming Mercedes.

2 *Negritude from* SENEGAL TO CAMEROUN

The dominating trio

Three exceptional novels were published in Paris in 1956: *Le vieux nègre et la médaille* by Ferdinand Oyono, *Le pauvre Christ de Bomba* by Mongo Beti and *Le docker noir* by Sembene Ousmane. This was two years before the publication of Chinua Achebe's *Things Fall Apart* in London. These three authors were to be the dominating francophone writers, partly because they sold so well in English translation in the African Writers Series. Mongo Beti and Ferdinand Oyono were from Cameroun, a near neighbour to the Igbo part of Nigeria from where came several of the most outstanding African writers in English. Sembene came from Senegal whose capital, Dakar, was even more advanced as a cultural crossroads than Ibadan. The only other novel from French which outsold any of this trio was Camara Laye's charming autobiographical *The African Child* (Collins Fontana 1954) which was published in Paris in 1953 as *L'enfant noir.*

Just along the Rue des Ecoles from the Sorbonne in Paris is Présence Africaine, founded by the Diop clan from Senegal. Behind the bookshop among the book stacks sat the powerful Madame Diop presiding over the regular publication of the substantial journal *Présence Africaine* and a most adventurous list of work by Caribbean and African writers in French. Abiola Irele from Ibadan and Clive Wake from Cape Town, with doctorates from the Sorbonne, were struck by this bookshop and journal. These scholars were also impressed by the fact that works of distinction from Africa, as well as the Antilles, were coming out from other well-established literary publishers in Paris. This was in marked contrast to London where, although West Indian authors were appearing from hardback general publishers, there was very little work from African authors published in English. The *négritude* movement went back to the 1920s and included work from Africa as well as the French Antilles. We included a translation of René Maran's *Batouala*, which had won the Prix Renaudot in 1924, in both the African and Caribbean Writers Series (1973 AWS 135).

Keith Sambrook remembers that he had no idea of this treasure trove until he was told in 1963 of its existence by Clive Wake who was editing, with John Reed, *A Book of African Verse* as the eighth book in the Series and which had examples of the poetry of negritude, as it became known in English. The African Writers Series, with the advice of Clive Wake, Abiola Irele, John Reed and Gerald Moore came to provide the major representative selection of work from Africa translated from French.

Ferdinand Oyono
The boy & the madam

John Reed was to translate Ferdinand Oyono's first two novels as *Houseboy* (1966 AWS 29) and *The Old Man and the Medal* (1969 AWS 39), of which he said:

> *Le Vieux Nègre* deals with a single incident – the presentation to Meka, an elderly African who has been a model colonial subject, of a medal by the French authorities and the events which immediately follow the ceremony. Through this simple narrative Oyono shows the nature of the colonial relationship and the folly of the African who abandons common sense and accepts white civilisation to the point of accepting its evaluation of himself. *Une Vie de Boy* is in the form of a diary written by the houseboy, Toundi. Like Meka, he is an innocent, fascinated and awed by the white world and the story shows how his eyes, again like Meka's, are opened to the realities of this world. At the end Toundi is destroyed because the Europeans cannot endure the gaze of the man whom they have disillusioned.
>
> In spite of this ending *Une Vie de Boy* is a comic novel and so, in spite of the harshness of Meka's humiliation, is *Le Vieux Nègre et la Médaille*. The comedy is bitter, and without sentiment or humour …
>
> Both books are extremely funny, yet at the same time a comment even bitterer than Beti's on the colonial regime in the Cameroons. Oyono seems less interested in Europeans, and perhaps because of this his Europeans are uniformly unattractive …
>
> Oyono's Africa world is gay – and some of its laughter is ribald. There are also some passages – such as that in *Une Vie de Boy* where Toundi discovers about the Europeans' use of contraceptives which might be considered to make these books unsuitable for use in schools. (Report by John Reed 1963)

Aig Higo was delighted by the translation of *Houseboy*:

> I've now read this translation which I consider terrific. As for the diary itself I know nothing quite like it in the use of details, good humoured mischief and precision … Somehow, purists will try to guard schools against it – which will be a pity – but the general reader will be acquiring a rare gem in African literature. (AH to KS 2 March 1966)

Ferdinand Oyono only published one other book. He rose in the foreign service of independent Cameroun; letters from Heinemann chased him at the embassies in Nigeria, Liberia, France, Italy and as representative at the United Nations in New York. He then became foreign minister. If he had continued to write with such bitter comedy about independent Cameroun that would have ended his career.

Mongo Beti
An affront to the church

Mongo Beti's *Mission to Kala (Mission Terminée)* was the first francophone novel to be included in the African Writers Series. It was easily available because it had been published in 1957 by Editions Buchet/Chastel in Paris and then in an English translation by Frederick Muller in London. It would have disappeared on to library shelves if it had not appeared as AWS 13 in 1964 in the second year of the Series; its sales were to be far greater in English than in French. In the early 1970s it was with amazement that we heard from George Bowman, the Inspector of English in Nairobi, that it had been accepted by the East African Examinations Council as a set book for Literature in English. Protests erupted, but not because the book was translated from French. Set books had to be chosen and ordered well ahead from England; many upcountry Roman Catholic schools in Tanzania thought that the title *Mission to Kala* sounded appropriate. When the books arrived the teachers, often in holy orders, were horrified not so much by teaching the scenes of gentle adolescent sex but by the obvious anti-clericalism. In Kenya a delegation of women sought an audience with the wife of the minister of education to protest about the affront to African womanhood. George Bowman was delighted and said to me, 'For the first time a set book is news!' As a compromise it was removed a year early as a set book to appease the complainers.

Le Roi Miraculé, Mongo Beti's third early anti-colonial novel, was included in the Series in 1970 as it had already been published in translation by Frederick Muller in hardback as *King Lazarus* (AWS 77). Mongo Beti's very first book, *Le Pauvre Christ de Bomba*, was one of that remarkable Parisian trio of 1956. Keith Sambrook wrote in 1965 to David Machin, Editorial Director of William Heinemann, in order to try and interest him in a hardback edition. He said:

> In many people's view, *Le Pauvre Christ* is by far the best of Beti's novels, and probably one of the best novels by any writer from Africa. It does, however, contain a well-known chapter which may have put off Muller some years ago, before the Lawrence case. This particular chapter has been translated by Ulli Beier in an issue *of Black Orpheus* and Gerald Moore, who is Director of Extra-Mural Studies at University College, Makerere and who has for some time been anxious to translate the novel in full. (KS to David Machin 26 February 1965)

Alan Hill sent the chapter to Michael Rubinstein, one of the solicitors who had appeared for Penguin in the Lady Chatterley case. Rubinstein reassured him that he did not think it went 'too far'; he merely seemed to be amazed that an educational company was proposing to publish it, which was an expensive way of getting irrelevant advice. Keith Sambrook told Gerald Moore that, having read James Baldwin's *Another Country*, he did not feel there was anything to worry about. Gerald Moore eventually translated the whole novel for £100 to occupy himself on a Union Castle voyage back to Britain after finishing his contract in the extra-mural department at Makerere. It was published in hardback and paperback as *The Poor Christ of Bomba* (1971 AWS 88).

During the 1970s a much closer publishing relationship evolved direct with Mongo Beti. Initially it was because he was suspicious that, in spite of the astonishingly good sales in Africa, he was not getting his correct royalties from Heinemann, Laffont and Buchet/Chastel. Authors put up with a great deal from their publishers but when they start to question royalty statements the publisher needs to get nervous. I wrote back on 28 October 1974: 'It was a great pleasure to get a letter direct from you as usually so many people are between us.' On 13 January 1975 I explained: 'The difficulty is that there are so many people along the line, all of whom have some share in the proceeds. There is an agent Rosica Colin, there is the original English publisher Frederick Muller ... there is your French publisher.' On 16 May 1975 I listed for Guy Buchet the exact print numbers of the ten impressions of *Mission to Kala* between 1964 and 1974, totalling 80,000 copies. On 8 December 1975 Mongo Beti was able to write to me saying: 'J'ai aussi parcouru avec étonnement les chiffres de vente.' He asked me to assure him that Heinemann had indeed paid the appropriate royalties to Buchet/Chastel.

Mongo Beti, unlike Ferdinand Oyono, found it impossible to accept the way that the post-colonial regime used the power it had been given by the French. From 1960 to 1994 he lived in Rouen. In 1972 the French authorities seized his pamphlet criticising the link between Ahidjo's one-party government in his native Cameroun and French profiteers, so he returned to fiction to spread his ideas. Two of these later novels appeared in the African Writers Series. *Perpetua and the Habit of Unhappiness* (1974 translated by John Reed and Clive Wake, 1978 AWS 181) is the story of young girl who becomes representative of all Camerounians who do not exercise power. *Remember Ruben* (1974 translated by Gerald Moore, 1980 AWS 214) recalls a young revolutionary killed in 1958; it was first published by Abiola Irele's New Horn Press in Nigeria.

He certainly felt himself the elder of the francophone writers. When there was a protest by certain South Africans at the Berlin Festival in 1979 (see photo p. xxxii), he clicked the button on his simultaneous translation microphone and firmly announced, without consulting anybody else: 'We writers of French expression dissociate ourselves from this protest.'

He died in 2004.

Sembene
Novelist & film-maker

The novelist Sembene Ousmane was, as Ousmane Sembene, equally well-known as a film-maker. It is common nowadays to elevate him to just Sembene. *Le Docker noir* (1956 but only translated for the Series in 1987) is an autobiographical

Sembene Ousmane
Frankfurt 1980

novel and tells of the lives of Africans working in the port of Marseilles. *Les Bouts de Bois de Dieu,* published in 1960, is a similarly realistic novel based on Sembene's experience of the strike in 1947–8 on the great Dakar–Niger railway line whose steel rails bound the French colonial empire together. *The Companion* comments that it is 'one of the great rallying resistance novels of Africa's late colonial era'. It was published in translation as *God's Bits of Wood* by Doubleday in New York in 1962, but did not appear in London until 1970 (AWS 63). I had an extended battle to get it accepted because it was so long and would be our first 'ten-shilling novel' when the ten-shilling note was considered to be a psychological barrier in sales terms. It has sold over 50,000 copies in the African Writers Series edition; this was helped by Advanced-Level and university sales but was an ideal book for anybody who wanted a good politically conscious read.

When Sembene returned to Senegal in 1961 he was shocked by how little impact his written work in French was having. After he failed to get an apprenticeship in film in Paris he went to train at the Gorky studios in Moscow. He most often shot his films in the Wolof or Diola languages of Senegal, with subtitles in French. It is with film that he has pursued his concerns about speaking to ordinary people and not just the elite; this is one of the many ways in which he begs comparison with Ngũgĩ who came to write his novels in Gikuyu and turned to plays with which to make political impact.

Film, book and politics overlap in all Sembene's other titles which appeared in the African Writers Series. *Le Mandat* (1965, translated by Clive Wake as *The Money-Order*, 1972 AWS 92), was made into a sadly witty film which shows how, for an ordinary man, the bureaucratic system erects hurdles of literacy and numeracy at every stage. By 1972 Sembene was in direct contact with us as he knew the importance of to him of publication in English. He published *Xala* in 1974 and issued the film in the French-speaking world in 1975. The publication of Clive Wake's translation (1976 AWS 175) was to be synchronised with the release in 1976 of the subtitled English film version in London and at the New York Film Festival. The businessman El Hadji Abdou Kader Beye gives his third wife her own European-style bungalow, car and servants. On the wedding night he finds he has a *xala*: he is suddenly impotent. The book is a sharp satire on the way Sembene saw that the new African middle class were exploiting the ordinary people in just the same way the colonialists had done.

In 1979 at the Berlin Festival Sembene made it clear to me that in future he wanted to deal direct with us over English-language rights. A substantial manuscript arrived in 1980 called *Le dernier de l'Empire* (1981, translated as *The Last of the Empire* 1983 AWS 250). Clive Wake's report starts:

> This is a political novel. It is set in Senegal. It deals with the failure and ideals of and aims of the present regime, leading to the fall of the President, and the problem of his succession in terms of the constitutional situation created by the President's own provisions for his succession... As the novel opens, the President, Leon Mignane (quite obviously Senghor) has disappeared … (Clive Wake to JC 7 July 1980)

Clive Wake said that it has a fascination for anybody interested in African politics and might have the same prophetic element as Chinua Achebe's *Man of the People*.

We asked Adrian Adams to handle the translation. She went to university in Scotland and was living with her husband, who had been a Senegalese sailor, near Bakel on the river which bounds Mauritania. She was more critical than Clive Wake of what she called 'patches of bad or at least careless writing, which means one has to decide what S. meant to say, before translating' (3 April 1981) The campaigning publisher Lawrence Hill had published the US edition of *Xala* and so had first option on the translation of *The Last of the Empire*. I came to an agreement whereby he would double the translation fee for Adrian Adams, who had to depend on her literary earnings. Unfortunately he got the translation read by a former US ambassador to Senegal who told Lawrence Hill that he must turn it down because it was so critical of Senghor. These were the days of the cold war and Sembene had of course been trained in Moscow. I told Adrian Adams that Lawrence Hill had agreed to pay a translation fee even though he would not go ahead with a US edition:

> The reason I am giving him a chance to get off the hook is that his whole business is under threat from a libel action of stunning size which is being taken out by an ex-CIA man. He did not, to his credit, use this as an excuse. I just know that he is under terrific pressure and his business may well be driven under. (JC to Adrian Adams 3 April 1981)

In fact John Watson and Tom Seavey were now building up the Heinemann marketing organisation in New Hampshire and were delighted to have the chance to promote a new novel by one of Africa's most renowned authors. A translation by a University of Cape Town team of two short novels by Sembene, *Nilaam* and *Taaw,* was added to the Series in 1992.

Negritude & an elegant tradition

The only time I met Léopold S. Senghor, the poet president of Senegal, was in the Banqueting House in Whitehall, from which Charles I had stepped out to lose his head. He was on a state visit. Clive Wake and John Reed provided elegant translations of his work. We took over an anthology of Senghor prose and poetry (1976 AWS 180) when Oxford University Press dropped it from the Three Crowns series. Clive Wake and John Reed translated the complete book of poems, *Nocturnes* (1969 AWS 71). They would be the first to admit that they were influenced by Senghor's 1948 anthology as to which writers of negritude to select for their own *Book of African Verse*. Later in *French African Verse* (1972 AWS 106) they provided French originals alongside English translations.

We set out, often with translations by Clive Wake and John Reed, to represent the poetry of excellence that appeared in French. David Diop's *Coups de Pilon*, again published in Paris in the landmark year 1956, was translated by Simon Mpondo as *Hammer Blows* (1975 AWS 174). It had the same totemic standing in

French as Christopher Okigbo's poetry did in English; this Senegalese poet, who had a Camerounian mother, also died young. There were only 17 poems in this collection and the rest of his manuscripts went down with him in the plane crash that killed him. Jean-Joseph Rabéarivelo's *Traduit de la nuit* (1935 translated by Clive Wake and John Reed as *Translations from the Night*, 1972 AWS 167) provided an example of a poet who had used Malagasy as well as French; he committed suicide young in 1937. We should have been more adventurous with representing work from French published in the 1960s and 1970s. A good model would have been Tchicaya U Tam'si's *Selected Poems* (1970 AWS 72), which Gerald Moore had chosen and translated from four collections published in Paris and Tunis, which were difficult to find in French.

Abiola Irele wanted students of French literature, in Africa and throughout the English-speaking world, to appreciate the range and sophistication of style among writers of French expression. In *Lectures Africaines* (1969), a book outside the Series, Abiola Irele provided key extracts in French from a range of novels with accompanying introductions and notes in English about the authors and their work. It was one of those excellent ideas for which there should have been a demand, but where publisher and author were ahead of the market. Would we have been able to sell it better if we had included the book in the African Writers Series? It did prove to have one substantial publishing benefit for the development of the Series. Abiola Irele introduced me not only to the texts but also knew when English translations were already available of whole books. He told me of the significance of Cheikh Hamidou Kane's *L'Aventure Ambiguë* (1962), which had been published in a translation by Katherine Woods as *Ambiguous Adventure* by Walker in New York in 1963. Sambo Diallo finds his situation is ambiguous. He has become estranged from the Muslim faith of his people in Senegal but he is unable to identify with the material civilisation he finds in France where he is sent to learn the secrets of the white man's power. *The Companion* (p. 250) describes it as: 'The first major African text to provide a defence against European ideology'. At that time I was reserved about the novel, as I was influenced by Sembene's criticism of Islam and Ayi Kwei Armah's view of Islam being another form of imperialism in Africa. Abiola Irele had to remind me several times before I proposed the book to my colleagues in Africa. It appeared as AWS 119 in the tenth anniversary year of 1972, has been reprinted at least 23 times and was chosen as one of Africa's 100 best books.

We did not get far in our representation of French-language writers from the Maghreb whose work often appeared on Parisian lists. Len Ortzen's anthology *North African Writing* (1970 AWS 73) gave a taste of writers such as the Moroccan Driss Chraïbi; William Heinemann published one of his many novels under the title *Heirs to the Past* (1972 AWS 79), in which the tape-recorded voice of the hero's dead father provides a shock for the family. Heinemann Inc was to get Evelyne Accad's *Wounding Words* added to the Series in 1996.

Francophone writers after independence

There was a good selection in the African Writers Series of novels from the French colonial period, but what was being written after independence? Abiola Irele said in *Lectures Africaines*: 'the novel in *francophone* Africa can now be expected to progress beyond the bounds and preoccupations arising out of colonialism'. He selected as an example the Senegalese novel Malick Fall's *La Plaie* which was published in Paris in 1967; Clive Wake translated it as *The Wound* (1973 AWS 144). Magamou was on the way to try and find work in Dakar. In a lorry crash on the road to Dakar he is accidentally but usefully equipped with an awful wound; this enables him to become a beggar which gives him insights into the society which he only re-enters when the wound heals. (Beggars also play crucial roles in later Senegalese work such as Sembene's *Xala* and a novel by Aminata Sow-Fall called *The Beggar's Strike*.)

Ahmadou Kourouma's *Les soleils des indépendances* was turned down in Paris in 1964; this may well have been because of his enjoyment of inventing new words and his experiments at conveying Malinke syntax in French. It took until 1968 for Les Presses Universitaires de Montréal in Québec to give a chance to another outsider to challenge the purity of the French language. The translation of *The Suns of Independence* (1981 AWS 239) by Adrian Adams was criticised in *The Companion* for not bringing Ahmadou Kourouma's word games across into English. It seems that he was aiming to tackle the same problems as Gabriel Okara in *The Voice* (p. 42) which was published in London in the year that Kourouma was failing to get his book accepted in Paris.

In 1968 Editions Seuil managed to build up some competitive bidding at the Frankfurt Book Fair for a Parisian literary sensation called *Le Devoir de Violence*. It was written by Yambo Ouologuem who was descended from an ancient ruling family in Mali. Seuil titillated the French press with press releases about the exotic and the erotic. Aubrey Davies, editorial director at Secker and Warburg, which was also in the Heinemann group, felt nervous about the sum he had put down to secure the British Commonwealth rights. He ran round to the Heinemann Educational Books stand to make sure that he could begin to cover himself by selling on rights to us for the African Writers Series. Our managing director, Tony Beal, assured him that we would support him. The novel proved to be an even hotter property when later that year it won the prestigious Prix Renaudot in Paris. *Le Monde*, in singular ignorance, called it 'perhaps the first African novel worthy of the name'. Peter Lennon, who interviewed the author in Paris for *The Guardian*, said: 'It is difficult to know whether Ouologuem will turn out to be a better sociologist and historian than novelist.' It certainly lived up to its title. The review in *The Times Literary Supplement* under a heading 'Genital Reminders' says:

> The grand course of African history is spiced with sorcery and unnatural death, a taste of cannibalism, black magic and eroticism. This element of human interest is centred principally on the various treatments of the human genitalia: they are tortured, worshipped, gratified, doctored, torn out, eaten, even used for procreation, rarely ignored.

When the translation by Ralph Manheim, under the title *Bound to Violence* (1971 AWS 99), was ready for production in 1970 it turned out that Secker and Warburg, having used us as a bargaining counter at Frankfurt, had been negotiating with Pan to sell all the paperback rights without mentioning the agreement for the African Writers Series. Alan Hill had to point out to Fred Warburg that, if they honoured their agreement with a fellow member of the Group, they would make more money:

> ... if you still wish to sell the book to a major paperback publishing house, we would not complain, provided you reserve the African market for us. Penguin themselves acknowledge that we sell African paperbacks much better in Africa than they do. This is because the market is primarily educational. Such a division of the market, if you were to decide on it, would benefit the author, the French publisher and you. We would be willing to pay a good advance for even these limited rights ... (Alan Hill to F. Warburg 3 December 1970)

The book continued to be sensational for all the wrong reasons. One morning I was summoned urgently down to Alan Hill's office in Mayfair. He was on the telephone at his enormous desk. His nervous tension was betrayed by the way in which he kept switching the receiver from hand to hand. He put his hand over the receiver and mouthed: 'It's the old Graham Greene!' As Alan Hill graphically told *The Times* (5 May 1972):

> Greene came on the telephone to me. There was a dry old-paper feel about his voice. You could almost tear it. I immediately turned up the pages and there it was. It was remarkable how it has survived in translation.

Alan Hill got me to compare specific pages in Yambo Ouologuem's book and in a copy of Graham Greene's *It's a Battlefield* published by William Heinemann in 1934. An Australian research student in Zambia had told Graham Greene that he had spotted that Yambo Ouologuem had transferred the words in the French translation of this novel from a Dover boarding house into a similar seedy setting in Africa but with different characters. Graham Greene was not pressing and accepted the immediate offer by Alan Hill that an appropriate acknowledgement should be included in copies. But, as *The Times* reported:

> Mr Greene's notification came just in time to stop a shipment of 250 copies of *Bound to Violence* being distributed in Ibadan but too late to stop 3,000 in Nairobi, where they had been put on sale for a few weeks.

The reaction by the New York publisher reads like a scene from a bad novel:

> The American paperback version was on the presses and the cover had been made when the presses were halted.
>
> Mr Williams Jovanovich, chairman of Harcourt, Brace, Jovanovich, the American publishers, said he had withdrawn 3,400 hardback copies of the book as soon as Mr Greene's agent in New York had asked them to do so. He was shocked by the news. Such a thing had never happened to his publishing house before. Even if Mr Greene were to say that he just wants an acknowledgement we would still go ahead and destroy the copies. 'If I cannot warrant it, I cannot publish it.' Total cancellation costs

Mariama Bâ
Frankfurt 1980

Amadou
Kourouma
Berlin 1979

would be about $10,000 which he hoped to recoup from the French publishers (*The Times* 5 May 1992).

Yambo Ouologuem later explained himself with a casual aristocratic arrogance. He was reported in the news weekly *West Africa* as saying that he was merely using a technique from the film cutting-room of splicing in different frames from all sorts of sources – it was amusing to hear him using the technical word '*clichés*'. It was a pity that all this newspaper energy was not used for the benefit of a better book. The brouhaha tended to reinforce the patronising prejudices of people like Fred Warburg about writing from Africa. *The Times* mentioned that it very much seemed to be a Heinemann family affair. There was a historic Heinemann Group subtext. Graham Greene had been published, from his first books onwards, by William Heinemann. Many of the older directors including Alan Hill had been at the board meeting when Graham Greene had not only resigned as a director but taken his future books off to Bodley Head.

In marked contrast was Mariama Bâ's *Une si longue lettre* which was published in Dakar in 1979. It was the first winner of the Noma Prize for publishing in Africa; the award was made at the Africa Year at Frankfurt in 1980. We worked with Abiola Irele on the translation which was published in 1981 by New Horn Press in Nigeria as *So Long a Letter* (1981 AWS 248). We arranged for initial publication in Britain to be by the new feminist imprint Virago which could get its green covers into a wider range of bookshops than Heinemann could achieve in the orange covers of the African Writers Series. It could be called keeping a foot in both ghettos. *The Companion* points out that: 'It is a pioneering work, as Bâ was among the very first female novelists from sub-Saharan Africa to explore the experience of Muslim African women.'

She denied that the work was autobiographical. Unlike so many of the other books from Senegal, it was not critical of the politics of Senegal's post-imperial elite. The recently widowed Ramayoulaye gives an account of her married life to her childhood friend Aissatou who had opted for divorce to escape from her polygamous marriage. In the novel she shows how women collaborate in the oppression of women for their own material security. Tragically she was suffering from a long illness and died in 1981.

There was happy coincidence in 2006 in that the Noma Prize was awarded at the first Cape Town Book Fair to another novel by an African woman writing in French, *La mémoire imputée* by Werewere-Liking; although the book was published by Nouvelles Editions Ivoiriennes in Abidjan, the author is a Camerounian.

3 *Magic & Realism from* GHANA, SIERRA LEONE & THE GAMBIA

The most famous Ghanaian name on Heinemann's list was President Kwame Nkrumah. Van Milne, who published the first titles in the African Writers Series, had published the president's autobiography at Nelson and then signed up two titles for Heinemann before going back to Nelson. These two hardback editions were launched with great ceremony at Christiansborg Castle with Alan Hill and Keith Sambrook in attendance. Kwame Nkrumah was deposed by army officers in the coup of 1967; I was shocked to see the announcement on an evening-paper noticeboard just outside John Murray's elegant house in Albemarle Street. We did not republish Kwame Nkrumah's titles in the Series along with the political titles by Kaunda, Mboya, Mandela and Odinga. (*Pan-Africanism* was for a time listed as AWS but never issued.) This was because June Milne had set up Panaf Publications to disseminate his writing from his exile in Conakry, both before and after his death in 1972. In 1973 Penguin published a book on the life and times of Kwame Nkrumah called *Black Star* by Basil Davidson; he told me recently, when James Currey Publishers reissued it in 2007, that this title sold worse than any of his other titles as, after his death, nobody wished to remember Nkrumah.

Some of the most of exceptional novels from Africa are by the Ghanaian writers Ayi Kwei Armah, Kofi Awoonor and B. Kojo Laing. All three authors were also poets of distinction who drew on rich oral traditions. Also included here is an account of how we worked with the poet Lenrie Peters from The Gambia and with Yulisa Amadu Maddy and Syl Cheney-Coker from Sierra Leone.

A literate tradition

Keith Sambrook had gone out from Edinburgh to work in the Gold Coast for Nelson, where he started the University College of Gold Coast Press. In a country with a history, newspapers and outstanding mission schools, he found there was a great deal of writing activity which could be represented in the African Writers Series.

Writers of verse, plays and short stories had been given encouragement by the expansion of radio broadcasting at the time of independence in 1957. Henry

Swanzy had used the BBC's 'Caribbean Voices' to encourage a whole new generation of Caribbean writers (p. 16). His ancient family trading company had been absorbed by Unilever United Africa Company and this was one of his reasons for spending the year 1957 in Accra launching a programme called 'Voices of Ghana' which did encourage writers in the country but not far beyond.

There was as strong a tradition of popular publishing as at Onitsha in Nigeria. Asare Konadu showed the same range of ambitions as Cyprian Ekwensi. He had started as journalist and radio reporter, wrote prolifically and set about publishing his own work in a variety of styles with different audiences in mind. *Night Watchers of Korlebu* was about the spirits and ghosts moving through the wards of Ghana's most famous hospital. Under the name Kwabena Asare Bediako he sold considerable numbers of copies of novels with titles such as *Don't Leave me Mercy*. He turned his hand to writing books for the African Writers Series and we published two novels of Ghanaian rural life, *A Woman in her Prime* (1967 AWS 40) and *Ordained by the Oracle* (1969 AWS 55).

The subject of Yaw M. Boateng's *The Return* (1977 AWS 186), set in the nineteenth century, explores the tragedy of the way that Africans sold one another into slavery for the benefit of Europeans. The subject captured the interest of the editors at Pantheon in New York and they accepted it for general hardback publication in 1977 at the same time as they rejected Ngũgĩ's *Petals of Blood*.

The first Ghanaian title to be included in the African Writers Series in 1966 was Francis Selormey's autobiographical novel *The Narrow Path* (1967 AWS 27), in which a boy grows up to learn that his Christian father's harsh behaviour to him was a mark of his love.

Amu Djoleto's *The Strange Man* (1968 AWS 41) was a novel of growing up under tyrannical headmasters. We first met him when he came to a textbook publishing course at the Institute of Education in the University of London. Professor John Lewis, whom Keith Sambrook had encountered at the University of Ghana, knew of his writing ambitions and made sure that he was placed on a training attachment with Heinemann Educational Books. His first novel was accepted when he was working for Heinemann and was published in 1968. This was the beginning of a long association. In his satirical novel *Money Galore* (1975 AWS 161) the politician Abraham Kofi Kafu is surrounded by a bumper crop of rogues and money-makers. A London reviewer, Jeremy Brooks, said:

> The amount of time and energy Kafu devotes to his own advantage, compared to how little time he spends on the interests of his electors reminds one of – well, mustn't get libellous … this inventive irreverent book is as sharp as a quince, and richly satisfying. O yes – Kafu gets his comeuppance in the end and that's satisfying too.

Jeremy Brooks included this book, and *The Minister's Daughter* by Mwangi Ruheni, in his review in the influential Sunday paper, *The Observer*, of the weekly crop of novels from publishers in London. He began his column by saying:

> Neither patronage nor inverted culture snobbery impels me to lead with two novels from Heinemann's admirable African Writers Series. It just

happens that there is nothing in the week's domestic fiction to rival the vigour, wit and underlying seriousness of the two paperbacks from Kenya and Ghana.

Amu Djoleto, as director of the Book Development Council in Ghana and an adviser on educational reform, made a brave contribution to the restoration of Ghana's literary culture after the collapse of Ghana's economy. Becky Ayebia Clarke, herself a Ghanaian working at Heinemann, took advantage of the liberalisation of Ghana's currency in the 1990s to get his and other Ghanaian titles available once again in Ghana.

Ayi Kwei Armah

Beautyful novels not yet published

I had only recently joined Keith Sambrook in 1967 when the revised manuscript of Ayi Kwei Armah's novel of corruption *The Beautyful Ones Are Not Yet Born* (1969 AWS 43) arrived from Aig Higo. Keith Sambrook told me of his, and Aig Higo's, high expectations. He and I team-read it that very morning seated on either side of his desk. Keith Sambrook, Aig Higo and I were determined to get it into the Series. Here was a writer of outstanding self-assurance. The imagery of shit is embedded throughout the whole book. There is a description of a handrail encrusted from unwashed hands. At the time of the coup the politician Koomson escapes through the night-soil hole into the lane at the back of the house and runs to plunge his stinking clothes into the sea in ritual cleansing. Our colleagues reluctantly let us take on the novel although, judging by their experience of what was acceptable in Britain, they never expected it to sell in schools in Africa. The managing director sighed as he agreed that the reports made it clear that it was quite outstanding and that we should accept.

It was the beginning of by far and away the worst relationship we ever experienced with an author. We are all servants of times we live in and much of what Ayi Kwei Armah said about the role of all of us at Heinemann was probably thought at one time or another by other writers, but rarely expressed. Ayi Kwei Armah was right to treat the offer of the advance of £50 as insulting. That was the standard advance offered for new manuscripts in the African Writers Series at that time, but we should have realised that this was not a standard manuscript. I was only months into the job but, as the son of professional writers, should have discussed increasing the amount with Keith Sambrook and Alan Hill.

Ayi Kwei Armah is sure that he asked Heinemann for an increase in advance and that we refused. Nobody at Heinemann can remember this request. Aig Higo has recently written in 2007: 'I had nothing to do with royalties or advances at this stage and the topic never came up between me and AKA at this point.'

Ayi Kwei Armah had spent some time in the United States and would be aware that a writer could expect a more substantial advance from publishers there. He sensibly appointed as his first agent in the US Ellen Wright, the widow of the novelist Richard Wright and she obtained a $2,000 advance from a US publisher. That sort of sum would have been way beyond Heinemann, as an educational company, could reasonably have been sure of earning back from a novel which was unlikely to sell in schools. Only in 1978 did Ayi Kwei Armah's second agent in New York, Bertha Klausner, tell us that he had had in mind to ask Heinemann for something in the range of £200–£400. If a request for this size of advance had reached Keith Sambrook, it would have been approved by Alan Hill.

Alan Hill and Keith Sambrook sent me to Paris in September 1967 to try to get Ayi Kwei Armah to tell us which publisher we should approach in the US to negotiate for Commonwealth rights. He believed that I had come to get him to renege on his contract with his US publisher. I do remember a polite tussle with him over his refusal to allow Heinemann to pay for the lunch. I also remember that I failed to persuade him that it would be to his advantage either to put us in touch with the US publisher or even to agree that he would tell that publisher to get in touch with Heinemann.

Charles Pick, the managing director of William Heinemann, was about to set off on a round of US publishers and Alan Hill told him that if he saw Ayi Kwei Armah's book on the list of books he was shown he should make an immediate offer. Charles Pick did not see it on the lists of the publishers he visited in New York. He went up to Boston and there he saw it on the Houghton Mifflin list and surprised his opposite number by saying without hesitation that Heinemann would take this first novel by an unknown African; Alan Hill agreed to an advance of £500.

The rights situation had eventually been resolved in a way that benefited both Ayi Kwei Armah and Heinemann Educational Books. He secured the kind of advance from Houghton Mifflin that helped him continue writing. Sadly for him Houghton Mifflin were not able to sell subsidiary rights to a US paperback house and Heinemann Inc was later to distribute the novel in the US to the burgeoning university market. We managed to make sales in Britain, Africa and the traditional British Commonwealth of a size which was rare in those days for a first novel by an unknown writer. We were proud to have another novel of such distinction in the Series. It quickly sold the initial 50,000 that we only came to expect for truly exceptional books. This was partly because it was prescribed as a set book in schools for an Advanced-Level exam despite my colleagues' gloomy predictions.

The story of misunderstandings and damaged pride on both sides was to continue. We expected that we should never hear anything more from Ayi Kwei Armah after we, apparently against his wishes, had secured the rights from his US publisher. His second novel *Fragments* (1974 AWS 154) was published by Houghton Mifflin in 1970. Chi Ude was making his mark at Doubleday and came to see me in June 1972 with the news that they had outbid Houghton Mifflin and were to be the US publishers of his third novel *Why Are We So Blest*? (1974 AWS 155). Entirely to our surprise, Ayi Kwei Armah approached us to offer us the Commonwealth rights including the whole of Africa for his second and third books. On 16 May 1973, after a detailed negotiation, he wrote to Alan Hill to say: 'If we deal satisfactorily with Clause 18 and the other points, I am willing to sign the contracts.' Unfortunately there were accidents; the wrong post office box number was used on the packet of contracts and Keith Sambrook was flung against a dry stone wall by a car in the Lake District. Ayi Kwei Armah, because of these delays in sending the memoranda of agreement, offered rights to East African Publishing House without saying that he had accepted our offer. When we told EAPH of this they agreed to our suggested compromise of a split of the African market: EAPH would have East and Central Africa and we would keep the reduced market in West Africa and the rest of Africa as well as in the Commonwealth market. Aig Higo flew to Dar es Salaam in November 1973 to discuss the amended contract. Unfortunately Ayi Kwei Armah delayed accepting this compromise, saying that he could not consider it while working on a new novel. Aig Higo, with the ceaseless support of Alan Hill, worked patiently for over five years to get the memoranda of agreement signed.

On 23 May 1976 Ayi Kwei Armah wrote to Aig Higo, saying that he was going to Ghana and inviting him to visit him there to negotiate the West African rights for his fifth novel *The Healers* (1979 AWS 194). Aig Higo sent his vivid report to Alan Hill on 22 June 1976. A tropical rainstorm meant that they had to circle for an hour before landing:

> There were no buses so we had to walk from the plane to the airport buildings after which everybody was soaked. We all arrived exhausted, nervous and wet and there was AKA and Dr Apronti waiting to receive me.
>
> I noticed that as we drove to the hotel that AKA was clutching a jiffy bag. It contained *The Healers* and he handed it over to me. We got into the hotel room about half twelve. AKA was rather anxious to start discussion … I decided to hedge and put him off till the following morning. I read some forty pages before dozing off. It is simpler in style than anything AKA has written but right from the first page one is not only conscious of the length (472pp) but also the vastness of structure of this historical novel. You begin hearing echoes from a strange but enormous world.

On 14 August 1978 Aig Higo wrote to Alan Hill at last sending the signed memoranda of agreement for *Fragments*, *Why Are We So Blest?* and *The Healers*. There were still outstanding problems in the contract for *Two Thousand Seasons* (1979 AWS 218). Aig Higo concludes his letter: 'He's also working on a novel which I would not like to miss. I did not see the manuscript.'

In 1976 Ayi Kwei Armah had published a savagely brilliant article which, among other things, gave his view of his attempts 'to find an African publisher as opposed to a neo-colonial writers' coffle owned by Europeans but slyly misnamed "African"'. ('Larsony or Fiction as Criticism', *ASEMKA, A Journal of Literary Studies* 4, University of Cape Coast, Ghana).

Kofi Awoonor

Prisoner & ambassador

Kofi Awoonor, or George Awoonor Williams as he was originally known, had a well-established reputation as a poet by the late 1960s. A man of versatile talents, he had been involved in broadcasting and was director of the Ghana Film Unit. Keith Sambrook and I had high expectations for his first novel *This Earth, My Brother* (1972 AWS 108). He said in a letter to Keith Sambrook:

> I am anxious about the American publication. What possibilities are there and what is the mechanism? I did show the Ms. to a good friend in Simon and Schuster and she thinks they can publish it outright. But I remember I made a promise to you over a distant meal in London. Let me know what can be arranged. (KA to KS 19 September 1969)

We sent his agent David Higham a contract in August 1970 but it had not been returned signed. Then we heard that Chi Ude at Doubleday had bought the rights; he had recently been given a big cheque book with which he had already signed up Ayi Kwei Armah's third novel (p. 74). Kofi Awoonor's novel was first published in the US to outstanding reviews. *Saturday Review* said:

> Like his hero, the young lawyer Amamu, Awoonor tries to come to terms in this novel with conflicting realities of independence. He presents the dilemma of those few African intellectuals who refuse to be self-satisfied about their newly gained status and the material possessions that accompany it, who ask themselves of what use is statehood if colonial injustices are replaced by political opportunism and social inequalities? … But for all its social commentary, *This Earth, My Brother* is not a political novel. Politics have been minimised to point up the moral plight of the hero, and changed into a metaphysical confrontation. At the end Amamu's frantic race to the seashore is an attempt to recover a unity with his soul. The sea woman who lures him, her lover, to her cavern, is Africa, but Africa is also the conflicting landscape of a butterfly field and the dunghill. (19 June 1971)

The New York Review of Books critic said:

> We have now a few books like *This Earth, My Brother* which are bound to stand, it seems to me, not only as chronicles of the first tragic era of African independence but as noble contributions to the art of the world.

The Observer in London remarked of African novels:

> They are not easy reading; history rattles through them at a pace which our sedate classics do not prepare us to cope with. Even the novels set in the French or Russian Revolutions do not approach the breathlessness of the African experience. (26 March 1972)

There was another very English reaction in *The Times Literary Supplement*:

> Among the enemies of promise now confronting African literature it is possible to include the American university. Kofi Awoonor is a learned Ghanaian poet with an evident gift for narrative (when he chooses to exercise it) and he ought to be a good novelist; but he is also Chairman of

> the Comparative Literature Program at the State University of New York and much of *This Earth, My Brother* seems not to designed to be read in the ordinary way but to be thrashed out in seminars. The chapters are headed 1, 1a, 2, 2a, etc. those marked 'a' being written in the style of a prose-poem and printed in smaller type than the unlettered chapters – which are generally excellent narratives, short sketches about growing up in West Africa ... All this is fascinating; and the sketches add up to a mysterious but not wholly opaque portrait of Amamu and an account of his disintegration. There is no doubt that Kofi Awoonor could write a very good novel. (24 March 1972)

Some ten years later there were mixed reactions to the manuscript of his novel *Comes the Voyager at Last*. By this time Doubleday had given up their policy of buying African novels. Simon Gikandi said in his report:

> In any case, those of us who noticed the jibe aimed at Awoonor in Armah's novel *Fragments,* do not need to study the Ghanaian novelist in *Comes the Voyager at Last* too closely to discover that he is a rather cheap and designing parody of Ayi Kwei Armah, which is in the novel simply because the author wants to repay an old debt; if authors want to fight their own private wars in their novels they are entitled to, but when this is coupled with rather heavy literary borrowings from the 'enemy', it is advisable to be prudent. (Report by Simon Gikandi 8 November 1981)

Robert Fraser, who had written a study *The Novels of Ayi Kwei Armah* (Heinemann), said:

> I do not know how amenable Awoonor is, but it might be worth telling him in principle the book is an admirable addition to the list, but that both readers are in agreement in finding the bar scene digressive and unhelpful. If he wishes to score a point against Armah, he has already done so by writing a book which is in many respects stronger than much in his rival. (Report by Robert Fraser no date)

Kofi Awoonor was not amenable to reworking the manuscript and wrote to me on 18 April 1984 from the Embassy of Ghana in Brasilia. With the debt crisis we were already struggling to get books into Africa. We had an unhappy period of engagement with Kofi Awoonor as the market slipped away and the new owners put ever greater pressure on Heinemann to reduce our publishing. Now he was an ambassador. Only a few years before he had been a political convict in Ghana. Shortly after returning to Ghana he was arrested for aiding a political fugitive. He submitted his manuscript on his prison experience called *The Cistern's End*. I also sent the manuscript to Simon Gikandi, who was now at Edinburgh and had recently worked on Ngũgĩ 's *Detained*, who said:

> Here we have the poet as philosopher, involved in larger than life moral tangles. And down to earth ethics, in the tradition of Soyinka's *The Man Died* ... This book should be published. There are too many good things to be said about it. But Awoonor should be encouraged to look at Chapters 4, 5 and 6 again, try to forget his persecutor, Acheampong as a man, put aside some of the polemics, underscore his role as poet, dilute his role as a

> party man, and make his own convictions (as outlined in the prison notes) the bases of his analysis. More importantly, however much he would like to kick the smalls of all those idiots who sustained and rationalised tyranny in Ghana, he shouldn't forget there is something called libel. (Report by Simon Gikandi 5 May 1971)

We sadly had to turn it down, telling him that it did seem to be too deeply involved in the details of Ghanaian politics. I am sure that we would have published it in the later 1970s. In spite of the rapid descent into the African book famine we did manage, after long waits for reactions from Africa, to accept his collected poems under the title *Until the Morning After.* Robert Fraser reported:

> As you say this is a major proposal. The poems in the present volume cover the major part of Awoonor's pioneer pamphlet *Rediscovery and Other Poems* (Mbari Club of Ibadan, 1964) together with the subsequent volumes *Night of My Blood* (1971) and *Ride Me, Memory* (Greenfield Press, New York, 1973). They thus afford a panoramic view of the work of one of Africa's most lyrically eloquent poets over a twenty year period. They also include all of 'Poems from Prison', smuggled out while he was in detention in Ussher Fort, Accra, some of which have not appeared in book form before. There is also a selection of excellent new work …
>
> Taken together, the contents of this book serve as a working document for the theory of African literature put forward in his treatise *Breast of the Earth* [*A Critical Survey of Africa's Literature and History* (1975)]. They have an architectural shape which reveals the hand of the novelist and critic. They are all worth saving, especially as much of his work is out-of-print, or merely obtainable in dribs and drabs of anthologies. To erect a plinth would be good work. (Report by Robert Fraser undated)

The book was announced in the 1984 African Writers Series catalogue as appearing in 1985. Sadly Kofi Awoonor withdrew his manuscript in the period of delays following my departure from Heinemann Educational Books. This was in spite of Vicky Unwin telling him on 13 February 1986 that William Heinemann was strongly considering issuing a general-market hardback. This would have followed their hardback publication in that year of the *Collected Poems* of Christopher Okigbo, with a new preface by Paul Theroux, and of the first novel by a Ghanaian writer, B. Kojo Laing, called *Search Sweet Country.* I have described elsewhere the civil war that developed following my departure between Heinemann Educational Books and William Heinemann over the possession of rights to the work by B. Kojo Laing (p. 297).

B. Kojo Laing

Magic realism v. marvellous realism v. fantastic realism

B. Kojo Laing offered his first novel *Search Sweet Country* to the African Writers Series. Robert Fraser said in a profile in the literary magazine *Wasafiri* (autumn 1985) that he considered it to be 'the finest ever to be written in Africa'. *The Companion* says:

> Kojo Laing, a much younger writer from Ghana than Armah and Awoonor, injects new energy into the Ghanaian novel by his bold experimentation with language and his use of magic in *Search Sweet Country.* The world of the witch Adwoa Adde defies space and time. Doors and windows open on their own in her presence as she cruises over Accra at night. But these magical feats are perhaps less exciting than Laing's original and concrete metaphors, which stand out as fresh and innovative in their context. The novel is not as overtly political as those of his predecessors, but it is the more intensely satirical, since the author exposes the folly of public life as well as that of private lives. (p.188)

Early in the book the principled Okay Pol has to supervise the illegal import of racehorses at the airport. They break out of their crates and panic strikes the crowd. He announces:

> I must warn you what you see here is not true ... the government needs your support ... you are in the name of the law asked to remain here until further notice ... you may continue to look but don't pass water – I mean pass judgement. (*Search Sweet Country* pp. 40–1)

Pietro Deandrea of the University of Turin in *African Literature Today* 20 has made a study of the three novels; *Search Sweet Country* (1986), *Women of the Aeroplanes* (1988) and *Major Gentl and the Achimota Wars* (1992). The first two were published by William Heinemann in hardback, and then under the up-market Picador paperback imprint. The third title appeared in the African Writers Series. Pietro Deandrea puts these books in the context of more recent work:

> ... a new generation of narrators from Nigeria and other African countries; authors like Ben Okri and Syl Cheney-Coker managed to pave new, still untrodden paths for West African Literature, and ended up by being branded with the theoretically vague definition of 'magic realism'. The one novelist, whose work should strike the literary critic as unique and groundbreaking is the Ghanaian Kojo Laing ... (p. 158)

Kole Omotoso was to argue for the description 'marvellous realism' and Deandrea argues for 'fantastic realism'. In fact Kojo Laing defies all categories.

Reviewers were extravagant in their comparisons with the great of the western canon. *The Listener* called him 'an African Balzac'. The *National Times on Sunday* said:

> ... as idiosyncratic as Joyce and oblique as Woolf ... it is fun to be assaulted by poetry and exhilarating to be trepanned by so deft a surgeon ... It is a sprawling digressive *Tristram Shandy* of a book, and, like *Tristram Shandy*,

always under control when we least expect it to be. Read it. At least twice.

Robert Fraser saw it as breaking intellectual and literary moulds which had set hard twenty years before. Edward Blishen also placed it within the African rather than the western canon. His review in *The Times Educational Supplement* was a shout of vindication and a celebration of the vivaciousness of Ghana:

> The beauty of this novel is that, in it, the ideas are completely embodied in the characters made richly real. And everywhere there are the voices of individual Ghanaians, in markets, filling the elbowing streets of Accra: whole chapters filled with their amusingly, excitingly, and often elevatingly inventive voices. I love this novel because it raises a new and invigorating question proposed by some of the first generation African writers. Is it possible that the continent has powerful wisdoms to add to the powerful, but ill-balanced, wisdoms of the West? I recommend *Search Sweet Country* not only as a book good to read but also as a marvellous affirmation of African positiveness.

The Companion says: 'As a poet and a novelist Laing approaches language inventively; he pushes English to its limits and beyond by fusing Oxbridge with West African Pidgin, elements from African languages, and his own coinings, aiming to create one gigantic living and truly cosmopolitan language.'

As with Kofi Awoonor, B. Kojo Laing's strength as a poet comes across in his novels. A collection of his poetry called *Godhorse* was published by Heinemann in 1989. Pietro Deandrea points to how the 'utter lyricality' of the language' shows 'how much Laing's writing is affected by oral narrative style in general, and Akan poetic style in particular'.

A tradition of verse & drama

Working on the novels of B. Kojo Laing, Pietro Deandrea said that he noticed in Ghana 'a great predominance of poets over novelists, and most Ghanaian poets conceive their poetry as oral deliverance considering it as a communal act more akin to theatre than to the novelistic genre' (*African Literature Today* 20, p. 158).

The wide range of Ghanaian poetry was reflected in the anthology *Messages* (1971 AWS 42) which Kofi Awoonor and G. Adali-Mortty edited. Individual collections followed by A.W. Kayper-Mensah, *The Drummer in Our Time* (1975 AWS 157) and Joe de Graft, *Beneath the Jazz and Brass* (1975 AWS 166). Fortunately, in the depressed year of 1984, I managed to get accepted Kofi Anyidoho's poetry collection *A Harvest of our Dreams* (1984 AWS 261). The original idea was that it would make a good pairing with Kofi Awoonor's hoped for collection (p. 78). As Robert Fraser said in a report: '[Awoonor] was the first to extend the Ewe lament into a vehicle of political criticism. A contribution taken up by his younger compatriot Kofi Anyidoho both in his poetic work and in his research on the native lyricist, Henoga Domegbe.' (undated)

Joe de Graft was first and foremost a playwright and Henry Chakava at Heinemann East Africa initiated the publication of his play *Muntu* which was first performed in Nairobi. We rarely did collections of plays by a single playwright. However, we decided in 1980 to accept a collection by Asiedu Yirenkyi under the name of the main play *Kivuli* (1979 AWS 216). We also published, though outside the Series, a collection by Martin Owusu. Plays had a long concert party tradition in Ghana. Kobina Sekyi's plays were published in the 1930s and 1940s, but his satirical play *The Blinkards* was not published until 1974 by Rex Collings in hardback and paperback (AWS 136). It had been performed at the Cosmopolitan Club in Cape Coast in 1915 and satirised middle-class Fantis who embraced anything they thought of as western (p. 21).

Lenrie Peters
A scalpel probing

Lenrie Peters, a writer from The Gambia, worked in the 1960s as a surgeon in London and Northampton. In his novel *The Second Round* (1966 AWS 22) the main character, a British-trained physician, is a victim of 'the massacre of the soul' caused by westernisation. He returns full of noble ideas to work in his country's capital. However it is in an upcountry hospital that he finds that he can immerse himself in the traditional experience. He submitted a manuscript called *The Third Round* but that was not accepted.

It is as poet that he has stood out. *Poems* (1964) had the distinguished imprimatur of the pioneering Mbari list. He wrote on 5 June 1966 to Heinemann suggesting a new collection. Keith Sambrook wrote on 4 July 1966 saying that schools and universities only had anthologies to read and that they needed more collections by individual African poets. Longman was doing well with a collection by another Mbari poet, J.P. Clark. He asked Lenrie Peters:

> Would you be agreeable to a collection? This would probably have to include some, if not all, of the poems in the Mbari volume, as this contains some of your best work. No doubt Ulli Beier would be co-operative. He usually is, as he wants the best market for the authors he has launched and supported.
>
> You know that I certainly regard you as amongst the best contemporary poets and we'd be glad to have a selection on our list. (KS to LP 4 July 1966)

His work contrasts with the work of many of the poets in Ghana and Nigeria in that it owes little to the oral tradition. *The Companion* says:

> He is a cosmopolitan poet whose densely packed minimalist stanzaic structures accommodate the broad universal spectrum of human experience: ageing and death, the risks of love, the loneliness of exile. In … *Satellites* the poet-doctor's surgical detachment is a metaphor for the individual's painful existential isolation, his scalpel's probing 'at the cutting chaotic edge of things' an image for the imaginative piercing and spiritual penetration which are the real goals of the poet's quest.
>
> He is generally regarded as one of the most intellectual poets of his

> generation. Ideas – about politics, evolution, science, and music – orchestrate his images in the form of debates. Though he rages at the frustrations of Africa's underdevelopment, he reflects on blind, ill-considered modes of 'progress' …

In 1979 at a meeting of the African Literature Association in Bloomington, Indiana he and I discussed publishing *Selected Poems* (1981 AWS 238) in which he would choose from his 1964 collection published by Mbari and the two former collections in the Series, *Satellites* (1967 AWS 37) and *Katchikali* (1971 AWS 103). To this he would add some of his more recent work especially about America. Robert Fraser, in a long, informed and constructive report in October 1979, reacted to the selection Lenrie Peters had made:

> We can see his poetic style change from year to year, as he takes in and reflects the varying influences to which he has become subject, from the stringent self-deprecatory tone of fifties British verse, to the concentrated density of sixties poetry, to, finally, the more expansive gestures of anglophone African writers. His own style has demonstrated a certain consistency despite these superficial vagaries, and we are left with a feeling of a satisfyingly replete oeuvre, albeit with dull patches.

However, in his consideration of what had been included from *Katchikali*, he regretted some of the exclusions:

> I am alarmed to see that Peters has left out some of my old time favourites. Despite its imperfections 'The English summer brooks no delay' is a lovely cameo piece of an African medic prowling around Primrose Hill … There are, however, bound to be disagreements about what to leave out and what to leave. I am glad to see that Peters has decided to keep the excellent pieces near the end where the theme is the attempts of a newly qualified poet-doctor to square his medical detachment with the equally strong artistic demand for empathy.

He then considered the fresh material and suggested that some of the work 'would be included at the poet's peril'. He goes on to say:

> But for my money the most finely handled language occurs in the American sequence, which I like very much. For some reason Peters seems to be a poet who flourishes under the impetus of foreign travel … (Report by Robert Fraser October 1979)

Writers from Sierra Leone

The Sierra Leonean critic Eustace Palmer has argued that the novel in his country has suffered from the cultural complacency of the country's educated class the Krio, who were not concerned with those cultural questions that interested other African novelists. 'Black Victorian' is one of the descriptions used about *The African* by William Conton who was born in The Gambia. The manuscript had been published in hardback by Little, Brown in Boston in 1960; it had been picked up by an American publisher on an early swing through West Africa looking at the potential for American educational publishing in the region. In 1964, when the search for any books to reprint in the African Writers Series was intense, it was published as AWS 12. The immaculate English of the author, who rose to be the chief education officer of Sierra Leone, ensured massive sales in schools.

Yulisa Amadu Maddy was a total contrast; his threat to kill Dambudzo Marechera was only a joke (p. 287). A letter from him in 1971 says, 'I am here for my trial at the Old Bailey', but gives no clues. He had theatrical training in London, was influenced by Brecht and the theatre of the absurd and won the Edinburgh Festival Award in 1979. When we were considering publishing a collection of his plays *Obasai* (1971 AWS 89), he went to work with Michael Etherton at the University of Zambia. Michael Etherton had just got the students at the University of Zambia to build the Chikwakwa Theatre against the wall of a ruined tobacco warehouse. It was an inspiring time in Lusaka. However, culturally it was a step too far south for Yulisa Amadu Maddy, and Michael Etherton described how he found it difficult to come to terms 'with the role of the theatre in the sort of community that Lusaka is, and becomes frustrated when things don't work out as he thinks they ought'. Pat Maddy, as we called him, was to find himself as an inspired and witty user of pidgin; in the late 1970s and early 1980s his plays and productions became popular in Freetown and West Africa.

He also wrote a novel, *No Past, No Present, No Future* (1973 AWS 137), in which three young men try to escape the social complexity of their native Sierra Leone. It was in one way a pioneer as it was one of the first African novels to include a homosexual character. He responded to a series of tough reports and welcomed the helping hand of the novelist Richard Lister. Ros de Lanerolle was positive about the much rewritten script:

> I like this. Plenty of power, feeling, energy. And the shape of the book now Okay. But I'd edit with rather a heavier hand than Richard Lister … (Ros de Lanerolle to JC 9 October 1970)

The Companion (p. 188) says: 'Sierra Leonean literature begins to enter the mainstream of African literature only with the work of such writers (mostly poets) as Syl Cheney-Coker with his magic realist novel *The Last Harmattan of Alusine Dunbar.*' It was published in the African Writers Series in 1990 and won the Commonwealth Writers Prize. This lyrical novel has been compared with *One Hundred Years of Solitude* by the Colombian writer Gabriel García Márquez. In marked contrast to the Ghanaian poets, Syl Cheney-Coker tends to draw more strongly on European rather than African culture. We published his second collection of poetry *Concerto for an Exile* (AWS 126) in 1973. In 1977 he submitted his third poetry collection, *The Graveyard Also Has Teeth* (1980 AWS 221). Aig Higo's report was: 'Lethal!' We decided that, as we had sold over 3,000 of a first print run of 4,000, we would include the earlier collection with the new collection to save a publishing space in the African Writers Series. It then took three years for the last thousand copies to sell out and Keith Sambrook and I strained his loyalty with the repeated postponements and might well have lost him. In 1990 another collection of his poetry, *The Blood in the Desert's Eyes*, was added to the Series.

African Literature Today

As it happens, one of the most important contributions to the establishment of the study of the new wave of writing from the continent came from Sierra Leone. *African Literature Today*, a thematic annual, was edited from 1968 until 2001 from Fourah Bay College in the University of Sierra Leone by Eldred Durosimi Jones with, at various times, Eustace Palmer and Marjorie Jones. When Heinemann dropped it in 1985 it was continued by James Currey Publishers. Since 2001 the editorship has been taken over by the Nigerian Ernest Emenyonu.

Eldred and Marjorie Jones kept *African Literature Today* going through the Sierra Leone civil war in the 1990s. The edited manuscript of one issue was posted to England by Marjorie Jones in the Freetown Post Office on a Saturday. With inflation the packet had to be smothered with stamps and Marjorie Jones made sure that every last stamp was cancelled by the clerk at the Post Office On Sunday there was a coup. Marjorie Jones then had to seek the personal intervention of the postmaster general to extract the parcel. It was given to a Sierra Leonean journalist who was setting out to get, somehow, to London. He had to wait for weeks in Guinea-Bissau for his British visa. The manuscript eventually reached us.

At one time Eldred and Marjorie Jones had to lie on the floor of their house for a day and a half with the Nigerian peacekeepers on one side of the house and the rebels on the other. In one lull Marjorie opened their louvred windows so as to give the bullets a chance to whistle through without breaking the glass. At a later date Eldred and Marjorie Jones joined a delegation to Guinea to try to negotiate peace. On one occasion they had to return overland from Guinea. I said that it sounded like Graham Greene's *Journey without Maps*. Eldred Jones replied that, for much of the way, it was a 'Journey without Roads'.

Lenrie Peters (*left*) and Yulisa Amadu Maddy

PART 2
Writers from EAST AFRICA

George Hallett

George Hallett

Based on EAPH edition

Michael Harvey

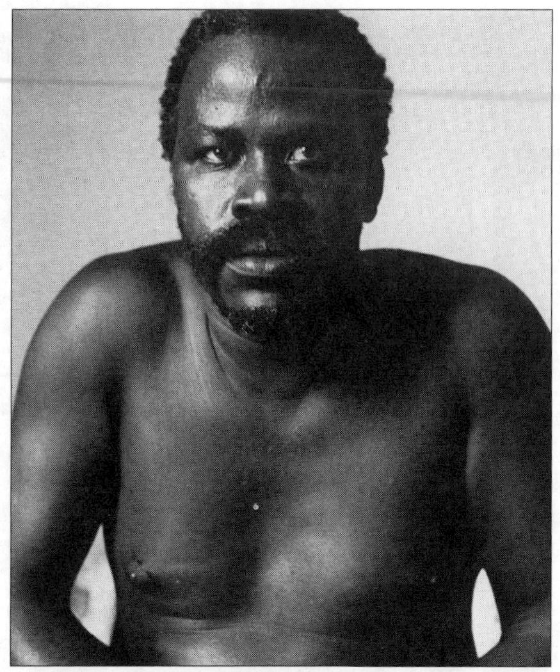

Taban lo Liyong
Hotel am Zoo,
Berlin 1979

Meja Mwangi
Berlin 1979

4 *Towards the Oral & the Popular in* KENYA, UGANDA & TANZANIA

Fortunately Ngũgĩ's promise had been recognised by Chinua Achebe in 1962 at the Mbari conference at Makerere (p. 3). However, by the time of the tenth anniversary in 1972 there were only a few books by East African writers in the African Writers Series. This was in marked contrast to West Africa where the team of Aig Higo and Chinua Achebe had made Heinemann the publisher of first choice against competition from other publishers in London and Nigeria.

In the three East African countries of Uganda, Tanzania and Kenya the Series was being marketed effectively from the Heinemann-Cassell sales office by Bob Markham and was introducing the writers from western and southern Africa to bookshops, universities and schools. In its second decade the Series was to flower with bold experiments from all over Africa. Many of the initiatives were now to come from Nairobi where Henry Chakava, in collaboration with writers such as Ngũgĩ, Okot p'Bitek and Taban lo Liyong, revealed on the printed page the influence of the oral tradition. At the same time, Henry Chakava with the help of editors such as Laban Erapu and Simon Gikandi, gave chances to a new generation of exceptional writers such as Meja Mwangi, Mwangi Ruheni and Rebeka Njau, who used the imported form of the novel to reveal the social realities of life in East Africa and the deep scars of Mau Mau.

The effort to work with East African Publishing House

East African Publishing House (EAPH) was founded in Nairobi in 1965 in collaboration with the imaginative London literary publisher André Deutsch. The managing director, John Nottingham, had resigned as a district officer during the war against Mau Mau because he was so disgusted by what the British colonial authorities were perpetrating. Its Modern African Library made an important contribution to the establishment of a lively literary scene, particularly round the universities in Nairobi and Kampala. It quickly captured the authors and the market.

In 1966 EAPH published Okot p'Bitek's *Song of Lawino,* which rapidly became one of the landmark texts of African literature. Keith Sambrook and Alan Hill were deeply impressed by the Modern African Library and by the way that EAPH was publishing academic work by the new generation of scholars, such as the historian Alan Ogot. So in 1967 an agreement was made for Heinemann Educational Books to distribute EAPH books in the rest of Africa and in the Commonwealth market. Heinemann Educational Books would not need to set up its own editorial department in the Heinemann-Cassell sales office in Nairobi; EAPH would continue to publish the best of writing from East Africa and we would make sure that the voices of these new writers could be heard as well in Nigeria, Ghana, South Africa and across the world. For instance, in 1967 Keith Sambrook suggested to John Nottingham that we might work together to publish work by the then unknown Taban lo Liyong. Successful publishing is all a matter of detail and, in those days when communication was more expensive, our own marketing department from EAPH could not get the flow of information that was needed to make the list known internationally. Sadly the arrangement broke down. Against our wishes we went back to being competitors rather than collaborators. John Nottingham and we were all trying to come to terms with publishing in a changing post-imperial situation. I am not quite sure whether he believed that we were as much the neo-colonial exploiters that he later made us out to be in the Kenyan press. As individuals we tried, at considerable personal effort, to use the international assets of Heinemann to make the EAPH list known outside East Africa. He could have taken advantage of that.

Peter Palangyo, Bonnie Lubega, Robert Serumaga & John Nagenda

High-flying young men

When EAPH failed to make the details work we just got on with building up the East African contribution to the Series. We already had in hand manuscripts by several young men who were to rise high in their newly independent countries and who never published further novels.

'I think I have found a good Tanzanian writer … very impressed by the drive and energy of his writing … it seems to me to be the first novel from Africa that really tries to get inside somebody's mind. At the same time, without being in the slightest anthropological, it gives the European reader a surprising insight into the life and customs of the Nyakyusa tribe of South Western Tanzania.' Thus wrote Professor Molly Mahood from the University College at Dar es Salaam on 28 September 1965. The author, Peter Palangyo, was a biology teacher in Iringa but, aged only 27, he had been appointed headmaster of H.H. The Aga Khan Boys' Secondary School in the capital. He quickly sought release from the burdens of running this prestigious six-stream school. He wrote to me on 26 June 1968 to say, 'I am going to the University of Iowa to "study", God help me, creative writing!' He went into the diplomatic service and rose to become ambassador to Canada. His *Dying in the Sun* (1968/1969 AWS 53) was the first Tanzanian novel published in English. Sadly we did not find another from the country to put in the Series. I had great entertainment from him during a visit to Dar in February 1968. He introduced me in a lift to a friend who turned out to be the head of the Tanzanian armed services. This soldier apparently had rung Peter Palangyo recently to ask him to tell him why Lawrence Durrell's Alexandrian quartet of novels was important. Apparently President Nyerere had told him at a meeting that he must read them and, as a good officer, he obeyed orders and had read the copies he borrowed from Peter Palangyo. The only Durrell this officer had known was the author of the algebra books.

It was Uganda that produced the most promising East African proposals at this time. Bonnie Lubega, who had been born in Buganda, was an experienced journalist and we hoped for a flow of work from him. *The Outcasts* (1971 AWS 105) was an elegantly simple story of the underdog getting his own back. Baganda cattle owners employed the services of Ankole kraalmen to look after their wealth – their cattle. They despised them as a dung-encrusted lower tribe whom they rarely visited. Some of the owners would give the occasional bull calf to their kraalmen. However, the hero Karekyesi sets out to penetrate his exploiters' psychology. The occasional cow calf goes away to his kinsmen in the hills and, after he has accumulated his own cattle wealth, he builds up a quarrel with the owner and goes off. Bob Windsor called it, in a report dated 1 June 1970, 'a ripe bawdy, earthy book', which includes burying the grandmother in the dungheap and the father taking the young bride on the wedding night.

Robert Serumaga was an actor and playwright. After taking a second degree in economics at Trinity College, Dublin he worked with the BBC before returning to Uganda to set up Theatre Limited. He tried his hand, with his usual elegant style, at a novel called *Return to the Shadows* (1970 AWS 54). An economist returns home to Africa but gets caught in a military coup. I do remember him on a visit to the Heinemann offices in London accusing the BBC of being prejudiced in its coverage of Idi Amin. However, he was arrested in 1977 for allegedly plotting to overthrow him. He fortunately survived and became minister of commerce in Okello's government but died in 1980 at the age of only 41.

In this period around 1970, when we were anxiously trying to find more work from East Africa to balance the West African output, I had hoped that the debonair and worldly-wise John Nagenda would produce a novel or collection of short stories. He had edited *Penpoint* at Makerere. I had first met him when he and I were colleagues at Oxford University Press where, for many reasons, he had become a legend. In his laconic style he agreed to play for the Oxford University Press Sunday cricket team on its annual visit to Sandon in Essex where the renowned typographer and artist Lynton Lamb lived. OUP did not mind that they always lost. Each year the village won comfortably and they all adjourned for a friendly evening in the pub. Sandon was, as usual, doing well when the OUP captain, Andrew Lamb, asked John Nagenda if he could bowl. He took the ball and more or less disappeared behind the pavilion to start his run. His deliveries came with the force of an African storm and Sandon was skittled out. He had not bothered to mention that he had played as a fast bowler for East Africa. Sandon felt that it was not playing the game for OUP secretly to bring a whirling dervish on their side. The villagers were furious and early in the evening grumpily slipped away from the pub.

John Nagenda worked as a radio and TV producer in Kampala, New York and London. During his exile, in the Amin-blighted years of the 1970s, he read and gave me advice on novels being considered for the Series. Typical of his style was when he started a report on a controversial South African novel with 'How pleasant to some across a MS you actually enjoy!' (p. 194). In the late 1960s, I started discussing with him the ideas for a novel, which eventually ripened into *The Seasons of Thomas Tebo* (1986 AWS 262). Some 60 or 70 seasons were to pass before it grew to maturity. Indeed I think that the original plan was to have four seasons as in the year, but that he never quite finished the fourth season. He first submitted a manuscript in 1974, sent in a revised version in 1981 and after further revisions it was only published in 1986 after my departure from Heinemann.

Richard Lister, experienced novelist, responded with a professional's enthusiasm:

> The book is entertaining, highly readable, often moving and perceptive; in all three sections the sense of real experience is high. The style is refreshingly direct. This is a very original talent. (Richard Lister to JC undated 1974)

By 1981 Simon Gikandi was working on his thesis at the University of Edinburgh and I asked him to report. I wrote doubtfully to Henry Chakava:

> He originally submitted this novel in about 1974 and he almost pulled it off in publishing terms. Here is Simon Gikandi's reaction to the revised version. I dreadfully fear that it is a question of 'almost pulling it off' again. (JC to HC 28 September 1981)

Simon Gikandi saw in it 'the talents of John Nagenda as a short story writer' but also the problems which that produced:

> What we have here are, in fact, three different stories, united only by the presence of the major character and an unacknowledged historical moment and, in my view, the problem posed by *The Seasons of Thomas Tebo* is largely one of unity rather than credibility. In any case it is only the first part of the novel which demands greater suspension of disbelief. The rest is familiar. And yet this unusual mixture of a folklore legend (part one), a novel of political intrigue (part two) and romance (part three) has a 'newness' to it which this reader finds rather appealing.
>
> The folk legend begins with 'his unusual conception when his teenage mother goes to bed with "a dark stranger" from across the sea; his growth into a child sexual monster, who goes to bed with his mother's agemate at the age of nine; ending with his departure for "further" studies overseas … So what? This is a monster direct from myth and his story is entertaining.' (Report by Simon Gikandi 25 August 1981)

Twenty-one years later Thomas Tebo hires a mercenary to assassinate President Mandu Manduku, the civilian tyrant of his native country Dondo (by this date the replacement in John Nagenda's native Uganda of the soldier Amin by the civilian Obote was not looking altogether happy):

> The would-be mercenary is in fact a London businessman called Jones, who, having been caught up in the crossfire during the troubles in the then Congo, has built a false image of himself as a tough-going dog of war. He undertakes the mission of extermination to Dondo, accompanied by Tebo. The two develop an intimate relationship as they set out to find the target with the help of some rebel army officers. Jones succeeds in killing the president but is killed by their army collaborators who are in desperate need of a scapegoat. Tebo is paid off by the new military elite and returns to his London lair disillusioned. (Report by Simon Gikandi 25 August 1981)

In the third part Nagenda switches to the role of romantic entertainer and Simon Gikandi sees 'a bit of the child monster in the middle-aged Tebo, but, again this is a world we can recognise'.

Vicky Unwin commissioned a report in 1985 from the playwright and actor Nick Owen who had done much work for the British Council in Africa. It could not have really been the report she hoped for:

> I was totally enchanted with Book One; some of the most exciting and distinctive African writing I have read for a long time ... The problem is the central character starts off as an enchanting kitten only to end up as a fat sluggish tom-cat ... Book 2 particularly never rises above stereotype: both of character and situation. It's a bad political assassination thriller; the hard drinking hero who gets the beautiful girl (of course she melts in his arms: in fact the role of women in this MS is generally seen from the typical African he-male point of view). (Report by Nick Owen 14 June 1985)

Vicky Unwin went ahead with publication and included the novel in her plans for 'relaunching of the African and Caribbean Writers Series'. On 28 May 1986 she invited John Nagenda to be one of the 'writers in conversation' in a Writers' Festival at the Institute of Contemporary Arts, London. I am sure that he would have put on a stylish performance. This was during the months when Museveni's army was advancing from Tanzania to seize control of Kampala later that year.

John Nagenda's involvement with the new regime had rather too much of the drama of a novel. He was made chairman of the Uganda Human Rights Commission. He appeared daily on TV and he was an easily recognisable target in this process, which predated South Africa's Truth and Reconciliation Commission. When I was in Kampala in 1992 in connection with the *UNESCO General History of Africa* we spent a cheerfully social evening in Kampala together. He insisted that, leaving him at the hotel, I be taken back to the rest house at Makerere University in his army Land Rover pick-up with an armed soldier standing on the back with his gun cocked. Perhaps like Mr Jones I might have been a decoy. When we reached the gates of Makerere the night porter waved the Land Rover past a queue of cars which he was searching. We roared up to the rest house and the manager rushed out expecting the worst as the Land Rover skidded to a stop. After the Human Rights Commission John Nagenda was to become a personal adviser to President Museveni and I am sure that he charmed the British aid ministers, Lynda Chalker and Clare Short, when the restored Uganda was at the height of its popularity with its old colonial master.

Peter Palangyo, Robert Serumaga and John Nagenda, living in and out of the political centres of their rapidly changing countries, all had lives which were a bit too much like plots for novels.

Ali A. Mazrui

The novel as political science

The Mazruis ruled Mombasa in the eighteenth century. Ali Mazrui, after working on the buses while at the Huddersfield Technical College, went on to Columbia University, New York, and to a doctorate at Oxford. I had failed to convince my bosses to accept one of his first political collections when I was at Oxford University Press. By 1970 he had published the first of many provocative books on politics and culture. He took over from Colin Leys in 1965 to become the first African Professor of Political Science at Makerere in the heyday of the magazine *Transition*. He was even then beginning to build up a remarkable international reputation, which meant that in 2005 the American journal *Foreign Policy* selected him as among 'the world's 100 leading intellectuals'.

In April 1970, three months after the end of the Biafran war, he wrote to Alan Hill apologising for not having written a promised book on Greece and Rome in Africa:

> In the midst of all my other commitments, the Nigerian civil war had such a tremendous hold on my imagination that I had to write a novel about it. Symbolically I was particularly moved by the death of Christopher Okigbo, the gifted poet who died for Biafra on the war front in a major's uniform. I never knew him, but I knew and admired his work.
>
> My novel bears the title of *The Trial of Christopher Okigbo* [1972 AWS 97], and uses as the central focus an imaginary courtroom in the hereafter at which Okigbo is charged with the sin of putting his tribe before his art as a poet. Many of the massive issues of contemporary Africa, from violence to aesthetic freedom, hold the stage in the Court Room. Behind it all is the Nigerian Civil war as a symbol of a continent in torment.
>
> Mine is a novel of ideas – violence, thought, sex and poetry. A lot of Christopher Okigbo's own poetry is woven into the narrative. (AM to Alan Hill 30 April 1970)

In his letter he particularly mentioned his friendship with Bob and Susanna Markham. Bob Markham had run the ESA bookshop at Makerere before taking over the Heinemann-Cassell office in Nairobi. There is an excited note from Susanna Markham to Tony Beal:

> To me who is neither a bookseller nor a publisher, but just an ordinary reader of books, the novel is phenomenal – I mustn't say any more about it – except I am thrilled to the marrow. (Susanna Markham to Tony Beal 8 May 1970)

We were all nervous about Nigerian reactions. In the chapter on Nigeria (p. 54) there is an account of the difficulties with Mbari over the publication in the Series of Christopher Okigbo's poetry in 1971 under the title *Labyrinths*. Aig Higo wrote to Chinua Achebe, particularly criticising Ali Mazrui's overuse of adjectives:

> It seems to me very well-written. I think he should disguise all the names – of people and places – for the sake of history and good taste. On the other hand, I doubt the validity of the thesis 'we were trying Christopher Okigbo for Nigeria and its agony, in relation to a primordial curse in Africa's fortunes'. This Trinity Theory vis-à-vis the dead, living and unborn seems to me far-fetched and irrelevant. His deft use of time and space, history and meta-history, Herebefore and After-Africa all seem fascinating especially in the Trial Chapters. The early chapters have the aura of the Tolstoy of Anna Karenin. (AH to Chinua Achebe 20 July 1970)

Ali Mazrui pointed out recently to me that the concept of 'the curse of the trinity' in the novel was the germ of the idea which culminated in the theme of the 'the triple heritage' in his television series and book *The Africans: A Triple Heritage* (BBC/Public Service Broadcasting 1986) (AM to JC 11 October 2006).

Chinua Achebe came back with a carefully argued criticism in which he explained:

> I have now read Ali Mazrui's novel and have mixed feelings about it. A 'novel of ideas' has to surmount a fundamental problem of keeping the ideas in rein so they don't run away with the novel. The middle sections of the book surmount this problem quite well and often attain heights of beauty and distinction. The beginning is not so successful. The initiation of the reader into After-Africa is rather heavy; the 'suspension of disbelief' takes too long to achieve. The weakness of the end of the book is even more serious. If in the early pages the ideas run away with the novel one might say that in the closing chapters in the novel run away <u>from</u> its own ideas....
>
> All the same the novel deserves to be published for braving such new ground. Some of the heaviness in the story can in fact be easily removed. (Chinua Achebe to KS 7 August 1970)

I wrote to Ali Mazrui accepting the book on 15 September 1970 and sending him the letters from Aig Higo and Chinua Achebe and said, 'You are of course, used to your writing creating controversy and this novel is no exception.' In his reply he said that he was disappointed that we were not going to publish it first in hardback. We felt that it was a novel which needed a detailed knowledge of the politics and philosophy of Africa. This was an amazingly timely book and we wanted it to be out at the same time as Christopher Okigbo's *Labyrinths* (p. 54) and before people's memories about the Biafran war faded; a hardback would have delayed its appearance in the African Writers Series.

> I am surprised that in your assessment you feel that this book is so African that the response in the United Kingdom is likely to be limited. I would have thought no serious book on the Nigerian Civil war could be so distant from British interests. (AM to JC 25 September 1970)

In my reply I gave an overview of the changing relationship of paperback and hardback publishing at the time:

> Marketing novels in the U.K. market is becoming a more and more frustrating business unless they are in paperback. Hardback sales, except of the best sellers at the top of *The Evening Standard* list, are now almost exclusively to libraries …
>
> We have got William Heinemann to produce a hardback of a novel on the Biafran war by S.O. Mezu called *Behind the Rising Sun*. Despite publicity for it which we obtained in *The Sunday Times,* interest has been extremely limited. And the booksellers, travellers and William Heinemann insist on a gap of eighteen months to allow them to get rid of the hardback … William Heinemann are afraid that the Biafran setting may now be a disadvantage because Biafra has faded from the television screens of comfortable, middlebrow Britain.
>
> On the other hand, to look at the position positively, the people who have a continuing concern on Biafra are people who know about Africa ….And they are the people who buy the African Writers Series in Dillons, Collets, Blackwells, Heffers, University of Sussex bookshop and so on. (JC to AM 8 October 1970)

It was decided with Bob Markham that, in publicity terms, it would be worth the exceptional expense of airfreighting 250 copies of the book to be launched at the Makerere Arts Festival in November 1971. However, there were diplomatic problems and Ali Mazrui wrote that he had had to reassure

> … the Nigerian High Commissioner and our own Foreign Minister that they could attend the launching of the book without taking a diplomatic risk … it would be diplomatically impossible for [the High Commissioner] to launch a book if the book contained a message which said 'What a pity Biafra failed! What a pity Nigeria did not break up!' (AM to JC 11 November 1971)

Ali Mazrui was amused that my secretary had mistakenly addressed him as Professor of Literature instead of Professor of Political Science. Indeed at about this time he contributed an article to the OUP Nairobi literary magazine *Zuka* in which he cheerfully wrote his own example of 'a modern poem' and then, with his own criticism, cheerfully tore it apart.

As usual Ali Mazrui's work provoked reactions. The writer Okello Oculi wrote in a Kampala paper:

> One's instinctive reaction to *The Trial of Christopher Okigbo* is that Mazrui has committed an act of profanity. He has exported Political Science to heaven. And in addition one gets the alarming feeling that Mazrui would like to see himself as the All-Africa Professor of Political Science (and public administration) in the united Africa that exists in the world after death.

Okello Oculi was a junior in Ali Mazrui's department and in this review, with sharp wit, attacks Ali Mazrui as 'an Africa Anglo-Saxon Liberal'.

Ali Mazrui sends an annual newsletter to his supporters and family; in the one which covers his international doings during 2005 he recalls an incident during the period of the publication of his novel at the end of 1971. In January of that year Captain Ochima had announced on the radio that Idi Amin had taken over power in a coup from Milton Obote, who was Langi. By the time that the novel was published it was suspected that hundreds of Langi soldiers had already been killed by other soldiers in Idi Amin's army. Ali Mazrui was told that Okello Oculi, who was also a Langi, had been seized by soldiers on the Makerere campus. Ali Mazrui confronted the soldiers and asked by whose authority they were taking his colleague away. One of the soldiers replied 'Ask Captain Ochima!' Ali Mazrui immediately used his connections:

> In 1971, my own standing with Idi Amin's regime was high. After all I had been a critic of Milton Obote when he was president. I was a high profile Muslim intellectual in postcolonial Uganda. Idi Amin's office did pursue the ominous capture of Okello Oculi urgently. We waited anxiously for feedback. Finally Amin's private secretary called me to say that Okello Oculi had been located and would be returning to Makerere within the hour. (AM personal newsletter for 2005)

Ali Mazrui was immediately in touch with the local representative of the Rockefeller Foundation so that Okello Oculi, who had to get out of Uganda, would be certain of a bursary in another country.

This novel was the beginning of a long personal publishing association. At Heinemann we published several of Ali Mazrui's books of political science, including the BBC Reith Lectures under the title *The African Condition*. Work with him on the eighth volume of the *UNESCO General History of Africa* called *Africa since 1935* continued with my own firm. James Currey Publishers has published four of his books including, most recently, *Islam between Globalization and Counterterrorism* (2006). Like the other young East African novelists, Ali Mazrui has never published another novel.

Poetry unknown outside East Africa

Writers were writing and being published in East Africa but were largely unknown in West and South Africa. Nigerians accepted their international reputation as their natural right. It was brought home to us in 1974 how badly East African poets were known in West Africa, especially after the demise of *Transition* magazine in Kampala. Wole Soyinka delivered to Secker and Warburg the massive manuscript of the anthology *Poems of Black Africa* (1975 AWS 171) which they had commissioned. Secker, who were in the Heinemann group, had subcontracted the book to Heinemann Educational Books for a paperback in the African Writers Series. Keith Sambrook and I, when we saw what was offered as the final manuscript, were quite shocked by what poor representation there was of work from East Africa. Wole Soyinka had mainly relied on our AWS anthology *Poems from East Africa* (1971 AWS 96) edited by David Cook and David Rubadiri. Clearly, as was his right, he had not shared the taste of those editors. However, he showed little knowledge of the EAPH list and the active literary magazines. We collected for him photocopies of poems and recent books from a range of East African publishers, as well as our own books of poetry in the African Writers Series by Taban lo Liyong and Jared Angira's *Silent Voices* (1972 AWS 111). Wole Soyinka, having got the job off his shoulders, was annoyed to have to reopen consideration of the work from East Africa; however, on the basis of the poetry we supplied he did enlarge the East African representation. Tom Rosenthal at Secker was also annoyed because the more representative East African selection led to a longer book and increased permissions fees.

The appointment of a publishing editor in East Africa

Bob Markham and Keith Sambrook decided in about 1971 to find a young editor from East Africa to develop school textbooks and to encourage East African authors to come to the African Writers Series. David Hill, second son of Alan and Enid Hill, was sent out to set up an editorial department in the Nairobi office and to help select an East African editor. Ngũgĩ had recommended one of his outstanding students who had gone on to postgraduate studies. However, this candidate felt that he had made such a mess of the interview with Bob Markham and David Hill that he rushed back to the university to get Ngũgĩ to ask that he be re-interviewed. He was interviewed again and got the job. That person was Henry Chakava, whose imaginative contribution to building up the Series quickly made it the first choice in East Africa, as it already was in West Africa. He was to make a central contribution to the flowering of the Series in its second decade.

The potential in oral culture

From his earliest days in the job Henry Chakava pushed forward efforts to handle oral culture within the written confines of the book. He came to London for a six-month training period in the Charles Street office and lodged with the South African exile publisher and editor Ros de Lanerolle, whose name appears on so many reports about manuscripts in this book. He may have learnt from me. I certainly learnt from him. My ambition was to show the world that writers from Africa could use the imported form of the novel as inventively as the Irish, the Australians and other writers across the English-speaking world. He saw oral literature as just as important in the African tradition.

On that visit he began to engage with me on the need for a better representation of oral literature through the medium of English. Chinua Achebe and Aig Higo had been key in the establishment of the dominance of West Africa in the first decade. The second generation of Nigerian writers felt that the first generation was too concerned with explaining Africa to readers in America and Britain. Indeed, Ngũgĩ's first four novels were so accomplished that reviewers in Britain praised them as 'Conradian'. Henry Chakava and Ngũgĩ were equally concerned with Africans writing about Africa for Africans. In 1978 Henry Chakava's publishing philosophy moved on to a new plane when the university failed to re-engage Ngũgĩ after he was released after detention for nearly a year without trial. As recounted in the section on working with Ngũgĩ (p. 133), Henry Chakava gave him a desk in his office and they debated, argued and worked out the literary and financial realities of publishing in African languages.

Writers in East Africa showed themselves to be even more inventive than writers in western and southern Africa who had in various ways engaged with the central problem of how to handle ephemeral oral culture in print. Chinua Achebe is most at ease when writing poetry in Igbo and his novels in English are oiled by proverbs. Ahmadou Kourouma had his work rejected by publishers in Paris because of his sophisticated experiments with Malinke syntax. The Ghanaian poetry of Kofi Awoonor derived much of its depth from its roots in Ewe. Masizi Kunene was writing epics in Zulu, although he could not get them published in South Africa and had to resort to translating them into English. All writers in African languages have to engage with the fact that their audience changes as soon as they resort to a European language.

In East Africa we were already beginning to work with Taban lo Liyong who had contacted both EAPH and Heinemann in 1967. We were soon to become his major publishers. In 1972 Okot p'Bitek, the most outstanding transformer of the oral tradition into English, with his classic *Song of Lawino,* approached the Heinemann office in Nairobi about his own work, which had originally been in Acoli. Okot p'Bitek's zesty approach showed how there was no need for work to be folksy and frowsty. So Henry Chakava, with Ngũgĩ, Okot p'Bitek and Taban lo Liyong, had three adventurers in the oral tradition with whom to work.

Before Henry Chakava joined the firm, Bob Markham and I had started publishing work from and in Swahili. This *lingua franca* is used for trade across Africa from Zanzibar to Kinshasa. However, the classic literary activity is concentrated on the coast of Kenya and Tanzania and most of its poetry has been passed on in public performance. We set out to represent work from the language with two anthologies of translations into English by Jan Knappert in *Myths and Legends of the Swahili* (1970 AWS 75) and in an anthology of love poetry called *A Choice of Flowers* (1972 AWS 93). There were accusations on the coast against Jan Knappert of stealing the poems because he wrote them down at public performances in the streets and square; his English renderings were unquestionably his own. He collected *Myths and Legends of the Congo* (1971 AWS 83) from printed sources. We also published, though not in the African Writers Series, a substantial collection of six *Tendi* with English translations by J.W.T. Allen; these classic stories from the Koran were familiar to readers of the Bible. In 1977 we republished in the Series a compact *Anthology of Swahili Poetry* edited by Ali A. Jahadhmy (1977 AWS 192), which gave originals in Swahili with parallel English translations of poems of romance, tragedy, valour and comedy.

Okot p'Bitek

Songs of charm

In 1966 EAPH published the English version of Okot p'Bitek's *Song of Lawino,* which showed how traditional oral literature could be enchanting, provocative and entertaining in English. Like Mazisi Kunene, he originally wrote in his own language, Acoli. The success of this long poem was to encourage writers and publishers to try to come to terms with what an African audience wanted, even through the medium of English. *The Companion* says:

> Okot p'Bitek's early Acoli-language novel [written in 1953] … was followed by the long poem *Song of Lawino*, first composed in Acoli rhyming couplets in 1956 and published in English in 1966. Described by some observers as the most influential African poem of the 1960s, not only in Uganda but throughout Africa, *Song of Lawino* is comprised of a series of complaints by Lawino, an Acoli wife whose husband Ocol has rejected her for a younger, more Westernised woman. *Song of Ocol* (1970) is the sophisticated, self-serving response of the unrepentant Ocol who has embraced the new culture as fervently as has his new spouse. Ocol sees nothing worth preserving in the old ways and has few reservations in saying so. The future, he asserts, is with western culture and the technology that makes it so dominant.

Okot p'Bitek studied law at Aberystwyth and then worked on a thesis on Acoli religion for a further degree in social anthropology at Oxford. In 1966 he returned to Uganda and became director of the Uganda Cultural Centre, later founding arts festivals in Kisumu and in his native Gulu. Under Idi Amin he kept his life but not his job and died in exile in 1982, all too young at the age of 51, while teaching at Nairobi University.

EAPH correctly saw his songs as one of their most valuable publishing assets. We would have sold a great many of the original 1966 edition outside East Africa if our distribution agreement in 1967 with EAPH could have been made to work. I wrote to the editor Leonard Okola offering a joint imprint and an advance of £1,000:

> I do feel very strongly that easier access to the text through the AWS would ensure that it was even more widely studied not only in Africa but also in Scandinavia, Britain, Australia, the Caribbean, Malaya, the Philippines and wherever there is an excited new audience for writing from Africa. As you will realise the Nigerian market is on its own very substantial and local stocking is crucial for supply. … I did discuss this years ago with John Nottingham but nothing came of it.
>
> As you will realise in the case of the two Ayi Kwei Armah novels, we are scrupulous about keeping our edition out of the East Africa market. (JC to Leonard Okola 5 May 1978)

I have typed on to the bottom of the copy for Henry Chakava, 'Can I ask you if you see Chief the Honourable Okot to put the advantages of this scheme to him.

Is he back from his *Song of Texas*?' Henry Chakava correctly told me off in a memo dated 26 May 1978 for not having got him, as the man on the spot, to do the liaison work, especially as Leonard Okola had left the firm. Nothing more happened until 1982 when his successor Richard Ntiru tried, as a condition of letting us have Okot p'Bitek's two songs, to get us to take 12 other EAPH titles for the African Writers Series. In the bargaining we managed to reduce this list just to the one popular novel by Charles Mangua called *Son of Woman*. Soon after Okot p'Bitek's early death Richard Ntiru requested on 28 July 1982 the rights to include two titles originated by Heinemann, *Horn of My Love* and *Hare and Hornbill,* in a commemorative edition of the collected works. It was not until 1984 that we managed to publish *Song of Lawino*, together with *Song of Okol* (AWS 266), in the African Writers Series across the world outside East Africa. Soon afterwards sadly EAPH went into liquidation when the German trade union backers withdrew their support. Henry Chakava bought the rights of several of the texts in the Modern African Library including *Son of Woman* and extended their publishing life in East Africa.

In 1972 Okot p'Bitek had approached the Heinemann Nairobi office to discuss a book on the oral literature of northern Uganda. David Hill wrote:

> … is it possible to have the translation and text side-by-side on the same page? I gather from Okot that his translation is in any case not a very literal one; his object being to translate the spirit not the letter; this might be an argument against a very close side-by-side arrangement. (David Hill to JC 11 April 1972)

Gerald Moore, who had been in the extramural department at Makerere, wrote from the University of Sussex:

> It does include some of the material we recorded together, but also a good deal of the other stuff of his own collection … I am strongly in favour of parallel translation, especially as Okot's are not free-ranging, and do stick as faithfully as possible to the text. (Gerald Moore to JC 4 May 1972)

We did not take up Gerald Moore's offer of an introduction as Okot p'Bitek could easily speak for himself; however, we did agree to the more expensive inclusion of the original text. When the book was printed in 1974, with the title of *Horn of My Love* (AWS 147), Henry Chakava rightly complained that his office had not received an advance copy although:

> For almost two weeks now, a rumour has been going round that Okot has received an advance copy of his book. Taban came in this morning and confirmed this; Okot and he have had several drinks together welcoming this new baby. (HC to JC 16 May 1974)

There was a friendly swipe at Taban lo Liyong in the opening paragraph of the Preface to the book:

> When, recently, my friend Taban lo Liyong, wept bitter tears over what he called *the literary desert of East Africa,* he was suffering from acute literary deafness, a disease which afflicts those who have been brainwashed to believe that literature exists only in books. Taban and his fast dwindling clan are victims of the class-ridden, dictionary meaning of the term literature,

> which restricts literary activity and enjoyment to the so-called literate peoples, and turns a deaf ear to the songs and stories of the vast majority of our people in the countryside. In this book I have presented the poetry of Taban's own people, the Acoli of Uganda. (p. ix)

He was teasing Taban lo Liyong who had, four years earlier in 1970, published in the African Writers Series *Eating Chiefs: Lwo Culture from Lolwe to Malkal* (AWS 74). Taban lo Liyong was later to claim his ancestry as being from the Kakwa in Sudan.

In 1975 Okot p'Bitek gave Henry Chakava the manuscript of what was to become *Hare and Hornbill* (1978 AWS 193). There is a significant letter from Henry Chakava in which he took up my reservations about collections of folk tales with which to represent oral literature in the African Writers Series:

> We have just received these folk tales from Okot p'Bitek. They are very well written indeed – most are shorter and more concentrated than Mvungi's stories in *Three Solid Stones* [stories from Tanzania] …
>
> I know that generally you are not very keen on folk tales in the AWS. On the other hand I have always insisted, oral literature is becoming more and more important here, and it is quite clear that from 1977 oral literature will form the basis for the teaching of literatures in secondary schools.
>
> It is not quite clear what the requirements for teaching oral literature will be. Last Friday we had a special meeting on oral literature. We decided to approach Mr. Henry Owuor-Anyumba who is the best man in this subject, to write a book tailored to the requirement of the new oral literature syllabus. We already have other names lined up in case Anyumba does not accept to do this. But this still leaves the problem of supplementary material, of which Okot's book is an example. Would you like to consider it for the AWS or would you rather we publish it here? Or should we turn it down? Our sales figures show that we have sold about 1300 copies of *Horn of my Love,* in East Africa alone.
>
> The other day I was visited by Rebeka Njau who has compiled some folk tales. I think the time has come for us to arrive at a definitive policy as far as oral literature is concerned. (HC to JC 6 October 1975)

In reply I said that I thought that he had made the crucial point when he said that oral literature needed to be 'very well written indeed' in English. I said to him later in the month that, of the books we had already included in the African Writers Series, I liked Taban lo Liyong's Luo tales *Eating Chiefs* (1970) and *Not Even God Is Ripe Enough* (1965 AWS 48), which were robust Yoruba stories told by Bakare Gbadamosi and Ulli Beier. However I did feel that *The Way We Lived* (1969 AWS 61), Igbo stories by Rems Nna Umeasiegbu, and *Three Solid Stones* (1975 AWS 159), Tanzanian stories by Martha Mvungi, lacked lustre. I asked:

> What about some anthologies of oral literature in the AWS? Perhaps one for the whole of eastern Africa from Somalia to the Congo and Zambia mostly from published work. Okot? Taban might have done it.
>
> I hope my feelings sound more positive now than you have thought them to be. (JC to HC 21 October 1975)

Richard Lister, in London, was certainly not positive when he assessed Okot's revised manuscript:

> He also refers to the difficulty that they are told in unsatisfactory circumstances, without an appreciative audience to which the teller can respond. This certainly must account for baldness and lack of life ... (Report by Richard Lister 2 April 1976)

In the mid-1970s the Ministry of Education drafted a syllabus for teaching oral literature in secondary schools. This was part of the sequence stemming from the revolutionary document 'On the Abolition of the English Department' at the University of Nairobi dated 24 October 1968 which had been signed by Ngũgĩ, Henry Owuor-Anyumba and Taban lo Liyong.

Henry Owuor-Anyumba had been a teacher when Henry Chakava was at Friends School, Kamusinga. He agreed that he would do a University/Advanced-Level textbook by April 1976. Henry Chakava said that teachers were hostile to this revolutionary syllabus because 'they do not know how to teach it'. He concluded:

> I have always urged Anyumba to write a book on oral literature for us. He has always replied in equivocal and evasive terms. But on this occasion there was no such thing. He has realised that the time has come, and if he does not write the book now 'the hawks and academic pretenders' will cash in with hastily prepared manuscripts, and because there is a dearth of material, these people will steal the [lead] ... (From report of meeting between HC and H. Owuor-Anyumba 1974)

It actually took Henry Chakava until 1982 to publish a School Certificate course on *Oral Literature* written by S. Kichamu Akivaga and A. Bole Odaga.

Taban lo Liyong
Delight in royalties

On 21 February 1968 Taban lo Liyong came into the Heinemann office in London on his way back to East Africa after five years in the US. He was the first African to receive the pioneering MFA (Master of Fine Arts) degree in creative writing from the University of Iowa. In some ways that was to show in his writing. He was an original who enjoyed breaking established rules. Keith Sambrook was in two minds about his work and wrote to Ngũgĩ to ask him to read the manuscript, which at that time was called *The Education of Taban lo Liyong and Other Stories*:

> The writer is obviously intelligent and full of ideas. But a lot of the ideas do not seem to me to come off in terms of writing. Some of the pieces seem to be pretentious and one would assume from others that the writer has no idea of self-criticism. (KS to Ngũgĩ 22 February 1968)

Keith Sambrook also wrote at the same time (22 February 1968) to John Nottingham at EAPH, with whom Taban lo Liyong had left another manuscript, to ask 'whether there is a chance that this is an author we could work together on in launching in East Africa in the hope that there would be a wider interest in his books later on'. Ngũgĩ, in encouraging us to 'publish a volume of his stories, however thin', said:

> Taban lo Liyong is a tough nut to crack and one must, I think, be on one's guard, must indeed be in the right mood, when reading him, else it would be easy to dismiss him as a tedious eccentric. (Ngũgĩ to KS undated)

Keith Sambrook wrote to offer to publish the book, which eventually was called *Fixions* (1969 AWS 69). Taban lo Liyong wrote back:

> I am delighted with your letter. Your selection is very good. All the stories you have selected have concision, graphic and dramatic precision. Hence they form a united piece. (TlL to KS 29 October 1968)

It was the beginning of a delightful association. *The Companion* remarks on how he employs 'pun, irony, humour, and wit to elaborate his satirical perspective'. He had a talent for good titles for his collections of poems: *Frantz Fanon's Uneven Ribs (including Poems More and More)* (1971 AWS 90) and *Another Nigger Dead* (1972 AWS 116). He dallied for years with a reader for students to be called *Radical Thoughts by East Africans*. He sat one Sunday morning on the terrace of Bob and Susanna's Markham's house in a lush suburb of Nairobi and said that out of the profits of his writing he was going to build a palace called 'Royalty House'. He liked the idea. Practical realities like the smallness of his writing royalties did not concern him. His poetry drew heavily on his fascination with the way that Africans rendered their own poetry. He introduced his own people's royalty in a collection called *Eating Chiefs: Lwo Culture from Lolwe to Malkal* (1970 AWS 74). He corrected his proofs with such cheerful abandon that it led to deductions from his royalties. When we received the corrected pages I had to tell him:

> It looks as though some linguistic genius has got at your proofs … Corrections cost a fantastic amount because they have to be done by hand whereas the original type is set on a machine. (JC to TlL 16 March 1970)

Business details kept evading his interest. I pointed out to him:

> … if you need money for Royalty House or for any other reason you can do yourself a service by returning your tax exemption form, having had it signed by the Kenya tax authorities. It is entirely academic talking about advances until this is signed. (JC to TlL 5 April 1972)

He and I indulged ourselves in another royal excursion. He had been delighted to discover in the Howard University Library in Washington a book called *Uganda's Katikiro in England: Being the Official Account of his Visit to the Coronation of His Majesty King Edward VII by his Secretary Ham Mukasa* (the coronation had happened in 1902). This had been translated from Luganda by the Reverend Ernest Millar who had accompanied the royal group from Buganda. Taban lo Liyong saw in this book a mirror image of the excitement of the British explorer John Hanning Speke when he described to the Royal Geographical Society his first reactions when he 'discovered' the court of the Kabaka of Buganda. Taban lo Liyong and I worked out the title for the edition which he edited for the African Writers Series as *Sir Apolo Kagwa Discovers Britain* (1975 AWS 133) by Ham Mukasa. The use of the word 'discover' was our joke. The Europeans always said that they 'discovered' land when they first went to a place which had been known since the dawn of time by the people who lived there. David Williams, Editor of *West Africa,* appreciated the reissue of the book when he reviewed it for *The Sunday Times*:

> Both these agreeable, intelligent men are lost in wonder, love and praise at what they see. The pipes of the St Paul's cathedral organ are like the stems of a green banana. Everything is so big. Tower Bridge lifts itself miraculously in half on great hinges, steam fire engines squirt water-jets as high as the tops of very high houses; the Army and Navy Stores have almost everything including mackintoshes, which are an A1 priority because the weather is foul though not complained of. (15 February 1976)

Roy Bridges of the University of Aberdeen said, 'It was a splendid idea to reprint Mukasa's work' but was critical of the editing. I wished that I had got a scholar as understanding as him to report on the introduction and notes before setting. Keith Sambrook and I had found the editing tricky, as is shown in a letter I wrote to Taban lo Liyong:

> Keith and I think that it's an excellent idea to cut out the return journey which is a bit of an anticlimax. I'd cut out the anti-Semitism if you are cutting out all the other racial prejudice, e.g. against Somalis ... we do have doubts about the editing of the racialist bits. You put a quotation at the beginning which is very appropriate. 'History is the appraisal and reappraisal of past situations, people and their deeds in the light of contemporary experiences in order to guide our choices.' Following that adage one should not censor Ham Mukasa because he expresses the prejudices of his day and class. He may have been reflecting the prejudices of the Revd. Mr Millar. (God rest his soul.) One suspects in particular the attitudes towards the Germans reflect his attitudes. However some of the prejudices may be their own. (JC to TlL 1 November 1972)

Long delays in editing and production led to a gentle enquiry from Taban lo Liyong:

> There has been a news blackout on our English discoverer, Onwami Apollo Kagwa and we are very concerned about it as you must realise His Highness The Katikiro is an important personage in our kingdom and his mission of discovery is of the greatest significance to our continued prosperity as well as the maintenance of cordial relationship between our two august kingdoms. Hence we must be kept informed of his movements and good health. Should we not hear by the next mailboat, we shall be obliged to fit a Find Kagwa Expedition under a young intrepid member of Our Royal Geographical Society to go and comb the whole United Kingdom in search of our just citizen and a scholar in his own right, the Honorable Sir Apollo Kagwa, The Katikiro of Uganda.
>
> Trusting in your dutiful English character, we are sure a prompt reply to this note will be immediately dispatched to our satisfaction, thus rendering our next step, namely: gunboat diplomacy, unnecessary. Respectfully Taban lo Liyong. (TlL to JC 2 May 1974)

In 1979 when Taban lo Liyong arrived for the Berlin Festival he found that the organisers had caged all the writers in the Hotel am Zoo. He started ringing round the other writers saying: 'The Germans have put me in the Zoo. Bring me a banana!' The classic portrait George Hallett put in his *Portfolio of African Writers* is of Taban lo Liyong, acting the part stripped to his waist, sitting on his bed at the Hotel am Zoo (photo p. 86).

Mwangi Ruheni & Samuel Kahiga

A popular book market develops

Nairobi had become a vivacious intellectual centre by the early 1970s and work by Kenyan and Ugandan authors was appearing. Books with a Kenyan background were selling well and a popular general market, for African as well as imported books, was being added to the established school market. By now the Nairobi offices of British publishers were becoming competitive in their efforts to sign fiction writers for their lists. The active international marketing of the African Writers Series was its biggest attraction; a writer could appeal to a Kenyan audience but be confident that his voice would be heard throughout the English-speaking world.

Mwangi Ruheni's first novel *What a Life!*, when published in 1972 by Longman Kenya, was considered to mark a new trend in the Kenyan novel. *The Companion* says: 'His novels are characterised by the combination of social criticism moderated by a happy ending or by the humorous attitude of the protagonist to the problems they encounter and the entertaining spirit of popular literature, without its pornographic or thrilling extremes.'

Henry Chakava and David Hill managed to secure Mwangi Ruheni's second title *The Future Leaders* (1973 AWS 139). It is a witty and entertaining story of the troubles of a Makerere graduate who finds that his degree does not automatically make him a leader. He went back to Longman Kenya for his third novel.

There was a substantial division of opinion in Heinemann about his fourth novel *The Minister's Daughter* (1975 AWS 156). Richard Lister said that 'as a swift moving light novel this was absolutely first-rate of its kind'. Ros de Lanerolle, with her taste for serious work, saw it as entertaining 'but this time the weaknesses are more intrusive' (10 May 1973). Keith Sambrook wrote to Henry Chakava:

> … I thought it was a let-down after *The Future Leaders*. In *The Future Leaders* the cynical, throw-away style fitted the first-person hero splendidly and was well sustained throughout. By comparison, the author does not seem to me to make the heroine of *The Minister's Daughter* anything like so credible … It is therefore a question of local sales on this one, I should say. If it were a first novel I'd be doubtful about taking it on without some revision. However, if you think that it will sell on the reputation of his other books, then go ahead. But, with his gifts, he ought to do something better next time. (KS to HC 19 July 1973)

Mwangi Ruheni did some further work and, when it appeared in 1975, the orange covers took the attention of Jeremy Brooks in *The Observer*, who said:

> Mwangi Ruheni is a gentle humourist who extends the rare warmth of his understanding even to his wickedest characters. It's very difficult to pin down in a few words the exact nature of his originality. He has an odd knack of being able to imply the nature of the milieu through the cadences of his prose … One of the things she [the minister's daughter] is taught is the need, in this city jungle, to lie and deceive, to pursue her own ends at the expense of others. She becomes involved in a complicated web of petty crime, which eventually leads to her having a direct hand in a murder. And yet through it all, Jane preserves her wide-eyed innocence; from being charming it has become dangerous, a defence against responsibility. In this witty and engrossing book Mr Ruheni displays the true novelist's gift: he doesn't argue, he shows. (*The Observer* 1975)

When Mwangi Ruheni retired in 1990 after 22 years as government chemist for the Kenyan government, it turned out that he had chosen as a public servant to write under a pseudonym. In 1974, he politely declined to attend a book launch given by Heinemann for his own book *The Minister's Daughter* in order 'to maintain a low profile in my writing'. Usually authors are very keen to have a public launch of their work.

At the same time we were considering *The Girl from Abroad* (1974 AWS 158). The author, Samuel Kahiga, worked in television and journalism, and was a composer. Henry Chakava sent this 'superb little novel' on 16 August 1973. I acknowledged it guardedly saying that I found it 'teeters on the edge of banality'. Ros de Lanerolle was dismissive. Again it was the professional writer Richard Lister who was admiring:

> So it is a simple story of boy meets girl and loses her, and of course with a story as simple as that everything depends on how it is told. And Kahiga tells it superbly. It flows from one incident to the next in the most effortless and natural manner; nothing is forced; towards the end the girl's leaving him is foreshadowed so that the after-mood of melancholy is dealt with on the way through, and the story ends with a smoothness and immediacy and with no loose ends. Technically it is in fact quite remarkable. This is perhaps more than the ordinary reader will worry about, but the effect of course of this skilful telling is to make the book a delightfully easy read. It is very entertaining, often witty, mostly amusing, from time to time quite moving … a small-scale work but a quite charming one … (Report by Richard Lister 26 October 1973)

Henry Chakava was on attachment to the London office and so was able personally to argue for this book to be accepted at the Wednesday meeting of editors and directors. He was able to give a picture of the liveliness of the fiction market in Nairobi. He and I hoped that with such a popular book he would be able to report that there would be new ways of marketing such books in Kenya. Unfortunately Bob Markham felt otherwise:

> I see no way of obtaining a special order … [even] if you give me a special

> price. I agree that this is the sort of book we should be able to get into the popular market and as you know by the time Kahiga's book is received we should be engaged in promoting and selling our own Spear book for the same market. (Bob Markham to JC 30 October 1974)

Henry Chakava had persuaded Bob Markham that there was a middle-brow market, alongside the African Writers Series, for thrillers and romances in the well-established general book-trade in East Africa and he set up Spear Books. They initially thought that they would not sell in the education market; the sales director Johnson Mugweru, when he saw nuns at a convent school picking up these books from his common room display, suggested that they might not be suitable for the girls. The nuns laughed and said: 'We don't mind what the girls read as long as they read.' Unfortunately Heinemann in Nigeria did not fully realise the sales potential of these middle-brow titles. Macmillan in Nairobi set up a rival popular series called Pacemakers and, although they did moderately well in East Africa, it was their Nigerian company which found a wide market and often outsold the high-brow titles in the African Writers Series.

Bob Markham, Johnson Mugweru and Henry Chakava were responding to this popular fiction market. The late 1970s was a period when people were buying books in East Africa for entertainment as well as for education. Okot p'Bitek's *Song of Lawino* brought the cult of the short line into Kenyan popular publishing. The remarkable way in which *Song of Lawino* could speak to a popular audience was brought home personally to Clare Currey and me when a young Kenyan Quaker was staying with us one Christmas while studying at a Friends' college in Birmingham (Kenya has the largest Quaker membership in the world; its 40,000 members go in for evangelical hymn singing as much as for silence). He lamented that his reading speed was so slow. We asked him what he was reading and he told us that he was labouring page by page through the Victorian sermons of Moody and Sankey. I gave him a copy of *Song of Lawino*, even though I expected he might find it rather improper. Not at all. He came back delighted. He above all loved the way that he could speed through it because of the short poetic lines.

The popular success of Okot p'Bitek's two books gave the struggling writer David Maillu the idea of writing an extended account in short if unpoetic lines of the experiences of a Nairobi prostitute, which was called *The Flesh (Part One)* and *The Flesh (Part Two)*. The short lines enabled the reader to rush on to one lush experience after another. When David Maillu could not get any of the established publishers to accept his manuscripts, he set up Comb Books to publish his own work, with typesetting machinery paid for by Danish aid. He also started the cult of the tiny book for the handbag. One of his runaway sellers was *After 4.30* which revealed the sexy experiences of secretaries after the office doors closed at the end of the working day; it was bound in a tiny format so that the secretary could discreetly slip the book into her handbag along with her comb when the boss came in. At the end of the 1970s it was boom time for coffee, which was called 'black gold' and there was a lot of money around to buy books for entertainment. David Maillu had a rocket-like popular success with his books in Kenya until he crashed in a cash crisis with his knickers in a twist, as so often seemed to happen to his heroines.

Rebeka Njau

A woman's madness

Rebeka Njau was Kenya's first female playwright and a pioneer in the literary representation of women. Her manuscript 'Alone with the Fig Tree' won the prize in an East African novel competition in 1964, the year in which Ngũgĩ's *Weep Not, Child* was first published. She worked on a substantial revision of the earlier manuscript to which she gave the new title *Ripples in the Pool*, and in 1975 it was published by John Nottingham's TransAfrica Press. Henry Chakava wrote to me on 2 March 1977 saying that Rebeka Njau had asked him to take it over as TransAfrica had gone bankrupt, and a subedited and reset edition appeared in the African Writers Series (AWS 203) in 1978. Henry Chakava sent me the typescript of his review of the original printing for a magazine in Nairobi:

> ... it explores the lives and relationships of two groups of people; the new elite who have tasted urban life, and the rural folks whose lives are close to the soil and in the mainstream of a long-established tradition ... In Selina, she has created a memorable character who will for a long time to come, remain the most intriguing female character on the East African literary scene ... In addition to the superb characterisation, is the author's effective use of symbolism. At the centre of these happenings, and possibly influencing them, if not remotely controlling them, is the sacred pool – mysterious, awe-inspiring, divined only by Muthee who watches over it, and endowed with a curse of death or blessing to whoever comes near it ... there is no doubt that this is one of the most outstanding novels to come out of East Africa in the recent past.

Ripples in the Pool was published soon after Bessie Head's novel of schizophrenia, *A Question of Power*, and the German critic Flora Veit-Wild makes comparisons between the main characters in both books in her recent study *Writing Madness* (2006). Selina is a high-class prostitute in the city. She celebrates her freedom as a modern independent-minded urban woman who is proud of her beautiful body. Eventually she decides to marry. She chooses a younger and innocent man, Gikere, whom she can dominate. When Gikere and she return to live in the village his mother calls her a 'respectless city woman' and, after she has a miscarriage, 'an infertile witch'. Gikere tries to reassert his authority, that is by beating his wife up. She had escaped the dirtiness of the slums and an abusive father by becoming a prostitute. Her way out in the village of this new violence and domination is by hysterical auto-aggression. Selina's body reacts with infertility. As she feels more and more isolated she directs her physical sexual needs towards her husband's younger sister Gaciru. Flora Veit-Wild says:

> This distinct homoerotic dimension particularly hinting at a lesbian situation, was very unusual in African writing at this time ...

Confronted with the 'dirtiness' around her and excluded from any human community, Selina's personality is gradually corroded and she becomes insane. When she hears that Gaciru has fallen in love with a young man from her own village, Selina loses the last bit of control. In a terrible nervous fit, she breaks into hysterical sobs of laughter, flings herself on the ground and bites into the framework of her bed. After people have tried to calm her, she drinks large quantities of alcohol. Drinking drives her into an extreme state of excess, in which she first wants to hang herself but instead strangles the sleeping Gaciru. When she realises what she has done, Selina flees the house into the fields and becomes a roving beast, barely recognisable as a human being. Once proud and beautiful, Selina ends as a monster, roaming the wilderness, one of the 'stray women' that earlier in the century were put into lunatic asylums.

With *Ripples in the Pool,* Rebeka Njau has produced an impressive literary figuration of what would happen if a woman did not submit to the rules laid out by a male-dominated society. Since the novel was written in the early 1970s, this act of independence can only take on the form of a nightmare, as it did in Bessie Head's *A Question of Power.* (*Writing Madness*, James Currey 2006, pp. 136–40)

Meja Mwangi
Mau Mau & tough towns

Henry Chakava got off to a good start at Heinemann with the capture of Meja Mwangi. Heinemann's reputation for paying royalties on time and getting books published with some despatch certainly helped attract authors who had already started to publish in Nairobi. Meja Mwangi had had his first novel accepted by EAPH, but Henry Chakava and David Hill managed to get manuscripts from him and Heinemann published his second and third novels before EAPH had published his first one. *The Companion* says: 'Mwangi's work, more than any other Kenyan writer's, provides a representative view of the country as a whole, reflecting its main concerns and the direction of its evolution.' His themes were the underworld, the slums, the working class and the Mau Mau struggle.

The title of *Kill Me Quick* (1973 AWS 143) refers to a powerful prohibited drink called to *chang'aa*. Meja Mwangi was the socially concerned kind of author who appealed to Ros de Lanerolle, as her brisk report makes clear:

> Really quite a find – 3rd person autobiography (written as a novel, but hero is named Meja Mwangi) of village boy who comes to Nairobi with his secondary certificate to find a job – only to find that like thousands of others he is unwanted. Makes friends with another boy in the same position, living off the rubbish in the backstreets. Their hopelessness, but determination never to go home to shame their families, comes through marvellously. Then gradually each lose heart. Both make attempts eventually to seek help from their families, with tragic consequences. They end up among the

> gangsters of the shanty towns, where they find comradeship but no escape from despair. Meja becomes a habitual criminal, his only home in jail. (Report by Ros de Lanerolle 14 December 1972)

Her concluding remark, 'Written with no skill or art – but absolutely honest', was objected to in Nairobi.

Carcase for Hounds (1974 AWS 145) was an ambitious novel about Mau Mau. Ngũgĩ was very interested and produced a critical but constructive report (6 June 1972) in just three days with suggestions about rewriting the novel: 'Mwangi writes well. He has material for a good novel … Action! Would he like to rewrite the novel?' David Hill wrote on 12 January 1973 to say that Meja Mwangi had responded effectively to Ngũgĩ and enclosing a report by Henry Chakava:

> This for me is the first novel which really penetrates the inside organisation and activities of the Mau Mau liberation forces, their strategy, and why the colonial government took so long to defeat the Movement. The book clearly brings out the four basic divisions in the struggle; the British Colonial army on one extreme and the forest fighters on the other, with the uncommitted Villagers and Homeguard stooges in the middle. The scene is the Laikipia District of Kenya and the action centres mainly on three men; Haraka, a legendary general, once a government chief but now a Mau Mau leader; chief Simba, a childhood friend and rival of Haraka, and now a colonial chief – cum stooge; and Captain Kingsley, a former District Commissioner now charged with the responsibility of capturing Haraka and his men. (Report by HC 12 January 1973)

Going Down River Road (1976 AWS 176) goes back to the world of *Kill Me Quick*. Richard Lister reported:

> The story of Ben, a building labourer who works on a 25-storey skyscraper being built in Nairobi. He is living when the story opens with Maria, a prostitute, in Maria's room in a rooming-house. With them is Baby, Maria's four-year-old son. Maria has improved herself to the extent of working as a secretary; when Ben met her she was prostitute at the New Garden Bar. She is now pregnant again; Ben presumes he is the father.
>
> We learn in a flashback that Ben was once lieutenant in the army. He got mixed up with one Mbugua, the Gorilla, who wanted him to supply a mortar and shells for a raid on the bank. The loss of the mortar was discovered and Ben and all his platoon cashiered. The criminals however blew themselves up in the bank raid, and Ben never received the promised money … It is an extremely powerful and unusual novel. (Report by Richard Lister 9 August 1974)

Akin Thomas in Ibadan sent a report by Michael Echeruo which showed clearly that in reading the manuscript he had been surprised by what he discovered about urban life in Kenya:

> … an important and impressive novel. It is important for what it introduces into modern African fiction in narrative style and in the use of dialogue. It is important, too, for its subordination of the story line to theme, its concentration on locale and mood at the expense of history and plot. It is

> impressive for its steady candour; its ability to mix the putrid and the gentle not only in a character like Maria but even in a cot like Baby's. [This novel] will, of course, serve for a long time as the guide to Kenya night life (Pilsner, Karara, Chang'aa and all) and will be taken (vide Oculi) as an exposé of an aspect of the African scene which brings it much closer to the life-style of the African ghettos of South Africa and – say – Harlem than one would have thought possible or desirable. The difference, which is also Mwangi's strength, is in the unsentimental tone of Mwangi's narration, and almost matter-of-factness of voice which belongs either to a lost or innocent civilisation. It is difficult to tell which it is, and perhaps [this novel] with its oaths, its Indians, its new tourist hotels overlooking its brothels and its shanty towns, is meant to leave us wondering what East Africa is really like or going to be. (Report by Michael Echeruo 10 February 1975)

Meja Mwangi won the Jomo Kenyatta Prize for Literature twice and also the Afro-Asian Writers award of the Soviet Writers Union and these prizes gave his sales a lift. He had the skills to write for a range of markets: he accepted an advance from Longman Kenya to write two thrillers which Henry Chakava would very much liked to have added to his popular Spear Books:

> I quite understand the pressures on you to make ends meet. I must say that Henry and I were a little disappointed over the question of the two thrillers for Longmans. I am not worried about you writing different books for different markets. That's fine. Many writers have done it. However, don't hesitate in future to consult Henry or myself about your needs. (JC to MM 6 May 1977)

Michael Echeruo's surprise at the manuscript of *Going Down River Road* reflects how Kenyan authors were writing about the town life of Kenya in a way that was being little done in West Africa. Henry Chakava and I were impressed by a rough manuscript, handwritten on both sides of the sheets of an exercise book, called *The Slums* (1981 AWS 241) by Thomas Akare. Eddy and his friend Hussein make a living of a kind washing cars in the slums of Nairobi. Because the big people come to Majengo to have their cars washed, Eddy is taken on and taken out to the other Nairobi by the attractive Zakia. Thomas Akare speaks from the centre of the slums and his picture is hard, realistic and unsentimental. We sent positive reports to him and we encouraged him to work on it and to resubmit. He laboured on it and we regretted that, when he sent in the revised manuscript that, although he had strengthened the plot, his writing had lost some of its vitality. We decided to go ahead and publish and not to endanger the book further by asking him to do yet more.

Ngũgĩ
London 1979

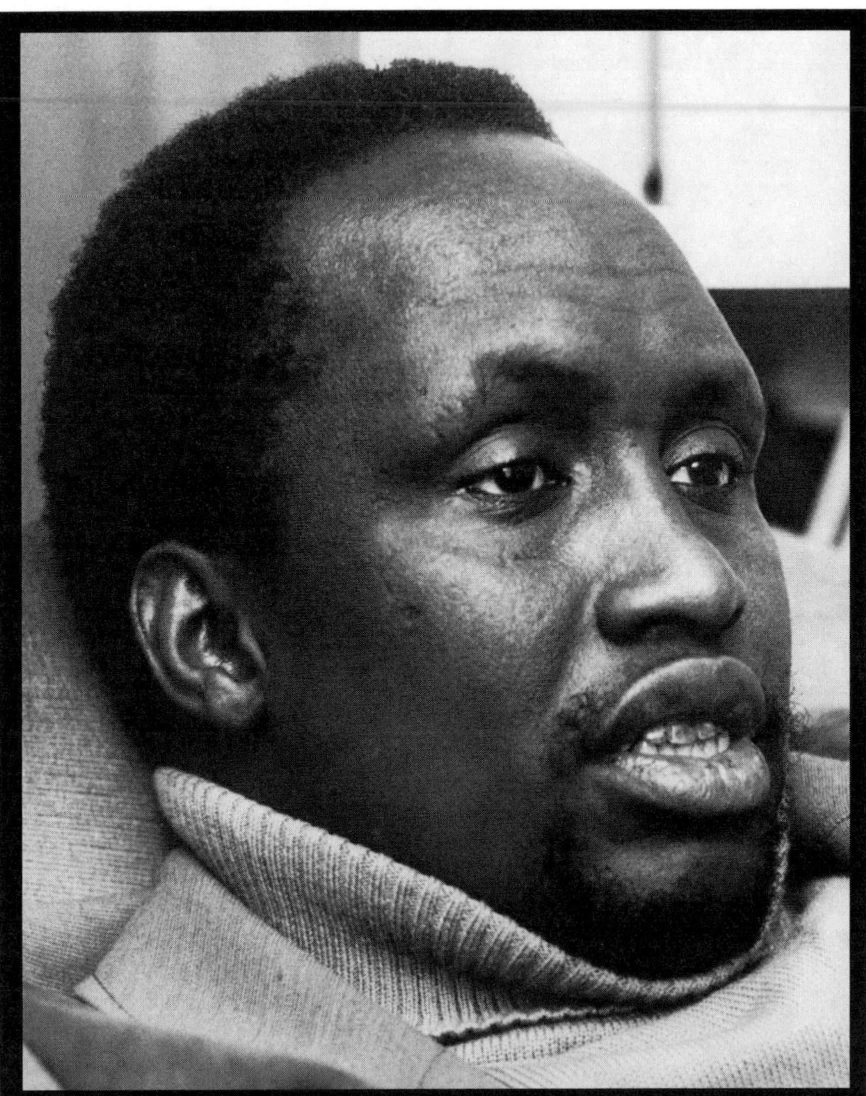

PUBLISHING

Ngũgĩ

Ngũgĩ was born in Kenya in 1938. By the time he was 30 he was already known internationally with the publication of the novels *Weep Not, Child* (1964), *The River Between* (1965) and *A Grain of Wheat* (1967), and of the play *The Black Hermit* (1968). The first Heinemann letters were addressed to him as an undergraduate at Makerere University College, Uganda as J.T. Ngũgĩ. He chose to publish the first titles under the name James Ngũgĩ rather than Thiong'o Ngũgĩ. He finally settled on Ngũgĩ wa Thiong'o but is now generally called by his own name as Ngũgĩ. Keith Sambrook worked in careful detail with Ngũgĩ on the first two novels, which had been written while he was a student at Makerere. While completing a postgraduate degree at the University of Leeds, he wrote *A Grain of Wheat*, which ran forward with Conradian strides.

Homecoming (1972) was a collection of his work on African writing and culture with a section drawing on his work at Leeds on George Lamming and other Caribbean writers. At that time his short stories were gathered under the title *Secret Lives* (1975 AWS 150). He had now settled on the name Ngũgĩ wa Thiong'o for future books.

Ngũgĩ was one of the first writers in Africa to try to survive on his income from writing. In 1969 he resigned from his first job at the University of Nairobi in the Department of English in support of five students whom he considered had been victimised by the administration. His argument as reported in *The Sunday Nation* was that:

> 'When admitted to the University they swear in front of the Principal, the Registrar and the general academic body, to seek the truth.' And says Mr Ngũgĩ, 'Free circulation is absolutely essential to any quest for truth and knowledge.' (*The Sunday Nation* 2 March 1969)

His bravery at confronting the authorities with awkward truths was showing itself.

Fortunately in 1973 the university appointed him senior lecturer and acting head of department, with the writer Taban lo Liyong to share responsibilities. They successfully campaigned to get the Department of English changed to the Department of Literatures.

But what was he writing? Keith Sambrook expressed the worries felt in Heinemann:

> I am a bit puzzled by Ngũgĩ; he seems to have come to a full stop. The short stories are good but, in confidence, I don't think they show any advance on his previous, admittedly high, standard of writing. He is full of ideas, young, famous – what serious writing is he doing or planning? (KS to David Hill 9 January 1973)

The seriousness of the next stage of his work was to overwhelm everyone and especially the Kenyan ruling elite. The reaction in Nairobi in 1975 to the play *The Trial of Dedan Kimathi,* which he wrote with Mĩcere Mũgo, taught him the power of performance. But it was his work with the Kamĩrĩĩthũ Cultural Centre in 1976 which concentrated his developing philosophy, particularly about the use of his own language and the vital importance of plays, as opposed to novels, in communicating with ordinary Kenyans. *Ngaahika Ndeenda,* which was written with Ngũgĩ wa Mĩriĩ, was performed by the villagers in their open-air theatre which they built as the play was being written; the excitement and popularity frightened the district commissioner who withdrew the licence to perform. At the time of the publication of *Petals of Blood* in English in 1977 Ngũgĩ said that in future he would write work in Gikuyu, a language which 'my mother, my peasant mother' could understand. Mwai Kibaki, who was to become president of Kenya in 2003 and who was then minister of economic affairs, launched the book in Nairobi City Hall. But the Kenyan leadership continued to move against him.

Ngũgĩ was detained without trial on the last day of that very year, 1977, and for almost the whole of 1978. In his cell he managed to write *Caitaani Mũthuraba-inĩ* on interleaved sheets of toilet-paper. It was published in Kenya in 1980 and then in an English translation as *Devil on the Cross* in 1982. *Matigari* (1986, English translation 1989) continued this allegorical and fantastic sequence set in the village of Ilmorog. The musical *Maitu Njugira* (*Mother, Sing for Me*, 1982) went into sustained public rehearsal, waiting for a licence for the National Theatre, before it was banned. His novel and his play in Gikuyu were read aloud, acted and recited in the homes, bars and villages of Kenya. Since the unsuccessful coup of 1982 he has lived in exile, first in England and then by teaching in the US. A satirical and inventive new novel in Gikuyu is being published by Henry Chakava in three parts; Ngũgĩ has translated it into English under the title *The Wizard and the Crow* and it was published in New York and London in 2006.

It was a significant gesture of support when Ngũgĩ agreed that his influential set of essays, *Decolonising the Mind*, should come out under the new imprint of James Currey Publishers in 1985. It was co-published with Henry Chakava's EAEP in Nairobi and with John Watson's Heinemann company in the US, as were his books of essays, *Moving the Centre* (1993) and the rethought *Writers in Politics* (1997). As with the rest of his work, his lectures and essays took people's imaginations where they had never been before.

Weep Not, Child

Published by William Heinemann in English in hardback 1964
(1964 AWS 7)

When Keith Sambrook took over from Van Milne at Heinemann on 1 January 1963 the manuscript of *Weep Not, Child* was on his desk. On 14 May 1964 Ngũgĩ wrote to him:

> I have gone through my exam. I was placed in Class II Upper Division. The results came out and three days after *Weep Not, Child.* A very eventful week. I celebrated the publication of the book by donating a pint of blood; I was dragged into it; I was feeling in no virtuous mood. (Ngũgĩ to KS 14 May 1964)

A year later on 30 July 1965 Keith Sambrook was writing to Ngũgĩ to tell him that his first published novel had been made a set book for the West African Examinations Council School Certificate. Such was the speed of take-off.

It has already been shown (p. 000) how this was the moment of take-off for the Series, when Heinemann Educational Books, as publisher of the paperback, became the originating publisher. Alan Hill and Keith Sambrook proposed that William Heinemann publish hardbacks of the outstanding writers so that the books could get reviews and library sales. A tussle ensued between Heinemann Educational Books and William Heinemann about the details of how this would work. I have already examined the politely tough 1963 memo from Keith Sambrook to William Heinemann (p. 12). Heinemann Educational Books wanted the paperback edition of *Weep Not, Child* to come out at the same time as the hardback. William Heinemann insisted that there must be the conventional gap of some 18 months between their hardback publication and the paperback publication in the African Writers Series. The benefit of the high pile was that Keith Sambrook was able to tell Ngũgĩ, 1,600 copies out of the 2,000 hardbacks of *Weep Not, Child* were sold in the first year and that this covered his advance on royalties. This arrangement with William Heinemann for publication in hardback did not last beyond the publication of *A Grain of Wheat* in hardback in 1967. After that Heinemann Educational Books published hardback editions of Ngũgĩ's novels under the imprint of Heinemann at the same time as the African Writers Series edition.

The River Between

Published by William Heinemann in English in hardback 1965
(1965 AWS 17)

Ngũgĩ wrote *The River Between* before *Weep Not, Child* and originally its title was *The Black Messiah.* The manuscript had won the prize in the

East African Literature Bureau competition. Charles Richards, the director of EALB, passed the manuscript to Van Milne at Heinemann. Keith Sambrook had written to Ngũgĩ: 'We'd like to have *The Black Messiah* ready to follow up.' (4 September 1963)

Ngũgĩ wanted to go to Britain for further studies. He wrote to Keith Sambrook from the YMCA in Nairobi:

> It may be that I am not going to Leeds after all; getting a scholarship seems much more difficult than I had thought. I am very angry about this as I had hoped that a new country & different environment were just the things I needed for a novel I have in mind. Images keep haunting my mind but I cannot get settled soon enough to grapple and come to terms with them. Kenya depresses me; although I have always written about this country I have never written a thing while I was actually living there; not even on my vacations. However this novel will be the most challenging thing I have done so far, if only Kenya will let me get on. The prospect excites and agonises me. (Ngũgĩ to KS 17 April 1964)

At the last moment the scholarship for Leeds was cleared. This was largely thanks to an intervention by Simeon Ominde, a geographer who had been the very first African to be hired at the Royal College, Nairobi and who was to become the Chairman of Heinemann in Nairobi in the 1980s. Ngũgĩ was met in London by Keith and Hana Sambrook. He wrote in early October thanking them and giving them his first impressions:

> Leeds shocked me, threw me into bewilderment from which I am slowly recovering. It seems to be a city that – mushroom fashion – had sprouted without a planning hand. Black soot seems to be the only clothes the buildings wear to fight off the cold.

Ngũgĩ went back to talk about the London visit:

> You remember the talk Judith [Verity] you and I had over the novel in Africa at one of your pubs. I said that the great novel from Africa must take count of the impact of African nationalism, that it seemed to me that this one big movement that has affected the lives of so many millions, could not possibly be left out of any creative writing that aimed at capturing the whole vision of Africa. I mentioned Peter Abrahams as one of the writers who had tried. Perhaps I did not make myself clear. I did not mean that the novel had to be merely political or a mere study of the rise and spread of African nationalism.
>
> Nationalism itself was born of many forces. All these plus what Achebe and others are trying to do will however be embedded in the intellectual and emotional consciousness of a group of characters, this consciousness which must capture the temper of 20th c. Africa – will have to emerge in the characters' day to day

human relationship. These characters need not be educated, or politicians or be necessarily intellectually articulate.

African workers to-day stand in relation to their community, in the same position as the late 19th c. Russian novelists, the Elizabethan writers (16th c) and Greek dramatists (5th B.C.) – who gave expression to the emotional & intellectual consciousness of their society poised between the past and the new era.

Whether African writers will have as big hearts as their counterparts remains yet to be seen. Of those writing now, Achebe has the best chance of doing this, if he lets his heart go. (Ngũgĩ to KS 12 October 1964)

A Grain of Wheat

Published by William Heinemann in English in hardback 1967
(1968 AWS 36)

The University of Leeds was the place for Ngũgĩ to go. It did realise the importance of this young African writer. The publication of *The River Between* was celebrated on 25 January 1965 by a party at the University of Leeds with a cluster of professors from across the disciplines.

The English faculty was pioneering, under their enterprising Irish professor, Derry Jeffares, a new course on 'Commonwealth Literature'. This reflected on the way in which the language of the imperial masters had been kidnapped across the English-speaking world; the concept has twisted and turned through 'Post-colonial Literature' and is now emerging under the description of 'New International Literatures in English (NILE)'. It was Leeds which gave the subject a journal and a base for exceptional graduates. Wole Soyinka, with the help of Martin Banham, had premiered new plays at the West Yorkshire Playhouse. Eldred Durosimi Jones not only wrote on Soyinka's work but also on *Othello's Countrymen* as they appear in Shakespeare. Aig Higo, Nigerian poet and headmaster, studied at Leeds before taking over the management of the Heinemann operation in Nigeria. In contrast to Leeds, when Richard Rive went to Magdalen College at Oxford to work on Olive Schreiner for his doctorate, that university was not able to find a supervisor and he had to travel to London.

Leeds gave Ngũgĩ the chance to carry out his ambition of writing *A Grain of Wheat*, which had been growing in his mind in the YMCA in Nairobi. He wrote to Keith Sambrook :

> I've become lazier and lazier at doing things. I suppose it's the climate here and the time moves so fast. There's only enough time for sleeping! ... I want to finish the first draft by the end of this term so I can properly work on it during Summer. I'm however stuck: problem of time. For the whole action is supposed to be contained

> within 10 days around independence in Kenya. (Ngũgĩ to KS 22 April 1965).

He developed his characters with Conradian skill. The story, which reflects on the Mau Mau struggle, also prophesies that in the post-independence period Kenyans will battle against Kenyans for economic and political ascendancy.

William Heinemann took 1,800 sets of sheets for publication in hardback. Some amusement was caused by the typesetter's readers who had red-marked certain passages, in spite of the fact that this was five years after *The Lady Chatterley* trial. Roland Gant, editorial director at William Heinemann, wrote:

> As legal adviser to HEB (speciality translation into 4-letter English from African languages) I would say that the passages which have been marked in *A Grain of Wheat* are extremely unlikely in the present climate which prevails, to lead to police action against your company and the printers of the book. Similarly, the jocular reference to the (admittedly punishable) offence of bestiality is unlikely to attract the attention of the non-existent censors in this country. I would therefore say that from the point of view of HEB this is a fair business risk.
>
> As Nigel Viney points out, it is extremely unwise to send books which contain words more explicit than 'drat' or descriptions more down to earth than 'tummy' to these particular printers. A cherub lurks among this printer's devils and we have had lot of trouble with them.
>
> I hope that this reassures you and secures me my usual inordinately high fee. (Roland Gant to Tony Beal 18 July 1966)

Ngũgĩ's work at Leeds on Caribbean writers was of singular importance to his developing philosophy. For his postgraduate work he chose to focus on writing from the Caribbean, and in particular on George Lamming, whose novel *In the Castle of my Skin* had made such an impact on publication in 1954. The 1950s were the time when so many of the Caribbean writers, to whom Ngũgĩ refers in *Homecoming*, such as C.L.R. James, Edgar Mittelholzer, V.S. Naipaul and Sam Selvon, had made their first appearance in Britain. He asked Keith Sambrook to find him a copy of the trilogy by Roger Mais which was already out of print.

The publication of writers from the Caribbean was a decade ahead of those from Africa. There had been many chances for publication in journals in the Caribbean and in books from well-established and adventurous publishers in Paris and London. There was lots of work for Ngũgĩ to find. Little from Africa had been published in London even by the mid-1960s, although Mongo Beti, Ferdinand Oyono and Sembene had already made a mark in French alongside the other Caribbean writers of negritude such as Frantz Fanon and Aimé Césaire.

Ngũgĩ says of George Lamming in *Homecoming*:

> He evoked through a child's growing awareness a tremendous picture of the awakening social consciousness of a small village. He evoked, for me, an unforgettable picture of a peasant revolt in a white-dominated world. And suddenly I knew that a novel could be made to speak to me, could, with a compelling urgency, touch cords deep down in me. His world was not as strange to me as that of Fielding, Defoe, Smollett, Jane Austen, George Eliot, Dickens, D.H. Lawrence. That was in 1961. (*Homecoming* p. 81)

A lengthy and well-informed interview of Ngũgĩ, by a quartet of students in the Leeds *Union News* of 18 November 1966 before the publication of *A Grain of Wheat,* reveals how far he had already come in his beliefs. Frantz Fanon was central to his philosophy. These students no doubt had, as I had, welcomed the independence of Kenya only three years before in 1963. Ngũgĩ made it clear to them how the new elite was running the country at the expense of the peasantry who had actually fought the liberation struggle.

The Trial of Dedan Kimathi

A play by Ngũgĩ wa Thiong'o and Mĩcere Mũgo
Published in English (1976 AWS 191)

Internationally Ngũgĩ is famous as a novelist. In Kenya it was his plays, especially in Gikuyu, which were to lead to his detention and ultimate exile. His play *The Black Hermit* (1968 AWS 51) was written at the same time, and with some of the same themes, as the novel *The River Between* (p. 115). Over a decade later in 1975 *The Trial of Dedan Kimathi* was born out of intense controversy. Henry Chakava, put the situation in context:

> This is a play about the now legendary Dedan Kimathi, the leader of Mau Mau who was arrested and hanged by the colonial government in 1958. The version [by Ngũgĩ and Mĩcere] is made up more of truth than imagination, and the angry tone of the playwrights can only be explained in the context of recent events on the Kenyan Theatre scene.
>
> Some time this year, April or May, a play by Kenneth Watene (published by Transafrica) entitled *Dedan Kimathi* was performed at the National Theatre. The play depicted Kimathi as an emotional, murderous, lusty terrorist, built up and destroyed in a Macbeth-Othello type fashion. It was written in verse and even some lines were borrowed verbatim from Shakespeare's tragedies. Although the play received very hostile press reviews it was extremely well attended and went on non-stop for 3 weeks.

> I was not there at the performance when Mĩcere Mũgo and Ngũgĩ are reported to have walked off. But I know they did walk off – and for many people, including myself – the Watene play was myth-shattering, adapted unscrupulously from Ian Henderson's book *The Hunt for Kimathi*.
>
> Ngũgĩ and Mĩcere swore that they would write a play which would restore Kimathi's historical role as daredevil freedom fighter, a hero and a patriot of Kenya's independence. This was partly due to their desire to put the record right, but more immediately to stop Watene's play from being entered and performed at the All Africa Arts Festival in Lagos (now postponed) by presenting a 'better' alternative. I am personally so involved in the dispute that I cannot say which is the better play in strictly dramatic terms. I enclose a copy of the play Ngũgĩ would like us to publish.
>
> Because of the foregoing, I cannot dare give it to anybody here for a report, because I am sure that it will be difficult to obtain balanced reaction. I personally would have no objection to seeing it in the AWS although I realise that the single-play days of *Black Hermit* are long gone. The ideal thing would have been to publish it here (to coincide with the theatre production which Ngũgĩ is laying on) but unfortunately it would be a one-off as we have no series that could accommodate it. What do you think? (HC to KS 14 November 1975)

There was little difficulty about accepting it in London. After all, the play was by one of our best-known authors and was about a national hero of the anti-colonial struggle. It was described as 'very powerful' by Edward Thompson, the director of Heinemann's drama list which, along with those of Faber and Methuen, was considered one of the most innovative in London publishing. Henry Chakava wrote to me on 5 December 1975 saying, 'I am very impressed by this quick decision, which I have already conveyed to a happy Ngũgĩ.'

There were two points at issue. Ngũgĩ wanted to have the play performed before publication. I had always argued with Nuruddin Farah how important that was (p. 162). It would mean losing the undoubted sales that would be made in Nairobi at the time of first performance but would incorporate the lessons learnt in rehearsal on how to make the writers' words walk on the stage. In the end copies were rushed out in Nairobi at the time of the first performance. Also there was the question of whether Ian Henderson, who was still alive, could take legal action for defamation.

Keith Sambrook wrote to Ngũgĩ on Christmas Eve 1975 to offer publishing terms. Ngũgĩ was one of the first writers to try to survive on his writing rather than as a secondary income to a university or civil service salary. Heinemann had to keep his advances within sight of his potential earnings. Alan Hill was always responsive to Keith Sambrook's and my appeals for advances as long as they were carefully argued to keep the accountants off our backs. Keith Sambrook had managed to rationalise a very substantial advance which Ngũgĩ needed in order to build a house. This house at Limuru was designed by an architectural student at the University of Nairobi and was called the Seven Huts because it set out to make a traditional compound work in modern terms. Keith Sambrook pointed out to Ngũgĩ that his royalty account was still in the red but that, as the school edition of *Weep Not, Child* had sold in Nigeria alone 50,460 copies in October 1975 and 4,006 copies in November 1975, a new advance could be managed.

Ngũgĩ was certainly benefiting from international distribution. It was difficult to sell the series continent-wide except from a British base. Intra-regional trade in Africa remains poor to this day and direct sales from Kenya to Nigeria remain difficult; air freight is expensive for books which are called 'dense cargo' by the shippers because they have low value in relation to their heavy weight.

However, the publication of this play led to fresh thinking about the way the African Writers Series might expand outside its London base. In a memo to Henry Chakava I proposed a new development for the publication of *The Trial of Dedan Kimathi*:

> *One off publication by HEB(EA).* As there is a rush this is probably the answer. You should originate the publication because the play is going to be of the greatest interest in East Africa. Keith and I feel that this may be the occasion for you to contribute your first title to the African Writers Series. We should subcontract for the market outside Kenya, Uganda, Tanzania, Zambia, Ethiopia and Malawi. You would sell us 3000 copies or so for the rest of the world. (JC to HC 8 December 1975)

This led Henry Chakava to propose a development of this idea reflecting the offer of scripts by Francis Imbuga and Joe de Graft and the publishing possibilities in East Africa:

> What would be your views if we proposed starting a single play series with a Heinemann (East Africa) imprint for which you would have the option to do an AWS edition for the rest of the world? Once started we would get all the local playwrights to publish with us since there is no active Drama series in East Africa at the moment. (HC to JC 3 August 1976)

He was disappointed when we decided, as our international sales expectations were growing, that London should pay Heinemann (East Africa) an offset fee of half the setting costs and that we should print our copies in Britain. He complained: 'This is where reciprocity seems to work only one way.' I pointed out that as long as Heinemann (East

Africa) did not reduce its price the offset fee would be clear profit to them.

Henry Chakava tried to get Joe Osadolor and Aig Higo to take more than the cautious order of 50 copies direct by air freight for the Festival of African Arts and Culture (FESTAC) in Lagos. I had remarked that all authors expected that the festival would sell thousands of their books, but cynically added: 'It is not just the streets which are going to be choked with traffic but all the book supply lines are going to be choked as well.' (JC to HC 5 December 1976)

Henry Chakava told Aig Higo that due to public demand there had been repeat performances of *The Trial of Dedan Kimathi*, and that they had sold 300 copies of the text outside the theatre:

> For the first time, the African in this part of the world has come to realise the relevance and meaning of cultural independence. You will realise that you West Africans are far more advanced in this area of authentic African theatre than we are. (HC to AH 8 December 1976)

Ngũgĩ and Mĩcere's alternative play, in contrast to that by Watene, pointed up the way in which the emergency had split Gikuyu and Kenyan people. Their message was that the British had made the decolonisation deal with the loyalists and that the ordinary peasants, from whom the freedom fighters were drawn, were robbed. This was not what the Kenyan elite wanted to hear.

I Will Marry When I Want

Ngaahika Ndeenda Published in Gikuyu 1980
A play by Ngũgĩ wa Thiong'o and Ngũgĩ wa Mĩriĩ
Published in English (1982 AWS 246)

Kamĩrĩĩthũ is the transforming name. One of the most moving passages in *Detained* is when Ngũgĩ reflects in solitary confinement on his memories of his return in 1955 to his childhood village from Alliance, one of the top African boarding schools which was in distant Nairobi:

> I came back after the first term and confidently walked back to my old village. My home was now a pile of dry mud-stones, bits of grass, charcoal and ashes. Nothing remained, not even crops, except for a lone pear tree that swayed slightly in sun and wind. I stood there bewildered. Not only my home, but the old village with its culture, its memories and its warmth had been razed to the ground. I walked up to the ridge not knowing whither I was headed until I met a solitary old woman. Go to Kamĩrĩĩthũ, she told me. (*Detained* p. 73)

Everybody had been concentrated in an 'emergency village'. At that time a youth centre had been built, but in 1976 the University of

Nairobi Free Travelling Theatre, when it put on some plays including extracts from *The Trial of Dedan Kimathi,* had to perform on the grass round the abandoned classroom buildings. Ngũgĩ joined the new management committee and in December 1976 he and Ngũgĩ wa Mĩriĩ were commissioned to write what was to become *Ngaahika Ndeenda*. The performances were to begin on the symbolic twenty-fifth anniversary of the declaration of the State of the Emergency and the beginning of the armed struggle in Kenya. Ngũgĩ says:

> The six months between June and November 1977 were the most exciting in my life and the true beginning of my education. I learnt my language anew. I rediscovered the creative nature and power of collective work. (*Detained* p. 76)

Ngũgĩ emphasises the totally transforming nature of the enterprise; it raised money for health projects and it reduced drunkenness. The villagers not only wrote a play with the Ngũgĩs, they not only produced a play in public rehearsals with shouted criticisms, but they built a whole theatre. Ngũgĩ conveys his astonishment at the enterprise:

> I saw with my own eyes peasants, some of whom had never once been inside a theatre in their lives, design and construct an open-air theatre complete with a raised stage, roofed dressing rooms and stores, and an auditorium with a seating capacity of more than two-thousand persons. (*Detained* p. 77)

District Commissioner Kiambu, who had not even bothered to come to see the performance, on 16 December 1977 withdrew the licence and sent in the askaris to close the theatre. On 30–31 December 1977 Ngũgĩ was taken in chains to Kamĩtĩ Maximum Security Prison. *Detained*, his account of these events, will be discussed later (p. 129).

A few years on, when I was on one of my regular visits to Kenya, Henry Chakava and Ngũgĩ took me on a quiet Saturday afternoon in the rainy middle of the year to see this remarkable achievement. I saw with my own eyes the size of the earthen banks which had been flung up for seating over 2,000 people and the circle of bamboo stake fences driven into the ground. I could only share Ngũgĩ's pride but also his astonishment at the panic reaction of the Kenyan ruling class to such a desirable social achievement.

On that same Saturday afternoon Ngũgĩ took us to meet members of the cast. They were seated on benches up against the walls of the room. I was introduced to the actors in the name of their characters and Ngũgĩ acted as translator. Henry Chakava and I were given seats in the circle and a drinking horn of mead circulated. I was much moved by the whole experience and told Henry Chakava my excited reactions as we drove back to Nairobi. He said: 'It's all very well for you. I have to go back each Christmas to my village and sit round like that for days on end.' He remarked that they took me, as a *mzungu*, a white man, absolutely for granted but that they had found him strange because he could not speak Gikuyu, and they had asked many questions about how far away he came from and whether it could possibly be from within Kenya.

It was indeed all very well for me. I could go back to Britain and have no fear about what I published. I had the additional advantage that whatever was newsworthy helped sell books. But Henry Chakava was in the front line as Ngũgĩ's publisher. On one occasion after another he showed firmness and bravery. He suffered a savage panga attack when his car drew up at the gate to his house. There was no attempt to demand his watch or wallet. When you shake hands with Henry Chakava you feel the small finger curled permanently under his palm despite all the careful medical treatment he received. He could have lost the use of an arm or hand. He was repeatedly phoned afterwards in Gikuyu and English with threats issued against a background radio to confuse the sounds and prevent identification of the voice. It was a good guess that GEMA (Gikuyu and Embu Association) were behind the calls. The male voices always made references to the hospital visit on the exact date of the panga attack. He even had money demanded with precise details about how it was to be delivered at night on the veld at Thika. These messages were ones of political intimidation, even if Ngũgĩ was not specifically mentioned.

Henry Chakava was much pressed to become an MP and no doubt could have done extremely well by accepting. One midnight he took me to the substantial suburban house of Mudavadi, the power broker of Kenyan politics. It was for his wake. Huge bonfires at the four corners of the well-watered lawn threw columns of sparks up into the black sky. Henry Chakava was whisked off into the family cabinet meeting, appropriately held in the kitchen, to discuss the emerging political situation. Mudavadi's son was second-in-command to Raila Odinga in the stolen election of December 2007. The title of Oginga Odinga's book *Not Yet Uhuru* (1967 AWS 38) remains apposite. Fortunately, for his authors and for Heinemann, Henry Chakava stuck to publishing.

Maitu Njugira

A musical play by Ngũgĩ wa Thiong'o 1982
Title in English: *Mother, Sing for Me* (or *Mother, Ululate for Me)*

On a Monday afternoon at the turn of February and March 1982 Ngũgĩ came into Henry Chakava's office in Kijabe Street, just round the corner from the University of Nairobi, the Voice of Kenya, the National Theatre and the Norfolk Hotel with its Delamere Bar. I had arrived the previous midnight from a winter London via Amsterdam and Cairo. He told us how the Kamĩrĩĩthũ Community Theatre had applied for a licence for their musical play in good time in November 1981 but that the request had been ignored by the authorities. The play was heavily booked at the National Theatre and the production had been planned to make use of their technical facilities. A cinematic technique was to be integrated to project scenes from colonial history, such as the burning of passbooks. The whole performance was packed with songs in Luhya, Kamba, Kisii and Kalenjin, as well as in Gikuyu and Swahili. In the meantime rehearsals were being continued in hope in the theatre of the Education Department at the University of Nairobi.

This remarkable occasion is recorded in a series of interviews by Anne Walmsley in *Index on Censorship* 1/83 with Ngũgĩ, Nancy Murray and James Currey. Ngũgĩ remarked in his interview on the perversity of the Kenyan authorities:

> The musical dealt with Kenya during the highly repressive colonial period. So what is surprising is that the authorities should feel sufficiently strongly to suppress an anti-colonial play. It's very strange. But there is in Kenya a pattern where the authorities actively support, even financially, foreign, anti-Kenyan cultural offerings. This was in fact dramatised in our own case – at the same time that they were banning, or refusing to grant us a licence for the musical, they were showing *The Flame Trees of Thika* by Elspeth Huxley. It is a novel which is basically racist, it isn't Kenyan, it isn't African. It was shown on Kenyan television as a seven-part serial. The government actually spent money on it.

Ngũgĩ suggested that Henry Chakava and I should come along to that evening's rehearsal. I imagined it would be like other rehearsals I had attended; I had been taken in 1962 in Lagos to *A Dance in the Forests* which Wole Soyinka himself was producing. There had been a small cluster of people in the stalls round that now familiar head. But on that Monday in the University of Nairobi the theatre was bursting with excited noise, every seat was taken and the performance about to begin. As Nancy Murray explained when she was asked in *Index on Censorship* what the authorities were afraid of:

> But if you could see the crowd at this rehearsal you would see what they were scared of. Remember there hadn't been any advertisement. There hadn't been a poster. It was spread just by word of mouth. And people came in buses from far, far away. People came who had been to Kamĩrĩĩthũ and seen the previous play *Ngaahika Ndeenda*, people came who had gone to Kamĩrĩĩthũ but found the play had been stopped. It was a kind of national occasion.

To our surprise we realised that we were not going to get in. Henry Chakava and I went round to the stage door where we were embraced by Ngũgĩ wa Mĩriĩ. He found us two of those rather uncomfortable canvas stacking chairs and then sat us in the wings almost in sight of the expectant audience, as I described in *Index*:

> Yes, we were on the stage. Now really with the first tableau, all company on for the opening scene, immediately one felt one was in it because everyone was picking up their chains, and the whole thing was symbolic of slavery, they had yokes … Into the middle of the full company – I don't know how many there were, about 50, a lot of people – is drawn a cart, drawn by a black man, and in the cart is a white district officer/government figure, sitting with his solar topee. And then the musical gets going. Quite honestly Henry and I thought that perhaps we'd just get a taste of it and go off after a bit. But we were absolutely gripped, although neither of us understands Gikuyu … It was three and a half hours long without an interval, but it was totally engaging … after three hours the opening tableau was re-established. Everybody came off and collected their chains, their yokes and everything. The same cart drawn by the same black man was rolled onto the stage. But this time [in the cart], wearing the solar topee, was a black man.

There was a strong Brechtian drama holding this play together under the emotional and uplifting song, mime and dance. The white settler Kanoru (The fat one) uses Mwendada (Lover of one's stomach) to control the farm workers. Kariuki (The one who has been resurrected) leads the armed struggle.

After the performance Ngũgĩ wa Mĩriĩ took me to talk to the cast, translating what I said into Gikuyu. I told them that I had been so excited that my canvas seat broke. Days later, on 12 March 1982, not only were the rehearsals stopped in Nairobi, but the district officer in Limuru sent in three truck-loads of askaris to break down the Kamĩrĩĩthũ Theatre which they themselves had built. Before Ngũgĩ's detention in 1977 the theatre had been closed. Now it was destroyed.

I have chosen to write about *Maitu Njugira* at this point so as to put it in sequence with the other plays and the events surrounding the Kamĩrĩĩthũ productions. I now return to the Ilmorog sequence of novels which started with *Petals of Blood*.

Petals of Blood

Published in English in hardback 1977 (1977 AWS 188)

Ballad for a Barmaid was the original title of the fourth novel which Ngũgĩ was struggling to write during the early 1970s. Many writers have the problem of a second novel. Ngũgĩ's first cluster of novels drew on the formative influences of Gikuyu social and cultural tradition, western liberal thought and – however much he resented it – the language of the Bible. He had become famous and the longer people waited for his next novel the greater was the level of public expectation.

By the mid-1970s his philosophy had been transformed by pan-Africanism and the black power movements. The Caribbean writers he had studied at Leeds had influenced his work and thought.

Ngũgĩ wrote to Keith Sambrook:

> I am alternately elated and depressed by the novel. Hope alternates with despair. It will take me longer to write than any of the other novels – but I hope it will be worth it.
>
> The main problem of several voices, several levels of time, is to get the kind of action (+plot) that would make everything cohere, that would make a reader keep on reading the novel etc. (Ngũgĩ to KS 13 May 1974)

After this long gap, with only collections of short stories and of essays, we were anxious to get attention for Ngũgĩ's writing in literary circles in Britain and the US. Efforts to place the hardback rights within the Heinemann group failed. Tom Rosenthal, then the managing director at Secker and Warburg, is believed to have been an inspiration for the well-lunched figure in the Snipcock and Tweed publishers' cartoon in *Private Eye*. He wrote to Alan Hill:

> In other words, none of us feels that it sufficiently crosses the border between Africa and a British market sensibility and given the rather heavy load that I am already carrying for 1977 in terms of distinguished non-English books, many of which I fear will lose money, I think we will have to pass this up … (Tom Rosenthal to Alan Hill 8 December 1976)

There was much more sense of Ngũgĩ's importance among general publishers in the United States. The distinguished campaigning publisher Lawrence Hill had taken the collection of short stories *Secret Lives* on the understanding that he was going to have the next novel. When I sent him the manuscript I said:

> Indeed it's long, but it is closely worked and well worth spending effort on. It really needs a list of characters in the style of translations of Russian novels. Keith Sambrook and I are very taken with it but the elaborateness of his flashbacks means it needs close attention. It needs some editorial work and we are getting Richard Lister, a novelist in his own right and a careful guardian of authors' individuality, to work over it. (JC to Lawrence Hill 17 February 1976)

Ngũgĩ, who had taught at Northwestern University in the US, was handling US rights and asked Lawrence Hill for an advance of $15,000 which was far more than he felt his imprint could earn. I was having success placing African writers with Tom Engelhardt, an editor at

Pantheon within Random House, who was the original publisher of the Palestinian radical Edward Said's *Orientalism*. He wrote to me:

> Ngũgĩ was recently recommended strongly to me by someone whose opinion I respect highly. With your urging coming as it did, I would indeed like to reverse myself and give careful consideration to *Petals of Blood*. Please do send me the page proofs as soon as possible. I would also appreciate it if you could also send me his previous book *A Grain of Wheat* and anything else you might think useful to me in getting to know Ngũgĩ's work. (Tom Engelhardt to JC 17 January 1977)

Pantheon did decline *Petals of Blood* after all and it was not until early in 1978, after Ngũgĩ's detention, that it was considered again by Doubleday and then accepted by Dutton.

Ngũgĩ visited London for the British publication on 27 June 1977 of *Petals of Blood* and there were widespread reviews. However, it was the almost simultaneous launching in Nairobi a few days later in July which was the remarkable occasion. There were over 1,000 guests and all 500 airfreighted hardbacks sold immediately. (There were to be sales of some 20,000 paperbacks in Kenya alone in the next 18 months.)

Ngũgĩ had managed to get Mwai Kibaki, future preseident but then the minister of economic affairs, to give the launching speech. Our surprise was that it was economics which Ngũgĩ had chosen to study at Makerere, where Mwai Kibaki had been his teacher. The reason became clear in Ngũgĩ's speech:

> The headmaster of Alliance High School had said that Economics was that terrible subject which only Americans studied. Certainly not a subject fit for sober English gentlemen. Well I did not want to be a sober or unsober English gentleman, hence I studied Economics. (*Writers in Politics* p. 95)

Ngũgĩ had movingly started his speech with:

> I would like to start by introducing to this audience the woman who has all along inspired me. The woman who in fact made me go to school to learn how to read and write. I am referring to my mother, my peasant mother. (*Writers in Politics* p. 94)

He had also invited the actors and builders from the Kamĩrĩĩthũ Centre who, like his mother, could not understand English. Ngũgĩ had decided that in future they should be the first to read his work and that in future he would write in Gikuyu.

Henry Chakava handled with great skill what could have become an awkward incident. There is a great sweep of civic steps in front of the Nairobi City Hall. At the top welcoming the guests were Henry Chakava, Joe Osadolor from Heinemann Nigeria and myself from Heinemann in London. Okot p'Bitek wandered hither and thither in a vaguely diagonal direction up the steps and fell headlong in front of us. We leapt forward to restore him to his feet. Henry Chakava was most solicitous and said: 'Okot. Do go in that door. You will find the bar to the right.' Henry Chakava later told us that he was sure that Okot p'Bitek had put on this performance in order to get refused entry to the Ngũgĩ party. He had indeed been asked, for good reason, to leave a previous Heinemann party.

This party marked an important step in the development of an outstanding Kenyan company. Bob Markham had established the company on a sound basis and hired Henry Chakava as an editor straight out of university. Henry Chakava had recently been made managing director while only just 30. He was to back all the publishing of his old teacher Ngũgĩ whatever dangers the books presented, whether political or commercial. Ngũgĩ was determined that the first publication of his books should be in Gikuyu, although on past record books in the languages of Kenya did not sell. Ngũgĩ was later to write children's books in Gikuyu, which no publisher had tried before. The political risks to the Kenyan company remained even after Ngũgĩ went into exile in the early 1980s. Alan Hill and Keith Sambrook gave Henry Chakava the right to decide what he should publish, whatever the risks. We talked through the dangers with him. He and his staff were in the front line. It was their jobs which were at risk. I believe that the British directors of any other large educational company would have told Henry Chakava to stop publishing such politically sensitive material which would endanger their school textbook publishing and jeopardise their dividends.

As we listened to Mwai Kibaki that evening in July 1977 one could not foresee that members of the administration to which he belonged were becoming so frightened of the power of Ngũgĩ's writing in Gikuyu that, on the very last day of that year, he would be detained.

Detained

A Writer's Prison Diary

Published in English in hardback 1981 (1981 AWS 240)

> … some time in December 1977, two gentlemen, highly placed in the government flew to Mombasa and demanded an urgent audience with Jomo Kenyatta. They each held a copy of *Petals of Blood* in one hand, and in the other, a copy of *Ngaahika Ndeenda*. (*Detained* p. xvi)

Ngũgĩ's detention order was signed by D.T. Arap Moi, then minister for home affairs. Ngũgĩ was taken in on the last day of December 1977. What can a publisher do at a distance for a writer incarcerated without reason given? It must be remembered that communication, even on urgent matters, was mostly by return of airmail letters; telexes and cables were clumsier than text messaging is now, and you had to get an operator to send them. Telephone calls were majestically expensive and had to go through secretaries, operators and switchboards.

On 30 January 1978 Lisa Drew of Doubleday wrote to me in two capacities. First, she wondered what the International Freedom to Publish Committee of the American Association of American Publishers could do to campaign in the US about Ngũgĩ's detention. Second, she asked whether Doubleday might be able to have a new option to reconsider *Petals of Blood.*

I told her that Henry Chakava in Nairobi and we at Heinemann in London were acting as a clearing house for information and that we were encouraging the following:

> 1. Concerned people in the literary world to write to the press, particularly in Kenya.
> 2. People with contacts in the Kenyan government to write personal letters of concern.
> 3. Official bodies to protest.
> 4. Informed stories in press. (This, of course, becomes more and more important as the months roll on so that he is not forgotten.) (JC to Lisa Drew 9 February 1978)

Lisa Drew continued to be most devotedly active even after Doubleday declined *Petals of Blood.* She wrote to tell of efforts to raise the case with Vice-President Moi and Attorney-General Njonjo who were visiting Washington in the first week of March 1978. She said that her committee would ask the State Department to track what happened at Ngũgĩ's trial. I had to tell her:

> [Henry Chakava] regrettably says that there is absolutely nothing to give hope under the present law that Ngũgĩ would have to be brought to trial within three months of his arrest. This law, like so many governments have, has no date. (JC to Lisa Drew 3 March 1978)

Faith Sale, who was active in PEN, managed to get Dutton to make 'a very strong bid' for *Petals of Blood.* But Henry Chakava reported that Ngũgĩ's wife Nyambura was not being allowed to see him until 31 March 1978 when she would have to obtain a proxy to enable her to sign the contract. Mondo Sha, the Japanese publishers, had cabled doubling their advance on hearing of his arrest. At that time sales were made of Swedish, Italian, Japanese and East and West German translation rights. William Ash of BBC Radio wanted to give Ngũgĩ a commission from the European Broadcasting Union which would lead to his work being broadcast by radio in many countries. My letter suggested:

> I think that there would be great psychological advantage in

> writing directly to him care of his wife Nyambura, making this offer of a joint commission. I am sure that news of it may get through to him and help him in his ordeal. As a result when, and we obviously hope sooner than later, he emerges from detention, he will, health permitting, be anxious to consider your exciting offer. (JC to William Ash 15 June 1978)

William Ash was almost certainly put in touch with us through Mary Benson, with her South African sensitivities about political imprisonment, and who later wrote a radio dramatisation of *Petals of Blood*.

A practical and informative letter came from Cherry Gertzel, professor of politics at the Flinders University of South Australia and author of *The Kenyatta Election*, which we had co-published with EAPH in 1962. There had recently been a lunchtime picket outside the Kenyan High Commission in London, in support of all the Kenyan political prisoners, which had been joined by the easily recognisable figure of Ali Mazrui. Cherry Gertzel had visited me soon afterwards on the way back to Australia and wrote:

> I understand that only four people have significant power where detention/release are concerned: the Vice President, the Attorney General, the Permanent Secretary, Office of the President, and Head of C.I.D. I myself doubt if petitions or demonstrations outside the High Commission would have influence upon events. It seemed to me one would have to go right to the top, preferably in a quiet behind the scenes way. Have you been in touch with the Foreign Secretary? Someone suggested to me that the only language the Kenyan government understands is the language of commerce! (Cherry Gertzel to JC 22 June 1978)

Although approaches were made to the Foreign Office I did not have much hope about the British exerting pressure. The problem was that indeed the only language the British government understood about Kenya was commerce. The British authorities showed themselves willing over the years to watch Kenyan dissidents as proxies for the Kenyan government in order not to jeopardise British trade with Kenya. In 1982 I was to travel back from the Zimbabwe Book Fair with Ngũgĩ's co-author Mĩcere Mũgo and to witness discreetly, soon after dawn at Gatwick, the three-quarter hour interview she had with British immigration just to obtain a transit visa to Heathrow to get her onward flight that day to Canada. Although Cherry Gertzel was dismissive of demonstrations, Ngũgĩ gives examples in *Detained* of news getting through prison walls. One has to try everything.

Cherry Gertzel also gave her analysis of why the detention had happened at all:

> It seems to me (very obviously) that Ngũgĩ was detained because he challenged the present hegemony of the Kikuyu capitalist

> society. It is true that there was a strike at the Bata shoe factory, as I told you, but more significant is the fact that it was the local GEMA Chairman who was initially responsible for the arrest. But more significant than the challenge to the capitalist strategy of development is the form which that challenge took; an appeal to Kikuyu identity. (Cherry Gertzel to JC 22 June 1978)

A Colonial Affair was the original title of *Detained*. This was because Keith Sambrook had managed in 1967 to get a contract under that title from William Heinemann at the time of Ngũgĩ's return to Kenya after three years at the University of Leeds. The book was originally to concentrate on the shocking history of the settlers and to reflect the way the period was portrayed by the writers Karen Blixen, Elspeth Huxley and Robert Ruark. He had found the subject so degrading that he had put the book aside. In prison in 1978 Ngũgĩ was haunted by this title:

> A colonial affair …the phrase keeps intruding into the literary flow of my mind and pen … a colonial affair in independent Kenya … It is as if the phrase has followed me inside Kamiti Prison to mock me. (*Detained* p. 29)

He was suffering in Kenyatta's independent Kenya from authoritarian laws and procedures which mimicked those of the settler colony.

Henry Chakava posted the draft manuscript of *Detained* to me in London in April 1980. It centred on his imprisonment without charge or trial in Kamiti maximum security prison from the last day of 1977 until his release, soon after Kenyatta's death in December 1978, over 11 months later. Henry Chakava pointed out how an account of his detention had been used as a starting point for political and cultural arguments:

> It is very much what I expected to find, a broad personal survey of Kenyan life and society seen in an historical and continuing perspective. Ngũgĩ's ideological inclinations have obviously coloured the approach. In many ways it deepens our understanding of Ngũgĩ the man, his writings, what he considers the reasons for his detention, and his own views about prison life and detention laws. As usual it is full of biblical undertones. (HC to JC 16 April 1980)

I wrote to Ngũgĩ after reading the manuscript:

> It has made me reflect deeply on the realities of incarceration. You have handled the whole problem of writing of the essential boredom of prison life with real craftsmanship. (JC to Ngũgĩ 6 May 1980)

We were going through all the usual publishing processes comfortable in our salaried jobs but Henry Chakava brought me up short with the day-to-day realities of Ngũgĩ's life. The university had cancelled his contract after six months of detention and avoided re-employing him:

> Ngũgĩ phoned from Limuru yesterday afternoon. When I informed him that the contracts had arrived, he decided that he was going to drive to Nairobi and sign them so that I can post them back the same evening. We kept the office open for half an hour waiting for him. I have never seen him sign anything so fast.
>
> All this shows how desperately in need of money he is at the moment. He has been coming in to check on his mail twice a day. I suspect he visits his bank several times a day. When we spoke on 6th May on the telephone you said that you had not been aware that it was the money he needed more desperately than the contract. You said you would put it in hand immediately. It is now more than 10 days and, as he says, his children have been thrown out of school. He is at the moment quite demoralised and seems to feel that Heinemann is changing its previous cordial relationship with him. (HC to JC 16 May 1980)

Henry Chakava was trying to get Ngũgĩ to let us have the revised manuscript of *Detained* by the end of July so that we could get it edited and photocopied in order to show it to potential buyers at the Frankfurt Book Fair in October. I was also, far too optimistically, pressing him for the English translation of *Devil on the Cross*. 1980 was Africa Year at Frankfurt and, following the special programme on Africa at the Berlin Festival in 1979, we were working hard to sell translation rights of our best-established writers in West and East Germany and elsewhere. Amy Hoff, the rights manager, had already sold 12 translation rights in *Petals of Blood*.

> We are preparing material for Frankfurt because it is the great place for selling rights. As I mentioned to Ngũgĩ now that he is a full-time writer the best way of increasing his income is to sell translation rights. It is regrettable but a fact that sales of translations have increased since his detention. (JC to HC 11 July 1980)

He could ill afford it but on 19 January 1981 he instructed us to give 5 percent of his earnings to the Writers Association of Kenya.

The manuscript had arrived on 16 July 1980 and there followed the classic misunderstanding between author and publisher, which so often follows the late delivery of a manuscript, when the author expects the lost time magically to be recaptured. Nevertheless, from the file I am not altogether clear why it took us a year to publish the book, although extra documents were being inserted into the manuscript well into the new year. I wrote to Henry Chakava:

> I am terribly sorry if you and Ngũgĩ were under the illusion that we would publish this autumn. As the manuscript arrived on 16 July and we had already sent the list to press, it would be counter-productive to publish before Christmas. Apart from anything else

> it is essential to have a major book three months before publication in Great Britain. I know that you can rush out books in East Africa but the whole marketing situation is different here in Britain … Our efforts to rush through *Writers in Politics* were disastrous as you know because of the confusion over the accents. (JC to HC 14 October 1980)

It would indeed have been useful to have had the manuscript earlier so that we could have had printed copies of the book at the time of Ngũgĩ's visit to London towards the end of the year. This followed a trip, together with Bessie Head, organised by the Danish Library Association. Ngũgĩ had caused a national sensation in Denmark. Both writers were on a popular television interview programme which went out each Saturday evening at 6 o'clock. The interviewer of course asked questions about the Danish writer Countess Karen Blixen who wrote *Out of Africa*, which is set in the Kenya of the book Ngũgĩ never wrote, *A Colonial Affair.* The outcry, after hearing Ngũgĩ's attack on their national heroine, jammed the switchboard at the broadcasting house in Copenhagen.

We kept up our efforts to get Ngũgĩ publicised to a wider international audience. Dagmar Heusler, who ran the Africa Year at the Berlin Festival in 1979 was commissioned by a West German television station to make a film about Ngũgĩ in Kenya. Ben Shephard at BBC/TV, who has South African connections, tried to make use of the film:

> As you will have heard from Dagmar Heusler, we showed her film to Anthony Rouse last Monday. It was not a great success.
>
> I chose Rouse because a film on Ngũgĩ could easily have fitted into his 'Writers and Places' series and, not least, because he's one of the few people with the sort of money to spend that the subject requires. But he clearly has no residual sympathy with things African and started off by saying that Ngũgĩ was Marxist and finished by saying that he was 'too political'. So we were confronted by a very English art-for-art's sake approach which would have needed a pretty considerable film to overturn it …
>
> I shall explore other avenues but the immediate outlook is not hopeful. Rouse had some of Achebe's books on his desk, and perhaps he will find that more accessible. I'm going to keep working on him, and perhaps next time one of your writers is over you should invite him to a do. (Ben Shephard to JC 12 June 1981)

Africa was the place where people were interested. It had always been hoped that it would be possible to print an edition of *Detained* in Kenya. But the problems were that there might be administrative action to ban the book's circulation or that certain of the individuals criticised by Ngũgĩ might sue for libel. Henry Chakava decided to airfreight in some British copies, get reviews in the papers and test the situation:

> I attach copies of the reviews of *Detained*. You will be interested to hear that we have sold just over 5,000 copies since it was published 2 weeks ago.
>
> There was an agonising silence after we had put out the 500 UK copies. Then we decided to publish. There has been no action so far, and there is unlikely to be any now since the book has already travelled widely and has been read by the highest authorities. (HC to JC 12 August 1981)

Devil on the Cross

Caitaani Mũthuraba-inĩ Published in Gikuyu 1980
English translation published in hardback 1982
(1982 AWS 200)

Ngũgĩ excitedly told Henry Chakava and me that a new entertainment had entered the bar life of Kenya following the publication in 1980 of his novel, the first to be written in his mother's own language. A man literate in Gikuyu would read Ngũgĩ's novel aloud to the drinkers until his voice and his glass had run dry. He would then lay the novel page downwards on the bar until another drink was bought for him. Literacy paid off.

The script of the Ngũgĩs' *Ngaahika Ndeenda,* which had been produced with such drama in 1978 at the Kamĩrĩĩthũ Cultural Centre, was published at the same time. Ngũgĩ told us that when he had entered one bar a person, previously unknown to him, introduced himself by the name of one of the characters in the play. Then other people in the bar cast clustered round him shouting out their own characters' names. Play-reading had broken out across Kenya.

There were of course political dangers in publishing Ngũgĩ in Kenya. Henry Chakava explained with clarity the worries for them:

> As far as the strategy for publication is concerned, we have had detailed discussion, and some disagreements. I do not want to go into details, but in the end we agreed that *Ngaahika Ndeenda* and the Gikuyu edition of *The Devil on the Cross* will be published simultaneously. In this way the novel will draw some fire from the play, but not so much as if the novel had been published first. I have decided to launch the two in a series, say the African Languages Series, and I am sure the authorities will appreciate this as a policy decision rather than a deliberate attempt to embarrass them with this one play. Indeed if these two books do well, we could add more writings in indigenous languages such as the Luo, Luiya, Kikamba, Maasai, etc. (HC to KS 8 July 1979)

In addition there were commercial problems. Lip service was paid to publication in Kenyan languages, but it had proved almost impossible to sell the few titles which had appeared unless they were chosen as set books for exams. If the Ngũgĩ books in Gikuyu were banned by the government they would be unsaleable outside Kenya. However, even though district commissioners might ban performances of plays, there was no record in Kenya of them banning published books. Every detail of the strategy of publication was carefully considered in the Heinemann office in Nairobi. Johnson Mugweru, the sales director, described how, in order to register copyright, a copy was taken to a government office where an Indian clerk took the fee in shillings and gave a receipt. It was thus registered for copyright but it did not have to wait for any official approval. That was all. It was a formality. Johnson Mugweru explained how the orders, which had been gathered from across Gikuyu country, would be invoiced out in advance and the books would be put by the printers straight into the boots of the reps' cars and taken off to the shops to sell before any local administrative action could taken, as it had been by a district officer against the production of plays.

There had been signs that the reception for these two books would be exceptional. Ngũgĩ, annoyed, had rushed into the office to see Henry Chakava because he had been told by a friend that he had bought a copy of the play. Why had the authors not seen a copy? Henry replied that no more had he. He rang up the printers who said they were still binding the book. So somebody had slipped the very first copies out of the works and on to the streets of Nairobi. Ngũgĩ was hot enough to steal off the stack at the binders.

Ngũgĩ wrote to me in 1977 about the book he had started years before in English:

> I have been working on a new novel whose working title is 'Devil at the Cross' or 'Devil's Angels'. I am a third of the way through … The novel plays around the Faustus theme; it is about a woman, who, to get wealthy in a money based society (i.e. in a society where one's status is determined by the size of one's pocket), sells her soul to the Devil.
>
> She is then given the secret of five ways of making it to the top which, of course, she utilizes with consequences that will be examined in the novel. The whole manuscript should be ready the end of June, at the very latest, but I am hoping sooner. It is coming on well, and it will be the first novel I shall have written in the head, so to speak, before putting it on paper.
>
> It is very character based and it is also full of action. So with the main emphasis being on character and action the woman will be at the centre of the novel. I am sure that you will find it interesting – at least I am enjoying writing it. (Ngũgĩ to JC 10 January 1977)

By the end of that year he was in detention. At the end of 1978 he emerged from Kamĩtĩ maximum security prison brandishing the manuscript of *Devil on the Cross* written in Gikuyu on toilet-paper:

> Writing on toilet-paper? Now I know that paper is about the most precious article for a political prisoner, more so for one like me who was in detention because of his writing. At Kamĩtĩ, virtually all the detainees are writers or composers … These prisoners have mostly written on toilet paper. Now the same good old toilet-paper – which has been useful to Kwame Nkrumah in James Fort Prison, to Dennis Brutus on Robben Island, to Abdilatif Abdalla in G Block, Kamĩtĩ, and to countless other persons with similar urges – has enabled me to defy daily the intended detention of my mind. (*Detained* p. 6)

In those days the paper was hard, non-absorbent and came interleaved in flat packs. The written sheets could be concealed at the bottom of the box. He had started to write years before in English. Prison solved the language question. Then the manuscript was found in a prison search. He started again in Gikuyu. Ngũgĩ was determined on a third start with his words written between the printed lines of a Bible. Unexpectedly, after three weeks the first Gikuyu manuscript was returned by a prison officer to Ngũgĩ with the remark: 'You write very difficult Kikuyu!'

Henry Chakava was pleased to hire Simon Gikandi full time as an editor in 1977 in the interim before he went to Edinburgh to work for his doctorate, having just graduated at Nairobi with the only first in the whole faculty of arts. As a student he had reported with singular confidence and perceptiveness on a whole range of writers, including Meja Mwangi and Nuruddin Farah. His report on the original Gikuyu *Caitaani Mũtharaba-inĩ* is full of positive appreciation, though not without criticism for Ngũgĩ's tendency to lecture his readers. He puts his finger on the problem of what audience is the author addressing:

> Since this is a very long novel, it will be expensive to produce. It will appeal largely to the 'literary people' – what Arnold Bennett used to call the professional few who find excitement trying to delve into the intricacies of style and meaning. So, if Ngũgĩ has the 'ordinary' readership in mind, he might discover that most people consider reading long and somehow complex novels trying. The play, *Ngaahika Ndeenda* has the advantage of being short and straight-forward. The novel has an intricate structure built on flashbacks, dreams and allegory, and unless I am under-estimating the literary nature of the rural peasantry/working class, this is one of the problems we have to contend with. (Report by Simon Gikandi 6 July 1977)

It had been assumed in Nairobi, as in London, that the novel would outsell the play despite being published in full. The demand for both books was almost equal. By the end of 1980 three impressions totalling 15,000 of the novel and 13,000 of the play had been printed. Douglas

Killam asked me in 1982 to estimate the readership. I took a conservative guess that each copy would be read by an average of six or seven people which would mean at least 100,000 readers for each book. There was a ready second-hand market going on the pavements down River Road. In addition, how many people had heard the books read aloud?

Ngũgĩ had come out of detention at the end of 1978 even more determined to push forward his writing and publishing philosophy without compromise. Keith Sambrook wrote:

> Ngũgĩ is certainly not modifying his views as his full page in the Kenyan supplement of *The Guardian* the other day clearly shows. Being his publisher will no doubt cause us some awkward moments from now on but we shall retain the most important writer in Africa on our list. (KS to HC 15 June 1979)

The Ngũgĩs and Henry Chakava decided, in a memo dated 8 July 1979, that Heinemann Educational Books (East Africa) should now be the originating publisher for these two books. They wanted all translation rights and US rights to be handled by the Kenyan company rather than by the company in London. The central problem was that Kenya, even if the politics had been more certain, could not provide enough income for a full-time professional writer who had to depend upon his writing. The Ngũgĩs pushed the realities as hard as they could.

Henry Chakava and we in London over the next few years developed a policy whereby his company would have exclusive market rights in East Africa and open market throughout the rest of Africa, and at various times this allowed the Kenyan company to make sales, particularly in Zambia, Malawi, Ethiopia and Mauritius. In 1981, soon after the Zimbabwean settlement, I wrote to Ngũgĩ about the offers we had had for locally printed co-publications with the newly founded Zimbabwean Publishing House.

The Ngũgĩs insisted that all their work must be translated from the original Gikuyu and not from the English-language translations. Dagmar Heusler, adviser on African writing to the distinguished Frankfurt imprint of Suhrkamp Verlag, looked round Nairobi in vain for a Swahili-speaking German with literary ability. With Germany's historic association with Tanganyika that should not have proved too much of a problem. But I could foresee problems with smaller languages. My cousin Alice Martin who organises translations from English for the largest Finnish publishers, WSOY, tells me that the translation in 2007 of the 700 pages of *The Wizard and the Crow* had to be from Ngũgĩ's English.

There was also the problem of audience. Ngũgĩ expected a substantial advance for *A Devil on the Cross* from one of the renowned US literary imprints; it was declined as 'a tough sell' by Doubleday, Pantheon, Dutton, Putnam, and Farrar, Strauss and Giroux. Kathleen Anderson at Norton summed up the problem:

> The most interesting thing to me about the novel is Ngũgĩ's challenge to those African intellectuals who, although they give lip service to the struggle for liberation, are still so wedded to their bourgeois privileges that they are unable to act when the time for action comes … While *Petals of Blood* left some novelistic pleasures for a general reader, the current novel is so passionate in its political convictions and so enamoured of the Brechtian political rhetorical devices it uses to display its points that its audience is exclusively those who care about current developments in contemporary African literature or current Marxist thought. Consequently, I don't think it would transcend that specialized audience for the general reader. (Kathleen Anderson to JC 29 October 1981)

In fact the company which could get at just such an audience was Heinemann Educational Books Inc, Heinemann's very own and very new company in the US. Their sales director, Tom Seavey, just before I was going to see Ngũgĩ in Nairobi at the end of February 1982, wrote in a brief and practical memo:

> An interesting updated figure to use judiciously in dealing with Ngũgĩ regarding Inc. In 1981 we sold 4,512 (net) copies of his novels. In January 1982, we sold 901. Projecting this last figure at the growth rate of Inc. as a whole gives us a possible 6,700 total for '82. Inasmuch as all four novels we have are old, I have no doubt that we could reach 4,000 copies of *Devil on a Cross,* a new and frequently ordered title.(Tom Seavey to JC 29 January 1982)

Matigari

Published in Gikuyu 1986
English translation published in hardback 1989 (1989 AWS)

Here is the fairy tale as told by Ngũgĩ in Germany in 1989:

> Matigari, the main character, is puzzled by a world where the producer is not the one who has the last word on what he has produced; a world where lies are rewarded and truth punished. He goes round the country asking questions about truth and justice. People who had read the novel started talking about Matigari and the questions he was raising as if Matigari was a real person in life. When Dictator Moi heard that there was a Kenyan roaming around the country asking such questions he issued orders for the man's arrest. But when the police found that he was only a character in fiction, Moi was even more angry and he issued orders for the arrest of the book itself. That's why, in February 1987, in a very well co-ordinated police action, the novel was seized from all the bookshops and from the publisher's warehouse. The novel

> is now published in English for a readership outside Kenya, the first case, in our history of a fictional character being forced into exile to join its creator. But this was Moi's Kenya where facts are stranger than fiction, where state actions in the streets here induced more terror in its citizens than that of their nightmares, where the words of the head of state, spoken in all seriousness, would more than match those of the cleverest of satirists. (*Moving the Centre* p. 175)

It was always essential to get Ngũgĩ's books out fast across Gikuyu country: fill the boots of cars direct from the printers with orders from across the country and scatter. In fact by the time the Special Branch raided the Heinemann offices there were only a few file copies left. Ngũgĩ had been out of the country and it was impossible for him to return after the 1982 attempted coup.

But Henry Chakava was still there in Kenya facing up to the realities. He told me another episode in the fairy tale. Professor Simeon Ominde was the gentle and considerate chairman of Heinemann (East Africa). He was the person who had made sure that Ngũgĩ could go on to the University of Leeds in 1965. When he heard about the Matigari raid, he came into the office to tell Henry Chakava that he must insist that in future the board approve the acceptance of all books. Henry Chakava said that he regretted that he could not agree. Simeon Ominde said that he therefore must resign the chair and that he must go to State House to tell President Moi that he was doing so. On the appointed day Simeon Ominde sat in the ante-room able to hear the raised voice of the president, a former primary school head, shouting at the people who had just gone into the presence. Simeon Ominde's knees were knocking as in his own schooldays. Eventually he was ushered in, but as soon as he said that he wished to resign, President Moi said: 'You can't. I put you there to watch those people.' I asked Henry Chakava how he knew this and Henry said: 'Simeon was so relieved that he came straight back from State House and told me.'

PART

3 Writers from THE HORN & NORTH-EASTERN AFRICA

Painting by Ghassan Kanafani

Bill Heyes

George Hallett

George Hallett

Pierre Makambo Bambote, James Currey and Nuruddin Farah, Berlin 1979

5 *Emperors in* ETHIOPIA

Chinua Achebe was keen that the African Writers Series, which was initially dominated by work by Nigerians and Ghanaians, should represent the whole continent. When I showed Tayeb Salih's collection of stories *The Wedding of Zein* to him, he was not only delighted by their undoubted quality, but remarked that it would be the first book in the Series by a Sudanese. The arrival of the *The Afersata* by Sahle Sellassie, the first manuscript from Ethiopia, was of particular interest. We all hoped that, in that closed imperial country, the publication of a novel by an Ethiopian could draw the attention of his compatriots to new writing from the rest of Africa. Even more important, it should encourage the submission of further work in English from a country where there was already publishing in Amharic.

I had a fascination for Ethiopia. John Gardner, my housemaster at Kingswood School, Bath, had been appointed by the British Foreign Office during the second world war as tutor to the Duke of Harar, heir to Emperor Haile Sellassie I. He told us stories of ancient French trains from Djibouti and of the caves where the court had been set up behind great woven curtains and sheltered during the Italian air attacks. The emperor, during his exile from 1936 to 1941, had made his court in a house in Bath. The conservatory's glass had been painted white to turn it into an Ethiopian Orthodox chapel. The jewellers of Bath were relieved that their bills were paid when he was restored to the throne after the British drove out the Italians. The Duke of Harar later unsuccessfully tried to stage a coup against his father.

When I first visited Ethiopia in 1968 Oxford University Press had a substantial office in Addis Ababa run by Tsefaye Daba. His editor was Mary Dyson, with whom I had worked in Oxford University Press London. She and I shared an enthusiasm for Rex Collings's Three Crowns series, in which plays by Ethiopian playwrights had appeared, as well as *Travellers in Ethiopia* by Richard Pankhurst. She too had worked with Denys Johnson-Davies on his translated anthology of *Modern Arabic Short Stories* (p. 171). As Oxford University Press did not publish contemporary novels, she was able to help us in our contacts with Ethiopian novelists. She was later to marry the economist Paulos Abraham and they both worked for the World Bank.

Sahle Sellassie
Emperors of the past & present

Sahle Sellassie had studied at the universities of Addis Ababa, Aix-Marseilles and California. He wrote in three languages. His own language was Guraginya, in which he wrote his first novel, but there was little market for it. The University of California Press published in 1964 *Shinega's Village: Scenes of Ethiopian Life* which he had translated from the original, which was in Chaha, a dialect of Amharic.

Sahle Sellassie sent us *The Afersata* (1969 AWS 52*)* which was his first novel written in English. The manuscript, which had all the calmness with which Ethiopians cope with crisis, was an anthropologically revealing story centred on an investigation by collective means at a village level of the burning down of a hut. Sahle Sellassie's controlled use of English meant that his short novel lacked drama, but we felt that it could be useful to see whether we could get it used in Ethiopian schools. Charles V. Taylor, an English-language teaching (ELT) adviser in the Ministry of Education, in a letter dated 8 November 1967 pointed out: 'There are, of course, quaint "Ethiopianised English" idioms.' He also suggested that the author might consider removing 'words like "piss" or even veiled descriptions of connubial activities'. Mary Dyson has pointed out that when she used *The Afersata* in teaching agricultural extension workers they had other concerns and that 'some complained that it was shaming to read of one's countrymen barefoot, wiping feet on the grass' (Mary Dyson to JC 15 November 2006). When the book was published in 1969 in the last years of imperial rule we still did not know whether it would be censored. Ethiopia and South Africa were the only African countries where there was a formal system of censorship and Chinua Achebe and we felt that the Series could give work from these countries an international readership even if the work could not be easily read in the author's homeland. Sahle Sellassie wrote after publication:

> I hear that there was quite a fuss about the book in the censorship department here, that is whether it should be banned from Ethiopia or not. The final verdict is, however, quite satisfactory. Bookshop owners are allowed to import it. Mary Dyson called me a few minutes ago to inform me that Meno bookshop has ordered some copies. (Sahle Sellassie B. Mariam to JC 18 June 1969)

Keith Sambrook annotated the letter to say that the Giannopoulos bookshop had ordered 100 copies. It was a breakthrough. Sahle Sellassie's international skills were of value to the Addis Ababa office of the British shipping company Mitchell Cotts, the main agents bringing in books for the office of Oxford University Press.

When I visited Ethiopia in March 1968 Mary Dyson introduced me to people who could tell me about the history of novel publishing in Amharic. I commissioned Sahle Sellassie to write a report on a novel by H.E. Haddis Alemayehu, which several Ethiopians recommended. The central love story is of the beautiful Seble, daughter of a nobleman Meshesha, who at 24 is still unmarried because no suitor is considered noble enough. Bezabeh is assigned to her as a tutor and they fall in love:

> Masterfully grafted to this love theme unfolds another, more serious story – the relation of the traditional nobleman Meshesha and his peasant-tenants, a relation that ends in a peasants' revolt, and the subsequent humiliation of the captured Meshesha. The leader of the peasant revolt does not kill Meshesha. He prefers to make him a laughing stock to all who know him by capturing him alive and taking him to the provincial court …
>
> *Feker Eske Mekaber [Love Unto Death]* is not only the longest Amharic novel so far written (about 106,000 words), but also the best in many ways. The language is clear and beautiful although sometimes ecclesiastical jargons that are inevitably sprayed here and there are difficult to understand for those readers (including myself) unfamiliar with Geez, the classical Ethiopian language. Otherwise the words are vivid and reveal the imaginative grasp of the author …
>
> For the post war Ethiopian generation *Feke Eske Mekaber* is a social history; a social history that is groaning under the pressures of modernity, but that is not totally dead and buried.
>
> A proper translation of the book into English and some other languages will reveal that the theme is closer to the social setting of Europe and Russia of the pre-industrial era than to that of the present day Africa. It bears no resemblance to the themes developed by other [African] writers of today. (Report by SS March 1968)

However, Sahle Sellassie told Alan Hill on a visit to Ethiopia in October 1969 that he could not spare time from his own writing to handle the translation. The reference to Russia certainly fitted with my own impressions of Addis Ababa at the time, which sent me back to read Chekhov and Dostoevsky. I wish that we had found somebody at least to translate a couple of trial chapters to glimpse back into this feudal society in these last years before the deposition of the emperor in 1974. Mary Dyson says that it has now been translated as *Love Beyond the Grave.*

Unfortunately we had to decide to turn down the manuscript of Sahle Sellassie's next novella, even after he had responded to criticisms by the readers. Henry Chakava found his third manuscript *Warrior King* (1974 AWS 163) 'entertaining', and pointed out how there was 'great potential for oral material in East African universities':

> This is an epic of Kass Hailu, symbolizing at the same time the rise of powerful emperors in Ethiopia in the 19th century, and the corresponding fall of the feudal system of government … I do not think therefore that this work should be made to bear the weight of creative originality; and for this reason do not agree with you when you criticize it for dealing with 'the battle of political guile in straightforward terms.' There should be no pretence in concealing the epic nature of this work, and although I am unable to comment on its historical accuracy, I am certain that it is founded on historical fact, and that as work of art, it falls under that genre. Indeed it

> compares very favourably with that famous epic *Sundiata; an Epic of old Mali* although comparatively this one is a bit lacking in colourful and proverbial expressions. (HC to JC 9 May 1973)

Henry Chakava was not altogether accurate it classing it as 'oral', as Sahle Sellassie had been able to draw on much written material. When Sahle Sellassie sent the revised manuscript he explained his intention:

> As yourself and the other readers have clearly pointed out it is a story told in a simple, straightforward manner, the story of a man who starts life from the dust and raises himself to the status of an emperor. My intention was to show that a man is what he makes of himself. It is not true that men are made rulers over others by God. They make themselves so. And then I had some other intentions in writing the book. But I would rather leave that to the readers, especially the Ethiopian readers to discover for themselves. I have used many sources in writing the book. I read all the books on Theodorus available to me, over fifteen of them including 'Chronicle of King Theodore' Amharic ed. I went to Gonder city and stayed there several days visiting historical spots, looking for vestiges of the emperor, and inquiring people about him. But obviously it is not a history book – it is a novel based on history. (SS to JC 21 July 1973)

Reduilf K. Molvaer wrote about Sahle Sellassie's views on the comparative value to him of reviews and of publishers' reports:

> Some reviewers wrote that a political debate about land reform in Ethiopia had no place in a novel. Others pointed to technical defects. Although Sahle-Sillase felt that some critics raised valid points, he was hurt and annoyed when he thought that some critics were unfair and that their criticisms missed the point, but he never responded to reviews of his books. The criticism he had learned most from is the pre-publication critique from manuscript publishers. He is grateful to Heinemann for such guidance, and especially to the then editor, James Currey, for technical advice. He has learned more from this than from books or from criticism after the books have been published. (Reduilf K. Molvaer, *Black Lions*, Red Sea Press 1996)

Daniachew Worku
Pilgrims & the cleansing of a stagnant society

Daniachew Worku's novel *The Thirteenth Sun* (AWS 125) is one of the most extraordinary novels to appear in the African Writers Series. The title refers to the fact that Ethiopia has 13 lunar months rather than the muddled jumble of 12 in western Europe. Ros de Lanerolle saw it as a novel where 'Characters are … subsidiary to atmosphere … It's a mysterious book … The kind of book that should intrigue reviewers though.' In her enthusiastic three-page report she said:

> Story of a pilgrimage to the shrine of Addo high in the mountains of Ethiopia – a young man is bringing his sick father, the Fitawrary … in the

hope of a cure. With them is the Fitawrary's young daughter, born of his association with a city woman, but unrecognised by him. The old man represents the old ways, old values (valour in war, conquest of riches and woman, respect for religion and the Emperor); while the young man holds these in contempt, seeing them as representing a long-decayed past. His commentary throughout the book shows up the human and social reality behind the ritual, the greed behind the ritual, the greed and poverty behind the preaching of 'spiritual values'. Story culminates in a ceremony to exorcise the illness with the help of spirits called up by a 'conjure-woman', in collaboration with her grasping peasant husband, and when they reveal themselves as frauds the Fitawrary shoots the peasant – and dies himself. The book ends with the descent from the mountain with the Fitawrary's rotting corpse, which it is his son's duty to bury according to his wishes.

The tale is used to expose decaying society, politically brutal, static and uncaring, corrupt and privilege-ridden. Its main strength is in its evocation of atmosphere, the beauty of the country in contrast to the decaying society and religion, whose priests are reduced to swindlers, preaching 'unworldliness' and loyalty to the brutal emperor and government. Natural descriptions are evocative, almost elegiac; conversation often almost drily satiric; revelations towards the end full of irony. I liked especially the procession to the lake, and the sermon punctuated by the *kyries* of the pilgrims, and the physical response of the conjure-woman to the preacher. (Report by Rosalynde de Lanerolle February 1972)

When I read the manuscript it had a particular personal resonance for me. In February 1968 Tsefaye Daba and Mary Dyson wanted to test a long-wheel-based Land Rover for the use of Oxford University Press. They chose a severe route which was Daniachew Worku's pilgrim trail to the holy lake of Addo. They invited various people, including Richard Pankhurst, the Director of the Institute of Ethiopian studies and his wife Rita Pankhurst, who offered to provide a traditional Ethiopian meal to eat in the open air. This tiny track wound up the face of the mountain, between boulders and round precipices poised high above the shining plains. As the rockfalls across the track became more frequent Tsefaye Daba had to call on all the driving skills he had learned as a lieutenant in the Ethiopian army in the Congo in the first great UN operation in Africa. In the end the mountain was too much even for him and the grinding four-wheel drive of the Land Rover. If we had had two or three days to spare we could have walked the pilgrims' way. Before we descended we all sat eagle-high on the mountainside round a great basket with *wat* stew heaped in the centre. The basket was lined with *injera* unleavened bread which we broke off to use to lift the spicy food.

When I wrote to Daniachew Worku on 25 February 1972 I said that I thought that *The Thirteenth Sun* was 'one of the most important manuscripts we have at the moment'. In thanking me for 'the good tidings' he made a statement which was probably genuine and was not just for the eyes of letter censors. He was to tell David Hill, who visited him later in March 1972, that he was having trouble with his post which he put down to censorship. He said in his letter to me:

> I do not agree either with the reader's view that Ethiopia represents a totally decaying society. It may be true that she is stagnant. But not putrid. I believe that we have streams of young conscientiousness surging upwards to cleanse her. The statement on the emperor is obviously out of place. Given the material of the novel, I do not think one would arrive at such a conclusion. I, for one, respect and admire the Emperor both for his human qualities and for his leadership. There are even times when I loved him. He is one of those rare human beings of the twentieth century who is stranger than fiction and yet alive and real. If I hadn't known him, I wouldn't have believed that such a man ever existed. Even an imaginary character could never measure up to him. And if they did, I'm sure they would be incredible .... I'd been a lecturer at HIS University for five years before I left it three years ago to devote my life to writing. (DW to JC 6 March 1972)

I had heard from Taban lo Liyong that Daniachew Worku had been on the creative writing course at the University of Iowa and that he had already written much in Amharic. Daniachew Worku told me that he was working on poetry, plays and another novel in English. In responding to a request to an increase in his advance on royalties on 13 October 1973 I explained:

> I'm sorry that the amount of money involved in writing is so small. But that's it. One can only hope that your sales will build up. I'm afraid that it's not much of a consolation but in a fairly recent survey by the Society of Authors it turned out that very few people get over £500 a year from writing. They have to make up their income from reviewing, broadcasting and other outlets. Only two of the authors in the African Writers Series come anywhere near being able to live off their royalties. The situation in Africa is even more desperate. I'll have to look at the question of your advance being affected by the floating of the pound and see if we can do something to help. (JC to DW 13 October 1972)

He had told me that there had been a hold-up at customs. I wrote back telling him:

> I was talking to Dr Bereket yesterday and he held out hopes that the censorship office would not see the subtleties of the book. I hope he's right, but I would have thought that that they would almost certainly censor it. Wouldn't you? That would be sad for Ethiopia. However we are quite confident that we will sell reasonable amounts elsewhere. (JC to DW 13 October 1972)

Bereket H. Sellassie certainly spoke from inside experience. We had recently published in 1970 his pioneering study *The Executive in African Government* in which he attacked what he called 'neo-presidentialism', which was spreading through the continent. He was involved in drafting the charter of the Organisation of African Unity. He had been a supreme court judge and acting attorney-general of Ethiopia. That had not saved him from being considered suspect on the question of the independence of Eritrea from Ethiopia. He had been taken in the middle of the night to the office of a high-ranking executive in the imperial administration. This man did not look at him as he was brought into his office and for an hour or more just went on working on his papers before he started to interrogate him. Soon afterwards Bereket H. Sellassie left the country. He pointed out to me on a visit in October 1972 that the previous time he had come to the Heinemann office in London he had been chauffeured in the sleek embassy car. He was touched that we welcomed him as a hero.

The Thirteenth Sun was published in 1973, and it was still not clear in early 1974 whether it would be censored in Ethiopia. When I arrived for a visit to Addis Ababa in February 1974 there were the first demonstrations of what turned out to be the revolution. In March I was writing to Bob Markham telling him that *The Sunday Times* in London was saying that the censorship was in disarray. I asked whether he could get some copies of Daniachew Worku's book in from Nairobi, if necessary on consignment, which would mean that the books were sent at our risk and if they were confiscated we would not get paid:

> The only way the book can be known is to take advantage of the irregularities of the situation. Mrs. Omara, at the United Nations bookshop, told me she has sold her 24 copies just like that, under the counter. (JC to Bob Markham 12 March 1974)

I had a letter from Sahle Sellassie dated 14 August 1974 asking when *Warrior King* would be published. He was glad to have heard from me that in the early stages of the revolution Heinemann was selling more of our Ethiopian books, especially in Asmara. He told me that Meno bookshop had a display of *The Afersata*. The main reason for writing was:

> It might interest you to know that his imperial Majesty Haile Sellassie I has had his autobiography published in Amharic – a very readable book in two volumes entitled *My Life and Ethiopia's Progress*. The first part deals with his early life and his rise to power. The second volume is almost entirely devoted to the period of the fascist occupation of Ethiopia, and the Emperor's diplomatic struggles with the defunct League of Nations. The second volume will be of great interest to the British public because a major part deals with the Emperor's life in exile [1936–1941], in Bath, and the great role of the British government in the Ethiopian liberation movement ... I would be interested in translating it into English if it is not yet translated. (SS to JC 14 August 1974)

A month later on 12 September 1974 the Emperor was deposed.

From King Solomon & the Queen of Sheba

Bahru Zewde gives a moving account of the events of 1974 in the second edition of *A History of Modern Ethiopia 1855–1991* (James Currey, Addis Ababa University Press and Ohio University Press 2001. It should be noted that in the quotes from this book Bahru Zewde uses more exact, if less common, transliterations of 'Derg' as 'Darg' and of 'Mengistu' as 'Mangistu'):

> The revolution erupted suddenly in February 1974, surprising both the

regime and its opponents. It started with the promise and buoyancy of spring. It ended with the sombre darkness of winter. What looked like an unassailable edifice cracked and buckled under the massive assault of a popular upsurge that involved students, factory workers, civil servants, soldiers and religious minorities. The cabinet reshuffle that the regime initiated as a placatory measure could hardly contain the storm. In the heady atmosphere that prevailed, the idea of smooth transition that the Endalkachaw cabinet could be said to have represented had few supporters. Much as the students had been the chief inspiration behind the revolution, however, they could not direct it. By fits and starts the military, which was itself affected by the popular movement, gradually came to assume centre stage … (p. 273)

The ruler who had portrayed himself as the caring father of his people was now portrayed as a greedy tyrant. Finally on the night of 11 September, the ultimate act of vilification was perpetrated as the public was treated to a doctored edition of a famous film on the 1973 famine produced by Jonathan Dimbleby of Thames Television. A canny collage of royal feast and peasant famine drove home the emperor's alleged callousness to the suffering of his people. The following morning, representatives of the Darg went to the jubilee palace proclaiming his deposition. He was bundled off in a Volkswagen 'beetle' to his place of detention at the Fourth Division headquarters, the very birthplace of the Darg. Thus ended not only one of the longest and most remarkable reigns in Ethiopian history but also a dynasty that traced its origins to King Solomon and the Queen of Sheba. (p. 235)

Landing in a revolution

When I arrived on an Ethiopian Airlines flight on 19 February 1974 there were no boards up saying THIS IS DAY 2 OF THE REVOLUTION. *The East African Standard* that morning in Nairobi had said that the day before in Addis Ababa there had been a taxi drivers' and a teachers' strike and that there had been some disturbance. This sort of outbreak was not uncommon in Ethiopia at the time and Clare Currey and I gave no thought to cancelling our visit. At Addis Ababa airport I was chiefly concerned about the loss of my bag. Several other passengers had lost theirs also. I said, based on previous experience, that we had to demand to be taken out to the aircraft to look for the baggage ourselves. As the expert, I climbed up into the luggage belly of the airliner and found everybody else's luggage but not my own. Clare Currey arrived half an hour later on an Air India flight with my luggage (as parents of young children we had chosen to come by different flights). The taxi driver drove us like mad along a well lit but empty highway excitedly turning round to tell us, in as far as we could understand, that on the previous day any taxi which moved had been stoned. What we did understand was his noisy imitation of the firing of guns, which had been the response of the police and soldiers. He drove us to the Ghion Imperial Palace

Hotel, which lived up to its name as it really was in the grounds of the royal palace and stood between the house and the royal stables. Our contacts told us on the phone that the situation was unpredictable. During the humid night we were awoken by a sound like an explosion and the drone of an aeroplane. It turned out to have been a crash of thunder.

On Saturday morning I rang up Richard and Rita Pankhurst about their invitation to lunch at their home. Richard Pankhurst told us that there had been shooting at the nearby police barracks during the previous night but that he would pick us up at midday. He strongly advised us to stay in the hotel but that, if we went out, not to go to the *mercato*, the picturesque market area which was much visited by tourists. We were expecting David Beer, an American lecturer from the department of English at Haile Sellassie I University. He took us out shouting above the roar of his Volkswagen beetle, 'These are great days. If I hear shooting I get into the car and go and see what is happening.' He took us straight off to the *mercato* which was sunny, calm and empty. We did not dare confess to this visit at the Pankhursts' traditional Ethiopian lunch. Late that afternoon we were again collected from our hotel by Merid Wolde Aregay, a historian from the emperor's university. Where did he take us? Straight back to the *mercato*. It was no longer quiet. Rivers of people poured down every street and it was hard to keep track of Merid Wolde Aregay. He was very excited. Everybody was very excited. He was heading for the elegant white modern market building which had been erected by the Italians. People were standing crowded around an outside flight of steps. The noise level rose. Women began to ululate and Merid Wolde Aregay said excitedly: 'It's the emperor!' Haile Sellassie was making his first public appearance since the disturbances. The crowd roared their welcome and he threw clouds of bank notes which fluttered like butterflies into the upstretched hands. (The emperor on his public appearances always did cast money into the crowds. According to Clare Currey we did not see this casting of *birr* to the populace and I have put the image into my memory because of other written accounts such as that by Gunnar Poulsen.) It was day 3 of the revolution.

Merid Wolde Aregay picked us up before dawn on Sunday and together with Richard Caulk, who taught history at the university, drove us in the dark up into the bowl of hills which rises above the street-lit city of Addis Ababa. He took us to Entoto Mariam, the nineteenth-century capital of Emperor Menelik, who defeated the Italians at the battle of Adwa in 1896. We reached the church in a brilliant freezing highland dawn. We stood in bare feet inside the round church with our backs to the whitewashed wall of the outer circle. We were within a ring of men in the white traditional garb of long white tunic over white trousers. Everybody was gathered as normal as they had done deep into the Christian history of the country. Remote, but within sight below, was the modern capital waking up to day 4 of the revolution.

Monday was full of publishing appointments. Daniachew Worku had kindly lent me his large American car for the day to go round the town. He gave me the keys, showed me the gears and flipped open the glove pocket. 'There's a revolver!' I did the rounds of the bookshops and the Ministry of Education. It was a normal first day of the working week. At dinner in a restaurant, with Sahle Sellassie and Daniachew Worku, we were told by the manager at about half past eight that there had been news and that they must close immediately. Day 5 of the revolution.

Clare Currey had rearranged our schedule. We had planned to fly north to Axum, ancient capital and home of the remarkable stone stele, and then on to Lalibela with its churches cut out of the rock. In the circumstances we flew in an ancient Dakota direct to Lalibela. The Ethiopian pilot brought us in skilful circles down through the mountains and we landed on a dusty strip. The hotel in the hills had been designed by the emperor's grand-daughter, Hirut, and was in the same traditional round form of the church at Entoto Mariam. The word 'monolithic' might have been specially invented for the churches sculpted out of the living rock. Their cruciform shapes are conceived downwards from the rock surface with substantial surrounding areas within 10-metre rock walls where white-robed church processions can circulate. The churches had the self-confident calm of Christian history. Day 6 of the revolution.

On the Wednesday we were to fly on to Asmara, in what is now the separate country of Eritrea, to join next day the Ethiopian Airlines flight for London. After breakfast in the princess's round dining room we were told calmly by the Ethiopian Airlines man that we were to be taken back to Addis Ababa for a night at the Ghion Imperial before being put on the same flight at its origin. He told us calmly that there was a strike at the airport at Asmara. Certainly a strike sounded less worrying than the mutiny by soldiers that it really was. We sat in the large round room for the morning. I was interested in listening to a group of four or five hotel staff who were clustered round a battered copy of John Gunther's *Inside Africa*. They were intently discussing in English why Ethiopia was at the bottom of all the economic tables. They suddenly all stood up together and I assumed they were going off to organise lunch. At midday I heard from the kitchens the call sign of 'Lillibullero' from the BBC Africa Service. It was perhaps better for our nerves that we did not hear what they were saying about the situation in Addis. The sound of the Dakota eventually came echoing through the mountains and a man with a bugle scared the birds and animals off the landing strip. Day 7 of the revolution.

The bus from the Ghion Imperial to the airport had broken windows down one side and when we got to departures it was crowded with anxious people and piles of baggage. Fortunately we were in the calm hands of Ethiopian Airways and the flight for London took off on time. We were in the insulated capsule of the best African airline. The airport was closed later that morning. We were out on Day 8 of the revolution. We arrived just too late to vote in the British general election when Harold Wilson replaced Edward Heath. Our young son and daughter knew more about what was happening in Ethiopia than we did, thanks to the children's television programmes John Craven's News Round and Blue Peter, which had raised money for the famine in Wollo Province the previous year. Mary Dyson's husband Paulos Abraham was for a short time later in that revolutionary year made deputy-governor of the drought-stricken northern provinces where there had been accounts of landlords' barns full of grain. Mary Dyson says she remembers him describing 'how appalled he was to see a mother fighting for a meagre few grains' (MD to JC 15 November 2006).

On 1 December 1974 near the end of the year of revolution I received a letter from Sahle Sellassie. He was able to tell me that an order for 1,000 copies of *Warrior King* had arrived:

> I am still working on *The Convict of Kerchelay* ... It is set against the background of events in Ethiopia between June and September 1974, i.e. the second phase of the Ethiopian peaceful revolution. However the events serve me only as background to the story. I am concentrating more on the plot and the characterisation. I believe I have created one of the great villains of African literature to date in the person of Ato Kebret. The protagonist is called Bezuneh, a young man who falls victim of a vicious official. But I will send you a more detailed account of the story when I will have completed the book ...
>
> Things have certainly become easier for Ethiopian writers to write and publish books, since last February, And there is great interest to read among the general public. But there is no law abolishing censorship. Of late, however, people are becoming more cautious once again because of the turn of events. The sudden execution of sixty detained officials made many people wonder what was to happen next. (SS to JC 1 December 1974)

At that very same time Mangistu had eliminated his rival, General Aman Andom. As Bahru Zewde says in *A History of Modern Ethiopia*, 'Mangistu went ahead to eliminate one rival after another with nauseating regularity' (p. 230).

> What is more there is something inexorable about the rise of the obscure major to absolute, not to say *total*, power. Partly, it had to with the deep authoritarian traditions of the country, which was more conducive to the emergence of a strong man than the collective leadership the Darg aspired to give at the beginning. In the absence of any liberal democratic legacy, it is not surprising that the autocratic emperor was replaced by the totalitarian dictator. Marxist-Leninist orthodoxy on the fertile bed of Christian orthodoxy provided the requisite ideological recipe. The parallels with Russia are very striking in this respect. Both countries had a strong orthodox as well as imperial tradition. And in both instances, revolutions sprouted dictators. (p. 249)

The writing had started with 'the promise and buoyancy of spring'. We were never to publish another novel by an Ethiopian in the African Writers Series. Almost twenty years later in 1993 *The Case of the Socialist Witchdoctor and Other Stories* by Hama Tuma was published in the Series with an introduction by Ngũgĩ. It is thus a special pleasure that, under my own imprint, there are two editions of the distinguished history of his country by Bahru Zewde who, like many others, was to suffer imprisonment under Mangistu.

PUBLISHING

Nuruddin Farah

Nuruddin Farah was born in Somalia in 1945. His first novel *From a Crooked Rib* (1970) showed a particular sensitivity to the position of women in a Muslim society. *A Naked Needle* (1976) was full of daring experiment. The first two novels were published in paperback in the African Writers Series and not in hardback. He was determined to become established in the international literary market and held off the publication of his next books in the African Writers Series until his newly appointed agent, with active help from Keith Sambrook and myself, sold the hardback rights. Allison and Busby published hardbacks of *Sweet and Sour Milk* (1979), *Sardines* (1981) and *Close Sesame* (1983) with the undertaking that paperback publication in the African Writers Series would follow. This 'mature and complex' trilogy, as *The Companion* described it, is about the realities of a Soviet-guided dictatorship in Siyad Barre's Mogadishu.

He explained to me early on: 'And after all, I am nothing but a Somali nomad' (11 May 1970). He rejected state employment in Somalia and was one of the first writers from Africa to set out to support himself as much as possible by his writing. He moved from country to country, sometimes teaching, always writing. He has continued to write with a professional intensity and to have his work published, reviewed and win prizes in Europe and the US. Simon Gikandi said perceptively on reading the manuscript of *Sardines* in 1981:'I honestly think Farah will become one of the great masters of the African novel.'

From a Crooked Rib
(1970 AWS 80)

Nuruddin Farah has always been amused that, when in 1968 he submitted the manuscript of *From a Crooked Rib*, I asked him whether he was a woman. The writer had certainly portrayed the heroine Ebla with a female sensitivity. I was taken with her spirit when she argued, after taking a second husband to escape her arranged marriage, that she was only following the custom of men in a Muslim society who could choose to have more than one wife

I was so excited the evening I read the manuscript that I took it to bed, to the annoyance of Clare Currey who objected to the noise of turning manuscript pages. I was still reading it on the tube the next morning when Keith Sambrook happened to join the same train. I could share with him my enthusiasm for this script, which raised so many questions about polygamous marriage, female circumcision and divorce.

Nuruddin Farah was also entertained by me interrogating him as to whether he was an African. Again I had reason to ask. He wrote from

Chandigarh in the Punjab. To be included in the African Writers Series at that time a writer was supposed to have been born in Africa. The boundary was geographical and not racial and, with near complete success, we did spot attempts by writers to cross with false passports. (One American sent a photo of his Ugandan servant with his script.) Nuruddin Farah wrote to me on 18 September 1968: 'I am an African native from Somalia – and I am 22 years old – presently I am in India.' He went on with firm confidence to say: 'I am a writer – I've written three novels and about a dozen short stories – and am at present writing a novel in verse.' He did not mention that he also wrote plays.

Sadly the reports for *From a Crooked Rib* are not in the file. I do not remember that they suggested much work, which was in marked contrast to his later novels where a succession of readers with widely varying views honed his professionalism. We tried to get William Heinemann to accept it for publication in hardback but Roland Gant, the editorial director, told Keith Sambrook:

> I think a tremendous amount of work will be necessary on this book if it is to be published as anything more than an anthropological curiosity and as it stands it is not very easy to read. (Roland Gant to KS 1 August 1969)

(It can be imagined that Keith Sambrook and I felt a particular pleasure when it was accepted in 2002 for Penguin Modern Classics.)

I wrote to Nuruddin Farah on 7 August 1969 to accept it. I clearly should have sent the edited manuscript back to him because he was to rewrite a great deal on proof and, in those expensive days of printers moving individual pieces of lead monotype by tweezer, he had exceeded his correction allowance of 10 per cent of the setting costs.

A photograph of the author always appeared on the back cover of the Series. There was no doubt that black faces on the orange covers gave people in Africa the confidence to start writing. Nuruddin Farah was resistant to having his photograph on the back:

> I must declare immediately that there are three institutions which I hate: Barbers, Doctors, and Photographers. But in spite of it I managed to collect myself together and get a photo taken. (NF to Ann Scorgie 11 June 1970)

The question of a photograph came up again in a more serious manner with his third novel when he thought that he ought to use a pseudonym as the regime in Somalia had become more and more repressive.

Regular letters came from Nuruddin Farah after his return to Mogadishu. He told me on 9 July 1970: 'My degree has been issued to me. After all the rigmarole. A degree worth a denaar. To say that I am "educated".' Very few young writers, whether in Europe or Africa, manage to survive without some sort of income from a salaried job. He reflected on whether to take the offers of a professional career in education or whether to devote all his time to writing.

> Besides there is a possibility of my being transferred to the College of Education where I shall teach Creative Writing something. Can one teach another to write? I wonder. Did you receive my letter from Addis Ababa?
>
> The novel is forming in my mind. It comes little by little and there are so many things to attend to, and there are so many things one should read. The reason I don't wish to be transferred to the University College is that I won't have any time to write. Peccato. (NF to JC 18 July 1970)

He was already sensing that if he took a job in the government's education service he would accept patronage that could compromise what he needed to say about his country. Early on he had a firm view of himself as a wandering writer drawing on a wider world, even if his work was to reflect on his own African society.

> I am sorry I keep moving from one place to another. All the correspondence is forwarded to me; that is the best part of it. And after all, I am nothing but a Somali nomad. (NF to JC 11 May 1970)

The news of the arrival of the advance copy of his first published novel was prefaced by news of an early penalty for his restless style of life:

> My wife has gone back to India and I am alone with my son. Terrible mess ain't it?
>
> Crooked came, beautifully bound, the cover cunningly attractive, etc. The Ministry of Education is presently considering it for a textbook. But … y'know, I have misgivings about novels being used as textbooks. (NF to JC 26 November 1970)

After the excitement of the first novel he felt himself neglected by his publishers and by me in particular. This was the result of his changes of address. Several of my letters had not reached him and his first bite of what he called 'royalty meat' had accidentally gone to his previous bank in India. No letter from me had reached him since February 1971 and so he wrote in December to Tony Beal, the managing director, reminding him of the option clause in the contract binding the author to offer his next work to the publisher, and threatening not to send the manuscript of his second novel *A Naked Needle*. He quoted Clause 18:

> If however the publishers decline the first of these works the author shall not be bound to offer them the second. SILENCE IS REFUSAL! (NF to Tony Beal 19 December 1971)

Nuruddin Farah was very pleased when he heard from Tony Beal by return:

> Currey never answered questions pertaining to money matters; he always ignored. The idiot I am thought there was something big in store, and I waited for Godot, and as usual Godot never comes

> in time. If he ever comes. And certainly, sir, I don't feel neglected or unhappy, as you wrote in your letter, but I feel terribly disappointed. Not for the money part of the deal. But about something that no one wishes to say, whatever that something is. But before I forget, I must say how thankful I am to you for having written immediately you got my letter. The gesture is worth a great deal in itself alone.
>
> Query, a question that one must ask oneself is: Does your royalty department send statements, advances, etc to Kwame Nkhruma care of the Osayegefo Presidential palace near Legon still? And what about Mboya? Do they send him care of the Government Road in Nairobi? Or have they updated their data? I hope they have, because if they haven't, nobody will have no more faith in your house. (NF to Tony Beal 8 January 1972)

Tony Beal, relieved about this joke about dead Heinemann authors, replied:

> I must say that our royalty department normally functions most efficiently. They don't send Kwame Nkrumah's royalties to the Presidential Palace in Ghana because he always insisted that they be paid into his (Russian) bank account in London. Sensible man. (Tony Beal to NF 12 January 1972)

Early that year Nuruddin Farah and I both hoped that we had re-established our original happy relationship, but there is a postcard dated 19 September 1973 from Hungary complaining that I had not answered a cable from Moscow: 'My God, What's your summery-silence coming to? Nothing's impossible y'know.' I replied: 'Communication with Russia seems to be as irregular as with Somalia.'

A Naked Needle

(1976 AWS 184)

Author and publisher both get nervous about second novels. Nuruddin Farah had had the encouragement of good reviews for his first novel. The manuscript of *A Naked Needle* was much more ambitious. I told him firmly on 26 September 1972, 'We shall certainly accept.' It was to take four years of work before it was published in 1976.

A year later on 11 October 1973 I told him of the opinions we had received from Ros de Lanerolle and Richard Lister:

> 'Immense merit', 'very impressed', 'penetrating insight', 'unusual and interesting' are some of the phrases you will find buried in the reports of *A Naked Needle*. There is no doubt we ought to publish it. It would not be impossible to publish it as it is. You have gone a long way since *A Crooked Rib* and you are pushing your writing

> to its limits. This is as it should be. But you have lost a lot of the clarity and brilliance of your first novel, especially in the opening movement but also in the conclusion. Conscious literary obscurity is a difficult thing to deal with and one wouldn't be without James Joyce …
>
> First movement: I really want you to work on this … But I do think you would be grossly unfair on your readers if you make them wade through this before getting on to a comprehensible book. In fact most of them will get left behind. Novel reading, even for intellectuals, should not just be a duty …
>
> I said that this letter would be disappointing because I had hoped that this revised version would be immediately acceptable. But it is the first time we have seen the full novel and one can never judge a novel properly unless completed.
>
> I must emphasise that we rarely get reports which are so unanimously full of praise, even though there is an apparent concentration on the criticism …
>
> I am convinced that you are among a small band of really talented writers and I hope that you will view all our criticisms with the realisation that we are expecting the highest achievements from you. (JC to NF 11 October 1973)

There is a sequence of three reports over a period of three years from Ros de Lanerolle. Her dialogue with Nuruddin Farah contributed to his perseverance in working and reworking the manuscript. 'More ambitious book than his first, but I think impressive', she says in 1972. A year later she asks:

> Is it not a politically perilous act to publish a book so full of hate and disillusion, if author continues to live in Somalia?
>
> Can he work on it further, cutting ruthlessly and clarifying? Particularly the last part. His writing is much too self-indulgent … Or am I making too much of the obscurity/confusion? (Report signed under maiden name Rosalynde Ainslie 5 June 1973)

The dangers of getting an author to rewrite appear. Ros de Lanerolle in her third report (30 April 1974) has 'the faint reservation that Nancy came over better in the first draft'.

Richard Lister, who had helped Bessie Head with such great sensitivity, turned against the book from the time of his original report dated 11 July 1973. In 1975 he says in reporting on the finally revised manuscript which had been sent by Nuruddin Farah for preparation for press:

> I'm afraid I had to give up this one. I usually manage to plod along to the end out of respect for the author and sympathy with his strivings, but after making my way to the middle of this one I couldn't pursue it any further … I gather from my report on the

> original version that I found the central section fascinating, but was bothered by the beginning and the end. The central section seems to have vanished. (Report from Richard Lister 15 April 1975)

In 1974 I had managed to persuade my colleagues in London to back this second book by a promising writer and to accept the book formally 'subject to a little further work'. Henry Chakava, soon after he had joined Heinemann, confidently wrote to Nuruddin Farah saying that he had not found 'any more obscurity than intended by you' (HC to NF 27 February 1972).

A richly enthusiastic report arrived belatedly from Nigeria which must have encouraged Nuruddin Farah after all this time and all these opinions. Molara Ogundipe-Leslie, writer and academic, had been commissioned to do a report by Akin Thomas in Ibadan. On 11 September 1974 I scribbled across the edge of my request of 22 May 1974 to him: 'I'm desperate for reply. Farah is due in U.K. for a year and it will be most embarrassing to turn down if he's here. Please let me have your verdict.' On 11 October 1974 I was sent Molara Ogundipe-Leslie's powerful report:

> An intellectual novel about an intellectual's dilemma in Africa, the work should be published for several reasons. Firstly for its linguistic and presentational daredevilry; secondly for its intellectual interest, it is one of the few novels of modern Africa which handles ideas of politics and culture not in any masturbatory or exhibitionist way but in their concrete and human relevance as a spectrum of members of a given society. Here are characters who actually live through contemporary ideas of culture, politics, economics etc through contemporary issues, who do not only cerebrate about them as in *The Interpreters*. We see the characters here live in a concrete social and human context not in some intellectual limbo. I have found this novel enjoyable to read and I hope other readers will. It is one of the few genuinely global and non-parochial African novels in which the contemporary African experience is a felt and living reality. (Report by Molara Ogundipe-Leslie sent by Akin Thomas 11 October 1974)

Molara Ogundipe-Leslie, like Ros de Lanerolle, advised that we check 'with Farah which stylistic forms are deliberate usages'. I asked him about a certain word which Ros de Lanerolle had said did not appear in the dictionary. Nuruddin Farah asked which dictionary she had used. I pulled down *The Shorter Oxford English Dictionary* and sure enough there was this word, of which I too had never heard, which referred to equipment in a butcher's shop and which was used with savage exactness.

A Naked Needle was published in July 1976 with a launch at the Africa Centre in London. A hitch was that, having sold some 8,845 copies of the first printing of *From a Crooked Rib* we had run out of copies at a difficult moment and I had to appeal to Johnson Mugweru, the sales manager at Heinemann in Nairobi, who replied:

> We received the following cable from you: GRATEFUL AIRMAIL OR AIRFREIGHT IMMEDIATELY 20 COPIES YOUR STOCK FARAH CROOKED RIB FOR USE PUBLICITY LAUNCHING NAKED CURREY.
>
> What with crooked ribs and launching naked, the cable must have caused some anxiety to the telecommunications people. (Johnson Mugweru to JC 5 July 1976)

A review in *The Guardian* commented: 'The intelligence, sensitivity, and linguistic adventure of this novel make it a considerable achievement in any terms.' The reviewer was the South African writer and poet, C.J. Driver, who took the chance to say:

> Nuruddin Farah's *A Naked Needle* is No 184 in the Heinemann's African Writers Series, and offers a good excuse for celebrating a series which has given a wider audience in Europe, Africa and elsewhere to a huge range of African writing – novels, stories, poems, autobiography, biography, plays, polemic – including some writing of an imaginative and political urgency unlike some of the insipidities celebrated locally. Nuruddin Farah's second novel is itself a notable success, a witty, wordy, hilarious celebration of a modern African dilemma. (*The Guardian* 29 July 1976)

Nuruddin Farah described this review on 30 July 1976 as 'a relief offering'. However, after the publication of *A Naked Needle* he learnt that he was in danger of prison if he returned to his country. A play and a novel extract published in Somali had been declared seditious.

During the period when he was still in Mogadishu I tried to help Nuruddin Farah in practical ways over getting his plays performed and broadcast and this continued when he was at the University of Essex where one of his plays was produced. My advisers did not feel that his scripts had been tried and developed under the pressure of actual performance. Nuruddin Farah correctly felt that I was being less enthusiastic about his plays than I was about his fiction.

I sent his scripts to Gwynneth Henderson and Veronica Manoukian at the BBC Africa Service in Bush House. I was keen that he should have an agent but he sneered at the advice that John Bassett at Curtis Brown gave him. I was in touch with Bill McAllister whose Interaction was running an experimental festival in the summer in central London. I sent one of his scripts to Michael Etherton, who was producing plays in an open-air theatre at the University of Zambia. Nuruddin Farah, annoyed, tried to guess the identity of the reader.

> As to 'The Offering'. The philosophy of African Theatre. It read like a lecture in the class-room. Was it Cosmos Pietres [sic] who

> wrote it? Or Lewis Nkosi? My god! What a blunder. Look I am a dramatist, not a novelist, James. I feel this from the flow of my pen. Anyway I don't mean to offend. But the butchery of a theory of one's philosophy!! I had thought of Martin Esslin too, come to think of it. Like a man drowning who knows he can save himself if he shouts for help, but won't. 'Cause it is his philosophy not to. No offence, James. Just thinking to myself. (NF to JC 22 October 1973)

I replied with concern because I did not want to lose him as a novelist by offending him as a playwright:

> You may well prove us wrong on the play front. It may be that in the end you prove an even better dramatist than novelist. There is no doubt in my mind that your achievements so far as a novelist are greater than your achievements as a playwright. I am most interested to find out that you are certain that you are a dramatist. You are a novelist. The one does not exclude the other. I did have two people read 'The Offering'. They were neither Cosmo Pieterse nor Lewis Nkosi. Your confidence in your own ability gives me hope that I am wrong. Let me have your revised 'A Dagger in Vacuum' and I'll give it to somebody else to read. I am sorry that the report read like a lecture in the classroom. Your reaction is absolutely right. If you are convinced of your own ability in the end then you will get published. But the question I want to ask you above all is how much performance has there been of your plays? In the end a play must work as a dramatic exercise. Then you can say whatever you like. It doesn't matter what philosophy of African theatre our readers have. If you can say the thing in effective dramatic terms then that is fine. Speeches are useless. In a conversation between two people you can get across far more. I know that you are such a good writer that you can turn your hand to playwrighting I am sure, and I am willing to help you. (JC to NF 31 October 1973)

Sweet & Sour Milk

Allison and Busby hardback 1979 (1980 AWS 226)

Nuruddin Farah had two particular concerns about *Sweet and Sour Milk*. One was that it should appear in hardback and the other was that it should appear under a pseudonym. Nobody has portrayed for me so well the mechanics of personal association by which dictators, whether Siyad Barre, Robert Mugabe or Saddam Hussein, control the social fabric of a country through the threat of fear. My acceptance letter shows these concerns:

> I am delighted to be able to give you formal confirmation of our definite acceptance of *Sweet and Sour Milk* for the African Writers Series. We should like to be able to publish it in hardback as well and will allow for this possibility in the contract. However I have explained our policy to you. I think as soon as we have the finally edited manuscript we ought to try William Heinemann. For special reasons I have little hope of the value of an approach to Secker and Warburg. As you know we are reluctant to issue hardbacks ourselves …
>
> Regretfully we should accept the necessity for publication under the pseudonym of Ahmed Mohammed although rather doubtful of the effectiveness of this cover …
>
> I am attaching a publicity questionnaire as usual. Please concoct an imaginary biography. We shall keep your photograph off *A Naked Needle* in the hope that the absence of a photograph on *Sweet and Sour Milk* looks less strange. Alternatively we could use the photograph [by George Hallett] of the guy with the Afro hair-do who appears on the front of *Naked Needle.* (JC to NF 18 February 1976)

One of our in-house editors, Ingrid Crewdson, wrote to me in Nigeria on 25 February 1976 to say that she knew I would be pleased that Nuruddin Farah had decided to continue to use his own name. On 4 March 1976 he came in to discuss the Heinemann offer with Keith Sambrook and wrote to me on 10 March 1970 that he would await my return to London; he was most unhappy that Heinemann would not publish in hardback:

> Keith and I talked for almost one and a half hours that Thursday afternoon. Keith and I talked in circles, we talked about circles – in effect which circle a man of my background and standing should belong to and why. We talked about economics, we talked about royalties, we talked about advances, and we laid our cards on the table. We dwelled a little on policies (your house's not liking to do hard-covers) and we also talked about the possibilities or lack of possibility of William Heinemann's or Andre Deutsch's interest in doing *Sweet and Sour Milk.* That must have been the moment when … Keith and I talked about agents. I said that I would use the services of an agent.
>
> I…!
>
> I made it absolutely clear that that should not be taken as an act of aggression on my part or that approaching an agent should not be interpreted as my saying, 'I am quite dissatisfied with the way you've handled my work.' Of course, I have one or two things I would have wished to be looked into again. All the same …
>
> Keith and I talked about rising royalties. We talked about

exploring together possibilities of getting Crooked and Naked translated into Italian (which to my way of thinking is as important in Somalia as getting the book out in the first place). And we talked about risks. But, James – all my life has been risk at any rate. Why should my contacting or using an agent be a graver risk? My writing the novel – isn't that a risk? My wanting to publish the novel – isn't that another? I remember very many things that were said either by Keith (who has been ever so kind, patient and understanding) or by myself (a man immersed in the deepest shadow of an undefined fear). But I do not remember my saying that …

A.D. Peters & Co of 10 Buckingham Street, London WC2 are from this moment on the agents who will represent me, and negotiate on my behalf. And by copy of this letter, I authorise A.D. Peters & Co, hereafter my agents, to place the manuscript of *Sweet & Sour Milk* with a hardback publisher. Barring other unforeseen technicalities, I want you to know that H.E.B. will be informed before sale of paper-back rights is concluded with another house.

However, I do hope that From a Crooked Rib and Naked Needle will prosper under the new format and that our relationship will survive the agonies of seasons and snowless months. (NF to JC 10 March 1976 All the ellipses at the end of paragraphs are those used by NF and do not signify that text has been left out.)

Keith Sambrook had written an internal memo to colleagues after his visit:

Of course he's right to hope for a hardback and complain that we don't do one ourselves or manage to persuade some other publisher to do so. But the reality of the position is that hardback publishers want <u>all</u> the rights even if they publish a relatively unknown Somali writer anyway. The fact that his stuff is 100% better than much they <u>do</u> publish is understandably discouraging but true. (KS to Elizabeth Ledermann and Susie Home 4 March 1976)

What is sad is that Nuruddin Farah had not got his courage together in the one and half hours to say that he had already found a good agent. Keith Sambrook would have been as delighted as myself. We had gone as far as we could do in nursing a promising writer.

However, Sheila McIlwraith at A.D. Peters found it no easier than we did to place this novel with a general publisher. After a year in March 1977 I had suggested that it might be sensible to publish in the African Writers Series for Africa only. His agent replied:

The typescript is currently being considered by Rex Collings, and there are still a number of hardback houses who haven't seen the novel which I feel will be interested in it.

> As I expect you know, Nuruddin is adamant that there should be a hardback first. (Sheila McIlwraith to JC 14 March 1977)

Two further years later, in 1979, Henry Chakava wrote to me from Nairobi:

> I remember reading this most interesting novel [*Sweet and Sour Milk*] and most enthusiastically recommending for publication in the AWS.
>
> This has not appeared anywhere and I do not see any advance publicity information about it. What could have happened to Nuruddin and his surrealistic novel? (Henry Chakava to JC 20 April 1979)

I annotated this memo: 'Allison and Busby are doing a hardback and that may do it some good. They have a good record of winning prizes. We shall issue the paperback next year. They are sharing setting costs. A & B have been terribly slow. It's taken 2/3 years to get this far.'

In a letter from Los Angeles about potential reviewers for *Sweet and Sour Milk*, Nuruddin Farah, having successfully delayed the African Writers Series and his agent having failed to place an American edition, tells me that all his friends are asking when the book is coming out in paperback:

> Good thing is that Watson HEB US and I have been speaking on the phone and has been ever so co-operative and punctual. I am impressed ... But that HEB in Canada don't want to provide the books asked for. There have been complaints in this regard. I wonder if you can do anything. And next time you write or speak to Henry Chakava kindly tell him to remember the name of Farah when compiling for bibliographical works a list of books of authors in East Africa. It is annoying to be deliberately omitted from every goddam list. I bet he won't even bother having S&S reviewed in the Kenyan press. (NF to JC 8 January 1980).

The criticism of his long-time supporter Henry Chakava explains the slightly laboured defence I wrote in February 1980:

> You will be surprised to hear that despite the conspiracy between Henry and myself and every other member of Heinemann not to sell *Naked Needle* we are actually reprinting. We will get the quote from *The Scotsman* on the back [by another supporter Angus Calder] and put the biographical material at the bottom.
>
> *Sweet & Sour Milk* will certainly not be on the stand at the Nice Commonwealth Literature Conference. Neither will Mongo Beti nor Senghor. Poor sods didn't have the benefit of being in the Commonwealth. Or do we treat British Somalia as an honorary member? As you know perfectly well we did make the mistake of getting some copies to Berlin. We do our best not to sell your book.

> I am terribly sorry but we have ruined the front cover of *Sweet and Sour Milk* by putting a photograph by George Hallett on it …
>
> You must remember that we are not even in a position to sell the book in Britain, Europe and America until November this year, due to our agreement with Allison & Busby. Anyhow we go ahead and print it fairly soon and get copies out to Africa even if we only officially publish the book in November. (JC to NF 18 February 1980)

Nuruddin Farah moved to the new University of Jos in Nigeria, which had also appointed Ali Mazrui as Visiting Professor. A postcard in March 1982, only a month before the Nigerian foreign exchanges closed, said:

> *Sweet & Sour Milk* copies have turned up and they are easily available; and I am content to give you the news. So are *Crooked* & *Naked*. Aig and Akin have delivered the goods. They've also flooded the 'walls' with 82-calendars and Hallet's portraits the size of his ego. (NF to JC March 1982)

Nuruddin Farah's patience in his long wait over the publication of his third novel was an important statement in his justified ambition to be accepted as a writer and not just as an African writer. As I hope has become apparent, this was equally our aim and we set out to co-operate with our most outstanding writers to provide bridges for recognition by reviewers, agents and general hardback publishers in Britain and the US – and by international prizes.

> May peace prevail – may reason and truth reign! … Twice, three times, ten? May peace prevail.
>
> In a letter I am not quite sure if I posted I gave you the good news that *Sweet & Sour Milk* has won the English-Speaking Literary Union and the prize money which is $2000 is really handy in this lean year of Khomeinis and Afghanistan and American paranoia. (NF to JC 30 January 1980)

Sardines

Allison & Busby hardback 1981 (1982 AWS 252)

> I honestly think Farah will become one of the great masters of the African novel. For me *Sardines* comes as a pleasant surprise. I left off Farah after reading *From a Crooked Rib* and *The Naked Needle* which were not so strong in comparison with other urban novels, but I seemed to have missed the potential that was evident in them. In *Sardines*, Farah brings to the African novel complexity and a consciousness of style unrivalled, except by that Soyinkan creation, *The Interpreters*. (Undated report by Simon Gikandi 1981)

This was the first opinion from Simon Gikandi after he went to Edinburgh to work for his doctorate on the novels of Fielding.

There are politically correct accusations that Heinemann imposed 'metropolitan standards' on the African Writers Series (p. 23). The files on the first four novels by Nuruddin Farah show that the assessments from Africa were the ones which swung the balance for publication. Henry Chakava, as a new recruit, was immediately confident in his support. Molara Ogundipe-Leslie from Ibadan spoke forcefully for *A Naked Needle*. And now Simon Gikandi began to provide many of the most perceptive and imaginative reports we had ever had.

Nuruddin Farah's *Sardines* would have been rejected if I had only presented the British reports to my colleagues. Richard Lister, the English novelist, had been important in encouraging Bessie Head over *A Question of Power*; however, he dismissed the first draft of *Sardines* as 'exploratory notes for a novel, of intolerable wordiness'(29 February 1980). John Wyllie, the Canadian detective-story writer sent his first report on Nuruddin Farah's manuscript. In it he said that 'there is no way in which the work could be published because it would need too much editing.' His opinion on the reworked manuscript was reserved:

> First after a very careful reading, the good points. A sensitivity which suggests that the author may not be a man, as the name Nuruddin suggests, but a woman using a pen name....
>
> The book has been very extensively re-worked ... and lengthened ... and I suspect the author goes about making a revision in the same compulsive way Marechera does. Perhaps a kinder parallel would be with Tom Wolfe, the First, (Look Homeward Angel) who needed the benevolent and understanding Maxwell Perkins to deliver him from his verbosity and his compunction to let words breed words and ideas until he wound up lost in infinity. In any case, the re-working has improved the MS very considerably by giving it a definable image and aim, one that the reader can trace, albeit with some difficulty, all the way through the book.
>
> Finally, 'Sardines' (still, I think, a ridiculous title) suggests, as no book I have read before does the intriguing (in two senses) intricacies, dangers and discomforts of life in the current Somalian dictatorship. (Report by John Wyllie 2 December 1980)

Simon Gikandi was annoyed by John Wyllie's report:

> This is definitely a book in the best sense of the word, and any attempts to deny it that quality leave me quite apprehensive because Farah made a very conscious effort to rescue the African novel from the limits of particularity and locality. *Sardines* is not just a novel about Somalia and Africa but also about the third world dilemma. In this respect, it is an important addition to the

> growing voices against tyranny in the body of literature unique in its universal application. The superficial expression of this important upturn is the 'troubadour' nature of the characters who, homeless and symbolically orphaned, roam across the whole breadth of Europe looking for a place to nest. These 'homeless' characters have already become legends in the black American novel ... These characters are like sardines compressed by the emergent African tyrant at home (the General in Farah's novel) and the intellectual arrogance of Europe (represented by Sandra in the novel). The title of the novel is hence ... pretty! ...
>
> We certainly get lost in the narrative at times, but once we have grasped the underlying stream of ideas, we find a way out of the labyrinth ...
>
> Editorial slimming? It would do the novel some good. The hatchet of a 'ruthless-to-be-kind' editor? Please no! If this work is mutilated, it will become as fetid as the abandoned corpse of a stillborn monster child. (Second report by Simon Gikandi 1981)

The trilogy *Variations on the Theme of an African Dictatorship* was completed with *Close Sesame* which was published in hardback by Allison and Busby in 1983 but, in the worsening financial situation, did not appear in the African Writers Series.

Nuruddin Farah has worked with great determination to become internationally accepted and in this he was actively supported by Keith Sambrook and myself. The African Writers Series and the support of his fellow Africans gave him a start. Simon Gikandi in his reports compared Nuruddin Farah with writers across the whole world of literature: Infante Cabrera, Wole Soyinka, Carlos Fuentes, James Baldwin, Dambudzo Marechera and John Williams. Unfortunately William Heinemann considered his first book 'an anthropological curiosity' and would not publish a hardback edition. After a second title came out in an African Writers Series paperback only, he found an agent who arranged hardback publication, before paperback publication in the Series. His more recent work has been published in London and New York and in 2007 Penguin in the US listed six of his titles as available in general market paperback. His work has been translated into Italian and other languages and in 1998 he won the Neustadt International Prize for Literature.

English is only Nuruddin Farah's fourth language, but London provided a crossroads for this nomad. Through polyglot English he could address his fellow Africans and, increasingly, an audience outside the continent. Somalia is at the crossroads of the Islamic world, but politics largely removed the possibility of Nuruddin Farah talking to his countrymen in his first three languages of Somali, Arabic and Italian.

6 *Arab Authors in* EGYPT & SUDAN

What were contemporary writers doing in Arabic? There was evidence that well-established writers in English wanted to find out. The novelist John Fowles said in 1978 in his introduction to Naguib Mahfouz's *Miramar*: 'Of all the world's considerable contemporary literature, that in Arabic must easily be the least known, which is one very good reason why the Arab mind remains something of a mystery to Westerners' (p. vii). Kingsley Amis reviewed regularly for the Arabic Service of the BBC in the 1960s. He compared Tayeb Salih's *Wedding of Zein* favourably with contemporary British fiction. He was enthusiastic about Fathy Ghanem's *The Man Who Lost His Shadow* (1980 AWS 223 + 1980 AA 14) though, with typical liverishness, he objected to us quoting him on the back cover when we included the book in the Arab Authors series. This novel, about the rise of a young and ambitious Cairo journalist, was remarkable for the way in which you discover in each of four parts that you have been there before and that you are seeing the same events again through the eyes of four different characters; this device had been used before in Arabic. Lawrence Durrell used the same technique in the four separate books of his *Alexandria Quartet* set in Egypt's fabled Mediterranean city. Did Durrell get this structural idea, which so impressed London reviewers, from Egyptian writing? He did not understand Arabic, but he could have got the concept through some of the literary chatter in Alexandria in French.

Arab Authors grew out of the African Writers Series. The first manuscript I ever showed to Chinua Achebe was *The Wedding of Zein* by the Sudanese writer Tayeb Salih. The short novel and stories had been translated by Denys Johnson-Davies who was to be described by the Palestinian writer Edward Said in *The Independent on Sunday* in 1990 as 'the leading Arabic-English translator of our time'. Arab Authors, which was Denys Johnson-Davies's idea, aimed to be a revelation of the realities of writing and publishing modern writing in Arabic. The series succeeded in giving an idea of what was being written in contemporary Arabic and of the struggles writers were having to fight against the religious and political establishments. Denys Johnson-Davies saw Heinemann's commitment to Arab Authors in a wider context:

> Arabs have, rightly, been disappointed with the one way stream in the so-called inter-traffic between East and West; some, in times when the

> relationships are strained, speak – again not unjustly – of cultural colonisation. Certainly in England our publishers, some of whom have done very well out of their markets in the Arab world, have shown great unwillingness to provide channels … (quoted from *Middle East International* in series publicity)

As so often in publishing, new projects take a long time to develop. In a sign-off paragraph of a letter dated 9 October 1970 Denys Johnson Davies said to me: 'Have you thought any more about producing an Arabic Writers Series?' The first three titles in Arab Authors were launched at the Cairo Book Fair in January 1976. Publication in London later in the year could be synchronised with the remarkable World of Festival of Islam which used the new oil wealth to introduce people in the West to the art, architecture and culture of a whole part of the world of which they remain so arrogantly dismissive. Jill Neville welcomed Arab Authors in a substantial review of all the first titles in *The Sunday Times*:

> The series should have the same success as Heinemann's Series on African writing. One is overwhelmed not by the awful spaces between Christian and Muslim sensibilities, but by their unexpected similarity at the deepest level. (*The Sunday Times* 2 May 1976)

After the oil price hikes of the 1970s there had been an increasing demand in the boom parts of the Arab world for books in English, especially among European expatriates. According to a member of the sales staff of Penguin, by the beginning of the 1980s Arab Authors came to occupy the key space on the fiction shelves in the Gulf.

Avoiding the African label

The African Writers Series set out to represent, through the medium of English, the best creative writing from the whole continent. Most of the titles published were originally written in English. So translations were an important way of giving some idea of what writing was also being published in other languages. Some writers – most notably Ngũgĩ and Mazisi Kunene – felt that they must write in their own languages and only, as a second stage, translate the work into English. We had tried, as the chapter on writing in Ethiopia shows (p. 145), to get Sahle Sellassie to translate novels which had been published in Amharic. There was a healthy input of writers in Portuguese. Some of the best writing from Africa south of the Sahara appeared in translations from French. There were only two examples of work by the distinguished Maghrebi writers who were frequently published in Paris; there was a novel *Heirs to the Past* (1972 AWS 79) by the Moroccan Driss Chraïbi and a collection of *North African Writing* (1970 AWS 73) translated and edited by Len Ortzen. Denys Johnson-Davies was certain that Arab Authors should only include translations from Arabic, as the Maghrebi writers, however distinguished, were despised in the Arab world for using French.

Egypt had by far the largest publishing industry in Africa. Yet there were only three token Egyptian titles in first 200 books in the first African Writers Series. There was a collection of plays, *The Fate of a Cockroach* (1973 AWS 117 + 1977 AA 1), by the leading Egyptian playwright Tewfik al-Hakim, who wrote plays which inspired comparison with Ionesco and who had a Cairo theatre named after him. The plays were translated by Denys Johnson-Davies with whom I had worked at Oxford University Press over the publication of Tewfik al-Hakim's *The Tree Climber.* There was also *Midaq Alley*, a novel by the popular novelist Naguib Mahfouz. Egypt tended to turn its back on Africa. There was no doubt that in the Arab world that the 'African' label on the Series was not an advantage.

Publishers in Britain had published remarkably few translations from Arabic for us to reissue in Arab Authors. The readable flow of Desmond Stewart's translation of Fathy Ghanem's ingenious *The Man Who Lost His Shadow,* which had been published by Chapman and Hall in 1966, made it a natural choice (p. 69). We included Taha Hussein's elegant autobiography *An Egyptian Childhood* (1981 AWS 228 + 1981 AA 16) which had been published in English translation by Routledge in 1931. Mostly it was a matter of our arranging new translations, sometimes with the help of UNESCO. New Egyptian titles also continued to appear in the African Writers Series. Both editions had the advantage of the inventive full-colour covers created by the Egyptian photographer Ahmed Mustapha. Although Arab Authors would inevitably be dominated by Egyptian writers, Denys Johnson-Davies set out to bring in outstanding authors from the rest of the Arab world.

When we launched Arab Authors in 1976 the African Writers Series was imported into the US by Humanities Press. Heinemann Educational Books Inc was only to be set up in 1978. In November 1976 I paid my first visit to the United States and met Don Herdeck in Washington DC, who had recently founded Three Continents Press. He immediately made an offer to co-publish and actively promote Arab Authors in the US. As a diplomat he had come to realise, during postings in Asia and Africa, that few examples of what people were writing in these two continents were available in English translation in his own 'third continent' of North America. Don Herdeck started teaching the Foreign Service course at Georgetown University in Washington DC and had seen an opening for publishing this literature and selling it to university courses and adventurous bookshops. With his wife Margaret, he set up Three Continents Press, using newly available computer typesetting in their garage and rushed out a pioneering range of books. We already had included in the Arab Authors launch list Denys Johnson-Davies's representative *Modern Arabic Short Stories* (1976 AA 3) which had only been published in hardback by Oxford University Press; we were pleased to be offered by Three Continents a parallel survey, Issa J. Boulatta's *Modern Arab Poets* 1950–1975 (1978 AA 6). Don Herdeck and I were to work together on many books including translations of Naguib Mahfouz, years before he won the Nobel Prize for Literature.

The art of seamless translation

Denys Johnson-Davies taught us the problems of translating Arabic into English and the skills needed to produce flow. He explained how the translator of works of literature must discreetly convey what the writer had in mind but had not necessarily expressed on the original page. Objects may have an exact linguistic translation but the translator must convey, without it being apparent, the social, political and geographical context which the writer takes for granted will be in the mind of the reader in Arabic. He gave an example of 'The doum tree of Wad Hamid' in a Sudanese village on the edge of the Nile which is the title of a story by Tayeb Salih. A botanically accurate name would have been pointless as it would not have been recognised among English-speakers. The important thing was to convey that this tree had heavy foliage so that its dense shadow reached right across the river at sunset. A Sudanese would find these features intrinsic to the name of the tree. This must be seamlessly conveyed to the writer in English.

He was scornful of a manuscript of translations of the Egyptian playwright Tewfik al-Hakim which were submitted by a Reader in Arabic at an ancient British university, with footnotes appearing in clusters at the foot of each page. Denys Johnson-Davies, who himself published performable translations of plays by Tewfik al-Hakim and other Egyptian playwrights, maintained that plays must be published in stageable form. He asked what happened when an actor came to a footnote. Did she or he wait while the prompt read out the annotation to the audience?

John Fowles learnt that for the translator there are problems arising from the style of Arabic:

> … stylistically Arabic has an odd conjunction of paucity of rhetorical device but great subtlety of syntax and grammar. A translator in English is faced with the constant problem of staying true to his text on one hand and making some accommodation to English stylistic conventions on the other. To take small examples, both ellipsis and repetition of words are favourite devices in Arabic … and in general the very reverse in English. (*Miramar*, p. viii)

Catherine Cobham, another translator admired by Edward Said, says in her introduction to Yusuf Idris's *Rings of Burnished Brass*:

> In my translation of these stories I cannot hope to have faithfully represented the originals, for 'faithful representation' is a far from unambiguous concept. This is not to say that I have interpreted rather than translated; in fact I found that I moved closer to literalness in the course of translating them, or found surprisingly that there was more scope for licence in the choice of words, but less in syntax, than I had anticipated. (*Rings of Burnished Brass*, p. xiii)

Yusuf Idris
The language of the Cairo streets

Arab Authors included novels, plays and poetry, but the series reflected the fact that short stories dominated publishing output, especially in Egypt. Newspapers in the 1950s, 1960s and 1970s were the major outlet for creative writing in Arabic. Not only did they carry a daily diet of short stories, but also novels were serialised. It had been the same in Britain before the days of television and colour supplements, where newspapers as diverse as *The Manchester Guardian* and *The Evening Standard* used to provide an income for aspiring writers. There are more than five books of short stories by Naguib Mahfouz, and his novels were usually serialised in a newspaper before book publication. In that way he became known to a wider range of Egyptians than if his work had only appeared in books. Arab Authors reflects the importance of the short story. Denys Johnson-Davies collected an anthology of *Egyptian Short Stories* (1978 AA 8) and introduced several other active writers. For example, *The Smell of It* by Sonallah Ibrahim (1971 AWS 95 + 1978 AA 10) made available through the medium of English a collection of stories which had been banned on its first publication in Arabic in 1966. *The Mountain of Green Tea* (1984 AA 19) was in page proof when their author Yahya Taher Abdullah was killed in a car crash. Denys Johnson-Davies then found that both sides of the family were convinced that the book would make a fortune and started quarrelling; one side of the family resorted to Islamic lawyers and the other to Napoleonic lawyers. As the dispute dragged on and delayed publication, I sardonically observed to Denys Johnson-Davies: 'There is nothing worse an author can do to his publisher than die on him!' The publisher deals with the author, perhaps through an agent. But once the author dies hosts of relations pop up, and they all think they know exactly what the author would have wanted and none of them can agree. Denys was in addition having to deal with two families split across traditional and modern lines.

Intense cultural and political struggles had to be fought by writers against the traditionalists. Writers were having to establish points which in Britain or the US writers could take for granted. Sometimes work which had appeared in newspapers was considered too controversial for publication in book form in Egypt and had to appear in the alternative publishing centre of Beirut. Yusuf Idris was described by Tewfik al-Hakim as the 'genius of the short story' because he set out to represent speech on the page in the way that it was spoken in Cairo streets. Wadida Wassef, who translated a collection of his stories under the title *The Cheapest Nights* (1978 AWS 209 + 1978 AA12) explains the intensity of the opposition to what the writer was doing:

> Idris's style is unique in that he is the first writer to have developed a mode of expression quite new to Arabic literary tradition by making full use of colloquial Arabic. He makes a deliberate distinction between the language spoken by his characters and that which he assumes when he himself takes

> over the narrative. This subtle alternation of classical and spoken Arabic enhances the realism of his work and his own individuality as a writer. Such a detail will escape the English reader as the same distinction does not exist in English. This innovation at first raised an outcry among Arab critics who saw his work as a deviation from the tradition and concepts of Arabic literature. (*The Cheapest Nights*, p. xii)

English is almost purely a vernacular language and the written form changes with the spoken. An Arabic writer in Morocco, 'the farthest west' country of the Maghreb, can read work by a writer in eastern Iraq with ease. If the writers met they would find one another's speech substantially different in a way that people would not expect in the English-speaking world. The classical form of Arabic is still fundamentally derived from the language of the seventh-century founding fathers of Islam. The Koran is always recited in the very language in which it was first written. Yusuf Idris was considered to have interfered with the sacred language when he tackled the technical problems of the notation of the vernacular in the cursive script. Writers were considered dangerous because they dared to write about social, sexual and religious subjects in a way that was attractive and could be understood by ordinary readers of Arabic.

Peter Owen, always an enterprising publisher of work in translation, published in English with the help of the UNESCO translation scheme Yusuf Idris's first collection of stories, *The Cheapest Nights*. We subcontracted the paperback rights for Arab Authors. The author came to London for the launching party, though sadly it appeared that he considered that the translator had made a selection which was rather too dominated by his youthful work from the time when he was fighting for the FLN in Algeria and opposing the Nasser regime. He wanted something that was more representative of his more mature work, and he very much wanted Catherine Cobham to be the translator. At the party he agreed with Peter Owen and his editor Dan Franklin, who was to go on to have a powerful influence at Jonathan Cape, that there ought to be a follow-up collection. In collaboration with Heinemann they commissioned Catherine Cobham to make and translate the collection which was to appear under the title *Rings of Burnished Brass* (AWS 267 + 1984 AA 21).

Ghassan Kanafani
A letter from Gaza

Other books in Arab Authors represented different struggles. Literature of excellence could give the reader in English translation some feeling of the realities of Palestine. The writer Ghassan Kanafani had been a spokesman for the Popular Front for the Liberation of Palestine and had died in a car which had been booby-trapped. His Danish widow Anni Kanafani was anxious that the Palestinian/Iraqi writer Jabbra Ibrahim Jabbra should do the translation, but he declined, saying that he did not even translate his own short stories into English. He acknowledged that Ghassan Kanafani was 'a leading novelist in the Arab world' and that people called him the 'Palestinian Maxim Gorky' (Jabbra Ibrahim Jabbra to JC 21 June 1977).

Hilary Kirkpatrick had offered us her translation of *Men in the Sun* (1978 AA 11), a novella which had already been made into a film. Anna Kanafani reported that some critics had considered this novel 'as the spark which started the resistance movement'. Three desperate Palestinian refugees pay a tanker driver to smuggle them into Kuwait to find jobs. At the border, with the three men hiding in the burning hot tank, as Ros de Lanerolle's report says:

> ... the driver's own past catches him up – the immigration officer has found out the secret of his experience in the 1967 war when his balls were blown off in a gun battle, and he keeps him standing, humiliating him about it. The delay is too long. The driver dumps the corpses in the desert. The stark horror of this story is totally unrelieved – it is relentless, angry, ugly. But the feeling is immensely sensitive, the telling and the style controlled and deeply impressive. (Report by Ros de Lanerolle 30 August 1975)

Other stories of his were added, including 'A Letter from Gaza', at the suggestion of Jabbra Ibrahim Jabbra. Ghassan Kanafani was a striking artist and his dramatic painting of a Bedouin horseman heading directly at you out of the desert had been used on a PFLP postage stamp; it not only made a dramatic cover for the book (p. 141) but also was used by Heinemann as a poster to promote the whole series. We took from Three Continents a collection of Ghassan Kanafani's stories called *Palestine's Children* (1984 AA 22), set between 1936 and 1967, giving not only a child's-eye view of the refugee camps but also of the dreams and hopes which come with each new generation.

Denys Johnson-Davies translated a collection of verse by Mahmoud Darwish, *The Music of Human Flesh* (1980 AA 7), who was described in an article in 2007 in *The Economist* as now being called 'the poet-laureate of Palestine'. Other books from outside Egypt included the prophetic novel *Death in Beirut* by the poet diplomat Tawfiq Awaad, which was published in 1972 and prophesied the civil war of 1976; the translation by Leslie McLoughlin was published in 1976 (AA 5).

Tayeb Salih

'An Arabian Nights in reverse'

I could not get Tayeb Salih's collection of stories *The Wedding of Zein* (1969 AWS 47 + 1978 AA 13) accepted for publication when I was at Oxford University Press, even though two of Denys Johnson-Davies's translations had appeared in *The London Magazine*, one of the most prestigious journals of the period. So I was free to take the manuscript to my first meeting in February 1967 with Chinua Achebe, who was immediately delighted to include the book in the African Writers Series (p. 5). An additional pleasure were the extraordinary illustrations by the artist Ibrahim Salahi, who had trained in Khartoum and in London at the

Tayeb Salih

Slade. One of my most memorable afternoons in Africa was when Ibrahim Salahi took me along through the plots near Khartoum, where peasant farmers were lifting water out of the river with machines that had been invented several thousand years before. This was the very Nile which is almost a character in its own right in Tayeb Salih's writing.

Then followed Denys Johnson-Davies's translation of Tayeb Salih's novel *Season of Migration to the North* (1969/1970 AWS 66 + 1976 AA 4). Tayeb Salih lived in London at the time as he was head of drama at the BBC Arabic Service. He had studied for an advanced degree in London. He speaks English with a gentle assurance and Denys Johnson-Davies was certain that he could have written English translations of his stories and novels. However, Tayeb Salih was firm about his need to write in Arabic and his diffidence about writing in English. Denys Johnson-Davies worked with him on what he called an English version. Together they developed a translation which was aimed at the British audience.

The Observer described the novel as 'an Arabian Nights in reverse'. Tayeb Salih had not only stood apart in language but also in context. The village scenes on the banks of the Nile are warm and realistic. The London scenes, set in the 1920s, are cold, harsh and violent; they parody the mythologies held by Westerners about the Arab world. As the contributor to *The Companion* says: 'Mustapha says he will appease his race by liberating Africa with his penis, thus reversing and re-enacting the rape of Africa. He exploits three British women who fall in love with him and [two of whom] eventually commit suicide. He meets his match in a woman who teases him, cajoles him into marriage and eventually coaxes him into killing her.' When the book was relaunched in Arab Authors in 1976 Jill Neville said in *The Sunday Times*:

> Having nibbled, in the past, at the edges of Muslim thought, I expected to have to hoe my way through dry, laconic tales ... Instead I was hurled in a cauldron of morality, tensions and psychological bombshells with Tayeb Salih's classic *Season of Migration to the North.* (2 May 1976)

Keith Sambrook and I made attempts to find a hardback publisher in London for this book, which was so shocking about the way men could regard women but even more revealing about the mythology with which different societies regard one another. The editorial director at William Heinemann said: 'I don't like it at all and I think it would very difficult to put over' (Roland Gant to JC 17 May 1967). It was Denys Johnson-Davies who, through his native English, had drawn attention to this exceptional novel. There have now been over 20 translations, most of which came from Denys Johnson Davies's English rendering, on which he had worked so creatively with Tayeb Salih.

The title was included in Penguin Classics in 2002. At a meeting in 2005 at the British Library a new generation of readers bought every copy of the book they could seize after hearing Tayeb Salih speak. In his introduction to the Penguin edition he remembers the initial reception in London as 'cool' and in particular that *The Times Literary Supplement* was 'haughty'. Tayeb Salih then remembers how well it was received in Paris:

> There were complimentary reviews in most of major newspapers. M. François Mauriac said 'we have never read anything like this before, we who have read everything'. Which made me wonder how a novel which could be so trivial in London could be hailed in such glowing terms in Paris! (Penguin Classics 2003 p. ix)

Naguib Mahfouz

'Earthier than Coronation Street'

Denys Johnson-Davies felt that, as the best-known writer in the Arab world, there ought to be a representative work by Naguib Mahfouz in the African Writers Series. He found it difficult to recommend which novel to start with. He told me that in Egypt *The Cairo Trilogy* was regarded as his greatest work. Naguib Mahfouz himself, according to *The Companion*, called the sequence 'a history of my country and of myself'. It follows the life of a family through three generations from 1917 to 1944. I asked Denys Johnson-Davies whether he would translate it. He said that it was so dense with historical and political references that it would need a concordance or heavy footnoting, which was certainly not how he felt this writer should be introduced to an audience in English. The *Trilogy* was completed in 1952, which was the year of the revolt by the young officers; however, it was not published until 1959 when Nasser was strongly established and there is a complex subtext in the books against the authoritarian regime. The artfulness of writers gives deep hope to readers in times of oppression.

Midaq Alley (1975 AWS 151 + 1975 AA 2) is a novel of the interlocking stories of people living in an ordinary Cairo street. It was published in 1947 (and in a first incomplete English translation in Beirut in 1966) and Denys Johnson-Davies felt that it would be representative of Naguib Mahfouz's early period and easily understood in English without notes. Trevor le Gassick's observation on his translation published in 1977 is instructive:

> Arabic is, of course, a language far different in syntax and sounds from English and gives expression to a highly distinctive people and a complex culture. The translator has, then, an almost limitless range of choices and dilemmas over vocabulary and arrangement when attempting to convey the spirit of a work of fiction. The present translation offers an approximation of how Mahfouz might have expressed himself had English been his native tongue … A few words, relating to aspects of Egyptian national and Muslim cultural life for which we have no parallel, have been given brief descriptive definitions in the text where essential. (*Midaq Alley*, p. viii)

Trevor le Gassick succeeded in conveying what had made Naguib Mahfouz such a popular success in Arabic. In a review at the time of its reissue in Arab Authors Jill Neville in *The Sunday Times* compared it with a popular British TV soap opera and the headline read 'Much earthier, more truthful and more vivid than Coronation Street', and she said that 'it deserves to be even more popular because Mahfouz knows how to keep the reader perpetually agog without teasing too much' (2 May 1976).

Attempted assassination

> It is not often that preachers lead their flocks into the streets to shout for the banning of a novel hailed by many as a masterpiece, nor that the editor of a great newspaper has to rely on his friendship with the Head of State to ensure that a serial is published uncut to the end. This is what happened in Nasser's Egypt in 1959 when the semi-official *Al-Ahram* printed *Children of Gebelawi*. (p. vii)

The translator Philip Stewart shows in his introduction that the reaction within Islam against this novel was every bit as extreme as that, at a later date, to Salman Rushdie's *Satanic Verses*. Naguib Mahfouz was in 1994 to survive an assassination attempt; this followed his being cursed by a cleric who was later to be arrested in the United States in connection with the first attack on the twin towers.

Naguib Mahfouz had suffered a religious crisis in his teens when he discovered Darwin; he worked from 1939 to 1954 in the Ministry of Religious Affairs. During the 1950s he engaged with the subject of religious belief in his religious allegory, *Children of Gebelawi*. It was set, like *Midaq Alley*, among ordinary Egyptian town dwellers. Hilary Kirkpatrick pointed out in a review that it expressed his interest in the rise of the three monotheistic religions, Judaism, Christianity and Islam, his preoccupation with the confrontation between science and religion in the modern world and his critical stand towards the authorities in Egypt. It was never to appear in complete book form in Arabic in Egypt, although a censored version was published in Beirut. The translator Philip Stewart says in his introduction:

> The reason for these strong reactions was that Naguib Mahfouz had boldly taken up the issues that most deeply divide Egypt and, perhaps, the world. The successive heroes of his imaginary Cairo alley relive unawares the lives of Adam, Moses, Jesus and Mohammed, and their aged ancestor, Gebelawi, represents God, or rather 'Not God, but a certain idea of God that men have made' as Mahfouz put it in the course of discussion with me, so that his fate takes on a dreadful significance. Most of the readers became so passionately involved that they could see in the novel only their own ideology. (p. vii)

Naguib Mahfouz rejected the accusation that it was atheistic, and indeed regarded it as a statement of the transcendancy of true religion.

Philip Stewart arrived in 1978 at the Heinemann office in Bedford Square on his bike bearing his translation of *Children of Gebelawi* (1981 AWS 225 + 1981 AA 15), the first draft of which he had made while a postgraduate in Egypt. He had an album into which he had pasted the cuttings from *Al-Ahram*. After the outcry the cuttings had been circulating from hand to hand in Egypt. Denys Johnson-Davies had told him of the café where Naguib Mahfouz held court with other

Egyptian writers and intellectuals. Philip Stewart sat on the edge of this group on various visits and then summoned up courage to tell Naguib Mahfouz of his translation. Naguib Mahfouz seemed amused by this long thin Englishman cutting out each episode from the newspaper and said that he did not even have a full set himself.

John Rodenbeck, director of the American University in Cairo Press, approached us about the programme they had initiated for translating into English the novels of Naguib Mahfouz. He said that the American University in Cairo Press had signed an agreement with Naguib Mahfouz for all the rights for English-language translation. The English version they had in the office bore a startling resemblance to that which Philip Stewart had carried out with Naguib Mahfouz's agreement. In the end Heinemann and the American University in Cairo Press came to an agreement. But then it turned out, 20 years after the original publication in Arabic, that they could not take the copies in English they had ordered from Heinemann because of Egyptian censorship. Philip Stewart's reaction to what he called this 'Cairene' situation, in a letter dated 10 July 1979, was: 'How unspeakably comic that they acquired the rights to publish something they cannot publish!'

Chattering about revolution

The furore created by *Children of Gebalawi* when originally serialised in 1959 led Naguib Mahfouz to a period of silence and *Miramar* was not published until 1967. This time the characters are confined, not within an alley, but within a hotel where they live on the sea-front at Alexandria. The reports by the African writers Laban Erapu in Kenya and Michael Echeruo in Nigeria are most perceptive. Michael Echeruo said:

> *Miramar* is easily misread. Because its centre of action is Alexandria and because there is abundant evidence of the profligacy one has come to associate with that city – in travelogues like Forster's *Alexandria*, as well as in fiction, like Durrell's *Justine* – we are likely to see *Miramar* as just another story of licentiousness. In fact, it isn't. It is the quest for the meaning of the good life undertaken inadvertently by one who has been made incapable of a morally relevant discrimination by personal, national and ideological rootlessness; made useless to his mind, so to speak, by what the novel calls the winds of revolution 'blowing his class's candles out'. There is therefore a lot of talk of the pleasures of the flesh, of cafes, hotels and pensions which house the mistresses, serving girls and procuresses – Greek, Syro-Italian, Egyptian, and Maltese: 'past fifty, fat and flabby, but still a woman.' 'All shapes and sizes'. The book appropriately takes its title from one of those new homes for the rootless, though the madame may want to distinguish between the 'transient' and the 'permanent' guests! There is also a lot of talk of revolution. Indeed *Miramar* can be also about the futility of revolutions. Although one cannot say this with certainty, there is a strong impression

> that the book is something of a *roman à clef*, with a gallery of personages whom a seasoned Egyptologist would have no difficulty identifying. The revolution is dated 1919 but it could well have been 1959. (Report by M.J.C. Echeruo to Heinemann Nigeria 1976)

John Rodenbeck had had the useful idea of commissioning John Fowles, who had spent a writing winter in Egypt, to provide an introduction. John Fowles's *French Lieutenant's Woman* had been made into a successful film and we hoped, unsuccessfully, that his introduction would convince William Heinemann to issue in hardback. Pantheon in New York did belatedly make a substantial offer but withdrew over a complication with the US rights.

The translation of *Miramar* (1978 AWS 197 + 1978 AA 9) by Fatma Moussa-Mahmoud had been commissioned by the American University in Cairo Press. It showed the problems that Denys Johnson-Davies had foreseen in providing attractive readable novels to an audience in English. She had a Cambridge degree but approached translation from rather too formal a standpoint. She did not totally overcome the conventional rule of literary translation, which is that the translator should translate into his or her own language and indeed culture. It was decided to confine the copious notes to the back of the book.

Unfortunately a whole cluster of manuscripts of novels by Naguib Mahfouz suffered from the translations which had been enthusiastically commissioned by the American University in Cairo Press from Egyptian academics. A pile of dead translations accumulated in a corner cupboard in my office. Denys Johnson-Davies recommended *The Thief and the Dogs* but felt that the translation provided would do a disservice to the original, considered translating it himself, but gave up because he thought that the original lacked 'bite'. I was much taken by the title of another novel called *Chattering on the Nile*; in as far as I could judge from the translation, the book consisted of existential chatter among literati on a houseboat, using the stream of consciousness technique. I was interested to see Edward Said point out in *The Independent on Sunday* (12 August 1970) how much Naguib Mahfouz has suffered from translations, 'some quite good, most of them, however, either indifferent or poor'.

The new management at Heinemann decided to drop Arab Authors after Keith Sambrook and I left the firm. With immaculate timing, they managed in 1988 to revert the rights in the novels by Naguib Mahfouz to the American University in Cairo Press just weeks before he was awarded the Nobel Prize.

'Arabic is a controversial language'

Edward Said, writing in 1990 in *The Independent on Sunday* at the time of the first Gulf war, gave an account of the 'comically symptomatic' reaction in the US press when Naguib Mahfouz won the Nobel Prize for Literature in 1988. There were profiles in half a dozen magazines such as *Vanity Fair*, *The New York Times Magazine* and *The New Yorker*.

All the writers, some of them accomplished essayists, were totally innocent

> both of Arabic and of Arabic literature. All of them regarded Mahfouz as a cross between a cultural oddity and a political symbol. Nothing was said about his formal achievements or about his place in modern literature as a whole … It is impossible not to believe that one reason for this odd state of affairs is the long-standing prejudice against the Arabs and Islam that remains within Western, but especially American, culture. (*The Independent on Sunday* 12 August 1990)

Edward Said said in this article that he had been asked, eight years before Naguib Mahfouz won the Nobel Prize, to suggest a list of third-world novels for translation by a 'major New York publisher known for his liberal and unprovincial views'. Two or three of Naguib Mahfouz's novels were at the top of this list. When Edward Said enquired a little later what had happened he was told: 'The problem is that Arabic is a controversial language.'

PART

4 Writers from SOUTH AFRICA

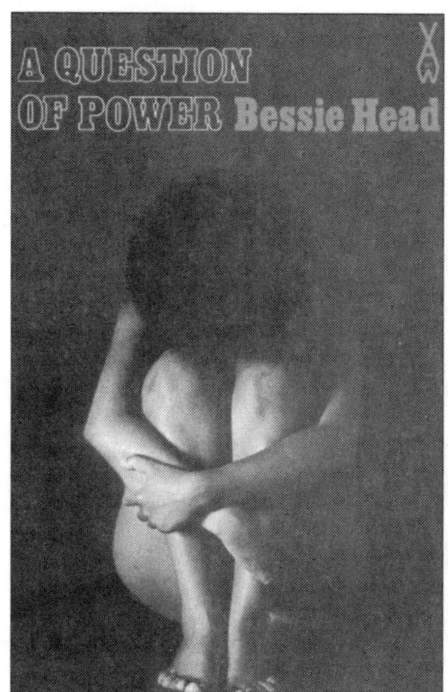

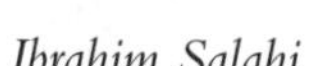
George Hallett

George Hallett

Ibrahim Salahi

George Hallett

Photographing the cover for D.M. Zwelonke's novel *Robben Island* (p. 190)

7 *Resistance in* SOUTH AFRICA

The books which appeared in the first 25 years of the African Writers Series reflected the changing circumstances for publishing South African work through the medium of English. This chapter shows the changing way in which writers from South Africa were represented in the African Writers Series, although there was no editorial office in the country. There was a William Heinemann sales office in Johannesburg run by Andrew Stewart to promote the sale of books from the English market. This was in contrast with Ibadan and Nairobi where Heinemann Educational Books had editorial offices which took an active editorial role in building up the Series. This chapter concludes with accounts of the way that publishing relationships developed with the South African writers in exile: Alex la Guma, Dennis Brutus, Mazisi Kunene and Bessie Head.

But how were writers to be found in South Africa itself? The network of South African writers, journalists and academics, both in the country and in exile, gave us leads, opinions on manuscripts and worked with us on three novels which revealed the realities of life for ordinary South Africans: D.M. Zwelonke's *Robben Island*, Modikwe Dikobe's *The Marabi Dance* and R.L. Peteni's *Hill of Fools*. It was difficult to find possible manuscripts; as Ros de Lanerolle wrote in reporting on *The Marabi Dance* 'black South African writers tend to short stories, in any case, seldom novels' (2 November 1971).

In the 1970s, a heroic band of independent publishers emerged in South Africa. By the 1980s writing from the country was mainly represented in the Series by titles which were subcontracted from the lists of David Philip, Ravan, Ad Donker and others.

A South African publishing apprenticeship

I was already alert to the South African literary scene when I was sent to South Africa by the Oxford University Press in 1959. My parents, both writers, were born in South Africa though they left during their childhoods. My father was the poet R.N. Currey and my mother Stella Martin Currey was a novelist and playwright. I had grown up in 1950s England familiar with names such as Jack

Cope, Roy Campbell and Guy Butler. My South African grandmother just referred to Alan Paton's novel with the one word *Cry*.

At Oxford University Press in Cape Town, David Philip and I both had the good fortune to have publishing apprenticeships under the distinguished Afrikaner historian Leo Marquard, who was the editorial manager. His philosophy of the publication of academic books with a serious political and cultural purpose is central to the policy of James Currey Publishers today. The OUP was my day job. Working in my spare time for *The New African* was to be an equally crucial factor in my apprenticeship in Cape Town as it introduced me to the new writers of Africa.

The New African was published in Cape Town from 1961 to 1964 and, in exile in London from 1965 to 1967. I suggested the name in reflection of the left-wing London journal *The New Statesman,* which influenced our group of young members of the South African Liberal Party. Our editorial policy, for what was called 'The Radical Review' on the front cover, was that we were interested in work on Africa in general and in South Africa in particular. Exciting things were happening to the north which were an antidote to the frustrations of South Africa.

Randolph Vigne, who had got me actively involved in the South African Liberal Party in the period before Sharpeville, was the editor of profound political commitment who brought *The New African* together each month, even while still working at the publishers Maskew Miller. The other editor was Neville Rubin, who soon went off to work at SOAS in London, and later, for the ILO in Geneva. He was well-placed to raise funds for the review's survival and to collect material from sympathetic organisations in Britain, Europe and America. When Randolph Vigne was banned he managed to continue secretly as editor, while Neville Rubin's name stayed conveniently alone on the masthead. I was in charge of design and printing. Every month built up to a '*New African* weekend' when I pasted up the galley proofs of typesetting and used the new invention of 'Letraset' to hand-letter the display headings; I adapted bold design ideas, particularly for maps of Africa, from *The Observer* and other publications in London and the new availability of offset printing enabled us to illustrate it with photographs.

Leo Marquard, a founder of the South African Liberal Party, differed in the radicalism of his politics from his OUP colleague of English descent who would have blocked my involvement with *The New African*. Leo Marquard said to me, 'Strictly speaking an employee of the OUP is not allowed to be a director of another company. However, I can't see that you will make any money out of *The New African* so I do not see it as a problem.' He turned a blind eye to the political dangers which he knew only too well in his own life.

The New African managed to survive in Cape Town for three years. In 1964, as the Rivonia trial was coming to its feared end in Pretoria, government pressure grew. The Special Branch blackmailed our printer to stop printing the review by threatening to renew his personal ban, which would have meant the closure of his whole business. A compositor, who was a member of the Liberal Party, secretly set the magazine after hours in the printing works in which he was employed. The April 1964 issue was seized by the Special Branch. The Rivonia trial came to an end and the head of police boasted in the Johannesburg *Sunday Times* that all resistance had been crushed. That night there were explosions in Cape Town and Johannesburg, which were carried out by the African Resistance Movement (ARM). It later transpired that Randolph Vigne, and several people associated with *The New African* were involved. On Thursday 12 July 1964 I used my British passport to buy a ticket on a Norwegian boat for me to travel to Montreal, but left Randolph Vigne aboard in my stead by jumping over the side. I was advised by the British and Norwegian consuls to leave South Africa as soon as possible. Fortunately Oxford University Press found me a day job in London. This was later to involve running Three Crowns, the series in which writers such as Wole Soyinka and J.P. Clark first appeared outside Africa.

We revived *The New African* in 1965 in London and, in all, published a total of over 50 issues. Thanks to the Congress for Cultural Freedom, we mailed each issue free to the original subscribers in South Africa. In the end, as Pretoria banned each issue, we had every month to invent a new name such as *Inkululeko* for the South African edition. Each '*New African* weekend' I was again pasting up work by writers with names such as James Ngũgĩ, Bessie Head, Wole Soyinka, Zeke Mphahlele, Dennis Brutus and Chinua Achebe. This was an appropriate literary apprenticeship for me when in 1967 I took over running the African Writers Series with Keith Sambrook at Heinemann.

The search for black writers

When the Series started in 1962 most of the South African writers published in London and New York had European roots. Keith Sambrook and Chinua Achebe had to hunt around to find black authors from South Africa. In 1963 they put, as only the sixth title in the Series, Peter Abrahams' novel of Johannesburg *Mine Boy* (AWS 6), which had been first published in hardback in 1946. Symbolically, his ancestry could be traced to the Khoisan, the original inhabitants of the southern end of the continent. In 1963 Chinua Achebe, four months after his appointment as Editorial Adviser to the Series, told Keith Sambrook of the publication in Nigeria by Mbari of a book which he reported had been 'smuggled out of South Africa' (CA to KS 1963); it was *A Walk in the Night* by Alex la Guma. Two early anthologies of work from the whole continent were made by South Africans; Clive Wake, with John Reed, collected *A Book of African Verse* (AWS 8) and Richard Rive edited *Modern African Prose* (1964 AWS 9) and these South African editors were delighted to discover how much work there already was from further north in Africa.

The historic contribution of the mission presses in the early part of the twentieth century was later to be reflected in the inclusion of two novels in the Series. Stephen Gray re-edited in 1978 for the Quagga Press the complete uncut text of Sol Plaatje's *Mhudi* (AWS 201) which, when originally published in 1930, was the first novel written in English by a black South African. It is a scathing attack on racial segregation and the Land Act of 1913. This historical epic, set among the Barolong, had been written by the person who in 1912 had become the secretary of the party which was to become the ANC. (Heinemann and James Currey Publishers were in 1984/5 to publish a biography of *Sol Plaatje* by Brian Willan.)

Thomas Mofolo's novel *Chaka* had been written in Sesotho right back in 1909. The missionaries at the printing works at Morija in Basutoland had reservations about the conflict between traditional beliefs and Christian values. It was eventually first published by Lovedale Press in Sesotho in 1925 and then in a bowdlerised and Bunyanesque English translation in 1931 which was used for the translations into Afrikaans, German, Italian and French. The French translation, published in 1940, was to inspire work by at least five francophone African writers including L. S. Senghor. The novel also led to writing on Shaka in Zulu and other southern African languages.

Daniel P. Kunene had persuaded my African colleagues and myself, especially in view of the enormous influence of the quaint 1931 version of *Chaka* and its translations, that there should be a full uncensored modern translation from the original 1909 Sesotho edition. He is an expert in Sesotho, one of the family of languages stretching north from the Drakensberg mountains. I had first met him when he was a 'language assistant' at the University of Cape Town. Robert Sobukwe, a founder of the Pan-Africanist Congress (PAC) which triggered Sharpeville, held a similar position at the University of the Witwatersrand. In the 1950s and early 1960s this was the highest position to which an African could rise in a South African university. The 'language assistant' was graciously allowed to help the white lecturers and professors who were strangers to his own language. Dan Kunene had to leave the country to be able to rise to being Professor of African Languages at the University of Wisconsin. We published his new translation of Mofolo's *Chaka* in 1981. (As it happens Daniel P. Kunene is no relation of Mazisi Kunene, author of *Emperor Shaka the Great*.)

Apartheid sends writers to prison

In May 1973, some ten years after the foundation of the African Writers Series, we held an event which can now be seen to have marked the end of the first phase of our efforts in London to represent writers from within South Africa. With the inspiration of Dennis Brutus, a cluster of South African books was launched at an evening meeting at the Africa Centre in Covent Garden, London. Tragically Arthur Nortje had died at Oxford before the publication of his poetry, *Dead Roots* (AWS 141). All the other writers had suffered imprisonment. There was a substantial collection of Dennis Brutus's poems, *A Simple Lust*; together with newer work, this book included his sequence *Letters to Martha* which had been disguised as prose letters to his sister-in-law Martha when he was serving 18 months on Robben Island (p. 207). At the centre of the event was the reissue of Nelson Mandela's *No Easy Walk to Freedom* (AWS 123) to mark ten years from the date of his first incarceration on 'The Island'; the new Foreword was by Ruth

First who would later be assassinated in Maputo. Albie Sachs was to survive an assassination attempt in Mozambique and as a judge in South Africa in the 1990s worked on the outstandingly liberal constitution of the new South Africa; on that same evening we published his academic study called, somewhat unconvincingly, *Justice in South Africa*. Then there were two novels of social reality, *Robben Island* by D.M. Zwelonke (p. 190) and *The Marabi Dance* by Modikwe Dikobe (p. 191); both of these had to be published under pseudonyms because the authors had been imprisoned and banned.

Later in the 1980s we were to reprint previously published books in the African Writers Series about the realities of being in prison in South Africa, such as Molefe Pheto's *And Night Fell* (1985 AWS 258). In 1982 we reissued *Bandiet* (1981 AWS 251) which was written from Hugh Lewin's experience of seven years in the hanging jail at Pretoria, after he was convicted for his part in the African Resistance Movement (ARM). I wrote to the Kenyan Simon Gikandi to get his opinion and he came back with: 'This is the most stark and horrifying experience of the South African prison system I have ever read ... What a terribly good memoir this is! ... no better book to read than *Bandiet*!' (Simon Gikandi report undated 1981).

What is an African writer?

The South African books chosen for the African Writers Series reflected first and foremost the realities of life suffered by people oppressed by the laws of colour. The criterion for inclusion in the African Writers Series was one of geography and not of race; writers had to have been born in Africa. We could have swamped the Series with reprints by well-established South African authors such as Alan Paton and Dan Jacobson.

Nadine Gordimer was pleased by my suggestion that, as an experiment, we should include a collection of her short stories in the Series. She and I agreed that I should try this idea on my colleagues in Ibadan and Nairobi to see if they thought that there would be a market. This led her to the idea that she would include from her several collections short stories set in Africa to the north and south. She wrote in 1976, the year of Soweto:

> I have chosen *Some Monday for Sure* [AWS 177] as the general title story because although written and set in the Sixties, and despite the ironies of a political refugee's life that the story recounts, the certainty of the title remains valid: some perfectly ordinary day, for sure, black South Africans will free themselves and rule themselves. (pp. 10–11)

The Cape Town photographer George Hallett produced an elegantly appropriate cover from his portfolio of photographs of District Six. He and we were pleased by Nadine Gordimer's reaction to the advance copy:

> I must tell you that I am delighted with the lay-out, cover, and generally high standard of production. I wish that Penguin might take a leaf out of Heinemann's book(s) ... My paperbacks with Penguin have been a series of

disasters, ugly and full of errors both of fact and taste. (Nadine Gordimer to JC 1 June 1976)

Cultural boycott & censorship

Should we have been circulating books at all in apartheid South Africa? The ANC had a cultural boycott. I was informed that the Senegalese novelist and film-maker Sembene was refusing permission for his films to be shown in South Africa. I wrote, somewhat nervously, to ask him whether he objected to our selling the English translations of his novels in South Africa. My memory is that he wrote that as far as he was concerned, whereas audiences for films were segregated, the act of reading a novel was solitary and not to his feeling subject to segregation. When we met at the Frankfurt Book Fair in 1980, he and I agreed that we must not reduce the chances of the voices of Africans being read in South Africa and that it was not for us to do the work of the censor. At the Berlin Festival in 1979 I met the leader of a writers' group which was based in Pretoria; he told me how his members avidly read the writers from the north in the African Writers Series. The Series was giving writers a view beyond the restrictions of South Africa. The problems began when our books were banned by the South African authorities. When I told the Zimbabwean writer Dambudzo Marechera that *House of Hunger* had been banned in South Africa, he exclaimed, 'I'm delighted!' To which I replied, 'And stop those writers you and I met in Berlin from reading your work?'

D.M. Zwelonke

Robben Island

I had first encountered D.M. Zwelonke when Randolph Vigne included work by him under this pseudonym in *The New African*. He was anxious not to use his own name. He was in exile in Swaziland and still felt he had to protect his identity from 'my adversaries here' (DMZ to JC 8 February 1972). His novel *Robben Island* (1973 AWS 128) was the story of a Poqo leader, murdered under interrogation during a long spell of solitary on the island prison. Hilary Mutch, herself a South African, wrote:

> I have no doubt that Bekimpi is modelled on a real individual; his reported stoicism under torture has the quality of a legend in the making. Bekimpi's sexual fantasies and detailed re-enactment of his past during the cruel ordeal of solitary is particularly well done … But [Zwelonke's] main fault is his inadequate melding of Bekimpi's and [the narrator's] stories. Although their political lives cross, and they share the same prison, the jumps from one character to another are brusque, disconcerting, and most important,

> extremely difficult to follow. This is where [Zwelonke's] inexperience as a writer is most evident. He is happiest with straight autobiographical reportage, where his unusual and exciting gift for metaphor is particularly refreshing … (Report by Hilary Mutch 10 November 1971)

Zwelonke responded to our first round of reports but, when he returned the revised manuscript, it was clear that further work was necessary. I wrote to the novelist Richard Lister:

> There is a book in this manuscript trying to escape from the author's lack of formal education. Can you gently ease it out? (JC to Richard Lister 19 January 1972)

Richard Lister wrote:

> … he writes like a poet; and his freshness and his vividness have to be preserved, along with his oddities of expression, while making the thing a bit easier on the reader. (Richard Lister to JC 13 February 1972)

The problems that Zwelonke's work presented are demonstrated in this letter:

> My editor has corrected my English mistake without destroying my style. His method was more that of wiping out, rather than adding to my phraseology – getting rid of redundance and repetitions. I found that I no longer could add or subtract from this work without making clumpsy the whole text.' (DMZ to JC 16 June 1972)

Christopher Fyfe, the historian, wrote in a review in *New Society*:

> … the blurb writer is justified in comparing this with Solzhenitsyn's prison novels, though it is briefer and soars sometimes from prose into poetry. Nor does Zwelonke share Solzhenitsyn's quietistic acceptance of torment. [*Robben Island*] ends with an impassioned hymn to rationality, an angry rejection of the irrational forces that have condemned his people to a life of degradation … (*New Society* 24 May 1973)

In 1973 not many people outside the South African network knew the realities of 'The Island'; Athol Fugard's play of that name appeared a year later in 1974. D.M. Zwelonke's novel and Dennis Brutus's poetry were part of a process of capturing the imaginations of people about what was happening in the South African gulag.

Modikwe Dikobe

The Marabi yards of Johannesburg

The manuscript of *The Marabi Dance* (1973 AWS 124) was sent to us by Professor Guy Butler at Rhodes University. We came to realise that the name Modikwe Dikobe, for very South African reasons, was a pseudonym. His friend, mentor and editor was Lionel Abrahams, who had been working on the manuscript with the writer for a period of some 12 years. The plot was simple. Martha Mabongo, brought up in a Johannesburg slum, would please her family by marrying her country cousin in Zululand. However she is in love with George with whom she sings in the Marabi dance. The characters, including the bogus Reverend Ndlovu, rang true. Ros de Lanerolle wrote in her report:

> … this is a truly African novel, such as is seldom achieved by more skilled African writers (certainly not by foreigners writing about Africa). Its beauty is in the caring of the characters for one another; and in the subtle slow paced encounters … Novels as emotionally true as this about South Africa are rare … (Report by Ros de Lanerolle 2 November 1971)

Jan Raath, a journalist who worked on publicity for some time under the manager Andrew Stewart in the William Heinemann office in Johannesburg, wrote:

> I have just finished reading THE MARABI DANCE and WOW! My first impression in the early stages of the book was that it would be just another bit of offal for the social liberals to capitalize on. As I went on I became more and more impressed. I am personally somewhat acquainted with the 'Marabi' side of Johannesburg and Dikobe has even conjured up the smell of stale Bantu beer and coal braziers and the gnawing anxiety that is so much part of black Johannesburg. Lionel Abrahams I have contacted. Guy Butler who lectured me at Rhodes I am writing to. I need a few well chosen words from each I can use in publicising. Daily newspapers including African ones will receive review copies. I shall also try for coverage on the air. (Jan Raath to JC 4 April 1973)

Jan Raath's enterprising ideas for publicity would have pleased most authors but a month later he was writing:

> I asked Lionel Abrahams where we could get hold of Dikobe and he came back a little later with Dikobe himself over the phone. The latter is employed by the Municipality of Johannesburg in some humiliating capacity or other, and feels publicity would jeopardize his position, through his bosses thinking him too clever.
>
> This infuriates me because I think he is taking an 'Uncle Tom' attitude (though being outspoken in South Africa is <u>always</u> precarious). Also because one should even <u>have</u> to think like that in this ridiculous country. (Jan Raath to JC 4 May 1973)

Later that year in November I received a letter, as Jan Raath put it, 'In true South African style, this comes by Andrew Stewart's hand, all very clandestine.' He clearly felt he had misjudged Modikwe Dikobe, who was certainly no 'Uncle Tom' as he explained:

> Modikwe Dikobe is an assumed name. The man behind the name is Marks Rammitloa and he is at present a Non-European timekeeper for the Johannesburg Municipality, and in 1961, was banned.
>
> He has quite a lengthy political history. In 1956 he organised a bus boycott from the locations in Johannesburg. Then with the advent of the urban areas act, he organised a strike and petition concerning the removal of blacks from their homes in Johannesburg to Soweto, in about 1958. He later joined the Labour Party and was a founder of the Garment Workers

> Union. Then came Sharpeville, the state of emergency and the banning of the Labour Party. Listed as trade unionist and as a member of the Labour Party, he didn't stand a chance. He was put in detention for a short while, released and given banning orders.
>
> Lionel realised this and in his own words 'we have deliberately deceived your company' (obviously with no malicious intention).
>
> The reason for his recent approaches to me were because he had been told by the Special Branch about two months ago that he no longer needed to report to the police station every day. He thought that this entailed the banning order was lifted, and thought, well, now I can be interviewed, quoted etc. and can give The Marabi Dance publicity …

Jan Raath went on to explain that he had been to the South African Press Association to consult the banned list and found that, though Modikwe Dikobe did not have to report to a police station any longer, he was still banned – and in consequence so were all his writings. Jan Raath thought that, if it was found out, then it would be difficult to prove that he and Heinemann knew anything. He was more concerned about the consequences for the author, as he wrote in the same letter:

> I hope that nothing does ever happen. Marks is over sixty, blind in one eye as result of a serious mugging by Soweto tsotsies, and has a serious heart complaint. He also divorced his wife five years ago, and consequently lives alone in the Johannesburg Municipal Bantu Compound. I think a shock of this nature could easily kill him … Although this is a tricky and worrisome situation, I am quite pleased about it all. (Jan Raath to JC 23 November 1973)

In the circumstances Jan Raath had to forget any special publicity. In the normal way review copies were sent out to South African newspapers and the book, hiding behind the pseudonym, was distributed to the booksellers among other newly published titles in the African Writers Series. *The Marabi Dance* was never specifically banned. As Jan Raath pointed out, the mere title of *Robben Island* ensured that that novel would be banned. Jan Raath's adventurous approach was to lead to him being expelled from Zimbabwe in 2005 when he was the correspondent for *The Times*, London.

R.L. Peteni
Faction fights in the Ciskei

A contrasting novel of rural social reality was *Hill of Fools* by R.L. Peteni (1976 AWS 178). The problem here was that its story of faction fights might find favour with the authorities. It produced the greatest range of opinions I can ever remember from advisers. The manuscript arrived in 1973, again from Guy Butler:

> Here, at last, is the typescript of the regional novel I told you about some time ago. It is interesting for several reasons I think: no whites in it at all;

> no obvious political or colour issue: a good sense of character, family, clear region; informed by a gentle stoicism; no hysteria whatever.
>
> I believe it to be written out of his own experience of a particular reserve, near the Hoggsback, where he experienced from childhood the ancient Montague-Capulet grudge of the Thembus and the Hlubis – the former being Xhosa, the latter Fingo, who, you may recall, came into the Eastern Cape as refugees from Chaka in the early years of the last century.
>
> The feud continues today, much to Peteni's distress. He has just had tea with me, and is off on his rounds, seeking election to the new Ciskei parliament. Friends say he may become minister of education. He hopes to act as a mediator between Xhosas and Fingoes – which he says wryly, might be like trying to mediate in Northern Ireland. A sober, thoughtful man, and trusted by the few remaining members of the old guard at Fort Hare, where he lectures in English. (Guy Butler to JC 16 February 1973)

Ros de Lanerolle, with her ANC background, was horrified:

> I feel not just disappointed with this one – but angered. How can a competent writer (he is) in S.A. in 1973 expend his energy on a tale of simple tribal life – a moral tale, what's worse? Zuziwe's love for a boy of another tribe leads to a 'faction fight' in which a boy of her own tribe is killed.
>
> All the more saddening when you remember that even ten years ago, black culture in S.A. was decades ahead of the consciousness of the rest of the continent, now writers elsewhere are growing points, and from S.A comes this pathetic piece of 'separate development'. (Report by Ros de Lanerolle June 1973)

Richard Rive 'became engrossed'. Henry Chakava, who had just joined Heinemann East Africa after studying under Ngũgĩ at the University of Nairobi, reacted to some of the concerns which so offended Ros de Lanerolle. In point 5 of an enthusiastic two-page report he wrote:

> I personally feel that, to remove the impression that this is the story of barbarians, noble savages full of passions and ready to cut … throats at the slightest provocation, it must be restated that this is a struggle between two villages, or what Ngũgĩ in his novels calls two ridges; and not two tribes. All references to tribe and tribesmen must be removed and the result will be a *Romeo and Juliet* type of story much more superior to *Weep Not, Child.* (HC to JC 19 July 1973)

John Nagenda, the Ugandan writer and publisher, wrote of the revised manuscript

> How pleasant to come across an MS that you actually enjoy! …
>
> … MS is studded with good sentences, like: 'You may still find a corpse on your lap instead of a lover.' Or '… when the blue fly buzzes round us as we lie helpless on the mat of death.' (Report by John Nagenda 8 July 1974)

These vivid phrases were drawn from usage in Xhosa. R.L. Peteni was to point out in a lecture at the National Arts Festival at Grahamstown in 1977 (*English in Africa* 31:2 p. 28) that he had been inspired by the way in which Chinua Achebe drew on Igbo. He wrote, 'I felt that Xhosa was rich enough in proverbs, flexible enough in turn of phrase, and wide enough in vocabulary to be treated in similar manner.'

The way out of such mixed reactions was to accept the manuscript for publication and see what the reviewers said. David Philip took 1,000 sheets to bind up for a hardback edition and sold 708 in the first year before the paperback was released in South Africa. He encouraged R.L. Peteni to translate the book into Xhosa for them. Lionel Abrahams was very reserved about the novel in a review in *The Rand Daily Mail.*

Publishers of resistance within South Africa

These novels took much concerned work and it was a disappointment that no further manuscripts arrived from these three writers within South Africa.

Over the years there had been occasional publication in South Africa of work by African writers in English. An example was Zeke Mphahlele's first book, a collection of short stories, *Man Must Live*, which was published in 1946 by the experimental South African publisher The African Bookman; this was founded by Julian Rollnick, with plans to have book buses distributing books in the depths of the Transkei and Ciskei where there were no libraries, let alone bookshops. He is a man of the most discriminating tastes, whether in imaginative writing or in typography. David Philip and I, when we were at Oxford University Press in Cape Town in the early 1960s, worked closely with him on the design of books. He then went to work for the publisher A.A. Balkema, who brought a new standard of Dutch typography to the Cape.

In fact publication of work by black Africans was beginning to take place again within South Africa itself. In the 1970s, when the struggle against apartheid gave every appearance of being unending, independent imprints of great bravery emerged in South Africa. I worked most closely with Marie and David Philip in Cape Town, and with Mike Kirkwood at Ravan, Patrick Cullinan at Bateleur and Ad Donker in Johannesburg. These new publishers showed that there was a general market for creative writing in English in South Africa. A wider range of South African writers could be published because there was an enthusiastic and committed audience who saw writing as part of the struggle. It may well have been that the lack of television was an advantage.

These publishers bravely pushed the limits of publishing as far as the restrictions of censorship would allow. They suffered raids, harassment and sabotage. They evolved various strategies of survival to get round their exclusion from the school book market, which was so profitable for the big established publishers who collaborated with the government education departments.

The independent publishers also worked to make South African writers first published abroad also available in the country. David Philip, with the ingenious advice of John Dugard, who was a professor of law at the University of the Witwatersrand, found a legal loophole and evaded the customs ban on the African

Writers Series edition of Alex la Guma's *A Walk in the Night* by reprinting their own Africa South paperback in South Africa. Authors looked for loopholes too. Alan Paton and Nadine Gordimer persuaded their London publisher Jonathan Cape that their new books must be published simultaneously by David Philip in South Africa. Mazisi Kunene had written *Emperor Shaka the Great* and his other epics in Zulu. He was banned in South Africa because of his work for the ANC and so tried to persuade Gatsha Buthelezi, ruler of the Kwazulu bantustan, to permit the publication of his Zulu originals to prove that in his bantustan he was outside the writ of Pretoria. The borders of course were porous; it became well-known that Robin Malan's bookshop in Swaziland used the banned list as an order form from foreign publishers.

In the 1970s the emergence of the independent publishers provided a wide choice of new books from within the country; through these lists we could see what was happening. In addition Mike Kirkwood and his colleagues in the collective at Ravan Press established the journal *Staffrider* to publish resistance literature. We were able to select titles to represent the new generation of writers in the Series, such as Mongane Serote's *To Every Birth Its Blood* (1983 AWS 263) and Sipho Sepamla's *A Ride on the Whirlwind* (1984 AWS 268). These books reflected the atmosphere in the aftermath of the Soweto schoolchildren's rising of 1976.

Anthologies were also included to give a sense of this ferment. So we took from Ravan Muthobi Mutloatse's *Africa South: Contemporary Writing* (1981 AWS 243) and Robert Royston's *Black Poets in South Africa* from Ad Donker (1974 AWS 164). Another anthology, Barry Feinberg's *Poets to the People* (1980 AWS 230), was published with the International Defence and Aid Fund in London and could not appear in South Africa. *South African People's Plays* (1981 AWS 224) gave examples by Gibson Kente and others of the *samizdat* plays which were being performed in the townships.

Johannesburg v. Cape Town

There always was a cheerful arrogant assumption in Johannesburg that it was more African than Cape Town. However, Cape Town reflects a wide range of cultural traditions which are equally part of South Africa. In the 1960s a wider South African literature had begun to develop round groups in Johannesburg and Cape Town. *Drum* magazine, founded in Johannesburg in 1951, was a general-interest weekly with many photographs. Its style and urban concerns were much influenced by the interest in black America where the south was still segregated. Its presentation was heavily influenced by the socially conscious illustrated *Picture Post* in Britain. *Drum*, alongside its sister newspaper *Golden City Post*, provided work for young black writers. Freelance writers clustered round the office and met up in the shebeens of Sophiatown. There were jobs writing features and in the early days some short stories were published. One of these young journalists was Can Themba, a selection of whose stories was to appear in the Series after his early death under the title *A Will to Die* (1972 AWS 104).

Richard Rive brought together for the African Writers Series *Quartet* (1963 AWS 14), the neatly titled anthology of four stories by each of four authors, Alex la Guma, James Matthews, Alf Wannenburgh and Richard Rive, who formed a literary group in the multiracial, working-class area of Cape Town called District Six. I shall show (p. 203) the way that the publishing relationship grew in exile between Alex la Guma and Heinemann after the republication in 1967 of *A Walk in the Night*, which is set in District Six. Cosmo Pieterse edited *Seven South African Poets* (1971 AWS 64), which introduced a range of writers of promise such as Keorapetse Kgositsile, C.J. Driver and Dollar Brand. Dollar Brand, already known for his jazz performances in District Six, was to become internationally famous for his music under his Muslim name of Abdullah Ibrahim.

A somewhat dishevelled romanticism has built up round the name District Six. Nobody remembers Districts One to Five. District Six was in central Cape Town and handy for providing labour for running the docks and the city. Immigrants, many from eastern Europe, first settled there after getting off the steamers. Hanover Street ran through its heart and down on to the Grand Parade in front of the City Hall, where all the big demonstrations took place. In the 1930s there was a vibrant cultural and political life in this tight network of streets. There were debating societies which competed with others from all over Cape Town. The front room of one man called 'the professor' was a library of books. People found an identity in 'brownness' and took an intense interest in people of mixed race such as Paul Robeson, Alexander Pushkin and Alexandre Dumas.

Under the Group Areas Act District Six had been allocated to Coloureds, the people of mixed race who might carry identity cards rather than the 'dompas' of the Africans. (Soon after our marriage Clare Currey pointed out that legally we should have identity cards but, safe in my whiteness, I told her I had never bothered to get one.) District Six exhibited the mixed cultures of a great international port. You could have Indian or Malay meals with people of any colour of the rainbow. The Cape Town office of *Golden City Post* and *Drum* at the bottom end of Hanover Street was a meeting place for journalists and writers. Dollar Brand and Chris McGregor played jazz on Sunday nights. It was a place of resort for young politicals of all colours. One Saturday in March 1960 the photographer Joe Louw, his English girl-friend and I looked down from his flat on the comings and goings in Hanover Street as on the radio the minister of justice announced the establishment of the state of emergency after Sharpeville; although this couple's relationship was illegal under the immorality laws, her raven black hair and sunburn meant they were in little danger in that part of town. Joe Louw, following the South African fascination with the American south, was later to record the assassination of Martin Luther King. He captured the forest of hands pointing to the murderer from the Memphis motel balcony. His photograph symbolised the struggle of black people everywhere.

Christopher Heywood in his book *A History of South African Literature* (Cambridge University Press 2005) has recently focused on the creole diaspora from

Africa to North America and the Caribbean, but also stretching across the Indian Ocean round the international gene pool of Cape Town and the other South African ports. He argues that 'South African creoles pioneered a South African identity for all South Africans' (p. 30). A famous resident was the trade unionist Jimmy la Guma, father of the writer, who claimed Javanese, Madagascan and Scottish ancestry.

District Six was living proof of the absurdity of apartheid, being at the centre of Cape Town, a city which stubbornly slowed down the imposition of racial segregation. In the 1960s the Cape Town Council still had Coloured councillors, such as Cissie Gool, from well-established Cape Town families. The audiences in the City Hall for concerts and ballet performances still did not have to be segregated. Apartheid on the council buses was successfully resisted for some time. It was appropriate that it was eventually to be from the Cape Town City Hall balcony that Nelson Mandela was able to wave to the world on his release. But by then District Six had been bulldozed by Pretoria. Even then the spirit of the place stubbornly prevented it being grabbed by the apartheid property developers and it has been left a ground zero at the heart of Cape Town.

The violence of District Six in Alex la Guma's *A Walk in the Night* was the foundation of the success of Christian Barnard's team at performing the first heart transplants in the world. The surgeons at Groote Schuur Hospital had been able to hone their skills because so many casualties with knife stabs to the heart were carted in from District Six each hard-drinking weekend. Bill Hoffenberg was the physician who did the tissue typing which was essential to the survival of the patient. As he was an employee of the government he was banned from any political activity, but covertly helped through all the changing crises of the struggle, such as getting Randolph Vigne, the editor of *The New African* out of the country and in running the underground activities of the International Defence and Aid Fund. When he was banned he was seen off at Cape Town airport by the staff of Groote Schuur Hospital in white coats.

Above the urban desert of District Six there is de Waal Drive, the motorway from Groote Schuur Hospital and the Southern Suburbs. As you sweep round its tight bends you can see out across the windy glittering sea that other scar on Cape Town, Robben Island. Bill Hoffenberg would never drive that way because of black thoughts. And as you steeply descend de Waal Drive under the walls of Table Mountain into the city you pass the Roeland Street jail which was Alex la Guma's 'stone country'.

Nadine Gordimer
Gaberone
1982

James Matthews and Richard Rive, Cape Town late 1960s

PUBLISHING

Alex la Guma

Alex la Guma came to imaginative writing through active politics. To what extent did that make his work propagandist, as was so often implied especially in South Africa? He saw himself as an African story-teller, recording events as told to him and fashioning a narrative which is both moral and entertaining. Some people maintain that his greatest strength was in the short story; but he applied his craftsmanship steadily over the years to several novels.

Born in District Six, Cape Town in 1925, he was son of the renowned trade unionist Jimmy la Guma. He was sacked from the Metal Box Company for organising a strike for higher wages. He then joined the Young Communist League in 1947 and the South African Communist Party in 1948. He was employed as a reporter by the political weekly *New Age* in 1954. He was one of 155 defendants in the protracted treason trial in the late 1950s. He was detained for seven months without trial under the state of emergency following the Sharpeville massacre in 1960. In 1961 he was arrested again for helping to organise a strike in protest against the establishment of an all-white republic. In 1962 *New Age* was banned, he was put under house arrest and was banned from publishing his own work. In 1963 he and his wife May were detained in solitary confinement under the 90-days law. While still under house arrest he was again detained in 1966; the 90-days law had now been doubled to 180 days. As he says in the autobiographical details he sent to Heinemann: 'By coincidence he was held in the cell recently vacated by fellow South African Albie Sachs.' His ban denied him the right to earn a living as a journalist and he and his family had to leave South Africa in 1966 to live in London. He went to Havana in 1978 to run the ANC Cuba office. He died in 1985.

A Walk in the Night was published in Cape Town in a rough stapled form and then in 1962 by Mbari in Ibadan, Nigeria. *And a Threefold Cord* was published in 1964 and *The Stone Country* in 1967 by Seven Seas Publishers in East Berlin. He was later taken on by London agent Tessa Sayle; she was already handling Albie Sachs, who was to write *The Soft Vengeance of the Freedom Fighter* about being blown up by BOSS in Maputo. She placed *In the Fog of the Seasons' End* (1972) and *Time of the Butcherbird* (1978) with Heinemann for publication in hardback and in the African Writers Series. Alex la Guma was awarded the Afro-Asian Prize for Literature in 1969.

A Walk in the Night (1967 AWS 35) was one of the earliest titles for the Series to be recommended to Keith Sambrook by the recently appointed Editorial Adviser, Chinua Achebe, writing on Voice of Nigeria paper from Broadcasting House, Lagos:

La Guma is a young South African. The ms. of his short novel was

> smuggled out of South Africa by Ulli Beier and published in Nigeria. If you like it I suggest you write straight away to Beier, c/o Mbari Publications ... Another publisher (I think Deutsch) is interested but I told Beier that the AWS was the better choice. (Chinua Achebe to KS 27 March 1963)

Lewis Nkosi, in a review of the original Mbari edition of *A Walk in the Night* in the *New Statesman,* says of this short novel set in District Six in Cape Town:

> What distinguishes La Guma's work is that it shows real people waging a bloody contest with the forces of oppression: they celebrate their few short moments of victory credibly enough, in sex, cheap Cape wines and stupid fights with one another.
>
> *A Walk in the Night* describes for us what happens to Michael Adonis, a coloured boy thrown out of his job for talking back to a white foreman, and a supporting cast of thugs, derelicts, spivs and neurotic cops 'doomed for a certain term to walk the night'. By the end of the night Adonis has killed a harmless, kindly old man; a jittery policeman has shot a small-time thug; a penniless man has been 'rolled' for the money he never had. (*New Statesman* 29 January 1965)

Mbari in Nigeria had printed 2,000 copies of *A Walk in the Night* but still had about 600 copies left which they hoped to sell in another year. Keith Sambrook offered to compensate them for unsold copies in order to avoid delaying publication beyond October 1964. William Heinemann thought it too short to bring out on its own in hardback and suggested that some short stories should be added, but still did not take the book for the general market. Ulli Beier sent four stories which had all appeared in the famous Mbari journal, *Black Orpheus*. In the margin of the letter from Mbari dated 20 May 1964 Keith Sambrook has written a question to ask Richard Rive when he next came into the London office: 'Is La Guma writing anything else?' He was indeed writing while under house arrest and we had missed it; this was *And A Threefold Cord,* a novel which he describes as being about 'life in a suburban shanty town' and which was published in 1964 in East Berlin.

Upon his release from another arrest in 1966 he finished a novel *The Stone Country* (AWS 152). George Adams is 'a political' in the stone country of the jail which stands below the walls of Cape Town's great mountain. He shares his food and listens to the tales of miserable lives. The prisoners have brought into jail the violence of District Six: Solly acting the clown in tattered rags, a scarecrow come to life; Josef the Turk, lean, sleek, dangerous as a knife blade; his sworn enemy, Butcher-boy Williams, a collector of tribute; and the Casbah Kid, who will hang for murder. The hierarchies within the jail reflect those within the apartheid police state. The guards have unquestioned power. Under them are the coloured guards but they are no more powerful than the cell bosses who collude with the guards to terrorise the weaker inhabitants. Even then prisoners spend their energy in personal hatreds among themselves instead of getting together to resist the power structure. It was not until 1974 that we were able to take over the rights for this title from Seven Seas, who had published it in English in East Berlin in 1967, and make it more easily available in the African Writers Series.

In the Fog of the Seasons' End (1972 AWS 110) was the first novel by Alex la Guma which we originated. It is an atmospheric novel of political organisation behind the newspaper headlines. This is what happens every day. This is the day-by-day work of dedicated people. Only at moments of crisis are dying bodies flashed up on television screens. But the political workers are always risking a tortured death out of sight at the hands of the security police. Keith Sambrook tried to persuade Tom Rosenthal at Secker to publish in hardback to secure reviews and library sales. But he thought it 'politically not sufficiently startling ... would certainly get rather sniffy reviews.' (T.G. Rosenthal to KS 30 July 1971). He wanted the headlines. In a letter to Alex la Guma's agent, Tessa Sayle, I said:

> I'm afraid that what you, Keith Sambrook and I like is the low key of the whole book. It is genuine. It makes you feel the grinding misery of organising politically. I personally know how authentic it is. (JC to Tessa Sayle 13 August 1971)

Alex la Guma set *Time of the Butcherbird* (AWS 212) in an arid Karoo town. Hlangeni's people have been 'endorsed out' to a bantustan to make way for mining interests. The grim Shilling Murile has returned from jail and is determined to take his vengeance on Hannes Meulen, a prosperous Boer farmer and prospective parliamentary candidate. The dramatically bloody cover is by George Hallett, the photographer who himself had come from District Six. It was difficult to persuade Tessa Sayle that the formal acceptance of such an accomplished novel was having to await consultation with our branches. I wrote: 'but you know the reasons. It makes all the difference in their attitudes towards selling the book if they are involved in selecting it.' (JC to Tessa Sayle 21 February 1972)

One of the last times I saw Alex la Guma was in 1983 when he was on the way back to Cuba from an Afro-Asian Writers Conference in Alma-Ata in Kazakhstan, many Aeroflot kilometres into the southeast of USSR. I too had been invited by Victor Ramzes, the secretary of the writers union of the USSR, who had done a great deal to get a range of African authors translated into Russian and other languages. He said if Heinemann could pay for me to get to Moscow then for the rest of the trip I would be a guest of the writers union. I was most excited by the chance. I was booked on a British Airways flight to Moscow, and then the Russians shot down a Korean airliner flight 007 near the Kamchatka peninsula. At the last moment I could not go because western pilots, boycotted Russian destinations. I think Victor Ramzes suspected that I had not gone as an act of Cold War protest whereas Alex la Guma could understand my disappointment at not going.

Alex la Guma was always gently friendly. He never talked much. His words flowed on to paper. Without his writing it was difficult to appreciate what an extraordinary man he was. Apparently at the time of his death he was at work on a novel called *Zone of Fire* in which, according to *The Companion,* he 'imagines the final phase of the protracted struggle for a democratic South Africa'. Only after 12 June 1986, the tenth anniversary of the demonstrations by the school kids in Soweto, did hope grow again. When he died in 1985 change still did not seem to be in prospect.

Cosmo Pieterse performing with Chris McGregor's Brotherhood of Breath, 1972

PUBLISHING

Dennis Brutus

Dennis Brutus was born to South African parents in 1924 in Rhodesia. He graduated from Fort Hare University, South Africa, in 1947 and taught in high schools for 14 years. He started studying law at the University of the Witwatersrand in the 1960s but was arrested. His first collection of poems, *Sirens Knuckles Boots*, was published by Mbari in Nigeria in 1963 while he was serving an 18-month sentence on Robben Island. His poems, *Letters to Martha,* which drew on that experience, were published in 1968. A substantial collection, which included other individually published books, came out in 1973 under the title *A Simple Lust*. A further collection, *Stubborn Hope*, was added to the African Writers Series in 1978. Slim volumes have continued to appear.

Letters to Martha

Paperback (1968 AWS 46)

One hot Mayfair afternoon in 1967, during my first summer of working on the African Writers Series, I was given the manuscript of *Letters to Martha* by the exiled writer Cosmo Pieterse. Dennis Brutus already had a Byronic mythology. He was arrested in 1963 but escaped while on bail. He had a Rhodesian passport and tried to escape through the Portuguese colony of Mozambique. The secret police, the PIDE, handed him back to South African security police. He told me that he realised that nobody would know of his capture and that he might be disposed of without anybody outside the police knowing; he made a desperate attempt to escape but was shot in the back in a Johannesburg street outside the Rand Club, while the owners of South Africa's wealth were at lunch. At least the newspapers now knew that he was back in South Africa, even if in hospital. After recovery he was sentenced to 18 months' hard labour on Robben Island. Dennis Brutus described *Letters to Martha* as:

> Poems, chiefly of experiences as political prisoner. On release from Robben Island Prison served with banning orders which made it criminal to write anything which MIGHT be published. This included poetry. Thus wrote poems but called them 'letters' and wrote them as if they were letters – this reduced the risk of prosecution and imprisonment. FURTHER NOTES TO FOLLOW c/o Cosmo (DB publicity questionnaire for Heinemann)

My first memory of Dennis Brutus is of him in the offices of *Contact*, the Cape Town liberal fortnightly newspaper, up in the eaves of Parliament Chambers opposite the Houses of Parliament. Patrick Duncan, the editor, enthusiastically used to bring in as many people with ideas as possible for editorial meetings. Dennis Brutus was one of them.

I had grown up in England as the son of writers who assumed that the worlds of politics and writing were separate. In South Africa writing was a political act. Writers and artists were forced by the socially divisive policy of apartness to take sides. Most of the authors at Oxford University Press in Cape Town were openly political in a way that they were not in London. Also in England in the 1950s it was assumed that sport had nothing to do with politics – and even less to do with poetry.

Dennis Brutus interwove the worlds of politics, poetry and sport. He was central to the development of the sports boycott which led to the exclusion of South Africa from the Olympic Games. Even more painful was to be the boycott by their rough and tough rivals the New Zealand rugby football team, the All Blacks. In the late 1970s Dennis Brutus, when a professor in the US, nearly lost his US work permit by working for the disinvestment campaign which put pressure on the universities and city councils to boycott banks and financial funds that invested in South Africa. These boycotts were to prove more effective than the UN trade embargoes which the multinational companies cynically circumvented. White South Africans could not evade the psychological effect of being unable to show off their sporting prowess against other nations. Dennis Brutus used poetic leaps of the imagination to develop the sports boycott and the disinvestment campaign, which were to prove to be as effective as any other methods in working in the long term for peaceful change in South Africa. According to the BOSS files in Pretoria in 1978 he was rated as 'one of the 20 most dangerous political figures overseas' (Gordon Winter *Inside BOSS*, Penguin, p.202).

It is now taken for granted that the best way for poets to sell books is at readings of their own work. In the case of Dennis Brutus the message of the poetry was immediate and political. By the time of the publication of *Letters to Martha* in 1968 he had been active in setting up SAN-ROC (the South African Non-Racial Open Committee for Olympic Sports). He was already jetting round the globe pursuing the cause of non-racial sport and wowing them with his poetry about Robben Island. Dennis Brutus writes letters in both an ordinary and an italic hand, according to his moods. In a letter written in ordinary hand on notepaper headed 'In Flight … Pan Am Jet Clipper' he scribbled:

> Sorry I was not able to make contact before I left: anyway will you please let me have another <u>doz</u> of 'Martha' on my a/c please. Am well pleased with it, tho' dismayed that the typos for which I sent corrections were not amended. (DB to JC 14 February 1969)

He was on the way to New Zealand for a lecture tour organised by CARE (Campaign for Racial Equality), which was fighting for the All Black boycott. David Heap, the founder of Heinemann's New Zealand business, was asking for copies to be airfreighted and he was always to show similar initiatives in promoting the African Writers Series in his small but concerned market.

It was during this period that the post-room at Heinemann Educational Books at 48 Charles Street, Mayfair entered the mythology of the SAN-ROC campaign, which was eventually to lead to the expulsion of South Africa from the Olympics. In February 1969 Randolph Vigne asked me if Heinemann could find a job for Isaiah Stein who, having been banned, jailed and house-arrested, had arrived on an exit visa with his wife and eight children. Alan Hill and Keith Sambrook immediately agreed to take him on to run Heinemann's extensive internal and international post. He used to have committee meetings of SAN-ROC in the basement at Heinemann. SAN-ROC had taken out subscriptions to sports journals to make up a calendar of political action to persuade sporting bodies round the world to boycott South Africa. Trevor Hook, the Heinemann paper buyer, analysed the golfing journals.

Gordon Winter spied for South Africa and maintained an effective cover by filing anti-apartheid stories for the Johannesburg *Sunday Express*. He spotted that Isaiah Stein was sending out extensive mail for SAN-ROC using the Heinemann franking machine to pay for the postage. Tragically he sent the GPO franking machine number 853 to BOSS in Pretoria so that all Heinemann's South African post could be monitored. When *Inside BOSS* was published by Penguin in 1981, Alan Hill was very annoyed because Gordon Winter assumed that this use of Heinemann postage was unknown to him and the management. It was certainly known to Alan Hill in 48 Charles Street that Isaiah Stein was doing this work, especially as at times there were complaints among the secretaries that he was being slow with Heinemann post. If, after hours, I put my head round his door, I had to wave to half the people at the committee meeting round the table. It was a way in which the money which Heinemann made out of Africa was discreetly recycled in a cause which would have been approved of by all the authors in the African Writers Series if they had known. The facilities of companies are used for the promotion of all sorts of outside interests from golf to charities, some of which may benefit the company. Heinemann's owners Tilling, round the corner in Lady Crewe's former town house behind the most expensive lawns in Mayfair, would have feared that such activities threatened their investment in the PUTCO bus company which carted labour into Johannesburg at dawn. Alan Hill, like Nelson, knew the advantage of a blind eye. There was poetic justice in that two of Isaiah Stein's eight asylum-seeking children were to play football in the English premiership. Isaiah Stein even used to boast that his son Mark Stein had had a trial for England.

Cosmo Pieterse's informal style led to accidents. A penalty for Dennis Brutus's jetting around was that he was remarkably casual about the collection and publishing of his poetry. He wrote to me in italic script from his home in Finchley, where he occasionally seemed to stay, that he was unhappy about the way that Cosmo Pieterse had arranged the first collection:

> Some time ago you wrote that *Letters to Martha* would be reprinting. I have been chatting to Cosmo Pieterse, who put it together and we have a suggestion: That a new printing be revised with certain poems omitted and a number of others added (Say 6). The omissions would be poems which do not properly belong to the *Martha* group: the new additions would be poems written in the *Martha*-period. The book would thus have a greater unity while remaining the same size. Do let me know what you think. I shall be reading at the ICA on the 29th with Ted Hughes and Carolyn Kizer. (DB to JC 27 July 1970)

I wrote on this letter when I passed it to Keith Sambrook: 'I'm not keen. I'd prefer another book.'

A Simple Lust

Hardback and paperback (1973 AWS 115)
Includes revised *Letters to Martha* and *Sirens Knuckles Boots*

> I was glad to see you on Saturday night and to have a word with you. I hope it doesn't sound ungrateful but I hope in time people will think of one, not as pigeonholed in the category of 'African poet writing in English' but simply as someone writing poetry in English. I think one ought to try and escape a racial or geographical classification. (DB to JC 3 August 1970)

This letter, written in careful italic, was accompanied by a poem (27 July 1969) – 'one I found around' – on the Algiers Casbah, 'where the bombed structures gape/in mute reminder of the terror of the French'.

I wrote to Dennis Brutus, then in Denver, at the end of the month:

> We shall be delighted to do another book of poems by you. In view of your understandable desire to have the book considered as poetry and not exclusively as African poetry, we would like to do a hardback under the Heinemann imprint. We would suggest that this included your own selection of all your own poetry to date including those already published in *Letters to Martha*. Some time after that we could separately issue a paperback collection, which is after all the one that would sell in the African Writers Series … Do let me know if you would like to talk about the selection, although in the first place I suggest you go ahead and make it and then get our reactions. (JC to DB 28 August 1970)

Dennis Brutus accepted the offer but said that Chi Ude at Doubleday had asked Bernth Lindfors to make the selection. I feared another muddle and wrote to him:

> I hadn't realised until the other day that it was Cosmo who made the selection in *Letters to Martha*. It is certainly very unusual for a living and writing poet to have such trust in his editors as you apparently have. I would rather that you chose what you wanted to put in. Doubledays can then decide whether they want to take that collection. (JC to DB 10 September 1970)

Dennis Brutus sent the suggested collection on 30 November 1970. Keith Sambrook and I asked Arthur Ravenscroft, a South African academic from the pioneering Commonwealth course in the School of English at the University of Leeds, to read the manuscript, but he took a long time to report:

> As someone who not only admires Dennis Brutus as a man and as a poet, but also includes his verse in a postgraduate course in African Literature that I teach, my first reaction to this typescript was of disappointment and unease. The poems seemed patchy and uneven, yet when I went through them a second time, more carefully perhaps than before, I realised that I had been reacting not so much to the quality of the poems as a whole but largely to their arrangement in the typescript. There seem to be two reasons for this reaction, both flowing from the nature of Mr Brutus's poetry:
>
> thematically his poems do constitute a decided movement through a series of phases corresponding roughly to his biographical experience – pre-prison experience in S. Africa, prison experience, exile and world travel, life in England, the latter not <u>only</u> of exile, but containing an almost unwilling reaction to English phenomena, then moving back to memories of pre-exile, yet clearly distinguishable from the unambiguous poems of exile;
>
> the general development of his verse, a shading gradually from the earlier, wordier, usually more metaphor-laden and 'rhetorical' poems to poems that are sparser, barer, more muted in manner, but by no means less powerful.
>
> It seems to me, therefore, that a more comprehensive collection of Mr Brutus's poems, like the hardback being envisaged, should reflect these two poetic considerations. More than with some poets, a sort of chronology in the arrangement would seem more important for his work to be more meaningful to the reader …
>
> Finally, without going into too much detail, I would suggest the omission completely of the following poems listed in Mr Brutus's Index among the previously uncollected poems, on the grounds that they are too slight, or too melodramatic, or too attitudenizing,

> or too forced – in short, that they seem to me to fall considerably below the quality of the rest of the poems submitted, and don't really do Mr Brutus justice as the very considerable poet that he is. (Report by Arthur Ravenscroft July 1971)

Arthur Ravenscroft had allowed me to reveal his identity when I wrote to Dennis Brutus:

> At last! Arthur Ravenscroft's report has arrived. I am sending it unexpurgated. You may find yourself disagreeing with his taste at the end. That will be up to you. You can, of course, include any of these poems if you feel strongly.
>
> Keith and I very much like the idea of including *Sirens Knuckles Boots*. Indeed I think that it would be very important and we can negotiate with Mbari.
>
> We also like the idea of the whole group of poems published in Texas as *Poems from Algiers* … (JC to DB 6 July 1971)

In a letter dated 8 July 1971 Dennis Brutus was in agreement 'with most of his suggestions – and criticisms', but raised the recurring problem that a supporter was negotiating, with all generosity, with yet another publisher. Professor John Povey, the South Africa editor of the Californian journal *African Art*, had also been in discussion with Bob Armstrong, the gentle and generous director of the Northwestern University Press, who was an anthropologist at the Herskovits Center. Bob Armstrong's own work was on Africa and he developed the first specialist list of any American publisher; he was later to become the director of the Ibadan University Press. He wrote to me:

> My position is very simply stated: I will do whatever is in the best interest of Dennis's poems … I told him that, in my judgment, there was little doubt that as between Doubleday and Northwestern University Press he should, given the opportunity, go to Doubleday. (Robert Plant Armstrong to JC 27 September 1971)

After all this Doubleday turned the Bernth Lindfors selection down. At about this time Chi Ude left the company, and they became reluctant to publish African authors from then on. We tried it on Hill and Wang, the adventurous publisher which was later to be bought by the prestigious literary imprint of Farrar, Strauss and Giroux. I was reserved in the way I wrote to Dennis Brutus about the possibility:

> The proofs are now with Arthur Wang of Hill and Wang. I have tended to think of him as drama publisher but he has taken Wole Soyinka's poetry and, although it has sold very poorly, he feels he ought to take some of the best African poets. I am afraid this sounds a bit defeatist about poetry but everybody in American publishing seems to be as defeatist about poetry as people in UK publishing are. It is a delight for us to be able to sell books of verse in Africa. (JC to DB 1 December 1972)

Fortunately on 23 January 1973 I was able to tell him that Hill and Wang had accepted the collection.

Ann Scorgie, the editor at Heinemann who had carefully brought his manuscript together for typesetting as he travelled from continent to continent, pointed out to him that the poem 'A Simple Lust' which Dennis Brutus had taken as the title for the whole book was missing. Dennis Brutus wrote to her from Northwestern at Christmas:

> This is not the poem I intended for the title piece; it is in fact a rehash, I think, of the idea – but not in the same lyrical vein. But it will have to do if I do not find the other – it is the first time I have succeeded in re-writing, sort-of, a lost thing. Since it is the last I am likely to write this year, it makes a suitable closing piece for the collection. (DB to Ann Scorgie 25/26 December 1971)

Dennis Brutus was always active in helping others despite the hyperactivity of his own life and investigated whether Ann Scorgie might take a degree at Northwestern (p. xxi).

Dennis Brutus's reaction to the finished copy of *A Simple Lust* gave me personal pleasure: 'I received a copy over the Easter weekend, and was, as you predicted, delighted with its appearance. It is really a pretty good job; I love the cover especially.' (24 April 1973) I had personally designed and letrasetted the restrained typographical cover and had used in large type a quote from the review of *Letters to Martha* in *The Guardian* by Myrna Blumberg, which said that Dennis Brutus's verse 'has a grace and penetration unmatched even by Alexander Solzhenitsyn'. Heinemann used this cover some 30 years later in 2002 in an advertisement in *The London Review of Books*.

Early in 1973 Dennis Brutus suggested he give a verse reading at the Africa Centre in Covent Garden to mark the publication of *A Simple Lust.* This initial idea grew into the meeting held on 24 May 1973 at which a total of six South African books were launched, and which now can be seen to mark the end of first phase of publishing books from South Africa in the African Writers Series (p. 188). In the week following that meeting I met Tony Beal, the managing director of Heinemann Educational Books, on a sunny summer morning when we were going to work through the handsome fanlighted doorway of 48 Charles Street. He asked me to come into his office where he calmly showed me a cutting from the Johannesburg *Sunday Express* which was headlined 'Brutus's poems published in S.A. under false name'. The reaction at William Heinemann, the general hardback publisher round the corner in Queen Street, Mayfair, had been anything but calm. Tony Beal had been told that the actions of one of his young editors was threatening the very existence of the William Heinemann company in South Africa. The cutting read:

> Several hundred copies of a book written by a banned South

African political figure have been openly on sale in the Republic for more than two years.

This disclosure was made to me this week by the overseas editor of the British publishing firm Heinemann, Mr James Curry.

Mr. Curry told me that the book, a collection of political poetry entitled 'Thoughts Abroad' had been secretly written by Dennis Brutus, 48, Coloured president of the South African Non-Racial Olympic Committee (Sanroc).

Mr. Curry said that Mr. Brutus had deliberately published the book under the false name 'John Bruin' so it could be freely published in South Africa.

The book was titled and published by Troubadour Press of Texas, America, in 1970. It consists of 24 poems written by Mr. Brutus in various parts of the world, including one written when he was a prisoner on Robben Island,

Further details of the book's contents cannot be given because Mr. Brutus is a banned person, whose statements cannot be legally published in South Africa.

But Mr. Curry told me: 'Mr. Brutus wrote the book as a little joke against apartheid, I think.'

'An initial consignment of 200 copies were sent to selected bookshops in Johannesburg, Cape Town and Pretoria. Complimentary copies were sent by Troubadour Press to newspapers and public libraries, which were unaware of the deception.'

Mr. Curry said that the hoax was successful and that more copies were requested after the book had received favourable reviews in several South African papers.

One book doomed for banning is 'A Simple Lust', published by Heinemann this week.

It contains all Mr. Brutus's previous works, including the poems he wrote under the name John Bruin.

Dennis Brutus is rated by Pretoria as 'one of the 10 most dangerous South African political figures overseas.'

The rating is understandable because Mr. Brutus is responsible for South Africa's almost total exclusion from international sport. (*Sunday Express* Johannesburg 27 May 1973)

Dennis Brutus had given an interview to Gordon Winter, the BOSS spy who used journalism as a cover. The devious Gordon Winter could not quote a banned writer, so he had put the words of Dennis Brutus in my mouth without telling me. I had not given this interview; only the quote about Dennis Brutus having 'a little joke' were my words. I suppose in this game of joke and counter-joke I would have told him the same story if he had actually interviewed me. Dennis Brutus had asked me, when assembling the manuscript, whether John Bruin's poems should be included in the collection and I had said that the time had come to reveal the joke, as the whole of *A Simple Lust* would in any case be banned in South Africa. In the end the joke was on me. (Another joke: 'Bruin' means Brown in Afrikaans and is used for describing coloured people.)

The reason that the managing director of William Heinemann in London was so upset was that the general manager in Johannesburg was in the middle of discreet negotiations with the Publications Control Board to clear the proofs of a new novel by the South African writer Wilbur Smith. The problem was not politics but sex. Wilbur Smith sold exceptionally well in South Africa especially to ladies' book clubs; while the maid was at work the madam would be romancing through Wilbur Smith's sweaty nights. The macho style appealed to men. The Dutch Reformed pressure on the board meant that a sex threshold had to be observed. Heinemann were waiting to hear which lusty passages would have to be toned down. So in effect readers throughout the world had what Wilbur Smith wrote cleared by the South African Publications Control Board.

Another South African title which was published at the Africa Centre meeting was a collection of poetry by Arthur Nortje called *Dead Roots*. Arthur Nortje was Dennis Brutus's former pupil at Paterson High School in Port Elizabeth. He took up a scholarship at the University of Oxford but died very young in 1971. Master and pupil had in 1962 entered for the Mbari prize in Ibadan and they had both won awards.

Dennis Brutus, while serving his 18-months' sentence on Robben Island, was summoned to the commandant's office and there to his surprise handed a cheque for £150 as his Mbari prize. This was a serious amount of money in those days and could have greatly helped his wife and children. The story, although recounted by Gordon Winter, rings true:

> As Dennis ran his eyes over the accompanying letter he noticed something which caused him to hand back the cheque to the commandant. 'I'm sorry, sir, but I must ask you to return this to the sender.'
>
> When the astonished commandant asked why, Dennis pointed to a clause in the rules stating that the poetry contest had only been open to non-Whites.
>
> 'Well that's all right,' smiled the commandant, 'You are a non-White.' Shaking his head, Dennis replied, 'It's true that I am classified by Pretoria as a Coloured person, but it's not all right. The contest was not open to Whites. That makes it racialistic, and I will not associate myself with anything of that nature.' (Gordon Winter, *Inside BOSS* Penguin 1981, p. 212)

Stubborn Hope

Hardback and paperback (1978 AWS 208)

Over the years Dennis Brutus has published at least eight slim volumes of verse with a range of publishers. His two collections *A Simple Lust* and *Stubborn Hope* draw on work in some of those books, but also include substantial bodies of previously unpublished work. In 1975 he sent me two short manuscripts together with other scripts. I had to point out to him that Heinemann could not publish a flow of slim volumes:

> One problem with the African Writers Series is not to produce too many titles so that we make sure that we can put enough effort into promoting those titles which we do publish. So that is one reason I am anxious not to put out two titles by you close together – otherwise it means cutting out somebody else. (JC to DB 15 October 1975)

In addition Dennis Brutus provided a new problem. He wanted us to publish them under pseudonyms. He wanted 'The Egyptian Sequence' putting out under 'D. UMBO', which only sounded African if you thought of Walt Disney, and 'Schizophrenic's Journal' under the name Peter Carson which did not even sound vaguely African. His campaigning fame had helped us get attention for his poetry under his name. He had successfully sold copies of his poetry at readings round the world. I had willingly agreed to reveal the banned poet behind the Afrikaans-sounding John Bruin.

Dennis Brutus had also sent the manuscripts to Arthur Wang in New York. Arthur Wang declined on 13 March 1975, giving him the reason that '*A Simple Lust* has not done well in the market-place. We have not succeeded (I cannot understand why) in getting the book reviewed in the right places. This indeed baffles me.'

Even before he had received the rejection letter from Hill and Wang Dennis Brutus told me on 25 February 1975 that he had accepted an offer from Don Herdeck, who ran Three Continents Press (p. 171), for a collection of poems and that he had given him world rights. As usual with Dennis Brutus, we were riding into confusion over publication rights. At times Don Herdeck tried to make out that Heinemann was an imperialist bully who elbowed out the small publisher, while in fact himself enjoying the role of the privateer. He was very sensitive about the division of market territories in far-flung parts of the globe. He wanted to have exclusive rights in the Caribbean and so I wrote:

> The only real problem – and it is a major one – is the question of the Caribbean. Our presence is already strong in the Caribbean. Turnover has doubled. We have established a company which goes into full operation next year with a young and energetic Jamaican

> Manager who has a deep personal interest in the literature. The Caribbean Writers Series is already well-established. The African Writers Series is also in great demand and we have stocking arrangements with Sangsters in Kingston. It would be a great disappointment at this time of growth of a strong publishing relationship if this were to stand between us. (JC to Don Herdeck 3 October 1975)

In the end he agreed that we should have the Caribbean market but 'excluding the American Virgins'.

Dennis Brutus again had shown reluctance to make his own selection and I had reluctantly suggested Arthur Ravenscroft, who would have taken forever, or Bernth Lindfors, who would have got on with the job. Somebody had suggested the Cape Town poet, artist and publisher Peter Clarke, but there might well have been a clash of personal tastes and there would certainly have been a security problem with working on the poems in South Africa. Anyhow, Don Herdeck, with a confidence I did not possess, did the job himself and had the typesetting done in his garage with reasonable results.

I sent to Ibadan and Nairobi the complete collection marked with the selection suggested by Don Herdeck. Henry Chakava in Nairobi replied:

> You ask if I think that the poetry needs further cutting down. As far as I am concerned the selection is excellent. Whoever did the selection has excluded a number of the poems which are weak, as well as others which tend to weaken the poet's vision. My own feeling is that a few of those in the latter category could have remained, if for variation only. However, that is a minor point and I hope you will want to go ahead straight away. (HC to JC 22 January 1976)

Aig Higo cabled at about the same time:

> MUST PUBLISH BRUTUS; A STUBBORN HOPE x SUGGEST ELABORATE INTRODUCTION PLUS NOTES ON EACH POEM AT THE END – HIGO+

Dennis Brutus was pleased by the reactions of Henry Chakava and Aig Higo and on 28 February 1976 said that he was 'willing to do short pithy notes to some of the poems'. Unfortunately this idea of notes was ill-timed as Dennis Brutus had other concerns. 1976 was an Olympic year and during it South African schoolchildren, despairing of their elders, had thrown the name 'Soweto' round the world like stones aimed at window mesh on a police Saracen. I wrote to Don Herdeck:

> I really am in absolute despair about this book. Dennis Brutus, to my mind, is grossly irresponsible about his poetry. I attach a copy of a letter from Wayne Kamin at Troubadour Press. This chap may be very good but I feel more and more that it would be better to

> get out the straight-forward selection you have already made and stop fooling around. (JC to Don Herdeck 26 October 1976)

Six months later I wrote to Dennis Brutus:

> I've just heard from Don Herdeck that he saw you in Boston at the African Studies Association Conference and that you promised him the manuscript of *Stubborn Hope*. What news? Don's selection looked fine to me. I feel more and more that we should let the poems speak for themselves and not worry about annotations. Let's have them! Let's price them! Let's publish them! Any hope? (JC to DB 6 April 1977)

On 28 April 1977 Don Herdeck wrote:

> Regarding Dennis Brutus and *Stubborn Hope*: Not much hope. I saw Dennis for 30 seconds at ALA meeting in Madison Wisconsin and he was very evasive. He said he had misplaced or lost the ms. (Don Herdeck to JC 28 April 1977)

Stubborn Hope was eventually published in 1978, although there had been the old problem about order and Dennis Brutus had to add a note to the English edition explaining which poems had been written some time before in South Africa. I was able to tell Don Herdeck:

> Dennis gave a very moving poetry reading at the Africa Centre in aid of Ngũgĩ. It became a strange sort of prayer meeting with writers like Amadu Maddy and Dennis contributing their experiences of imprisonment and how it must be affecting Ngũgĩ – if he lives. (JC to Don Herdeck 28 September 1978)

Dennis Brutus, ever the campaigner, wrote in February 1979:

> What news from Ngũgĩ now he's out? How's his health? Currently trying to do something for the Korean poet Kim Chi Ha … (DB to JC February 1979)

His letters often had enclosures. The file finishes with a 'Resolution on National Actions':

CALL FOR A NATIONAL WEEK OF ACTIONS, APR 4–11, 1979
TO DEMAND:

UNITED STATES OUT OF SOUTHERN AFRICA; DIVEST NOW!

SELF-DETERMINATION FOR THE PEOPLE OF SOUTHERN AFRICA!

NO TO RACISM FROM THE UNITED STATES OF AMERICA!

This campaign was based on a poet's perception that American banks would not want to lose the business of handling the incredible wealth of US universities. The committee mobilised the students to march to demand that universities only place their investments with banks which had disinvested in South Africa. They spread the campaign to the councils of cities where there are large black populations such as Washington

DC. These councils started to demand that their banks disinvest in South Africa or they would take away their vast accounts. The campaign gained strength during the years of Reagan and Thatcher. Dennis Brutus used his Commonwealth connections to lobby, among others, the Commonwealth Secretariat in London. In 1989, the year before the change in South Africa, Sir Shridath Ramphal was able to write in a foreword to a report to the Commonwealth foreign ministers:

> South Africa's apartheid economy is now trapped in a situation where it cannot sustain a satisfactory rate of growth without sufficient new sources of foreign exchange which are no longer in prospect. (*Banking on Apartheid*, Commonwealth Secretariat in association with James Currey 1989)

Dennis Brutus put his whole future in the US at risk. A campaign had to be run to make sure that Dennis Brutus's work permit was renewed. Letters, petitions and lobbying only saved him on appeal. His campaign was not popular with the university administration itself. He told me that when he was teaching at Northwestern about 40 per cent of its income came from the military-industrial complex.

The contributor to *The Companion*, published in 2000, makes the interesting point:

> Within South Africa itself Brutus is still not well known; unlike the poetry of Mbuyiseni Mtshali, Mongane Wally Serote, and Sipho Sepamla, his was not allowed to feature in school and other anthologies in the later days of the apartheid era. By the time his work was officially unbanned in 1990 and he had begun to pay visits to South Africa, readers had become less interested in the tribulations of the previous era, and indeed he seemed a visitant from the past. There can be little doubt, however, of his stature as one of South Africa's most important poets. His most memorable poems are those about or closely related to his concrete experiences as an opponent and a victim of apartheid. But as a citizen of the world and a person deeply concerned with human and cultural rights and freedoms he has continued to write thoughtful, delicately crafted, sometimes haunting lyrical poems.

PUBLISHING

Bessie Head

Bessie Head was born in 1937 in the Fort Napier Mental Institution in Pietermaritzburg, South Africa. Her mother had been consigned there after what may have been an affair with a black servant in her parents' household. Bessie Head worked in Cape Town for *The Golden City Post*, which was in the renowned *Drum* group. Her first two novels *When Rainclouds Gather* (1968/1987 AWS 247) and *Maru* (1971/1972 AWS 101) were set in Botswana, which had become her country of exile. She told Mary Benson that she was unable to write about South Africa because people there tend to think in racial groups. She had great trouble in getting *A Question of Power* (1973/1974 AWS 149) accepted but, with its revealing concern with schizophrenia, it has attracted the most critical attention of all her ten books. Acceptance for the African Writers Series, after it had been declined by the New York and London publishers of her first two books, gave her the energy to revise it. It now appears in Penguin Classics. The genesis of the collection of short stories about village women, *The Collector of Treasures* (1977 AWS 182), were the interviews she was making for *Serowe: Village of the Rain Wind* (1981 AWS 220). Her writing brought her international recognition and travel; she was in her early 40s when she left southern Africa for the first time. She died, a citizen of Botswana, in 1986 at the age of 49. With the strong support of Heinemann Inc. in the United States and David Philip in Cape Town several titles were added to the African Writers Series in later years.

A Question of Power

Hardback Reg Davis-Poynter 1973
Paperback (1974 AWS 149)

Schizophrenia is shocking. It is even more shocking in oneself. It is shame. How do you face the outside world? How, as a writer, do you dare to lay your very self bare? *A Question of Power* was clearly written out of awful personal experience.

Randolph Vigne, the exiled South African publisher, told me of the difficulties Bessie Head was having over getting her latest manuscript published. She was already known for her novels *When Rain Clouds Gather* and *Maru*, which had been published to good reviews by Scribner in New York and Gollancz in London. At the suggestion of Randolph Vigne, the manuscript of *A Question of Power* was sent to me in 1972.

Bessie Head had just sacked the famous agent Hilary Rubinstein, who had been star of the defence for Penguin in the Lady Chatterley trial. In her letter to him she exploded:

> Patronage galls me. I see that you are waiting patiently and hopefully for another book. Please do not bother. This letter is intended to end whatever business relationship we had. If you cannot wait for another agent to come and collect my affairs from A.P. Watt you are free to throw the whole bloody lot of my work out of the window … I don't need your patronage Hilary. You are not my type. You know what would happen with the fourth book: 'Poor dear, she's a loony.' I am supposed to write books that are rejected by you. I prefer to be rejected by both Gollancz and McCalls then see what I do next. This is goodbye. (BH to Hilary Rubinstein 16 June 1972)

Bessie Head's new agent was Giles Gordon, who had published her first two novels. It was somewhat surprising, as Bessie Head told me that he had rejected *A Question of Power* before leaving Gollancz:

> He rejected it with a very stupid letter, jumping about the hedge on my misuse of the English language. This is quite a thing with him. English is spoken perfectly over there, he has informed me, twice. (BH to JC 16 June 1972)

As long as Bessie Head lived I went on fearing that our publishing relationship might be explosively terminated. She was to quarrel with a whole sequence of publishers and agents who were not only a long way away in mail boat miles but distances away in cultural sympathy. She was as hair-springed as a landmine in detecting British people being patronising. Her exiled South African friends – Randolph Vigne, and the writers Myrna Blumberg, Ken Mackenzie and Mary Benson – managed to keep an airmail bridge with her in her own exile in Botswana. *A Question of Power* had also been turned down by Cape, Scribner, Doubleday, Houghton Mifflin and several other well-known imprints. The editor at Saturday Review Press said that it gave her sleepless nights but did not accept. Bessie Head expected the worst from me:

> The book has so far antagonised many people so should it antagonise you please land it straight on to Randolph. (BH to JC 28 June 1972)

I accepted *A Question of Power* on 24 August 1972, within six weeks of the arrival of the manuscript, apparently before getting an outside reading. Keith Sambrook and I felt as hopeful about it as did the South African network. Undoubtedly she was an exceptional writer and this difficult work should be published, even if the London literary press might give it critical reviews. The African Writers Series was riding on a high in its tenth year and I could be confident about getting colleagues in Africa and England to agree to accept it. I wrote to Bessie Head:

> *A Question of Power* numbs me. I go back and back to it … It is big. You throw the lot on us and I really can feel, feel, feel though I cannot always understand. I know that you have laid the inside

of your head on the paper and I think perhaps we are all asking you to do the impossible ... The book will never be easy. But it has to be slightly more accessible. It is a public exposure of a very private thing. Having got so far with your public exposure can you go a little further? Can you go back to it? Can you stand outside it? ...

> We are willing to give it exposure in African Writers Series as an experiment, seeing that it does not seem to be considered right for the UK hardback/paperback market. There is no better way to publish a book in Africa than in the African Writers Series. But if it is in that Series, distribution in the UK will mainly be through African Studies channels. You have got a lot to say about the human mind. It just happens to be an African saying it. One would like more people to be able to read it. (JC to BH 24 August 1972)

I had met Bessie Head through Randolph Vigne in Cape Town in 1960. It was the heady time after Sharpeville when, for a couple of months, the Afrikaner nationalist state had looked rocky. African countries to the north were bursting into independence. We had published some of her work in *The New African*. She wrote:

> Our paths crossed so suddenly. I remember seeing you in an office in Cape Town, with your head turned sideways looking at something. That's all. And the New African. I can't remember talking to you, so it is an odd feeling receiving a letter from you. (BH to JC 31 August 1972)

In the same letter Bessie Head lamented:

> You can't do much about re-writing unless you have a buddy who is putting his/her mind against yours and thinking with you.

I sent the book to be read by Richard Lister who as a novelist in his own right, I suggested to Bessie Head, might be that 'buddy':

> He won't want to touch it if he does not respond totally. He would work on a photocopy so you could reject it all and insist on it being all included ... Giles Gordon and I feel that if it proves possible to provide a catalyst in this way then he can try the London hardback publishers again. (JC to BH 21 September 1972)

Giles Gordon wrote to Bessie Head:

> [James Currey] still feels, as I do, that it would be a happier situation if the book could be published in hardback by a trade publishing house as well, as only then would it be likely to be widely reviewed and substantially ordered by libraries. (Giles Gordon to BH 21 September 1972)

After all the previous reports and rejection letters Richard Lister's letter was disarmingly straightforward:

> I think it is a wonderful book. I feel very strongly opposed to the idea that the author should be asked to do any re-writing. The thing is superb as it stands....I do agree that it could be slightly

> more accessible to the reader, but all that is necessary – or, I think, desirable – for this is a fair number of very trifling editorial amendments. These are very tiny points indeed; mostly, in fact, a matter of punctuation. Sometimes a sentence pulls one up and has to be re-read to grasp the meaning. Sometimes this is because it expresses something that is complex or demands a pause for thought; but quite often it is because the comma is in the wrong place…. it demands some effort of attention from the reader, and the effort is enormously rewarded. It is a considerable achievement, a prolonged spiritual crisis seen from the inside and powerfully described. (Richard Lister to JC 27 September 1972)

The result was that Bessie Head, having reacted against all the other reports, set to work on her manuscript with a new confidence even ahead of receiving detailed suggestions from Richard Lister who wrote to her:

> … it is an unfamiliar world, and one has to feel one's way through it with an open apprehension rather than reasoning. (Richard Lister to BH 9 November 1972)

On receiving a copy of this letter I wrote to Richard Lister:

> One cannot prophesy whether she will react against it or not. We will just have to wait with bated breath. Giles Gordon [is]… overwhelmed by the fact that you and we have got her to look at the manuscript again. (JC to Richard Lister 13 November 1972)

On 27 November 1972 I wrote to her to say that I was delighted to hear from Giles Gordon that a new left-wing hardback London publisher Reg Davis-Poynter had accepted it. I was keen that it should also be published a third way in a general market paperback. Caroline de Crespigny, a political activist who had had to leave South Africa on a one-way exit visa, had recently started the highbrow Picador imprint in London alongside the middlebrow Pan. I recommended to Giles Gordon and Reg Davis-Poynter that they should follow up this South African contact, although this did not work out. However, the book was accepted in 1977 for the American market by Tom Engelhardt, the bold editor at the distinguished New York imprint Pantheon.

On 20 November 1972 Bessie Head wrote three excited pages, finishing by philosophically saying that she was no longer the 'critic's pet' and expecting poor reviews but thanking me for 'sticking by a book with so many embarrassments it could simply be the work of someone insane.' A major aim in getting the book published in hardback was to get over the prejudice of literary editors of the Sundays and weeklies against reviewing paperbacks. So it was ironic that one of the best reviews was by Ronald Blythe in *The Sunday Times* where it was the Heinemann African Writers Series paperback edition which was specifically reviewed rather than the Davis-Poynter hardback edition:

> Bessie Head's vision of the separation of the mentally sick and her ability to give mind-suffering a kind of picture language convey a positively medieval horror. She brilliantly develops ascending degrees of personal isolation and is very moving when she describes abating pain. She herself is a South African exile in Botswana. Her novels – this is the third – have a way of soaring up from rock bottom to the stars, and are very shaking. (*The Sunday Times* 18 August 1974)

In 2002 *A Question of Power* went into Penguin Classics with, on the back cover, a quote in large type from Ronald Blythe's review.

The Collector of Treasures
(1977 AWS 182)

Women told stories to Bessie Head with Chaucerian vividness. She had been working on her book on the village or town of Serowe and in June 1974 suggested to me that she put together a collection of short stories which would include some triggered by tales she had heard from women. She sent the collection in 1975 to Reg Davis-Poynter and me under the original title of *Botswana Village Tales*, with a note for her two London publishers pointing out the sequence she had used to arrange the collection. She said that the last four:

> ... can be grouped together as they deal, in their different ways, with the complete breakdown of family life, especially in Bamangwato country where I live. All the data was given me by women who rear illegitimate children on their own. The really massive social analysis of the problem takes place in the story 'The Collector of Treasures' – (which I regard as my masterpiece). Since the problem of broken homes touches so deeply on my own experience, the story of other women's unhappiness has certain intrusions of my own forceful views on the subject, which appear to mar such stories like 'The Collector of Treasures' and 'Hunting'. So I wish to point out that I descended to preachy moralising only because the problem is so very desperate. (Note from BH for either James Currey or Mr Davis-Poynter undated)

At a later date she suggested that she used *The Collector of Treasures* as the title for the whole collection. In this title story the wife receives a note from her errant husband:

> Dear Mother, I am coming home again so that we may settle our differences. Will you prepare a meal for me and some hot water that I might take a bath.

On the evening of the husband's return the story continues:

> Satiated with food and drink, he had fallen into a heavy sleep the

> moment his head touched the pillow. His concubine had no doubt told him that the correct way for a man to go to bed was naked. So he lay, unguarded and defenceless, sprawled across the bed on his back. The bath made a loud clatter as Dikeledi removed it from the room, but he slept on, lost to the world. She re-entered the hut and closed the door. Then she bent down and reached for the knife under the bed which she had merely concealed with a cloth. With the precision and skill of her hard-working hands, she grasped hold of the genitals and cut them off with a stroke. A massive stroke of blood arched its way across the bed. (p. 103)

When the police Land Rover delivers her to jail the women warder, with 'a flicker of humour', puts her in a cell with four other women who have killed their husbands. It would be good if Heinemann (or even better Virago) reissued this book as a contrast to Alexander McCall Smith's lady detective from Botswana.

An author takes a great deal on trust from the publisher. The one regular test the author has of the publisher's integrity is the royalty statement. As Chinua Achebe has pointed out (p. 33), this is something which all too often publishers in Africa have tended to forget. Bessie Head expected the worst from publishers and agents and this led her in 1975 and 1976 to break with no less than three people who were genuinely trying to help her. From year to year I expected the same to happen to me. At least Heinemann had got off to a reassuring start. In a postscript she wrote to me: 'How is it that royalties started coming in so soon from your Heinemann edition of *A Question of Power*? Are sales good?' (26 May 1975)

Effective publication in southern Africa concerned me. As has been pointed out, several new independent publishers, such as David Philip and Ravan, had set up in South Africa in the 1970s. Among them was the Bateleur Press, started by the poet and writer Patrick Cullinan. He had visited Bessie Head in Botswana and had had enthusiastic discussions with her about publishing *Serowe,* the book of oral history which she had been working on for some time. Her interviews on this project had led Bessie Head to write new stories inspired by the experiences of women.

Her agent was working to overcome a technical problem which was cutting Bessie Head's earnings and her trust in her publishers. An alarmed Giles Gordon had written to me:

> As you know, largely because there is no double taxation agreement between Botswana and Britain or Botswana and America, Bessie Head has been losing to the tax man approximately two-thirds of her earnings on her writing. As she lives entirely off her typewriter this is a serious matter, and indeed she has gone on record not only to people in this country but to the President of Botswana saying that if the tax situation isn't resolved in such a

way that she loses substantially less of her income she will almost definitely write no more for publication in Britain or America.

With most people one would probably dismiss this as an idle threat. Those of us who know or have dealt with Bessie over the years absolutely accept that it's a threat she would most likely carry out.

The arrangement we have come to with Patrick Cullinan and Reg Davis-Poynter is that Bateleur Press will become Bessie's primary publisher ... (Giles Gordon to JC 8 September 1975)

South Africa had a double taxation agreement with Botswana and so could pass on her earnings without deduction of withholding tax. All this activity at the highest level just served to make Bessie Head feel more suspicious and persecuted. Reg Davis-Poynter had got the chairman of his board, the mighty Labour legal peer Lord Goodman, to raise her problem with the tax authorities. I do not believe Bessie Head realised in what high political regard Lord Goodman was held in Britain at the time. In November 1975 Giles Gordon sent me a copy of a sorrowful letter to Bessie Head:

I know that you've asked me not to communicate with you again but I'm just not prepared to lapse into total silence, to vanish into limbo (or would purgatory be more accurate?) after we have been in such regular communication for – how long? – over ten years ...

My first point concerns your tax situation. Frankly, I'm damned if I'm going to be blasted out of your life on this count ... It was only when Reg Davis-Poynter asked, after discussion with me, Lord Goodman to take an interest in your case at the highest level that the light began to be seen by the tax authorities ...

I assure you, dear Bessie, that nothing whatsoever you may or may not have said about my own writing has influenced my dealings with you or on your behalf as your agent. Truly, the suggestion is absurd. I suppose I represent about seventy authors. Some of them may think well of my writing, others loathe it, most I imagine haven't even read it ... I am sorry that you think that I am going through a personal crisis. I'm unaware of that ...

If I was victimising you why ... would I have spent hours and hours working with Reg Davis-Poynter and James Currey on your behalf – certainly not because I thought that Anthony Sheil Associates would get particularly rich on the proceeds ...

Bessie, I am not angry, I am sad. I admire you as a human being enormously. As a writer you are unique and unexcelled. I believe that I have acted throughout, first as your publisher and editor, later as your agent, not to your disadvantage ... (Giles Gordon to BH 25 November 1975)

Bessie Head did not feel easy with all the efforts of the Labour Party establishment on her behalf. Next summer I sighed when I received a letter from Reg Davis-Poynter saying:

> I am sorry to tell you that Bessie Head has decided that I am a crook, so that with great regret I have written to her to say that I can no longer be associated with her in any way. I don't want to go into the lunatic details in a letter. (Reg Davis-Poynter to JC 9 June 1976)

My reply showed that I feared the worst:

> How tragic. I certainly don't want to hear the lunatic details. It is too painful to see a person shooting down people on impulse. I will now step forward into the firing line expecting a bullet to the heart. (JC to Reg Davis-Poynter 15 June 1976)

Unfortunately the huge efforts made by Giles Gordon to find a hardback publisher had backfired. Bessie Head resented the fact that the hardback publisher took a proportion of the royalties paid by Heinemann.

She wrote to Randolph Vigne at this time: 'I feel a sense of relief more than anything else as I feel my affairs can at last be sorted out with people who make sense to me.' (25 June 1976). Bessie Head's letters to me began to become longer and more personal. I saw this as a danger. I was friendly but I set out to be brief and to the point in my replies. She tended to reply by return and I could not keep up that pace. I felt I could help Bessie Head by keeping a professional distance. I believed my first job was to help her get her work published rather than to become a pen pal. It is interesting to find in Patrick Cullinan's book, *Imaginative Trespasser*, on his correspondence with Bessie Head, that I appear quite remote.

She wrote to me on the same date accepting my offer of 15 June 1976 for the 'world rights excluding the United States':

> I could make a joke about your world rights … Heinemann AWS turns up everywhere, so get on with you! … I am grateful to you for your stand at this time, James, and I don't think it will go unrewarded. (BH to JC 25 June 1976)

I wrote to her about the enthusiastic marketing of the Series right across Heinemann:

> Your joke about world rights and Heinemann; just before your letter arrived I had been hearing from Keith Sambrook what a good display of the AWS, including your books, he had just seen in a university bookseller in Lund in Sweden. They also had our new Arab Authors displayed. They do get around. All our Managers round the World are enthusiastic about the Series. Our Australian Manager and Publicity Manager (his wife) thought up our annual AWS calendar. I am sending a copy of this for your amusement … (JC to BH 7 July 1976)

I had brought her to realise the advantages of publishing in the

African Writers Series. I had written to her the year before emphasising that we did not just make the decisions in London about whether to publish in London:

> I may have mentioned to you before that we feel that it is essential, with the development of editorial departments in our East African and Nigerian Companies, that they are integral to the process of selection as well as of selling the books once published. (JC to BH 6 May 1975)

I managed to convince her, as she wrote to me:

> I am happy to know that libraries will buy the AWS edition. Indeed, the AWS is more than a prestigious venture. I have been informed that people really regard it as a collector's item; they buy up each new edition, not so much through love for the writers but to have the whole collection. Something might be wrong here but that's the position. (BH to JC 10 December 1976)

Sadly she reacted against Patrick Cullinan publishing her stories in South Africa. Patrick and Wendy Cullinan were long-term supporters of Bessie Head and helped both with her writing and her finances. Patrick Cullinan has recently published their correspondence with Bessie Head, revealing what led to this hurtful break-up (*Imaginative Trespasser* Wits University Press 2005).

I contacted David Philip, my former colleague from Oxford University Press, Cape Town who, with his wife Marie, had set up their new imprint three years before. They accepted *The Collector of Treasures* for a South African edition and she was delighted:

> Only you and I know the ANGUISH of my life and I would have dreaded an adverse decision from him. As it is, I say, yippee! (BH to JC 17 January 1977)

There were postal hitches over the return of her manuscript for final work at this time. There had been sabotage bombs on the railway line through Botswana, but on 8 October 1976 she wrote:

> I had reduced the postal staff to the point of breakdown over the typescript. They went ashen at the sight of me; six of them were on duty to instantly report the appearance of the typescript to me. (BH to JC 8 October 1976)

Two editors in the US had particularly riled Bessie Head; ironically they were both women and both black. Wendy Wolf at Pantheon asked her to cut out the sections on white volunteers in her book *Serowe*. Bessie Head, who had a sound South African non-racial philosophy, was incensed. *The Collector of Treasures* had been sent to Random House. Unfortunately the novelist Toni Morrison, later to win the Nobel Prize for Literature, was only just getting back to her editorial job at Random House after a period at Yale; when she saw the title of the manuscript was *Botswana Village Tales* she rapidly sent it to the children's department. There is no record of what the children's editor made of the emasculation scene which is central to the title story!

The Collector of Treasures became a feminist passport for Bessie Head when she went, at short notice, to the US in 1977 to take part in the University of Iowa Creative Writing Program. She had never been outside southern Africa before. Her journey to the US was complicated by the rejection of her application for citizenship of Botswana. As she wrote to me at the end of 1977:

> I am tired of being a refugee and reporting to the police every Monday as I have been doing for the past 13 years (BH to JC 14 December 1977)

However, I was able at last to cable on 23 February 1979:

> CONGRATULATIONS CITIZEN OF BOTSWANA

London publishers then, and probably now, share a prejudice against collections of short stories. I and my colleagues at Heinemann would rather have had another novel offered to us. Now I share Bessie Head's feeling that the book contained some of her most outstanding work:

> I wish great things for that pretty book. It was the harvest of 13yrs of rural life in Botswana and I love village life very much. (BH to JC 14 July 1977)

Serowe: Village of the Rain Wind
(1981 AWS 220)

Mary Benson, who among many other books had written a biography of Tshekedi Khama, sent me the typescript of an article she had intended for *The Observer* in which she gave this vivid description of Bessie Head:

> 'Dumpy' she described herself to me: she could not know the impact of her presence and personality – the lighted face reflecting the animation and intensity of her thoughts, the spacious rhythmic gestures accompanying her talk, the husky yet always audible voice – all contributing to an impression of vitality and generosity.
>
> She has been unable to write about South Africa in any direct way because, she explains, 'people there tend to think in racial groups. It is as though, with all those divisions and signs, you end up with no people at all. The environment completely defeated me, as a writer. I just want people to be people.' (Mary Benson to JC 28 October 1976)

It was perhaps her feelings about writing set in South Africa which explained why she found working on *Serowe* so rewarding. The idea had come to her when reading Ronald Blythe's book *Akenfield*, which had been culled from the words and voices of Suffolk villagers in an England she had yet to visit. I was later to ask Ronald Blythe to write a couple of sentences to quote on the cover but his assessment was so enthusiastically extensive that, with his permission, we made it into a preface in the book.

Originally I had said to Patrick Cullinan that *Serowe* would not be suitable for Heinemann. Even when we had decided to go ahead the correspondence shows that we were doubtful whether a book with its unusual structure would fit into the African Writers Series or whether it should be published on its own. I wrote to the writer Laban Erapu, who was then an editor in the Nairobi office:

> … by using this technique Bessie Head makes people aware about their real roots in Africa. Although she uses Serowe in Botswana I feel that people anywhere in Africa could make comparisons with their experience in their own societies. (JC to Laban Erapu 17 April 1978)

Heinemann Nigeria reassuringly ordered no less than 1,500 copies from the first print run.

Penny Butler handled the editing with firmness and tact. It was overlong and Bessie Head tended to gush about people of whom she approved, and in particular Patrick van Rensburg. Reactions were mixed among the publishers' readers who had reported on the manuscript in detail. Bessie Head wrote a long piqued letter explaining her aims and answering their criticisms:

> How I see my Serowe book is as follows. It is a continuous picture of people producing things from its simplest beginnings like the self-sufficient traditional society to more complex forms of production.

She had used the lives of three men to provide a historical core:

> The three men hold together well, at least that aspect of their work that I deliberately selected. It was my intention to show that Khama, The Great, opened up the whole society to make it receptive to new ideas; and Tshekedi Khama laid the foundation of a type of education, free and experimental, that Pat van Rensburg could build on.

Various queries had been raised:

> You ask what people do in Serowe. I explained in the general portrait of Serowe in the introduction that Serowe is a traditional African village; in this sense it is not a place of employment but a place of rest. The work areas are at the lands where the people plough their crops and rear their cattle. When people are in Serowe, they are resting after the summer harvest. The bulk of the people keep this pattern up till this day. That is why it is so astonishing that that so much was done in a village like this to pioneer new forms of education, that is why it is astonishing that so much of the unexpected always happened here. I wonder why

> the readers did not see this. Was there something wrong with my introduction? Did it sound mad and unfactual? (BH to Penelope Butler 18 January 1979)

When the book was published in 1981 Elspeth Huxley said in a review in *New Society:*

> Ronald Blythe's *Akenfield* has become a classic in the literature of English social history. I should be surprised if *Serowe* did not win a similar place in the literature of post-independence Africa. Here is the warp of tradition and the woof of change. The pattern of the cloth confuses, as life confuses; there is no plain design. As for the book, every word rings true. (*New Society* 6 July 1981)

There had been repeated alarms as the publication of this complicated and highly individual book progressed. In 1979 the Berlin Festival ran a conference of African writers. One summer morning I arrived at the Hotel am Zoo where the writers were staying; the lobby rang with Bessie Head's high-pitched voice as she took the organiser, Dagmar Heusler, to task for her handling of per diems. As Bessie Head later wrote, 'We had enormous trouble from that lady.' Later in the day I found myself in the front line at a lunch in the Reichstag building. She set about accusing Heinemann of taking 80 per cent of income from rights such as those for translation, quotation and film, and only passing on 20 per cent to her. It was with some difficulty that I managed to persuade her that it was she who received the majority share. I wrote:

> It was good to see you in Berlin and a great relief to be able to explain that you had got Clause 14 … back to front … As I said to you we took the book on because we wanted to do it and there was no question of asking for charitable terms. If we do a book we do it on proper terms. (JC to BH 8 July 1979)

As it happened I had, in addition, already asked David Philip in Cape Town to pay royalties direct to Bessie Head in Botswana without deducting the proportion for Heinemann that the contract in fact allowed. Even this was misconstrued and Chris Green, her agent, managed to reassure Bessie Head that I was in fact being generous. Chris Green sent me a copy of Bessie's acceptance (30 December 1981) with a compliments slip on which she had written nothing but 'Phew!' Bessie Head had told her: 'I was thus very upset and immediately thought dark thoughts about Heinemann …'

Another misunderstanding arose between Bessie Head and myself about the free copies of *Serowe*, over and above the six books provided for in the contract:

> One of my problems is going to be how I am going to live in peace in Serowe once the book is published. There isn't a person in this village who will not want that book … I owe my 94 contributors a free copy each but the story will never stop there. I

> know this village. The fence of my yard will be broken down by the people. (BH to JC 19 July 1979)

I replied that 'if they honour you as a writer they ought to honour you by buying the book' (JC to BH 1 August 1979). She vented her annoyance with Heinemann to Patrick Cullinan. Certainly Heinemann did not expect to have to give 94 copies away, but in the end I got my colleagues to accept that we had to make an exception.

While Bessie Head was working on *Serowe* she was discovered by people from the UN and the World Food Programme. They found what she said in the book like *pula* (rain) in the desert. Without any evidence of her administrative capacities they wanted her to run a silkworm project.

> I know that I have always sounded like a poverty-stricken sort but with a job with U.N. and a few paid lectures here and there, I might be able to purchase large quantities of *Serowe, The Village of the Rain-Wind* from you with a grand flourish, with the accent on the grand flourish. I would certainly sell the copies in Serowe but without a dealers mark-up of profit ... The U.N. people said that the only way they could get any understanding of Botswana was through my books ... (BH to JC 20 August 1979)

She wanted us to sell her 500 copies for about £1,000, which she intended to borrow from the bank. I offered instead 100 copies charged against royalties which, once she had sold them, she could use to buy a further 100 from us. To my relief her bank manager in February 1981 refused to lend her money for the 500 copies and I wrote:

> I was desperately worried by your letter. It is essential that matters to do with selling books do not come between us in our editorial and publishing relationship. Neither you nor I are professionally experienced in selling large numbers of books. (JC to BH 30 January 1981)

Even then there was a letter which read like an incident recounted in the book itself. Thato Matome had contributed three stories but stipulated that none of the stories should bear her name:

> Thato Matome died suddenly on the 17th March this year. I approached her husband and asked if he would receive the Heinemann gift copy of the book for her as it was still her property, in spite of death. Her husband was dismayed to find out that all her stories appear under pseudonyms. He wishes to over-ride her stipulation ... (BH to JC 3 June 1981)

By now international recognition of her work was growing. In late 1980 Bessie Head and Ngũgĩ had been on a visit to Denmark at the invitation of the Danish library association. They then came on to London for a week to promote their work. There was a round of meetings, interviews and a press party. Jane Grant, who had been working on

Bessie Head's writing at the University of Essex, kindly asked her to stay at her home. I told Jane Grant that, if a whole week was too much for her and her family, Heinemann would pay for a hotel. She was driven to consider my offer seriously as Bessie Head talked excitedly to her all night.

Bessie Head was travelling with her son Howard who, though in his late teens, she treated in an obsessively protective manner. Howard sat silent in the corner of our meetings. In sympathy Penny Butler got her son, who was about the same age, to take him out in London one afternoon. Bessie Head was deeply concerned about which film would be suitable for Howard and the two teenagers were dropped from a taxi outside the chosen cinema in Haymarket. Penny Butler told me afterwards that she saw the boys go straight past the cinema and head off into Soho. Bessie Head got very agitated when the pair did not turn up for a long time after she knew the film had ended. During the week, in another cab, Howard proposed marriage to the newest member of the department, Vicky Unwin.

Bessie Head went back to Botswana via Zambia glowing after a week of attention from journalists and publishers; she was ecstatic about the expensive bottle of perfume that the women staff of my department, unknown to me, had got for her. 'My joy was limitless when I saw this gift.'

In 1978 I had sent her a copy of the AWS edition of *Mhudi*, the historical novel of the Tswana by Sol Plaatje, who had been the first secretary at the foundation of the ANC in 1912. This led her to experiment with writing a historical novel herself which was published in South Africa by Ad Donker in 1984 as *A Bewitched Crossroad: An African Saga*. We had considered it at Heinemann but sadly found it overburdened with chunks of history from textbooks.

After her death Heinemann and David Philip published a collection of her stories, *Tales of Tenderness and Power* (1990), a collection of her autobiographical writings, *A Woman Alone* (1990), which has been read on BBC Radio Four, and a novella *The Cardinals* with *Meditations* (1995), which she wrote during her time on *The Golden City Post* in Cape Town in the early 1960s. However, in many ways the most vivid posthumous publication is *A Gesture of Belonging* (S.A. Writers 1991), the exchange of letters from the years 1965 to 1979 with her most effective supporter, Randolph Vigne.

In the 1980s, during the early years of independence, the Zimbabwe International Book Fair took off and became pre-eminent in Africa. There was a symposium of African writers in Harare in 1982. The shocking news circulated that Bessie Head could not take up her invitation because she had cancer. I wrote to her expressing deep concern and she replied giving an explanation. My memory is that she told me, in a letter I have not found, that after accepting the invitation she realised that a certain South African writer would also be a participant at the Zimbabwe International Book Fair and that she had recently crossed swords with him at a writers' workshop in Gaberone. She panicked and gave cancer as an excuse. She had made up the sort of tale which could have formed the basis of one of her very own stories of women in her village. In 1986 she died, probably from something other than cancer, distressingly young at the age of 49.

Mary Benson describes Bessie Head on p.230

PUBLISHING

Mazisi Kunene

Ros de Lanerolle told me how, during endless ANC meetings in London at the beginning of the 1960s, she would become aware out of the corner of her eye that Mazisi Kunene was writing, writing, writing poetry in Zulu. Under the name Raymond Kunene he was supposed, as official ANC representative in London, to be doing something about the freedom struggle. Instead he was slipping away from his life of exile into drawing on what he had heard from his grandmother. Born in Durban in 1930, he was educated at the University of Natal before going to England in 1959 to pursue his studies. He returned to southern Africa to teach on the other side of the Drakensberg mountains in the University College at Roma in what was still the British protectorate of Basutoland. He was then appointed to teach African Languages and Literature in the pioneering African Studies Center at the University of California, Los Angeles.

The vast manuscripts of Mazisi Kunene's Zulu epics made us face up to all sorts of questions about what we were trying to do in the African Writers Series, which was centred on the un-African concept of the novel. They were originally written under his full name Mazisi ka Mdabuli w'Ekunene in Zulu, one of the most famous languages of Africa. Mazisi Kunene had in mind Milton's *Paradise Lost*. These epics were written by a man who loved the traditional trappings of African royalty and yet was committing his future to working for the liberation of South Africa through a modern political party. There was the question, which keeps coming up in Africa, of authenticity. Were the epics anthropology or literature? How did one handle history in imaginative literature? How did a publisher make the link to an audience reading the work of an oral tradition through the printed medium of English?

I felt insecure in my editorial judgements. I was certain that a Zulu should be presenting his own history. However, to what extent should he be presenting this history with a Zulu way of story-telling? Was I distorting African traditions by London-based demands for cutting, organisation and presentation? I had learned, working on the publication of books from Arabic, of how the translation of language is only the first problem; the translation into another cultural tradition is equally important. Fortunately my colleagues in the African companies were equally certain that the works needed more shaping and that in the format of a printed book the reader could be helped by chapter titles, section heads, running heads, lists of characters and all the mechanics of book publication. To what extent was Mazisi Kunene pushing forward our concept of what literature from Africa should be? Or was he being self-indulgent? His own society might expect long circuitous development. An audience approaching these epics through the western medium of English would probably be much less tolerant. Christopher Heywood felt 'he had emerged among the great South African poets' when he translated his Zulu poem into a language 'unaccustomed to hear the sung idiom of praise poetry' (*A History of South African Literature*, p. 164). Our correspondence went through periods of stress when he wished he had gone to other publishers and I was counting the cost of so much work over a period of four or five years. In the same years in the late 1970s Henry Chakava was coming to terms with the political, financial and cultural realities of publishing Ngũgĩ's work in Gikuyu (p. 129).

The importance of what we were both trying to do was brought home in a review I found of a historical novel on the Zulu king Dingane by Peter Becker published by Longman, no doubt to excite the reading clubs in Durban. The review was by the novelist Lewis Nkosi, who had been on *Drum* magazine.

> It is a shock for a Zulu, reading for the first time the story in English and by an outsider, to encounter terms like 'tyrant' and 'despot' used of kings who my parents never talked about save with very great awe and respect. Whatever its brutality, they always talked of this period as the finest in the history of the Zulus – perhaps as an antidote to the bitter pill of defeat. (*New Statesman* 29 January 1965)

Anthem of the Decades

Hardback and paperback (1981 AWS 234)

Diana Collins at the International Defence and Aid Fund passed on the manuscript of *Anthem of the Decades*, a creation epic in some 14,000 lines which describes the struggle among the gods for the future of man. Mazisi Kunene was banned because of his political work and so he could not publish in South Africa for the millions of Zulu speakers. For a long time he had refused to translate his work into English, holding that he was not an English poet and that he had to be read in his own language. In the 1970s he despaired and decided to translate this epic into English. He also began work on translating his Zulu manuscript of *Emperor Shaka the Great* (1979 AWS 211). He had finished five volumes in Zulu in his great scheme of ten volumes about his people. He had already established a reputation for reworking his short poetry in English with *Zulu Poems*, which André Deutsch had published in 1970. We had a happy time working with him in the early 1980s to publish *The Ancestors and the Sacred Mountain* (1982 AWS 235), which was two collections of poetry in one book.

I wrote, in a letter on 1 August 1974 asking to see the manuscript of *Anthem of the Decades,* that I hoped that his work would be as important as Okot p'Bitek's *Song of Lawino*. As one who wrote about gods and emperors, and whose reply was headed c/o Prince Mphoeng Khama, P.O. Box 2, Serowe, Botswana, he revealed large ambitions:

> Yes the 'Song of Lawino' is an epoch-making contribution to African literature. But then without sounding boastful I think you will find that the comparison with 'Anthem of the Decades' is like comparing 'Paradise Lost' and 'Song of Hiawatha'. (MK to JC 8 August 1974)

Ros de Lanerolle said in her report on *Anthem of the Decades*:

> He feels that prose and poetry traditions in French and English have now established themselves on the continent, and the time is now ripe for a new kind of breakthrough into something more Africa's own. And for this to happen, the great chasm between the 20th century writing in foreign languages and the ancient underground reservoir of popular myth and legend must be bridged. (Ros de Lanerolle 7 October 1974)

Richard Ntiru in Nairobi said in his 1975 report that the style was 'sometimes unnecessarily miltonic i.e. elevated' and that sometimes 'the difference between poetic prose and bad verse is difficult to establish'. Paul Edwards at the University of Edinburgh was working on a collection of translations of Icelandic sagas for Penguin. I told him we were seeking help from the 'Edwards Saga Advice Bureau' (8 January 1976). He was forthright and said that 'at its best it's likely to end up as Ph.D. fodder for some bloody careerist' (6 February 1976). After much revision we published *Anthem of the Decades* (AWS 234) in the African Writers Series in 1981 and Doris Lessing chose it in *The Observer* that Christmas as one of her 'three books of this year'.

Emperor Shaka the Great

Hardback and paperback (1979 AWS 211)

I was far more engaged by *Emperor Shaka the Great*, which we had published earlier in 1979. I prefer gods to take human form and be just as nasty. I was certain that there would be interest throughout Africa because the name of Shaka was already the subject of so many plays, poems and novels. This was chiefly due to translations of Thomas Mofolo's novel *Chaka* which he had written in Sesotho right back in 1909 (p. 188).

In his report in 1976 the historian Basil Davidson perceptively placed Mazisi Kunene's *Emperor Shaka the Great* in the tradition of the *izibongo*, the Zulu praise poem. At Nelson Mandela's inauguration as president in 1994 it was the performance of the Zulu praise-singer that was to be so memorable on the ground, as the fighter aircraft of the SADF flew overhead. Basil Davidson wrote to me (25 October 1976): 'it cannot but be a major advance to have a translation by a speaker from within the culture – and one moreover, for whom the oral history of the Zulu has always been a living part of his own culture.' In the gentlest way Basil Davidson encouraged Mazisi Kunene to provide breaks and titles for sections. 'It would help towards readability, because it would reinforce the sense of the story's being told.'

I had written to Mazisi Kunene on 15 October 1976 to tell him that we would include *Emperor Shaka the Great* in the African Writers Series but, as it was so monumentally long, only if he could secure the support he maintained was promised by UNESCO. (The poem was some 16,000 lines long and there are 470 printed pages.) I also said that the publication of *Anthem of the Decades* would have to wait on reactions to the Shaka poem. He was furious and replied (2 November 1976): 'I think [your letter] is a classic illustration of the commercialism that guides the selection of what must be published from Africa.'

Laban Erapu in Nairobi described it as an 'outstanding piece of writing', but pointed out:

> ... the author, instead of maintaining the focus on Shaka, often wanders off to deal with other characters who only indirectly influence the course of Shaka's life. The reader has a feeling at such times that the poet is concerned with depicting the entire history of the Zulu peoples ... the author could improve on the readability of the epic by adopting a different style of presentation which would start with tight prose (rather than loose verse) introductions to sharply defined and headed sections ... Great literary works are not made by bulk but by precise organisation of material into readable, impressive, organic form. (Report by Laban Erapu April 1977)

I sent this report to Mazisi Kunene asking whether he wanted to publish a work of anthropology or of literature:

> It needs cunning and artfulness or you will leave many a willing reader yawning. As with all great oral masterpieces it is necessary to translate to the medium of writing and not to go too far ahead of what people in a different society have come to expect ...
>
> This is dispiriting for you and for me. If I was being truly commercial, I should have told you a long time ago we couldn't publish. (JC to MK 2 May 1977)

His reaction was, to my relief, positive. A letter came back from UCLA where he had 420 students to whom he intended to prescribe his work. He was also cheered by the fact that he had signed a contract for the writing of a film script. He apologised for showing signs of 'anger and frustration'. He had cut out a great deal of material from the original translation:

> I realise myself that much of the original translation had many digressions acceptable to Zulu literary requirements but capable of slowing the pace of the English translation … epics are epics [but] they must do justice to the subject matter and form the basis of subsequent national literature. I did not indulge in length for its own sake. (MK to JC 16 May 1977)

He adopted Laban Erapu's idea of 'tight prose' introductions to each section. As the editorial work proceeded editors suggested helpful ideas such as a list of the important Zulu names and the need for more guidance to the historical and cultural background.

As it happens, the complete original version exists in a published Japanese translation by Satoru Tsuchiya. There were hopes that Professor Nyambezi would get Shuter and Shooter in Pietermaritzburg to publish a Zulu edition. Mazisi Kunene maintained that Prince Mangosuthu Buthelezi at the waPhindangene Royal Residence could under Bantustan rules designate 'it as an official document which means it cannot be banned' (MK to JC 28 September 1978). (Buthelezi was the man who threatened the first democratic election in South Africa in 1994 until, at the last hour, he agreed to let the Inkatha Freedom Party take part.)

The publication of both epics was made possible by their adoption for the enterprising UNESCO 'translations collection for work from lesser known languages'. Mazisi Kunene wanted the chance to be read across Africa. He expected to encourage writers to draw on their own histories. The backing from UNESCO allowed us to experiment.

Mazisi Kunene managed to confuse the UNESCO bureaucracy. Moenis Taha-Hussein, son of the Egyptian writer, spent the whole first page of a letter explaining the bureaucratic intricacies of a 'reimbursable advance'. However, on the second page he wrote:

> Now if you would like to be free of this 'advance' business, we could offer, as a unique measure, an order for a maximum of 500 copies. Actually we would prefer this since it would do away with the need of a contract not to mention other paperwork. (Moenis Taha-Hussein to JC 27 May 1977)

Only somebody of Mazisi Kunene's persistence and charm could have persuaded UNESCO that it was easiest for them to break their own rules. Every few months somebody in Paris forgot what had been promised. A letter as late as July 1978 apologised: 'This publication has been an exceptional case and we have got a little out of step with our formalities.' In the end their order for 500 hardback copies was crucial in enabling two such experimental volumes to go forward, especially when it proved impossible to find either a literary or academic co-publisher in the US. The book could not circulate in South Africa because Mazisi Kunene was a banned author in South Africa; he tried unsuccessfully to persuade Diana Collins that the International Defence and Aid Fund should buy some copies for free distribution in South Africa and round the ANC refugee camps elsewhere in Africa.

After all our struggles Mazisi Kunene saluted the arrival of the first copy in May/June 1979: 'Wonderful work congratulations on this masterly done book. I am certain that the hero himself will be pleased.' Again Doris Lessing was an enthusiast. I wrote to Mazisi Kunene quoting her: 'I am reading with total fascination, Shaka. What a marvellous thing.' (JC to MK 3 April 1980).

Mazisi Kunene was able in 1993 to return to be a professor of literature and language at his own university, which has been renamed the University of KwaZulu-Natal. At last in 1994, 1995 and 1996, as he originally planned, three of his books were published in Zulu. In February 2005 Pallo Jordan, Minister of Arts and Culture, conferred the inaugural National Poet Laureate Prize on Mazisi Kunene.

Mazisi Kunene died in 2007.

Pallo Jordan, now South Africa's Minister of Arts and Culture, was George Hallett's model for John Munonye's *A Dancer of Fortune* (p. 51); he was also the model for George Hallett's new cover for Chinua Achebe's *Things Fall Apart* (p. 37)

PART 5
Writers from SOUTHERN AFRICA

The Tongue of the Dumb
DOMINIC MULAISHO

George Hallett

Unattributed

George Hallett

Lyn Bruce

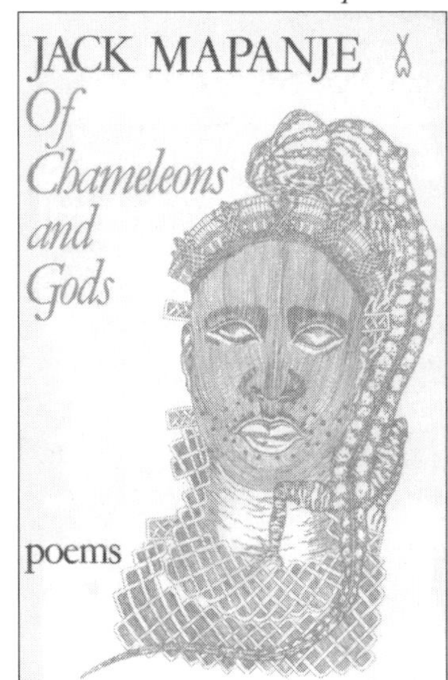

Cover and endpaper by Pedro Guedes

8 *Guns & Guerrillas in* MOZAMBIQUE & ANGOLA

The revolution in Portugal in 1974 led on to the collapse of the empire. Until that date Angola and Mozambique had formed with Rhodesia, Southwest Africa and South Africa a formidable peninsula of countries run for the benefit of settlers. Our active period of publishing work from Angola coincided with the final phase of the *chimurenga* guerrilla war which led to the Zimbabwean settlement in 1980. The struggle in Namibia against South Africa could be sustained from Angola after independence in 1976, as was made clear in John ya-Otto's autobiographical *Battlefront Namibia* (1982 AWS 244). The Angolan novelists and poets, whose books had emerged from resistance against the Portuguese empire, had something to tell readers of the African Writers Series about the way the struggle might go against the last redoubts of settler rule in southern Africa.

Luis Bernardo Honwana

A sharp eye on a mixed Mozambique

It was the *London Magazine* which introduced us to the Mozambican writer Luis Bernardo Honwana's story *We Killed Mangy-Dog* (1969 AWS 60). This influential literary journal had likewise published Tayeb Salih's story *Wedding of Zein* in the translation from Arabic by Denys Johnson-Davies. Outstanding collections by both these writers were published in the African Writers Series in 1969.

The translation from Portuguese of three stories by Luis Bernardo Honwana was made by Dorothy Guedes; she was the South African wife of an extraordinarily inventive architect in Maputo, which under Portuguese colonial rule was called Lourenço Marques. The school of art encouraged young painters such as Malagatana. By the early 1950s there were literary groups and journals in the capital and in the other port, Beira. There were a number of poets of whom the most famous was Craveirinha. In the 1960s Lourenço Marques and Beira had a southern European exoticism which contrasted with the Dutch reformed restraints of the Republic of South Africa. People of mixed blood called *mestiço* were in a stronger position legally than the coloured population of South Africa.

However, the country's notorious secret police the PIDE (International Police for the Defence of the State) co-operated with their equally racist opposite numbers in South Africa to stop political refugees escaping, as in the case of Dennis Brutus (p. 207).

I had an exchange with Dorothy Guedes over my draft blurb which revealed to me how much more careful writers in Portuguese had to be about what they wrote than was the case in South Africa in the 1960s. She was nervous about the way in which I had selected 'negative' elements for the brief biography:

> Luis Bernardo's prison sentence is made to seem the most important part of his life … nothing is mentioned about the educational and cultural opportunities offered to him …
>
> Please reconsider all this, and think of the possible repercussions on those who are not safely perched in parliamentary democracy!
>
> If the book has already gone to print, please return the publicity questionnaire I sent you, with the date on which you received it entered on it, plus your official stamp, with a covering letter telling me you are returning the document from which you took the information for the back cover. This will provide proof, if it is needed, that neither the author nor the translator were responsible for the selections or evaluations that were used. (Dorothy Guedes to JC 26 December 1968)

I apologised to her, saying that I had 'judged these stories from my five years in South Africa' and asked her to redraft the blurb but give the flavour of these stories: 'Somehow we must … make them attractive to pick up for people in Africa where their notions of Mozambique are extremely hazy.' (JC to Dorothy Guedes 1 January 1969)

Luis Bernardo Honwana's writing appealed to other writers. Lewis Nkosi, the South African novelist and journalist, wrote that the title story is:

> … a hauntingly beautiful story … whose simplicity of narrative conceals an extraordinary sharp poetic insight into the theme of life and death, the impulses of love and violence. 'We Killed Mangy-Dog' is a story which skilfully uses symbols in a manner which brings into artistic unity emotions of fear and hatred, protective love and cruel victimisation – a paradigm of a society in which brutality is equated with masculinity, love and protectiveness with weakness and cowardice. And yet, not once does Honwana speak directly of these things; not once does he raise his voice to harangue us. (*South Africa: Information and Analysis* vol 3 no. 1)

Jack Mapanje, who suffered imprisonment in Banda's Malawi because of his poetry (p. 259), was asked in a meeting in 2002 at the time of the fortieth anniversary of the African Writers Series to name the title which had been the most important to him. He touched on several well-known titles but in the end he told of how at secondary school in Malawi he had read with delight Luis Bernardo Honwana's stories which trained a sight on people in the mysterious neighbouring country of Mozambique. The African Writers Series had, as so often, given a young person the idea that Africans could write and get published.

Dorothy Guedes, in a revised blurb she sent on 7 January 1969, finished with the sentence: 'Throughout the book Honwana's eye looks at the details of life with the same concentrated attention of Ginho looking through the sights of his gun at Mangy-dog.' Jack Mapanje told me how in school in Malawi he used to gaze at the meticulous pen and ink drawing of just that scene (p. 244). It was by Pedro Guedes, the teenage son of the translator, who was to become an architect like his father.

It was not until the 1990s that further translations of short stories from Mozambique by the prize-winning writer Mia Couto were added to the Series: *Voices Made Night* (1990) and *Every Man Is a Race* (1994).

The history of resistance

Most of our other titles from Portuguese Africa were from Angola. This belated representation of writing from Portuguese was mostly due to the encouragement of Michael Wolfers, who had formerly been Africa correspondent for *The Times* in London. He pursued a radical path when, after 1969, he became associated with the support movement for Angolan liberation. He was invited personally to the independence celebrations in Luanda in November 1975 and in the following years worked as a journalist and broadcaster in both Angola and Mozambique.

Michael Wolfers selected and translated a substantial selection from the speeches of Amilcar Cabral under the title *Unity and Struggle* (1980 AWS 198). This guerrilla leader, father of Guinean and Cape Verde independence, had been assassinated in Conakry in Guinée in January 1973 just before the PAIGC achieved freedom in September of that year. It was appropriate that Basil Davidson should write the informative and rousing nine-page introduction; Basil Davidson had learnt the art of survival with the Yugoslav and Italian partisans and revived this skill while reporting the struggles against Portuguese rule in the rainforest.

We published at the same time a novel translated from the French original of 1976, by Williams Sassine from Guinée called *Wirriyamu* (1980 AWS 199). This novel was based on the actual massacre by Portuguese soldiers of the inhabitants of the Mozambican village of Wirriyamu in the dying years of empire in December 1972. The central character is the poet Kabalongo, who dreams of heroic deeds but gradually comes to terms with the realisation that he must go beyond words and take up the gun, for he has come to believe that in southern Africa the violence of colonialism will be overcome by force of arms.

Agostinho Neto

Angolan poets including a future president

Michael Wolfers said in an article in *The Guardian*:

> The constraints of Portuguese oppression, repression, and censorship meant that pre-independence writing was more often in the form of a poem or short story than of a novel or documentary study. The political aim of an ambiguously phrased poem could escape the censor's vigilance; poems if inaccessible to the illiterate could reach them in versions presented as popular songs.
>
> Poetry is the most typical form of Angolan writing, but even the most admired prose writers have built their reputations on short stories and novellas, rather than on long and leisurely novels. (*The Guardian* 2 March 1981)

African writers in English and French could freely publish in the old colonial capitals even if there were political or censorship problems in their own countries. Writers in Portuguese were hampered by the dangers for publishers in Lisbon. Some books did appear in Brazil.

Michael Wolfers, with the help of the Angolan Union of Writers, chose and translated an elegant selection from the work of 22 poets in *Poems from Angola* (1979 AWS 215). The country had been led to independence by the poet Dr Agostinho Neto. He was the son of a Methodist pastor and was sent by the church to study medicine in Portugal in 1947. He was imprisoned several times for political reasons during the 1950s and qualified in 1958. He returned to Luanda in December 1959 to set up a medical practice as a cover for his underground leadership of the Popular Movement for the Liberation of Angola (MPLA), but six months later was arrested by the PIDE in his consulting room. Prison in Luanda and Lisbon was followed by work as a doctor in Cape Verde under police surveillance, where he was then rearrested because he had shown people photographs of atrocities by Portuguese soldiers. An international campaign was launched to prevent the Portuguese authorities murdering the poet, as had happened to other political prisoners. Agostinho Neto was released in March 1962 and put under restricted residence in Portugal. MPLA organised his escape and, after some time in the freed areas of Angola, in December 1962 he was elected president of the MPLA at their first national conference in Kinshasa. On 4 February 1975 he returned to Luanda to a mass welcome from almost the whole city. On 11 November 1975 he became president of the People's Republic of Angola. Michael Wolfers says: 'His poems, many of which were written in and smuggled out of prisons, are the best known of all Angolan poetry and form the basis of popular songs and political mobilisation both nationally and internationally' (*Poems from Angola* p. 105).

J. Luandino Vieira
Speaking to ordinary Angolans

Another poet and campaigner in this anthology was J. Luandino Vieira. Angolan nationalists attacked prisons and police stations in February 1961 and this marked the beginning of the war of liberation. J. Luandino Vieira finished writing a novel *The Real Life of Domingos Xavier* on 10 November 1961 shortly before he himself was sentenced to imprisonment by a military court. The epitaph which stops the dance on the last page of the book shows the clear political message:

> My fellow Angolans. A brother has come to say that they have killed our comrade. He was called Domingos Xavier and he was a tractor driver. He never harmed anyone, only wanted the good of his people and of his land. I stopped this dance only to say this, not for it to end, for our joy is great: our brother carried himself like a man, he did not tell the secrets of his people, he did not sell himself. We are not going to weep any more for his death because, Domingos Antonio Xavier, you begin today your real life in the hearts of the Angolan people …
>
> And not even the wind dare rustle the leaves of the fig tree when Mussanda the tailor spoke thus. (p. 84)

A report by an unnamed reader made the point that: 'In fact this is not the story of Domingos Xavier alone, but the story of Portuguese oppression and the intricate way in which [the] liberation movement was kept alive despite the strong Portuguese spy system.'

The novel was first published, ten years after it was written, in a French translation in Paris in 1971. It was not published until 1974 in its original complex mixture of literary Portuguese, with cadences of Brazilian and Angolan black Portuguese and of Kimbundu, the language of Luanda. Michael Wolfers admitted in his preface that he had not tried to match the author's linguistic complexity but had used a fairly standard English. Fortunately Luandino Vieira, with the emphatic support of Michael Wolfers, insisted that the brief and powerful *The Real Life of Domingos Xavier* (1978 AWS 202) be published on its own. My colleagues had been pressing me to publish it together in a single volume with *Luuanda,* which consisted of only three tales. My letter to the author of 18 April 1977 started: 'It is a great pleasure to be writing to you in such completely changed circumstances.' Michael Wolfers generously asked to have his translator's royalties passed direct to the author. His translation was completed in Luanda on 10 November 1976, 15 years after the book had been written. The author had spent most of those years in prison.

November 1976 was the month I first met Tamara Bender at the African Studies Association meeting in San Francisco. I was later to publish in 1978, with the University of California Press, Gerald Bender's *Angola under the Portuguese: The Myth and the Reality*, in which he took issue with the Portuguese myth that they had integrated with the tropical peoples better than other colonial powers. (It was to be another ten years before I published Joe Miller's study of the British funding of the Angolan slave trade called *The Way of Death,* with its revelations about the way the business was funded by the London money market.)

We had been in touch with Tamara Bender since 1972 and she and Donna S. Hill had been struggling with the problem of J. Luandino Vieira's polyglot language in translating *Luuanda* (1980 AWS 222). We had contracted the stories on 8 June 1973 because Chi Ude, formerly of Doubleday, had set up Nok as a new imprint, and was making counterbids for total world English language rights. The three tales in *Luuanda* were set in the slums, called *musseques,* which surrounded the lovely colonial capital. The translators explained that the author had grown up among the *musseque* children in Luanda and that:

> [Vieira] used the Portuguese term *estórias* ('tales') as the book's subtitle, instead of the more traditional Portuguese term *histórias* ('stories') because he believed *estória* more correctly translated the Kimbundu word *mususo,* defined as moral story or allegory, fable, narrative, or tale. 'My intent in these narratives' he explained, 'was to take their structure from oral tradition, employing the stylistic and linguistic characteristics of the popular oral language so that the tales themselves could be told aloud.' ...
>
> Not surprisingly very few Portuguese, whether or not they lived in Luanda, could completely understand the language of Vieira's *Luuanda.* It is a Portuguese whose grammatical structure more closely approximates that of Kimbundu and whose vocabulary is liberally sprinkled with pure Kimbundu and 'portuguesation' of Kimbundu, especially in verb formations. Vieira refused to provide a glossary for his book because, as he explained, he wrote his *estórias* for the very people whose language he used, adding that ignorance of *musseque* speech was a problem of the Portuguese coloniser, not his. (Translators' Preface, p. vii)

It was certainly a problem for the translators. As they explained, their approach tried to reflect the adventurousness of the original. 'In order to preserve as much of *Luuanda's* original flavour as possible however, liberties have been taken with the English language in both phrasing and construction' (p. ix).

In 1965 the Portuguese Writers' Society, the country's oldest and most prestigious literary association, awarded the book its Grand Prize for fiction just as Salazar's regime was about to ban the book. The secret police closed down the headquarters in Lisbon. A clandestine edition appeared in Brazil. Dog-eared copies circulated. José Luandino Vieira was released from prison in 1972 but not allowed to return to Angola. After independence he was elected first secretary-general of the Angola Writers' Union. By 1978 the union, under his dynamic leadership, had published almost half a million copies of 32 different titles, including eight of his own.

The photograph on the back of the African Writers Series edition shows a mustachioed young man of film-star faroucheness and of predominately Portuguese blood. It is interesting to compare his efforts to reflect the language of ordinary Angolans with those being made by Ngũgĩ to speak to ordinary Kenyans.

Pepetela
What will liberation hold?

Pepetela wrote *Mayombe* in 1971 at the height of the guerrilla struggle in the Mayombe forest of the Cabinda enclave of Angola at the mouth of the Congo. The translation by Michael Wolfers was published in the Series (1983 AWS 269) in association with Zimbabwe Publishing House which printed copies for Heinemann in the liberated Harare. Antonio de Figueiredo pointed out in *The Guardian,* five years after Angola's independence, some thought-provoking discussions between the guerrillas:

> There are many passages in which the author prophetically explores the future which many people in Angola see as dangerously significant. One passage is in the form of a dialogue between two freedom fighters who figure prominently through the novel:
>
> ' … [You will be less tolerant] … when you are part of a victorious and glorious party which will take power and will regard as pagans all those who are not in it.' …
>
> 'We will take power and what will we say to the people? That we are going to build socialism. But that would take 30 or 50 years. At the end of five years, people will begin to say that such socialism did not solve this and that problem. And it will be true, because it will be impossible to sort out such problems, in a backward country, within five years …'
>
> The author's full name is Artur Carlos Mauricio Pestana dos Santos Pepetela, deputy minister of education. (*The Guardian* 2 March 1981)

A translation of Pepetela's *Yaka* was added to the Series in 1996.

In 1979 I received a letter from Antonio Jacinto, another of the poets in *Poems from Angola* and secretary of the National Council of Culture, inviting me to the meeting of the Sixth Conference of Afro-Asian Writers in Luanda. It would have been interesting to see the way this writers' union operated at the height of its powers. Sadly there was a Cold War clash with the West Berlin Festival and African writers' conference, to which I and many of my authors were already committed.

South Africa maintained its racist rule at the southern end of the continent for another decade. Angola's writers did have something to tell readers of the African Writers Series about how change might come in South Africa.

9 ZAMBIA
Shall be Free

Kenneth Kaunda's autobiography *Zambia Shall be Free* (1962 AWS 4) was one of the founding titles of the African Writers Series. A Methodist minister, Mervyn Temple, contacted Van Milne about the manuscript soon after the author had left HM Prison, Lusaka. It was to prove an outstanding seller with sales in its first 20 years of over 500,000 copies. In 1964 Kenneth Kaunda became president when Northern Rhodesia became Zambia. On a visit in 1967 Alan and Enid Hill and Bob Markham were invited to tea at State House, Lusaka and presented the president with a leather-bound copy of his book; in the background strutted the peacocks left behind by the last British governor of Northern Rhodesia.

Dominic Mulaisho
'The richest man in the world'

Dominic Mulaisho once said to me, 'If I owned what I controlled, I would be the richest man in the world.' As managing director of the Zambian parastatal MINDECO, he was the civil servant in charge of the government's 49 per cent shareholding in the mines. In the late 1970s the price of copper was soaring and Zambia, Chile and Zaire had formed an 'OPEC' for copper, to control output and keep the price from falling so that the rich world would not get its central heating installations too cheaply. He had also at one time been general manager of the National Agricultural Board. In 1965, the year after Zambia's independence, he had been made permanent secretary in the office of the president, Kenneth Kaunda.

Dominic Mulaisho's novels were convincing studies of the way power is used; the first novel, *The Tongue of the Dumb* (1971 AWS 98), is about a power struggle between a councillor and a chief; *The Smoke that Thunders* (1979 AWS 204) shows the colonialists in a country which is rather like Rhodesia deviously holding back power from the African nationalists (it was published in 1979 which was the year that the Rhodesians finally conceded majority rule at Lancaster House). Dominic Mulaisho's Roman Catholic schooling at Canisius College, Chalimbana gave the books an assured style which reminded us of the best-selling works of Morris

West (author of novels with a convincing Catholic background, such as *The Devil's Advocate* published by William Heinemann). Dominic Mulaisho was very much like the fast-rising young novelists in East Africa whose work we were publishing in the Series at about the same time. They had all benefited in the dying days of colonialism from a privileged education which gave them the confidence to take over positions of power and yet left them able to organise their lives so as fit in some writing.

Dominic Mulaisho, while permanent secretary at the Ministry of Education, wrote the manuscript of a novel which was originally called *The Vacant Stool*. He told me how he organised his writing. Government ministries ran along Ridgeway, Lusaka in both directions from the modern Anglican Cathedral and from State House. Its slopes ran down a mile or so to the commercial Cairo Road, its north–south axis reminding one of Rhodes's Cape-to-Cairo aspirations. The substantial Ridgeway Hotel, like the cathedral, had been built in the days of the Central African Federation and was expensive and unfriendly. So Dominic Mulaisho brought sandwiches and did a lunch hour of writing in his office every day.

The manuscript was first recommended to us by Gordon McGregor, reader in Education at the new university which had just been built with the same concrete assurance as the National Theatre in London. He wrote to Alan Hill about Dominic Mulaisho's manuscript:

> I fear it seems very much more than two years ago since we dined hilariously with yourself and your wife by the twinkling lights of the Ridgeway's ornamental pond, but I promised to keep you in touch with anything interesting that developed here in the African writing line … What makes this book different from almost everything that I have read by African writers, is a touch of satire and sardonic humour that runs through it. (G.P. McGregor to Alan Hill 23 October 1969)

Dominic Mulaisho responded effectively to reports on the first version from readers in Britain and East Africa. Bob Windsor felt the revision had improved it but still did not feel able to recommend it for the Series. I wrote to the author on 3 August 1970:

> We have now had a report from the same reader who was enthusiastic about your book before. He has made various suggestions. I have given it to another of our regular readers for a fresh opinion unaffected by previous readings.
>
> With the end of the Nigerian war we are now in contact again with Chinua Achebe who, as you know, has been editorial adviser on the series since it was started. He too will need to see the manuscript and our reports. I am afraid that this all takes time but rest assured that we wouldn't be doing all this if we weren't seriously considering your novel. (JC to DM 3 August 1970)

I called on Lalage Bown, director of extra-mural studies, when I was in Lusaka at the end of October 1971 and she saw this book as a natural candidate for their usual order of 200 copies. After acceptance we sent the manuscript to

Heather Karolyi to prepare for press, especially as she would be able to handle the Roman Catholic background. She had worked as an editor for Heinemann Educational Books and then married a musician who had fled from Hungary in 1956. She had been through the book twice when she wrote to me at the beginning of 1971:

> I still haven't come up with a brilliant title. *The Struggle Availeth*? *The Tongue of the Dumb* (see Isaiah 35.6)? (Actually this might be possible, since Mwape is one of the key links between the village and the mission, and the denouement turns on his cure.) It would spoil the story though to use the full quotation on the title page. Mmm, I'm rather coming round to this one: the assonance has a convincing ring. (Heather Karolyi to JC 7 January 197[1])

Dominic Mulaisho felt, now writing from MINDECO, that the '*The Tongue of the Dumb is* an excellent title and let's settle for it' (DM to JC 26 January 1971).

Operation full bar with toasties

Bob Markham suggested a launch party for Dominic Mulaisho to be held on 26 January 1972. Dominic Mulaisho got the agreement of President Kaunda, as the first Zambian author in the Series, to launch the first Zambian novel. The occasion would also publicise two other landmarks. *The Tongue of the Dumb* was AWS 98 and the very next month in London Chinua Achebe's *Girls at War* was to be launched as AWS 100 to mark the tenth anniversary of the African Writers Series. Also it would be announced at the party that Heinemann Educational Books was to set up an office in Zambia.

Bob Markham drew on all his organisational abilities. I wrote, full of admiration for his attention to every detail, including his haggling with the manager of the Ridgeway Hotel over the cost of 'toasties', which was what the settlers called cocktail snacks:

> Thank you for your raft of paperwork on operation full bar with toasties!
>
> We are naturally delighted about Dr Kaunda's acceptance to perform the launching. I see in a very self-effacing way, you suggest that either Currey or Markham should speak first. I am sure that the diplomatic order of precedence is Markham, if on his two feet, and only Currey if there is an emergency! I suggest that Dominic ought to say something. Anyhow that can all be tied up.
>
> We are arranging for leather bound copies to be prepared. (JC to Bob Markham 6 January 1972)

Bob Markham commanded the occasion with all the assurance of a flying-boat officer landing a craft on the Zambezi, which is what he indeed had done during the war. The first crisis was that President Kaunda's security people were turning away people who had not brought their invitations. My friend from Cape Town days, the South African poet Tim Holmes, knew everybody in Lusaka and attached himself to security to clear the guests. Bob Markham marched the president's bodyguard off to the kitchen and gave them a beer. Exactly at 8 o'clock he gave the command: 'Close the bar!'

Bob Markham gave a full account of the occasion to Alan Hill and was particularly pleased to report about his success with the biggest book chain in central Africa.

> President Kaunda twice asked to be remembered to you and Enid … Kingstons' book display sold 181 copies in one and half hours. Mulaisho was signing away at the rate of knots. I gave Kingstons a build-up in my speech thanking them for sharing the air-freight costs on 1,000 copies and they showed their appreciation by increasing their order for A.W.S. from 15 copies to 60 copies for every title. Markham scores again! (Bob Markham to Alan Hill 31 January 1972)

A political thriller

The title of Dominic Mulaisho's second novel, *The Smoke that Thunders*, was a translation of *Musi-O-Tunya,* the real name for the Victoria Falls, over which the River Zambezi throws itself in a cloud of spray. It was about a country called Kandahar, which was not quite north and not quite south of the Zambezi. Dominic Mulaisho had responded promptly and impressively to earlier reports. I urged my colleagues on 6 July 1976 to be quicker than usual because he was a well-organised executive who could not understand the slowness of publishers. I described it to Henry Chakava and Akin Thomas as 'a political thriller of the Morris West variety (with a touch of C.P. Snow)'. I enclosed a copy of Ros de Lanerolle's report which concluded:

> It is very complex, and though it has little to add to what we know about the forces at work in such a situation, the dramatisation is very effective. The characters, though sometimes one-dimensional, are very credible (the dialogue, including that of the whites … is amazingly successful): and the picture of the developing crisis very fair in its representation of exactly what Kenya, Zambia – and now Rhodesia itself – have had to contend with. Author writes with feeling as well as understanding: there are moments of great intensity, including the denouement. And some comedy – the special branch idiocies, the Indian conspiring to play each side against the other as insurance for the future. A novel very much worth considering for publication, and a writer of considerable sophistication. (Report by Ros de Lanerolle 16 April 1976)

It is now clear that 1976 was the beginning of the end for Smith's regime, although he managed to twist and weave, like the spitfire pilot he was, for another three years.

I tried to persuade William Heinemann that this was an African Morris West. Moira Lynd's report assumed that 'in this clever novel' the imaginary country was 'recognisably Rhodesia':

> The story has many ramifications, including a state of emergency declared

> by the Governor, and another state of emergency declared in reply by PALP. There are riots and executions which the Governor could have stopped, but he has not quite the courage. Independence comes, complicated by the supposed discovery of oil in Kandahar. And a surprise twist at the end shows the Africans cheated – the Coffee Syndicate too had ramifications that they did not know about … It is very publishable and indeed very topical and interesting. (Report for William Heinemann by Moira Lynd 28 July 1976)

William Heinemann rejected the chance to do a hardback which, with a subcontract to a general market paperback, could have placed an African author in the middlebrow library and bookshop market which they were so successful at reaching. Six months later I went back to Roger Smith at William Heinemann with news that a film company was interested in the work, and quoted a letter from Dominic Mulaisho:

> In fact the American film director, the screen play writer and the producer have been here for a fortnight and are still here. The local company has put in seed money – about K70,000 which should see the work to the point where the director hoped to secure Marlon Brando's signature. (DM in letter from JC to Roger Smith 13 January 1977)

At about this time Marlon Brando did play the role of a lawyer in the Steve Biko film. Would the part of Dominic Mulaisho's British governor have provided an opportunity for his growling talents?

Dominic Mulaisho, on frequent visits to London en route between Zambia and Chile, showed a fatalism about retaining power. When the price of copper was falling and his own power was waning, Dominic Mulaisho said to me with, with a sardonic laugh: 'These days you learn on the radio, while you are shaving, that you have lost your job.'

We never found other Zambian work to include in the Series although we received other manuscripts. Writing was certainly going on. The Northern Rhodesia Literature Board was just about the most productive of the institutions set up during colonialism to encourage the writing in the languages of the country, and it continued after independence. Their most successful author was Simon Mpashi, and at Oxford University Press in Cape Town in the 1960s we received a string of orders from the Board both for reprints and new books which could be put on the train for the long journey north. Simon Mpashi continued to be a successful author for the parastatal publishing company NECZAM, which was owned in a state publishing deal by the Kenneth Kaunda Foundation and Macmillan.

10 *Death & Detention in* MALAWI

In the footsteps of John Brown

Malawian writers in English have been altogether more exceptional than the Zambians. The colony of Nyasaland, which became Malawi, was the most successful outpost of the Church of Scotland. George Simeon Mwase, who went to a Free Church of Scotland school, wrote an account of the Chilembwe rising in 1915 when in Zomba Central Prison in 1931–2. He had been active politically but had actually been convicted of tax embezzlement. The 86 foolscap pages were shown by an administrator to the governor in 1933 'to enable him to form some estimate of the mental capabilities of the native'. The manuscript thus came to be lodged in the national archives, where Professor Robert I. Rotberg of Harvard read it in 1962. Its ringing biblical tones are apparent from the first sentence 'When at the first I took my pen in hand, that for to write, I did not understand that I at all should make any kind of a book in any kind of mode' (p. 1). Robert Rotberg saw that it was a remarkable document and prepared an edition under the title *Strike a Blow and Die,* which Harvard University Press published in 1967 and we included in the African Writers Series in 1975 (AWS 160).

John Chilembwe was sent to a Negro Baptist seminary in the US, where he learnt about slavery and emancipation and John Brown. He went back to Nyasaland in 1900 and set up a mission station. He turned sharply against British rule during the first world war when Nyasas began to lose their lives as carriers in Tanganyika, Northern Somaliland and Ashanti. He wrote a letter in October 1915 to the editor of the *Nyasaland Times*:

> As I hear that, war has broke out between you and other nations, only whitemen, I request, therefore, not to recruit more of my country men, my brothers, who do not know the cause of your fight … (p. 33)

He deeply resented that the censor forbade publication. At a meeting of chiefs and headmen in January 1915 John Chilembwe told them about:

> … a Mr John Brown of America, who after losing his hope, in succeeding the request in writing, to the authority concerned, in regard slave trading he determinate to strike a blow and lose his own life … They all came to a final conclusion of *'Let us strike a blow and die.'* (p. 36)

In a review in *The New Yorker* Stanley Edgar Hyman points out that:

> Mwase insists that the rebellion was purely symbolic – a voluntary martyrdom to touch the white conscience. He quotes – or, more probably, like Thucydides, composes – Chilembwe's instructions to his army, after prayers on that Saturday morning. (*The New Yorker* 27 July 1968)

John Chilembwe's words on 23 January 1915, according to Mwase, were:

> This is the only way to show the whitemen, that the treatment they are treating our men and women was most bad and we determined to strike a first and last blow, and then all die by the heavy storm of the whiteman's army. (p. 36)

Chilembwe was killed and the captured were executed 'singing hymns of their great God when [they] were escorted towards a scaffold for their last time in the world'.

George Simeon Mwase died in 1962 before independence and before he knew that his book would be published. Robert Rotberg says:

> In 1965, people in the Badawe area remembered Mwase as an exceptionally 'clever' man who managed to 'trick' the colonial government and to perform various legendary feats of magic. He was credited with managing to make leaves look like money. It was also said that he had at various time married five wives and sired thirty-one children. (pp. xl–xli)

Banda's detainees

The independence of Malawi was booked for July 1964. Clare Currey and I were in the capital, Zomba, in March 1964 for a visit to cousins who were working in community development. We had driven most of the way up from South Africa and had just visited the about-to-be-independent Zambia and the diehard Rhodesia. Independence was in the air. Clare Currey took a photograph of the Independence Office in Zomba which went on to the front cover of *The New African*. Dr Hastings Banda was every anti-colonialist's hero after the findings of the Devlin Commission. However, there were already rumours round Zomba that he was doing a deal with the Portuguese. We were being shown the staggering view from the Zomba Plateau over the valley towards Mount Mlanje when a small passenger aircraft flew north. Our hosts betted that this had to be Banda going to a rendez-vous on the Mozambique side of Lake Malawi. His alliance with Portuguese colonialists was to be extended to make the country a satellite of apartheid South Africa.

In that very month of March 1964 the Nyasaland Publications and Literature Bureau sent Keith Sambrook the manuscript of Aubrey Kachingwe's novel, *No Easy Task* (1965/1966 AWS 24). It was timely, as he used his journalist's skills to write about the struggle for independence in an African state called Kwacha (which meant 'dawn' and was to be the name of the new currency in 1964 for both the republics of Malawi and Zambia). Aubrey Kachingwe used all his contacts to get good publicity. The British Council in Zomba put on a well-orchestrated launch on 24 January 1965 to celebrate the publication of the first novel by a Malawian. The book had first been published in hardback under the Heinemann imprint. There was, however, a lesson to be learned. The price was all right for the new government ministers and diplomats at the party. Aubrey Kachingwe wrote on 7 February 1965 to Keith Sambrook: 'The Times bookshop hope to sell several hundreds throughout the country. I understand customers in the other towns are furious because they did not have in the local Times branch bookshops the hard-cover.' Bob Markham wrote to Keith Sambrook eight months later on 14 October 1965: 'The people of Malawi are looking forward to his book but the subscription of the 18/- edition was unenthusiastic, every bookshop stating that they would buy the AWS title.' The paperback edition followed in 1966.

It was our main rival Longman that published the first three novels by Legson Kayira, which gave a non-political portrait of rural Malawi. His third novel began to address, with a gently comic vision, the export of labour to South Africa, which was a fundamental source of income for this small agricultural country. He offered the African Writers Series his satirical fourth novel which he had written after going back on a visit to Malawi at the height of the repression of the Banda era. The first sentence of *The Detainee* (1974 AWS 162) begins: 'The only remarkable thing about Napolo was his simplicity – the naïve and trusting simplicity of a villager ...' The old man Napolo sets off from his village to go and see a white doctor in a distant town. On the way he falls among young thugs of the Youth Brigade who terrorise the land under the dictatorship of Sir Zaddock. He is taken away to a detention camp. It takes him a little time to realise that this is just not a rest camp.

Jack Mapanje

'Who will start another fire?'

Through Lan White and Adrian Roscoe, two British academics, we came to learn of a group of poets centred on Chancellor College in Zomba, which included Steve Chimombo, Frank Chipasula, Edison Mpina and Jack Mapanje. Should we do an anthology? However, it was Jack Mapanje's work which stood out. It was a time of economic depression and gross inflation. In 1980 in the first days of Thatcher the British Federation of Master Printers had given, without even a token fight with printing trade unions, a 25 per cent wage rise in the industry. I tried to get both *Of Chameleons and Gods* (1981 AWS 236) and a Malawian poetry anthology accepted by the Heinemann Wednesday editorial meeting. Sales of the Series were declining in Africa. I was told by my colleagues that it had to be one or the other; so I opted for the collection of Jack Mapanje's poetry. The managing director later in 1981 forced down the print run to 2,500 which was the lowest we had done in the African Writers Series. That turned out to be to be false economy and we had to reprint after ten months. (It should be pointed out that at the time a print run of 2,500 for a first collection by an unknown poet was the envy of the established poetry publishers in London, like Faber or Chatto.)

In his carefully composed Introduction Jack Mapanje said:

> The verse in this volume spans some ten turbulent years in which I have been attempting to find a voice or voices as a way of preserving some sanity. Obviously where personal voices are too easily muffled, this is a difficult task; one is tempted like the chameleon, who failed to deliver Chiuta's message of life, to bask in one's brilliant camouflage. But the exercise has been, if nothing else, therapeutic; and that's no mean word in our circumstances! (p. xi)

His poem 'Before Chilembwe Tree' ends with 'Who will start another fire?'

Jack Mapanje, who was working on his doctorate in London, felt guilty that it was his work that had been selected. He explained to me privately that, as the conditions in Malawi under Banda worsened, poetry was the last resort for coded opposition when everything was censored. The successor regime had all the worst aspects of the colonial regime and applied them more crudely. In January 1982 Jack Mapanje gave me the manuscript of an anthology under the title *Strangulado*. Could we sell an anthology of poetry from one small country? We hoped that we could offset some of the costs by doing a joint edition with the Dangaroo Press in Denmark where the typesetting was done on the kitchen table by two academics, the Australian Anna Rutherford and the Swedish Holst Kirsten Petersen. Paul Njoroge, who worked with Henry Chakava in Nairobi, reported on 28 June 1982:

> It is a good selection in the important sense that the poems voice responses to similar experiences. 'Strangulado' the poem which gives the title to the collection is about the strangulation of artistic expression as well as the imprisonment of the human spirit. The theme is a link to these poems from a land where repression and censorship are rife. The poems in this collection are … a gasp for free air, an expression of yearning for genuine human freedom.
>
> The virtue of these poems is their urgency: this urgency does not allow for the obscurities of some of West African poetry (Soyinka, Okigbo, etc.). It would be accessible to many readers. It would give joy to 'ordinary' readers. I have no hesitation in recommending it unreservedly. (Paul Njoroge to JC 28 June 1982)

The Nigerian foreign exchanges had closed in April 1982 and the pressure to cut titles in the African Writers Series redoubled. I again failed to get a Malawian anthology accepted. It was good that Steve Chimombo's *Napolo and the Python* was included in the Series in 1994. And it was Frank and Joan Chipasula who were commissioned to collect *The Heinemann Book of African Women's Poetry* (1995).

Jack Mapanje went back to Chancellor College in the University of Malawi to teach and continue working with his fellow poets. He was arrested in 1987. He is a Roman Catholic and God made sure that his priest saw him being taken away. Jack Mapanje was able to shout two words: 'Tell Lan!' Much distressed, the Father rang a friend in the priesthood in Galway and spoke in Erse, the Gaelic language of Ireland. He asked him to ring the lecturer and poet Lan White at the

University of York. So the news was spread instantly through the African network and into the international press.

Amnesty adopted Jack Mapanje as a prisoner of conscience. He was never charged. I did what I could but it was all too little and certainly nothing like as much as I was in a position to do over the detention of Ngũgĩ. Jack Mapanje was not released until 1991. Lan White, who had run the international campaign to stop us forgetting him over this long period, secured him temporary jobs at the University of York. For a time he was the visiting poet at Wakefield Jail. Some of Jack Mapanje's work written in prison was to appear in a collection which appeared in the African Writer Series in 1993 under the title *The Chattering Wagtails of Mikuyu Prison*. He also published in the Series an anthology of prison writing under the title *Gathering Seaweed,* whose title he took from Nelson Mandela's piece about Robben Island. No permanent position came along at that time. Robert Woof of Newcastle University got him selected as the Wordsworth Poet in Residence at Dove Cottage in Grasmere and, when that appointment finished, found him a permanent job at his university. At a party in London given for the Wordsworth Trust in 2004 Jack Mapanje introduced me to his grown-up daughters. Clasping my shoulders, his bearded face wreathed in smiles, he said: 'This is James Currey who got me into prison!' I gave a nervous grin. He roared with laughter, hugged me tighter and said: 'This is James Currey who got me out!' I am told that he has shocked several of his other supporters with the same drama.

11 *The Struggle to Become* ZIMBABWE

Doris Lessing was generous in the time she gave to helping two Zimbabwean writers of her generation. She worked on historical fiction by Stanlake Samkange and on oral history by Lawrence Vambe, both of whom were living in exile. We were equally on the look-out in the 1970s for young new voices from within Rhodesia. In 1975 we published *Waiting for the Rain*, the first novel in English by Charles Mungoshi, who won prizes for his work in both Shona and English. Five students, after being expelled from the University of Rhodesia for political protest, were given places in the University of Oxford and we published work by two of them. One was Stanley Nyamfukudza, whose first novel, *The Non-Believer's Journey*, reflected the civil-war realities of the second *chimurenga* freedom struggle which, by 1976, began to force real change. The other was Dambudzo Marechera, whose stories made a collection called *The House of Hunger.* It was Doris Lessing's review in *Books and Bookmen*, in which she had said that 'Marechera has in him the stuff and substance to make a great writer', which led to his being a winner of *The Guardian* prize for new fiction in 1979 (p. 279). After independence in 1980 the publishing of creative writing took off within Zimbabwe itself. By the late 1980s a new generation of exceptional talent was being published first in Harare and then subcontracted to international publishers, including Heinemann.

I noticed that Penguin had let Doris Lessing's first novel, *The Grass is Singing*, go out of print. Heinemann Educational Books had the only edition in print in their adventurous New Windmill Series. Should we offer a contract for it also to be included in the African Writers Series? There was a problem. Doris Lessing had been born in Persia, when her father was serving there in 1919. So far every author in the African Writers Series had, as far as we knew, been born in Africa. I suggested that we change the rubric to 'Books by writers who were born in Africa or who passed their formative years there'. Doris Lessing was only six when her parents moved to a large farm in Rhodesia and her novel draws vividly on her years of growing. She left for London at the age of 30 with the manuscript of *The Grass is Singing*, which was first published in 1950. The plot seemed naturally right in the Series. An English couple on a failing Rhodesian farm descend into physical and mental madness. The wife alternates abuse with dependence in her treatment of her 'houseboy'. The scene is set for her murder.

The book captures racial tension in a settler society and is one of the most atmospheric novels about Africa. My colleagues in Kenya and Nigeria thought it would be good to include it in the Series (1973 AWS 131).

Stanlake Samkange

'African with a cast of European'

Terence Ranger's *Are We Not Also Men*? (1995) is a collective biography of the Methodist minister Thompson Samkange and of his sons Sketchley and Stanlake. Terence Ranger said in his blurb:

> This is a book about the rise of elite African politics in Zimbabwe. But for the Samkanges the road to politics lay through religion. Nor was this only because training for the Christian ministry gave literacy and relative prestige. Thompson Samkange's political beliefs were deeply rooted in his religious beliefs. (Blurb for *Are We Not Also Men?* James Currey and Ohio University Press 1995)

Stanlake Samkange was a historian who, with considerable ingenuity, made use of his knowledge of Rhodesia's gloomy history to plot his novels. *The Companion* says:

> In his historical fiction Samkange draws heavily on published documents and has been criticised for a confusion of the historical and the imaginative. In all his writings the texts of imperialism or Rhodesian officialdom are refused the authority they claim for themselves and instead have the context a black writer allows them. The white voice is not silenced but is forced into a dialogue with a black voice, a narrative strategy with radical implications in the Rhodesia of the 1960s and 70s.

His first novel, *On Trial for My Country* (1967 AWS 33), is based on a clever idea. Cecil Rhodes and Lobengula are both put on trial for their respective parts in obtaining and granting the various concessions which gave the air of apparent legality to Rhodes's occupation of Mashonaland. Stanlake Samkange writes in his letter to Keith Sambrook dated 12 October 1965: 'most of the events recorded are historically correct except for the fact that there are two interpretations – the whiteman's and the African's' (SS to KS 12 October 1965).

His next novel, *The Mourned One* (1975 AWS 169), intrigued everybody. Doris Lessing forwarded the manuscript to us with her own two-page opinion:

> *The Mourned One* is – or Samkange so says in a preface – from material given to a kinsman of his by a man who was to be hanged in Salisbury prison. Of course it could be that Samkange is using an ancient literary device; but it looks to me as if in fact there was some sort of original manuscript to which he might have added, as well as smoothing it over. I don't know. However that might be, it is very lively, and a very funny story. Samkange's doubled eye, African with a cast of European, enables him to write of his people, the Vashawasha, and their customs, tribal medicine and so forth with a certain

> coolness. It is this perspective and flavour which gives the tale its value.
>
> In brief: Twins are born but twins are 'non-people' and traditionally must be killed. Through a series of chances – but there are no chances or coincidences in the thought of these people, everything is full of meaning – the twins' deaths do not take place at the time set for them by custom. One twin, the author of the book, considered dead, is rescued by a missionary and brought up as a white in a Mission near Marandellas; the other, as the sole heir of a famous hunter, gets a completely African education; the boys are different in every way. The educated one finally lands up in another Mission where, befriended by a white girl, he makes sexual advances, and, being drunk, attempts intercourse. Although the court established that 'penetration did not take place', the attempt was considered as good as a rape, and the man was duly hanged. I think it is historically accurate – I seem to remember a case of that kind.
>
> But it is not the bones of the story which are important.
>
> As one who lived in Rhodesia at the time of the events described, it is hard for me to assess what sort of interest the story would have for an ordinary white person. I would say that it is compulsively readable ... (Doris Lessing to JC 2 January 1974)

Ros de Lanerolle reported within the month and was of two minds about its provenance:

> I read this with the unquestioning assumption that it is the document that Samkange says that it is. Only when I finished did I begin to feel it to be perhaps too good to be true, too symbolically right, too complete in form and expression ... the question is NOT irrelevant. If this is a document, it is an extremely rare find, which would carry considerable extra value for its authenticity ... (Report by Ros de Lanerolle 29 January 1974)

Henry Chakava was also intrigued:

> I attach an enthusiastic report from [Philippa de Cuir]. I thought I could have a look through this manuscript and ended up reading most of it. I think it is a document very well written indeed and I unreservedly recommend it for publication with a hardback edition. The story is so sophisticated in construction and rendering and its application so current that it surprises me to hear that it comes from such a simple man, and refers to Rhodesia of the 1930's. It would still do well as novel but I think its impact is greater if it is published as a document, like Mwase's *Strike a Blow and Die* [p. 257]. I think Ros de Lanerolle's point about authorship (which also intrigues me) must be referred to Samkange. Because if it is true that this is the account of 'The Mourned One' himself, then this <u>must</u> be his book and Samkange its editor.
>
> I rate this book very highly and suggest that we accept it despite the present curbs on the AWS. (HC to JC 23 March 1974)

I wrote to Stanlake Samkange to accept the manuscript:

> Doris Lessing and all our readers are fascinated and cannot make up their minds to what extent you are its author. Either way it is excellent. If

> Ndatshana's manuscript does really form the basis then he ought to be at least credited as the co-author. What do you think? If you are its author may I congratulate you on an extraordinary achievement. If you are its editor I must thank you for finding it. (JC to SS 26 July 1974)

Stanlake Samkange wrote from Massachusetts to say our readers had reacted in the way he had hoped that they would:

> As regards authorship, there is, fortunately or unfortunately, no document. I use the device of a document to enable me to tell the story in the first person. There are, however, authentic features in the story; such as the fact that an African teacher named Ndatshana was hanged for rape of a white missionary woman in 1935. I read the transcript of his High Court trial. The case has acquired an oral tradition among Africans. This is given to me by Rev. M.J. Busike (Rusike) in his letter to me which is, also, authentic. Ndatahana [sic] was, however, a South African and not a Rhodesian tribesman. Mr Henry Chakava shows great perception when he says: 'The story is so sophisticated in construction and rendering and its application so current that it surprised me to hear that it comes from such a simple man and refers to the Rhodesia of the 1930's.' I did consider making the fellow, at least, a matriculant but there was only one African in the whole country who had gone that far at the time. So, I settled for one brought up as a Black European … (SS to JC 8 August 1974)

At this time in the mid-1970s, with the second *chimurenga* revolt having an effect, Stanlake Samkange went back to history with a novel called *The Year of the Uprising* (1978 AWS 190) about the 1896 Matabele and Mashona rebellions. In 1968 Heinemann had published *The Origins of Rhodesia*, which was his history of these events. Ros de Lanerolle (report 24 March 1976), with her South African political background, was full of anticipation when she read the script. After the first 30 pages she found it disappointing and felt that he had gone on writing out of a sense of duty. Perhaps, after the enthusiasm of our readers for *The Mourned One,* Stanlake Samkange had not worked on the final manuscript with sufficient thoroughness. After some three months, he asked Doris Lessing to enquire about what was happening about the consideration of his manuscript. I wrote to him on 20 May 1976 politely saying that the reports had been a been 'a little mixed'. Her letter of 28 May 1976 to Stanlake Samkange refers to the escalation of the war; it was indeed at that time that, under pressure from South Africa, Smith met Kissinger to discuss majority rule:

> I wrote to James Currey, and yesterday got a copy of a letter. I find it hard to interpret his letter, except that he is in a state of indecision! If it were me, I should publish it with the idea of interesting people specifically through the present crisis in Rhodesia … I do so hope that Heinemann's do accept it.
>
> In my view this book should be published with an eye to the future. A black, or mixed-race government in Rhodesia, would be bound to look kindly on this book. And I see it as required reading for an understanding of the Rhodesian problem now. But then I am not a publisher. And I am

> not in the position – which I understand many of them are, at the moment – of facing a crisis financially.
>
> I keep thinking that it is time Africa had a large all-African publishing house. It is long overdue.
>
> Zambia could do it. Or Tanzania. Or Nigeria. (Doris Lessing to SS 28 May 1976)

What neither she nor I knew was that, in the 1980s after full independence, Salisbury (renamed Harare) would become one of the most enterprising and imaginative publishing centres in Africa, as is shown at the end of this chapter (p. 273).

Her support tipped the balance for its publication. It was prepared for press by Richard Lister, who found the manuscript 'chaotic'. Unfortunately Stanlake Samkange reacted badly against his work, complaining:

> If you straighten things out, I would argue, you lose the African flavor so essential to keep. The writing ceases to be African. It becomes European … I found myself quite irritated by your editor's style or questioning. I have worked with several editors. I believe this is the first to irritate me. I could not help the feeling I was dealing with a mere pompous prig. (SS to JC 12 May 1977)

I told him that this editor had worked successfully with Bessie Head, John Munonye and other writers. I made it clear:

> It is your book. You must do things your way. The editor is one of the most humble men. I'm sorry that he struck you as a prig. He would be the first to say that you should ignore everything that he has suggested.
>
> The problem is that readers, both African and European, have been confused by the multitude of characters. It's up to you what you do. We raise the problems. You provide the answers. Some readers will be confused whatever you do. (JC to SS 19 May 1977)

Stanlake Samkange returned to Zimbabwe from America after independence. He had a taste for the English quaint. He drove round Salisbury in a Rolls Royce. He bought 'the only castle in Rhodesia' which a settler had built in 1940 at Hatfield on the airport edge of town. He opened a 'heritage' shop called 'The Professor's Den' to which he welcomed you smoking his pipe. He published two further novels in Harare. *Among them Yanks* (1985) used material from his exile in America. *On Trial for That UDI* (1986) went back to the formula he had used in his first novel about Rhodes and Lobengula. The British prime minister, Harold Wilson, is put on trial with Ian Smith, the settler's hero of the Unilateral Declaration of Independence (UDI). I suspect that Stanlake Samkange's personal style led people to undervalue his work in the new Zimbabwe. It is a pleasure for me to rediscover the ingenuity of *The Mourned One*. He died in 1988 at the age of only 55.

Lawrence Vambe

The landless

The first encounter we had with Doris Lessing at Heinemann Educational Books was made tense by hidden rivalries with the father firm William Heinemann. In 1970 she had approached Roland Gant, the editorial director, about a three-part autobiographical account of Rhodesian history by Lawrence Vambe, a Zimbabwean journalist who had been living in exile in London. William Heinemann, on the strength of Doris Lessing's recommendation, decided to go ahead with the first part under the title *An Ill-Fated People*. Lawrence Vambe sent a letter in 1970 to *The Observer* in London about the eviction of African tenants from Christian missions:

> I anticipated it even before the passing of the so-called Land Tenure Act because the squeezing of the Africans from these places began even before the Rhodesian Front came into power …
>
> In the old Zimbabwe, these people [the VaShawasha], who were once a part of the extraordinary Monomotapa empire, occupied the whole area of what are to-day Chishawasha and Epworth Missions, including parts of the land where modern Salisbury is situated. The Occupation of Mashonaland in 1890 by the white members of the Pioneer Column changed their fate entirely. They were made landless.

Lawrence Vambe's grandfather, Mashonganyika, was appointed chief by the white authorities after the defeat of the 1896 Mashona rebellion.

Alan Hill, then managing director of Heinemann Educational Books, was annoyed that we had not been consulted by William Heinemann about its acceptance and editing. The first he knew about the book was when he had suddenly been handed the complete page proofs; it had been taken for granted that we would accept it for the African Writers Series. Alan Hill, as is standard practice in academic publishing, sought a specialist opinion; he consulted Terence Ranger, then Professor of African History at UCLA, who had written *Revolt in Southern Rhodesia 1896–7*, which had been published by Heinemann Educational Books in 1967.

Doris Lessing expressed annoyance at 'this Professor Ranger business' in a letter she wrote to me:

> My attitude towards this book is this: for all I know the historical parts of it are all nonsense … I have no way of knowing. But I think that Mr. Vambe should be able to write what he believes is true and to quote the sources he feels are relevant; it is, after all, how the truth is eventually arrived at.
>
> This is the point that strikes me as forcibly as it strikes Mr. Vambe. It is that you, and others, automatically talk about 'historians' and 'history' meaning something written. In our culture 'history' is history when it is between covers. But at least two of the now official historians of Mashona life got most of their facts from Mr Vambe. But what Mr. Vambe says is not

> 'history'; and his manuscript has to be submitted to them for approval.
>
> It seems to me the faster he can get a book into print, when he can be a historian too, because of the magic of words on the page, the better … (Doris Lessing to JC 11 January 1971)

Anyhow Professor Richard Gray gave it the SOAS London academic seal of approval:

> … a most successful attempt to comment on Rhodesian history through the eyes and experiences of a small tribal community … It is also, academically, a valuable document combining much useful oral tradition on the rule of Vashawasha during the period of resistance with a convincing range of illustrations culled from the author's memories of life at Chishawasha as a young schoolboy and adolescent. Apart from these insights into the central theme of Rhodesian history, the leit-motif of the books is an analysis of the impact of, and the African reaction to, the work of one of the most famous Christian missions in Africa – the Jesuits at Chishawasha. I found this a remarkably balanced, critical and perceptive account, which gives the books a far wider relevance and interest than Rhodesia alone. (Report by Richard Gray, about February 1971)

After hardback publication by William Heinemann, *An Ill-fated People* appeared in the African Writers Series (1972 AWS 112). By that time Rachel Monsarrat, an editor at William Heinemann, was tackling the problem of how to publish the second and third parts of the book. She commented on the situation:

> Moira [Lynd] has summarised Lawrence Vambe's new book so I won't repeat the contents. But it is significant that in her enthusiastic report – which I wholeheartedly agree with – the story of Rhodesia from the African point of view continues to be a fascinating one – she deals entirely with the first half of the MS. She only gets onto the second half on page four of her report and it is dispensed with in a few lines. I also found in my notes that the contents of the second half can be summarised as briefly – but Lawrence has spread himself over 170 TS pages, more than half the book. (Rachel Monsarrat WH internal report 17 August 1972)

She got the agreement of Lawence Vambe to make a single book, which he wanted to call *A Hostage People in the Worst of Both Worlds*. I suggested the title *From Rhodesia to Zimbabwe* which suited everyone. However, our colleagues in Kenya and Nigeria shared our feeling that this personal historical account did not suit the African Writers Series. William Heinemann eventually published it in hardback in 1976.

Charles Mungoshi

Cold comfort

Charles Mungoshi writes in both Shona and English. He demonstrates the importance of there being prizes and a variety of publishing outlets to encourage young writers. His first novel, a love tale about the custom of pledging daughters, won a prize in a competition organised by the Southern Rhodesia Literature Bureau when he was only 21. His first collection of stories was published by Oxford University Press in East Africa (and banned in Rhodesia).

A collection of 20 stories was sent to us on 19 April 1971 by the Book Centre in Salisbury, which was run by the redoubtable Eleanor Tarica, one of those valuable bridge-builders who not only helped writers with their practical problems but told them how to get in touch with publishers in faraway London. Her southern African expressions brought one up short but, to her credit, in her no-nonsense way she helped the writers who diffidently wandered into her shop. There is a handwritten note which I have quoted in full to capture her style. She scribbled:

> I am glad that you have the Marachera Poetry. Do you like it? He says his short stories are not up to scratch but I am encouraging him to rewrite them. In true African Tradition in the fullness of time you will receive them.
>
> Mungoshi has just told me has a whole wad of stuff for you – but didn't know how to get it typed – so stupid – anyway I'll send them when they are typed.
>
> Victor and I are going to Greece for a month's holiday from tomorrow – maybe we will pop over to London – tell Allan and Hamish – (Eleanor Tarica to JC 20 September 1972)

I had caused this problem over the typing when writing to Charles Mungoshi about the revision of the 20 stories:

> Although your hand-writing is so beautifully clear we wonder if there is any chance of your gaining access to a typewriter. This is not so much a question of legibility as of safety. We are rather worried about your consigning your only copies to the post. Also whether you type or write the stories it will be more convenient if you use one side of the paper. It does not matter if you do not type very well but it does mean you have a carbon copy. Please double space your typing. (JC to CM 13 March 1972)

I hoped I was being practical. I was encouraging him to take into account the positive recommendation of the two readers and to resubmit with some more recent work. 'In the fullness of time' it had already taken us at Heinemann a whole year to get this far. I asked him whether he had tried his hand at a novel in English.

Ros de Lanerolle had said about the stories:

> Their strength is their really remarkable revelation of intense feeling … Guess the writer is young, exposed, his writing though not his perception immature.
>
> But he is [a] rare find. Southern Africa has plenty of 'social' writers, but few who try to convey the existential experience. The 'where it's at', terror, frustration, breakdown of personality, of being black in white-ruled Africa. Not much humour though! There is a book here, pruning and editing assumed. (Report by Ros de Lanerolle 25 January 1972)

We did not hear from Charles Mungoshi for another eighteen months:

> I am working on the stories as you suggested and I am afraid that this is going to take some time since I have to work myself into the mood in which I wrote these stories – and that was four-five years ago. A lot of things have happened since then, for instance the 'heavy' mood which seems to pervade the stories (could have been due to unemployment and still being very tied up with parents) – this mood anyway, has worn off a bit. So if I have to be sincere, I shall discard or completely recast some of the stories. Your notes only confirmed what I had begun to feel about the stories – too heavy, tense, and wavering – not satisfactory.

The second part of the letter gave the news we wanted to hear: he had posted the manuscript of a novel to us.

> … the book was already written and I had to get rid of it before it drove me into a nervous breakdown! So, please accept my apologies for loading you with it – more so, since I am aware of its defect as 'a story' in the normal sense. The idea was to do a family portrait. I did have in mind to call the book exactly that – 'Portrait of a Family' but by the time I came to put down the last line, my subconscious had perceived a kind of 'expecting' or 'waiting' element in the characters and I wrote down 'Waiting for the Rain' without any second thoughts. The 'seed' of the novel is a part of the twenty stories – hence the rather 'heavy' tone (Guess one just can't completely shake off the muck of origins!!) Anyway, there it is. I await your verdict. (CM to KS 16 August 1973)

A month later Ros de Lanerolle was celebrating *Waiting for the Rain* (1975 AWS 170), 'Beautiful – knew [he] could do it, didn't we?' Richard Lister read work by Charles Mungoshi for the first time:

> This is a strange book, quite powerful, rather puzzling … I'd definitely recommend this for publication, because the author has penetrating insight and puts some things across remarkably well, and is just too gifted to let go. If I take a slightly carping attitude, it's because, first, I find the whole thing a bit intense. The whole family is in a needless tangle; their habit of brooding on each other's attitudes – he thinks she thinks he thinks – is taken to such lengths that sometimes they seem more like a bunch of highly-strung intellectuals tearing at each other's egos in between analyses than a fairly simple family struggling for survival in a harsh world. Sometimes I was reminded irresistibly of *Cold Comfort Farm*. (Report by Richard Lister 20 December 1973)

Reaction from Africa was positive. A Nigerian reader said that his 'skilful blending of African expressions in English' reminded him of Chinua Achebe. Henry Chakava said:

> I like this novel for its psychological depth into the African imagination, its faithfulness to detail, and its very vivid presentation on an African family situation, with its rather simple people. True it is rather slow-moving, but there is dignity about this movement – quite representative of the people and society of its setting. (HC to JC 19 June 1974)

News came from the Book Centre, Salisbury, about their 1976 Award:

> This is an annual award made by this Company but administered by P.E.N. International in Rhodesia. This Award this year was divided into two sections so that instead of $500 for one writer we gave $300 for the best work in English published during the last year, and $300 to the best work in Shona or Ndebele. Two independent panels of judges worked on this and it was quite remarkable that Charles Mungoshi won the awards in both the English section i.e. *Waiting for the Rain* and for the work he has had published [1975] in Shona. (Book Centre/Textbook Sales to JC 15 April 1976)

This 'politically innocuous novel', as Stanley Nyamfukudza called it, was banned in the last days of Rhodesia. Charles Mungoshi went on to write in both languages and win prizes. He won the African section of the Commonwealth Writers Prize in 1988 and the Noma Award in 1992. In 1987 he translated Ngũgĩ's *A Grain of Wheat* into Shona.

Stanley Nyamfukudza
The struggle for Zimbabwe

In 1977 Stanley Nyamfukudza offered us *The Non-Believer's Journey* (1980 AWS 233), about the realities of split loyalties during the second *chimurenga* . The mood was far away from that in the comradely novels of the freedom struggle in Angola, where independence had been won a year earlier in 1976 (p. 247). I told Doris Lessing on publication in 1980:

> Interestingly enough, it turns out that Stanley Nyamfukudza was one of the five students given places at Oxford after being thrown out of the University of Rhodesia. Dambudzo Marechera was the only one of the five who didn't survive the academic hurdle race at Oxford. (JC to Doris Lessing 10 January 1980)

The first report was by Peter Rodda, a member of the South African *New African* network:

> Structurally and narratively there is a deft simplicity as the story is told, summarised in the excellent title, which of course has a symbolic resonance. Sam goes on a trip to the funeral of his uncle who has been killed as a traitor. It is Sam's last journey; he is killed as a non-believer in the cause of political liberation through armed-resistance. Those who are not for it are – must they be seen as against it? (Report by Peter Rodda December 1977)

Ros de Lanerolle felt in her report of 5 July 1978 that 'the ending is anti-climactic; the confrontation with the guerrilla can't bear the weight put upon it.' Laban Erapu in Nairobi sent a positive report by Wahome Matahi, but was himself firm:

> The war situation in which the story operates fails to gain intensity with the result that the final tragedy appears contrived and an afterthought … I am afraid that Nyamfukudza just has to sit down and try and rewrite this into a more serious novel. (Laban Erapu to JC early 1978)

The revised version was reported on by two practising novelists, neither of whom had seen the first version, although they were given the reports. John Wyllie (18 September 1979) felt: 'Mr. Nyamfukudza sees people and their background with the eye of a natural novelist.' Richard Lister thought that he had convincingly resolved the central problem of Sam deciding whether or not to take part in the struggle:

> He is a more than ordinary man caught up in a more than extraordinary situation, and he can't deal with it. So he tries to go along with the situation and yet not go along with it; he can't bring himself to ignore it entirely and go on with his own private life, but when he is brought into contact with the guerillas he sees too clearly their weaknesses – the disagreements between the communities, their dependence on 'spirit mediums' and worn-out ways of thought which his education makes him regard as nonsensical – and, with his natural truculence, all he can do is to attack an armed guerilla who, for all his contempt of him, has no intention of killing him; and so he arranges for his own happy dispatch, a solution he has intellectually perceived as the only one possible for him all along.
>
> I must confess that while reading the book I was often irritated by the necessity of concentrating on the meaningless idiocies of the unfortunate non-believer, Sam, while admiring the masterly portrayal of the revolutionary scene in which he's helplessly caught up, and it was a relief to find out when I'd finished that the author had it right; it's against the insignificance of Sam that the larger scene, with all its messiness and in-built flaws, stands out and justifies itself. (Report by Richard Lister 28 July 1979)

We had *The Non-Believer's Journey* and Dambudzo Marechera's *Black Sunlight* printed in 1980, the year when Zimbabwe became independent. Stanley Nyamfukudza, when he went back that year, was frustrated that the new books had not arrived and felt that this made his television and press publicity rather pointless:

> I do not think I will remain unemployed for too long, the main problem at the moment being that I want a job which is absolutely grey in political terms.
>
> It was somewhat surprising to find that most of the people I went to College with here are now Ministers, Junior Ministers and that sort of thing. The violence continues, but not on the scale one might imagine from the press out there … I am much more optimistic than when I arrived. (SN to JC 18 November 1980)

I told him of our efforts to get books into the country:

> Anyhow I am certain that that the thirst for Zimbabwean books will be even greater than ever. People felt that before they couldn't get hold of them. Now they will want them even more and can't get them. (JC to SN 9 December 1980)

Stanley Nyamfukudza was hired as an editor by College Press, the subsidiary of Macmillan, which was joining in the zesty scramble for Zimbabwean writers.

Heady years in Zimbabwe

I listened in March 1980 in Dar es Salaam to news of the unexpected election victory of Robert Mugabe's ZANU/PF; this, according to the settlers and their conservative backers in London, had opened the gates for communism. Within days I was in Salisbury for the first time since 1964. It was a throwback to my schoolboy memories of May 1945 and the end of the German war. White men in uniforms were everywhere. The classiest uniforms were taking their ladies out to tea in Meikles Hotel. The streets were crawling with a menagerie of camouflaged vehicles, with names such as Rhinos or Giraffes, which had steel plates welded at 45 degrees on to their sides to deflect the force of land-mines. The windows of the Monomotapa Hotel were being repaired after being shattered by an explosion in a church opposite, blown up by agents-provocateurs to destabilise the elections. On my way out of the country at the airport I was frisked in a discreet booth by a pukka Englishman who politely enquired when I had last visited Salisbury. I told him not since 1964 and he calmly replied, 'That's a long time!' as though nothing much had happened since then. When I got back to England an uncle enquired anxiously about a Rhodesian cousin, saying that she had told him that she would have to leave if the communist Mugabe got in. I said, 'Oh? When I saw her she was just off to the Borrowdale races in her hat.'

Heinemann Educational Books had never had an office in Rhodesia, although books were exempt from UN sanctions. We felt that this was the time when we would have an advantage over firms such as Longman and College Press/ Macmillan which had been established in Rhodesia in the years following UDI. Keith Sambrook and I were keen to investigate local reprinting. On my second visit Anita Wolfe-Coote came up from the William Heinemann office in Johannesburg and we paid a visit to Mardons, the best-established printer in what was still Salisbury. The manager, who was as English as Croydon, took us round the works showing us the ingenuity with which his mechanics had made spares to keep printing machines going in the time of sanctions. Everybody was talking of skilled whites leaving the country, so I asked about an apprenticeship scheme for Africans. He hastened to assure me that they were not going to let standards drop. I had quite forgotten that, as in South Africa, the skilled jobs in printing were reserved for whites. Anita Wolfe-Coote was much amused by these two Englishman failing to understand one another on issues of race.

Keith Sambrook and I went back to the strategy that Heinemann had tried out in the 1960s in East Africa, when it had been hoped that an alliance with the East African Publishing House (EAPH) would have saved us from having to set up an editorial office in Nairobi (p. 87). Keith Sambrook and I persuaded Heinemann Educational Books' managing director, Tony Beal, who had been dealing with the bookshops in Rhodesia, that this would be the most rewarding and politically adroit way of taking advantage of the new situation in the country.

It was decided to form an alliance with the Zimbabwe Publishing House (ZPH), which had been set up at independence. This initiative had been quickly taken by two journalists, David Martin and Phyllis Johnson, who had reported from Mugabe's ZANU/PF camps in Mozambique. (Most of the journalists concentrated their stories and the expectations of their readers on Joshua Nkomo who was more comfortably and accessibly established in Lusaka.) They wrote an influential book, *The Struggle for Zimbabwe*, which was first published by ZPH and by Faber in London in 1982. They were well placed with the new leadership; they played ping-pong with the minister of higher education who had become a close friend in Mozambique. When I stayed at their house, David Martin started telephoning his round of ministers and contacts at 6 am in the morning. David Martin and Phyllis Johnson persuaded the minister of education that the government must implement UNESCO policy which meant that, if a book was chosen to be prescribed or used in a substantial number of 1,000 or more in government schools, then the foreign publisher must license it to a Zimbabwean publisher for reprinting in the country. They would use their contacts to make sure that Heinemann textbooks, particularly in science, were included on the ministry of education lists. Penny Butler went out to Harare on several lengthy and demanding visits to work with them on the writing, editing and development of a new generation of textbooks and in training Zimbabwean staff.

I told Ngũgĩ that David Martin had said that, as far as African Writers Series reprints in Zimbabwe were concerned, ZPH would like 'progressive writers (yourself and Sembene Ousmane) and Zimbabwean writers whether progressive or not' (JC to Ngũgĩ 18 September 1981). David Martin and Phyllis Johnson wanted people to have a chance to read books such as Dambudzo Marechera's *The House of Hunger*, which had hardly been available. They had hopes of following up their connections in Mozambique and Angola and we planned to co-operate with them on the translation from Portuguese of three books, starting with *Mayombe* by Pepetela, who was now a minister in Angola (p. 251). Charles Mungoshi was hired as an editor by ZPH, where his office provided a shebeen for the young writers in Harare.

Keith Sambrook and I got the support of Tony Beal for the sublicensing of the rights for a select list of books in the African Writers Series for reprinting in Zimbabwe. The books had accessible Zimbabwe dollar prices, stock was easily available and sales multiplied. I was attacked after I left Heinemann for having adopted this policy, although it had brought in royalty cheques without investment.

During the 1980s a big enough market developed within Zimbabwe itself for a range of literary titles to be published. New Zimbabwean writers started to become viable in Zimbabwe alone. The best could be subcontracted for international publication in London or New York. Publishers competed for writers. There was an active interest in new writing in the daily press and in broadcasting, and new journals like *The Zimbabwean Review* were founded. This was literary publishing in Africa as it should be.

This desirable situation had previously only been achieved in South Africa after the independent publishers became established during the 1970s. The first South African titles in the African Writers Series had been by exiles. The pattern was similar for Zimbabwean titles; five of the first six writers in the Series were in exile in Britain or the US. By the 1980s we could depend on the new independent publishers in South Africa to subcontract key representative titles for the Series. Ironically, with freedom, there was a lull in adding new Zimbabwean titles to the Series. The Zimbabwean publishers had seized the initiative. ZPH, College, Longman Zimbabwe, Mambo and Academic were finding the new writing.

Hugh Lewin had spent seven years in the hanging jail in Pretoria, and a period in the London *Drum* office. He rang up from Zimbabwe one day in the late 1980s to say that he and Irene Staunton had started a new imprint called Baobab which rapidly became the most innovative literary publisher in Zimbabwe. Irene Staunton is one of those exceptional editors who can coax extraordinary writing out of authors. She introduced new writers – especially women – both within Zimbabwe and internationally and used a network of contacts to subcontract English-language editions and to sell foreign-language rights. Yvonne Vera's first novel was sold to the prestigious New York literary imprint Farrar Strauss and Giroux. Tsitsi Dangarembga's *Nervous Conditions* was published by Ros de Lanerolle's Women's Press in London, and later by Becky Ayebia Clarke. Several titles did appear in the African Writers Series including Shimmer Chinodya's *Harvest of Thorns* (1990), which won the Commonwealth Writers Prize, and Chenjerai Hove's *Bones* (1990) which won the Noma Award for Baobab. (Shimmer Chinodya's *Strife* won a Noma Award in 2007 for Irene Staunton's own Weaver Press.)

The early 1980s were heady years in Zimbabwe; it reminded one of the exhilarating atmosphere of the years of African independence in the 1960s. This excitement was fuelled by the Zimbabwe International Book Fair, which became a trading place for international rights throughout Africa, rather than just a local trade fair. The first fairs took place amid the Shona soapstone sculptures in the National Gallery and then they moved into the park under tents in the dry season, with marimba players round every grassy corner.

In 1982 the Fair organised a writers' workshop, which gave a chance to aspiring Zimbabwean writers to hear and meet distinguished authors from all over Africa. In the chair of the workshop was Emmanuel Ngara, whose radical books of literary criticism I have published over the years. He referred to me in his introductory remarks as the 'grandfather of African literature'. In the coffee break Nadine Gordimer greeted me with: 'Hello grandfather'. I must have looked slightly abashed as I was only 46 years old. So she said: 'It's a term of honour in Africa!' David Martin and Phyllis Johnson were delighted when an interview with me was headlined across the centre page of the *Herald* as 'The Godfather of African Publishing' which, according to them, was closer to the truth.

There is a picture from the journal *West Africa* showing our authors, Mongo Beti from Cameroun and Eldred Durosimi Jones from Sierra Leone, being introduced by me to President Mugabe at the first book fair. He took an active interest and spent so long going round the fair that the writers were delayed in their departure to visit the ruins of Great Zimbabwe. We set off on the four-hour journey in a bus with Department of Women's Affairs painted on its side. We were taken round by Stan Mudenge, whose book, *A Political History of Munhumutapa c.1400 to 1902*, I was later to co-publish with ZPH. Because of the late start we only arrived at the ruins as the sun set. He led us in the dark down into the round of the great walls. The stars twinkled in the early evening chill. In the last light the broken ruins were magically reshaped by the shadows and looked as they must have done when they were newly built. It was Saturday evening. Fires had been started. Drumming echoed in the hills. We had been carried back into African history. I misquoted Blake to myself: 'Wide through the language of [my] dreams the lordly Niger flows.'

'SA exiles, King Street, Covent Garden, London early 1980s' is the first picture in George Hallett's *Portraits of African Writers*. The exile artists and writers had been at a meeting in the Africa Centre, which had originally been opened by Kenneth Kaunda in the great period of independence of the sixties; it was right in the centre of London just by the Covent Garden fruit and vegetable market and along the road from the Royal Opera House (Heinemann nearly set up offices in the Charles II building on the left which had become a boxing saloon). The Africa Centre above all provided gathering spaces for performances and exhibitions by writers, artists and musicians from Africa and meetings and performances were held on all subjects from politics to history. There was a restaurant run by a Senegalese chef in the basement.

There is in this book a description (p.188) of the meeting at the Africa Centre in May 1973 when Heinemann launched six books by South Africans including titles by Dennis Brutus, Albie Sachs and Nelson Mandela.

In the period before 1980 it was often called 'Zimbabwe House' as it provided a meeting place for so many of the exiles. In that period it provided a stage for all sorts of performances by Dambudzo Marechera, as is shown in the next section. As the struggle for South Africa's liberation went on through the eighties the Africa Book Centre run by Tony Zurbrugg provided the South African exile community not only with latest books but also with news in *The Mail and Guardian*.

SA exiles, King Street, Covent Garden, London, early 1980s

PUBLISHING
Dambudzo Marechera

Doris Lessing said of the first book by this young man from the country where she grew up: 'We can't use the word *genius* now, it is so debased. But it used to mean something extra, the something nobody could have allowed for. Marechera has in him the stuff and substance that go to make a great writer.' She said this in June 1979 of his first book of short stories, *The House of Hunger*, in *Books and Bookmen*. I was already engaged in a long-running drama to get him to produce a publishable first novel and to establish him as a professional writer.

Dambudzo Marechera was born in Zimbabwe in 1952. He clashed with his teachers at St Augustine's, Penhalonga. He was expelled from the University of Rhodesia but his teachers managed to get New College, Oxford to give him a place. He was cared for, in spite of assaults on staff, by Lady Hayter, the wife of the Warden. He maintained that he was expelled for trying to burn the college down. He then wrote *The House of Hunger* (1978 AWS 207) in a tent beside the Thames – but then perhaps he did not, for he developed his own life-story with all the skill of a novelist and the self-regarding obsession of an actor. He stole the scene when his book won *The Guardian* fiction prize, the most prestigious prize for new writing, despite his sharing it with film-maker and writer, Neil Jordan. He displayed to the press like a peacock at the Berlin festival and the immigration services were so fazed by his performance at Heathrow that they let him back into Britain without any travel documents.

A publisher shares an author's nervousness about the second book when the first book has made an impact. My aim was to keep him writing and to keep his typewriter out of pawn. Short manuscripts emerged but all showed signs of having been written in keyboard-bashing highs fuelled by alcohol and other stimulants. His unannounced arrivals at the Heinemann offices put me on a state of high alert. The novel *Black Sunlight* (AWS 237) was published in 1980 to encourage him to keep writing and to earn him some money. After independence in 1980 he could go back to Zimbabwe. Chris Austin, a South African, made a film for Channel 4 Television about his life in London and about his reactions to going back in 1982 to the country which had emerged from Rhodesia. After a one-man civil war against the new authorities he died at the age of 35. Maybe his death was Aids-related. Everything to do with him had a touch of mythology to which I have no doubt contributed.

The growth of this mythology has been revealingly examined by Flora Veit-Wild who has collected the documents in *Dambudzo Marechera: a Source Book on his Life and Work* (Hans Zell 1992). She interviewed me twice in 1989 and 1991. Some five years had passed since my departure from Heinemann, and I said that I was sure that she ought to see if my memories were backed up by the Heinemann files. In 1992

Hans Zell gave me a copy of her 436-page book saying, with amusement, that I was much quoted. I read my letters with trepidation and was relieved to find that documents and memory were not too far apart. My son and daughter, then in their twenties, seized the book that Christmas to read about this man who had so invaded the lives of their parents when they were in their early teens. Flora Veit-Wild says: 'For Marechera, Heinemann – specifically James Currey – was a surrogate father.' She also uses the word 'friendship' about our relationship. I never chose to be with Dambudzo Marechera except for professional reasons. To be near him was to be on red alert. The curtain was always about to go up on some new drama which totally absorbed one's time. I always tried to keep a professional distance so that I could help him put together an income on which to survive. I needed to protect my time to look after my many other authors, several of whom really had become personal friends.

When on 17 February 1977 Dambudzo Marechera sent Heinemann his manuscript under the title 'At the Head of the Stream' he mentioned not only Charles Mungoshi but also the manager of the Book Centre in Salisbury, the supportive Eleanor Tarica. I sent the manuscript for a report to Ros de Lanerolle, whose South African background gave her an insight into the Rhodesian setting:

> One long and three (very) short stories by a Zimbabwean, all but one set in Zimbabwe. The long story tells the tale of a boyhood of a young man, told in flashback as he leaves home – and we are to assume, I think, Zimbabwe. Home and country are both The House of Hunger, the place of madness and violence and despair. The boy is formed in a home where tenderness has long given way to the tactics of survival, his father is drunken, his mother a constantly assaulted but young woman in a precise repetition of the model he knows. School is brutalising too – he remembers the beating of the weakest yet most obstinate of small boys – when he sees his picture in the paper as a guerrilla and a corpse. Sex is an instrument of domination, and a function of white domination. Township life is a prison, except to the whore, the police spy, the traitor. The hero goes to university, engages in political conflict, has an affair with a crippled white girl – each of them caught in the prison of race and skin colour. Both are beaten badly by white thugs, and the girl never recovers. His vulnerability is kept alive only by a nervous breakdown.
>
> It's as terrible a book as it sounds, raw and very powerful. I

> don't know another book about Africa that deals with the whole situation at such a level except perhaps Lessing or Head. Writer is clearly a most remarkable man. (Report by Ros de Lanerolle undated 1977)

I got photocopies of the manuscript off to Ibadan and Nairobi with this perceptive report and urged speed. In my memo to my African colleagues I noted:

> I detect a searing talent here. This is some of the most powerful slum writing and reminiscences I have ever seen. It still needs more work and a far more powerful title. (I suggested *The House of Hunger* to him.)
>
> The most powerful passages of the main story remind one of Mphahlele's *Down Second Avenue* or some of the Irish writers on their slum backgrounds.
>
> I'd be very grateful for speedy reports because Marechera is in a pretty bad state both psychologically and financially and he needs a lot of encouragement.
>
> I think it may be worth publishing these short stories first even though he is at work on a novel. (JC to HC, Laban Erapu and Akin Thomas 28 April 1977)

I was confident that I would get support from Africa. I had to plead a special case with my colleagues in London. On 23 May 1977 I managed, which was very unusual, to get an advance of £150 even ahead of formal acceptance because of the time it was taking to get responses from Africa. There does not appear to have been a Nigerian report. Then a politically correct report from Kenya, which Henry Chakava sent in late August 1977, was negative: 'It is clear that the writer does not have a high opinion of the black man. He is pompous and a bore, trying to fight liberation from Western capitals while all the time wishing that he was white … These stories are damaging to the morale of a world bent on liberation.' Henry Chakava did not bother with this opinion and his own report concluded: 'If this is Marechera's first effort, then he has a great future as writer.' (20 September 1977)

I could already see that this man needed to learn the tactics of survival in London while he wrote his first novel. *The House of Hunger* was not to be published until a year later in December 1978. Young writers, if they do not have another profession, need to put together an income from a range of activities such as the sale of short stories, broadcasting, reviews and articles for magazines. Ngũgĩ was one of a few African writers who had tried to survive on his royalties alone, and he had some chance of doing so because his early novels had been so quickly prescribed by exam boards. I put Dambudzo Marechera in touch with people who might be able to use his work. I mentioned him to people on the BBC Africa Service. I sent copies to Chinua Achebe for consideration for the journal *Okike*. I put him in touch with Hugh Lewin at the London offices of the Johannesburg magazine *Drum* in the hope that it would use a story. As the son of professional writers I knew that this sort of life needed organisation. In the days before mobile phones, how did editors and producers contact you when you lived in a squat in Tolmers Square? I would never give in to his requests for personal loans. What I tried to give him was a professional context within which to survive. It was difficult. The drafts of novels he brought in had inspiration but no development. Each was a new script. He had not worked over his previous work. He had scarcely taken into account the reports I had commissioned.

I was not surprised to receive a letter from Dambudzo Marechera in Cardiff jail dated 9 December 1977. Unfortunately prisons were an all too common problem for African writers. At the end of that very month in 1977 Ngũgĩ was to be incarcerated without charge in Kamĩtĩ Maximum Security prison in Kenya. We were in 1982 to include in the African Writers Series Hugh Lewin's *Bandiet* about his seven years in the Pretoria hanging jail. They were writers who were fighting political causes. Marechera was just incompetent. He was charged with stealing a book belonging to his, no doubt unpaid, 'landlord'. Cannabis came into the charge. The main problem was that he had not bothered to extend his visa when it ran out on 2 October 1975. As usual he played up the role of the professional victim:

> I believe I am in mess; and this time I don't think I know enough to get myself out of it. I have been in custody/remand for ten days and been remanded again in custody for another week starting from yesterday (8th December). They are threatening me left and right with deportation and I believe that they may just want to throw me out of the country through the quiet back door of Cardiff. All this is of course soup in which even a fly could not hope to backstroke it to the shores. Thanks to [my landlord] who has so astutely masterminded it all. Also thanks to 'my solicitors' who seem to be doing all in their power to have me drawn and quartered and disembowelled and grilled a la Cardiff. It is a cheerfull and moral meal that they are making out of me. (DM to JC 9 December 1977)

I sent a telegram on 13 December 1977 to Mr Marechera Prisoner No A87171:

> AS YOU ARE OUR CONTRACTED AUTHOR WE ARE FOLLOWING UP YOUR LETTER AND INVESTIGATING FULLY YOUR LEGAL POSITION STOP CHEER UP THERE ARE LOTS OF POSSIBILITIES

It was easy for me to testify to the solicitors about the stories that 'I have no doubts that the present government of Rhodesia would see them as highly critical' (13 December 1977). That was enough in the days of the premiership of Jim Callaghan to make sure that, though the magistrates sentenced him to three months, they made no recommendation for deportation.

Dambudzo Marechera's fantastic – I use this word carefully – 3,000-word letter written on 28 January 1978, the day after he left jail, started with how he had got back the edited manuscript of *The House of Hunger* which we had sent to his landlord's address:

> I came out of prison yesterday. I have given up the manuscript for lost because 'the landlord' who received it – I checked with the post office – refused to give it to me unless I went on my knees and apologized about my being a criminal. The first thing I did was to report at the Chapter Arts Centre where everyone was so annihilatingly the same as ever. They all seemed to regard crime as an occupational hazard for a writer. The administrator there however told me 'the landlord's' present address and I phoned … to demand the surrender of the manuscript to me. He refused. I went to the police and the CID man who arrested me two months ago on the strength of a statement from 'my landlord' told me to simply tell [him] that if he did not give me my property back there would be 'certain and strong legal measures' against him. I trudged to [his home] where I gave a deaf ear to some polite badinage about the uselessness of utopian human brotherhood in a situation rife with anti-social and criminal types. An hour later he gave me the manuscript and asked if I was going to write about everything that has happened. I assured him that I would whereupon he launched into a sermon about the moral obligations between host and guest. I reminded him that I was still suffering from a severe type of earnest boredom whose main symptom is sudden and inexplicable violence. (I think that some of my stories continually harp on this.) He slammed the door in my face and I immediately returned to the police station to tell that shifty looking CID type that strong measures would not be necessary. (DM to JC 28 January 1978)

He then went off to celebrate with a friend who:

> … crushingly informed her gin and tonic that I was not only the worst version of a blackman but also that Oxford had made me something which could not possibly exist. Such libel on my meagre character is of course now something of a tonic but it still unravels a lot of sentimental knitting wool out of me and before I knew it she and I had 'definitively' undertaken to be married. In fact she insisted on a footnote to the effect that we would be married on Monday (30th January 1978) which means there is nothing for it but to get those dentures because her parents told me

> once that there was something not quite right in a writer who did not have front teeth. I dont know much about marriage but I think that it is an assault on the nerves and also expensive. I think she and I will seethe pleasantly in this unwise marriage; though when I informed her that in fact marriage would not only cripple me into wisdom but also be rather convenient for my case at the Home Office she accused me of marrying her out of purely mercenary means … I think she thinks that I can persuade you to give me another advance on the book. She read in an obscurely scandalously Sunday paper about unknowns who suddenly become instant bestsellers and were paid astounding amounts by unscrupulous U.S.A. and Australian publishers. I have not been able to convince her that Mayfair is not exactly that generous to people like me. But there is nothing I can do but ask you for a sizeable amount to marry her … [and rather later he says] I think my hangover is lessening now because I can actually see what I am writing. And I don't like it. (DM to JC 28 January 1978)

My reply to his letter was realistic:

> I have told you that we are reluctant to start publishing any new author with a collection of stories but your writing is exceptional. The fact that your collection is judged exceptional by intellectuals is a sure fire indication that it will only sell to intellectuals. Please disillusion your fiancée. Big sales are made in the pulp paperback market to those people you encountered in jail, who despite being committed criminals, took a disgusting high-minded arrogant view of your being a terrorist/freedom fighter. I repeat that you can only make a living out of writing, unless you hit a freak jackpot, by regular work in reviewing, writing articles, broadcasting, writing TV scripts, etc. Book publication brings only a small amount of money. I cannot get a further advance for you. (JC to DM 8 February 1978)

He told me personally of his time in jail. His attitudes and middle-class style had provoked the most hostile and brutal response from other inmates. He had grown up in worse slum conditions than they had experienced but he did not know how to survive in the terms of British streets. He naively viewed them as victims of the British system. He learned in unpleasant ways that they viewed his heroic tales of the civil war in Rhodesia in the crudest racialist terms of his being on the other side against the white Rhodesians. That no doubt justified them in gang-raping him. At the same time he was addicted to being victimised. As always he slipped into playing roles.

During 1978 he did keep writing and brought into Charles Street no fewer than three aspirant novels. I had John Wyllie as an important ally. I hoped, enthusiastically, but probably naively, that between us we could get Dambudzo Marechera to produce a 'developed and structured novel' from a skeletal manuscript. Towards the end of the year, John Wyllie made a practical suggestion that these small-boned offerings be put together with, as an introduction, the autobiographical section which popped up in the middle of one of the three manuscripts. However, in December 1978, the month of the publication of *The House of Hunger*, I wrote to John Wyllie:

> I have given him a carefully edited version of your report. After some thought I have not given him the suggestion you make. I'm gratefully going to hold that in reserve. This is because he seems willing to try and produce a developed and structured novel based on 'The Black Insider' drawing on these three books. I'm half afraid he can't do it. His personal life is so fragmented that his writing comes out in pieces. I have made arrangements to pay him an advance of £50 a month through to March to try and buy him some writing time in his squat in Tolmers Square. (JC to John Wyllie 14 December 1978)

In September 1978 I had managed to get Alan Hill and Tony Beal to agree to an unprecedented arrangement for an advance of £50 a month for eight months so that there was something regular coming in. Initially Dambudzo Marechera thought it wonderful and would come in to collect the cash and then go off on a binge. By December he was writing:

> Your Christmas and New Year holidays are coming and I cannot enter 1979 by nervously lurking about Charles Street waiting for another furtive packet of £50 while trying to do serious rewriting. Indeed I loathe the whole set up, especially as it seems from the receptionist upwards I have become a kind of monkey for Heinemann's amusement. (DM to JC 12 December 1978)

This was the season when one was meant to be rejoicing over the publication of his first remarkable work but instead I was writing in fury:

> I'm fed up with all this money business. It's ruining everything.
>
> 1. We're fed up with you waiting for your payment. Please get a Post Office or Trustee Savings Bank account so you can avoid being treated like a monkey by our receptionist. I hate it. I should have insisted you had a cheque.
> 2. I have told you that we are not willing to make any change whatsoever in the present arrangements. They are generous when related to the sales expectations of the book.
>
> Stop being sorry for yourself. Get on with your writing. Some of it can be commercial and some of it can be self-indulgent.
>
> For goodness sake try your work on experimental publishers like Calder and Boyars and get their support for your unstructured work.

Have you put your poetry together yet?
Yours in annoyance and desperation. James Currey
(JC to DM 15 December 1978)

He could not even bother to get his poetry together. Henry Chakava, Aig Higo and I could have got a selection of his work into the Series. It would have earned him a modest advance. Fees would have begun to come in from anthologies and journals. I suppose that his poetry was scattered across his squats and the houses of people who had thrown him out.

The initial reviews of *The House of Hunger* were good enough for me to negotiate an award of £1,000 from the Arts Council of Great Britain to follow on in March 1979 when his Heinemann monthly advance came to an end. They too paid on a monthly basis. I was also delighted that Tom Engelhardt at Pantheon, one of the most serious New York imprints, had decided to make an offer and pay an advance for US rights in *The House of Hunger.* Suhrkamp in Frankfurt, another imprint of similar distinction, were to buy German-language rights a year later,

Heinemann Educational Books had moved from Lord Randolph Churchill's grand house and ballroom in Mayfair to three of the Duke of Bedford's even grander houses on the north side of Bedford Square near the headquarters of the Publishers' Association and at right angles to Jonathan Cape's publishing house. The plane trees in the centre of the square rustled with a firm determination in the late evening as I tried to reduce the pile of African novels which mounted with every post on the window-sill. The vast reception area and show-room were to become a new theatre for Dambudzo Marechera's charades.

I went on to red alert the moment the switchboard reported his arrival. 'Dambudzo is here disguised as an old woman.' And there he was in a grey wig. 'Dambudzo is here saying he is a photographer from *The Guardian.*' I rushed down to find him clustered with cameras, no doubt nicked from somewhere. 'Dambudzo is here disguised as a huntsman'. Indeed, there he was in black frock coat and bowler hat; had he just walked out of a Moss Bros fitting room? He tried to borrow £5 from me although he knew I always refused. He said he wanted to go to Oxford. I told him to hitch-hike. He replied, 'What? In this outfit?'

My concerns were least of all with his writing. I had a telephone call one Monday from an architect who had given Dambudzo Marechera Saturday lunch at his house. He was showing him his enlarged photographs of earth building in Kano when Dambudzo Marechera demanded some of them. The architect said that he was sorry but that he was mounting them for an exhibition, whereupon our author pulled a knife on his host and went off with some of the prints. Dambudzo Marechera never drew a knife on anybody at Heinemann but the knowledge concerned me. How could I, as a director of the company, get him off the premises without damage to my colleagues, the building or, indeed, to me? One time I had talked him to the large green front door with steps down to the square by telling him that *The House of Hunger* had been banned in South Africa. He said that he was absolutely delighted with this accolade. I said I did not see it as a cause for celebration when it stopped people with backgrounds like his from reading his work.

On one occasion my efforts to walk him out quietly developed into a wrestling match in the square underneath the plane trees. We finally both laughed at the absurdity and stood up to find that there were people hanging out of the four floors of Georgian windows watching this theatre (see photo p. xi). I think perhaps Dambudzo Marechera bowed to them.

Clare Currey could tell, just from my tone of voice when I rang home to tell her what train I was catching, if I had had a hard day at the office with 'damned Boozo', as our children loved to call him.

The Africa Centre in Covent Garden was another playhouse. They suffered even more from Dambudzo Marechera's theatre than Heinemann did; sometimes they turned it to good public effect when Marechera performed poetry with great drama at meetings there. It was not quite clear whether his poetry was a drama or whether his plays were poetry. In the last days of Rhodesia before 1980 the Africa Centre became nicknamed 'Zimbabwe House' as so many Zimbabweans used it as their club. Robert Fraser has described Dambudzo Marechera's extraordinary – even Edwardian – Oxford accent which infuriated other Africans. Murray McCartney, who with his wife Irene Staunton was later to found Zimbabwe's enterprising Weaver Press, told Flora Veit-Wild (pp. 242–4) that, when he was running the bar at the Africa Centre one evening, Dambudzo Marechera was drinking with the Ethiopian playwright Alem Mezgebe and Pat Maddy, the Sierra Leonean writer whose plays and novels we had published in the African Writers Series under his full name of Yulisa Amadu Maddy. These two writers were so provoked by Dambudzo Marechera that they attacked him, saying that they were going to kill him. Murray McCartney leapt across the bar shouting, 'Please, if you are going to kill anybody, can you go outside in the street and do it!' He shouted at Marechera to run. He probably sensed that there was a real danger that Dambudzo Marechera, the professional victim, would be tempted to find out whether they really would kill him. The director of the Africa Centre, Alastair Niven, who had included African writing in the course he taught at the new University of Stirling, had to deal with him on an even more complex and continuous basis than I did. Dambudzo Marechera had access all the many hours that the centre was open but, when the Senegalese chef told him he could not sleep there, he threw bricks at the plate-glass door which had survived since it had been first formally opened by Kenneth

Kaunda in the 1960s. Alastair Niven and I were burdened with liberal consciences and used to share opinions about how to handle this character who had all the hours in the week to try to turn both our buildings into arenas for his ego.

Repeatedly he dragged one into theatre. One's days were smashed with the casualness of tossed dishes. One sunlit morning a policeman rang: 'Last night I arrested Mr Marrycheera in Covent Garden for being drunk and disorderly. He threw a punch at me. That was all in the course of duty but when he threw a punch at the super at the station we had to charge him.' He was to come up that morning before Clerkenwell magistrates and I was asked if I would stand surety. I dropped all my other work on behalf of many other authors and cycled off. The policeman at the court was reluctant to let me see him. I pointed out that, if I was to stand surety, I needed to get the prisoner's assurance that he would turn up at court. Reluctantly he took me to the cell. Dambudzo Marechera was rattling away at the bars demanding that I get him out. When I could get him to listen I said that I was not going to risk my personal money if he was not going to attend court. 'Oh yes, of course I will. Get me out of here.' Rattle. Rattle. After a tense wait with adrenalin flowing I was up before the beak myself. The magistrate asked me whether I was sure that I could get the accused to court. I said that I would do my best. 'What will happen if you fail?' I took my long black Midland Bank cheque book out of my pocket and slapped it down with the force of a whip on the bar and said, 'I suppose that I'll have to pay.' The magistrate barked, 'You are not a fit person to stand surety!' I said 'Thank you,' and left the dock a free man. A producer from the BBC Africa Service also had his surety refused, so I did not feel too guilty about Dambudzo Marechera spending a week in prison before his case came up.

I got on my bike and headed westwards back to the Duke of Bedford's magnificent square. I was upset about the magistrate putting me in the dock. Near University College traffic was standing at a red light and I was cycling up the inside. A flood of Spanish students suddenly poured chattering through the cars and I ran into one of them. I threw my bike aside and chased him down the pavement as though he were Manuel in *Fawlty Towers* and gave him a kick up the backside of which Basil Fawlty would have been proud. Dambudzo Marechera's theatre was taking over my life and being transferred to the streets.

There was a period of professional relief in London when Christopher Heywood set out to get Dambudzo Marechera a position as a writer in residence in the English department at the University of Sheffield from February to June 1979. Christopher Heywood, a former Rhodes scholar from South Africa who had also been at New College, Oxford, told Flora Veit-Wild: 'James Currey had rung me to give an anguished intimation that a dark cloud was on the horizon, and something resembling a shower of locusts was about to descend' (Christopher Heywood to Flora Veit-Wild 18 August 1989). Even then I was not free, as I had to settle bills for accommodation and damages at the Sheffield YMCA where Marechera had turned a fire extinguisher on the night watchman. Also I had letters from a Sheffield vicar who doubted that Dambudzo Marechera would live much longer because of his dissipated life. I wrote, 'I only hope he can survive. The greatest assurance of this that I have is that he has managed to survive before. His past history is so chequered that it is amazing that he has got so far.' (JC to R.D. de Berry 26 April 1979)

The Marechera road-show was about to take to the air and move on to Berlin. There was a focus on Africa in the 'Berlin International Literature Days' in the last days of June 1979. The Berlin festival was part of the demonstration by the West Germans during the Cold War of how much more attractive was the capitalist way of life. I have never experienced a more lavishly funded display of African writers. The plan was to have not just public readings but a conference of the writers with simultaneous translation between French and English in the magnificent conference centre built by the Americans within sight of the Wall.

Dagmar Heusler, an organiser of the African participation, had during the earlier part of the year relentlessly telephoned me in order to widen the list beyond the best established writers. The list was dominated by authors who appeared in the African Writers Series: Chinua Achebe, Mongo Beti, Wole Soyinka, Bessie Head, Dennis Brutus, Taban lo Liyong, Meja Mwangi and Nuruddin Farah were among them. When I told her on the telephone of the review by Doris Lessing of *The House of Hunger* in the June 1979 *Books and Bookmen* she said; 'Get him here. Bring him with you. Heinemann buy the ticket. We'll refund you. We want younger, newer voices.'

On the day of departure Dambudzo Marechera arrived, quite late, in my office high up above Bedford Square. He lacked two things. He put his feet on my desk and I could see the soles of his feet through holes. I slung him the pair of veldschoen I had just bought in a sale. As we left the office for Heathrow I checked whether he had his passport. 'Oh no, I haven't got a passport.' Of course not. 'Well, have you got your birth certificate?' No, he hadn't because the original was in a safe at New College in Oxford. He brightly told me he had a photocopy. So I took him to a post office at Heathrow to try to get him a visitor's pass. The Pakistani clerk, well trained in the imperial bureaucracy, rejected the photocopy. I told Dambudzo Marechera that he would have to go to the passport office in Petty France and get his papers sorted out. He would probably be able to come on in 24 hours. He said he would give up and hitch back to Sheffield. With some annoyance I said, 'Let's see if we can get you to Berlin.' When you were with Dambudzo Marechera your middle-class training was in suspense. I assumed that he would not even be allowed out through passport control without papers. I spoke to the officer and we were waved through. He was no doubt delighted to see one less black face in Britain. We flew east with Dambudzo Marechera's excitement mounting with each miniature drink.

I told him to show the frontier police at Berlin the form which had been rejected by the clerk at the Heathrow post office. The policeman did examine it carefully but asked us both, very politely, to go into an office which had one wall of tinted glass. Over the next hour and half a succession of officers with greater and greater encrustations of gold braid on their shoulders peered darkly through the tinted glass at this crazy black man and this crazy Englishman. An officer eventually came into the room and addressed me politely, as though Dambudzo Marechera might not be able to understand his excellent English: 'I am afraid that your friend will have to go back to London on the ten o'clock flight, tomorrow morning, so he will be detained overnight.' Dambudzo Marechera later said I disappeared with a huge grin on my face because I was glad to get rid of him.

What I knew was that Dagmar Heusler was the only hope and that, in those days before mobile phones, the quicker I got to her the better. I found her at the Kunstlerhaus-Bethanien surrounded by broadcasting crews and making arrangements for the opening reading that very evening. She said, 'Leave it to me,' and disappeared. I was shown round this brightly converted asylum in the Turkish quarter of Berlin by David Sweetman, one of our authors who was there for the BBC Africa Service. As we wandered down corridors, he told me that he had found out that this had been the site of Nazi experiments on mentally handicapped people.

The readings began and just before the interval Dagmar Heusler slipped into the seat beside me and whispered, 'We've got him out!' She then announced at the interval to the audience that, as they had been able to release this young Zimbabwean writer from the foul grip of the frontier police, he would be able to read at the end of the evening. What a performance it was. He outshone the earlier writers with his brilliant reading of the story 'Rain' from *The House of Hunger*. He was immediately surrounded by the television and radio people.

Dambudzo Marechera basked in all the attention and played up the role of what Flora Veit-Wild has called the 'guerrilla writer'. His press conference, as recorded by *Deutsche Welle*, was full of exaggerations. For instance he asserted that his book was banned in Rhodesia. Heinemann had only been able to sell a handful there and very few people knew about it at all. He gave the journalists enough copy to make their readers feel guilty about the treatment of Africans under the Smith regime.

However, one journalist, after Dambudzo Marechera had told the news conference how his publisher had not helped him with the frontier police, said:

> What I heard, rumour-wise, is that you got out of the cell at Tegel, through almost illegal means. When I go to Nigeria the same thing happens to me, I am sorry to say. If I get to Nigeria without a passport or even without a visa or without a return ticket, the Nigerian police put me on the next plane back home to Europe. Finish. And I am put in a cell. Even to African friends that happens. (Edited transcript in Veit-Wild p.278)

Dagmar Heusler had known exactly who to go to in Berlin to get Dambudzo Marechera released. She pretended that he was due to perform that evening. He was not on the programme until that moment. Then, almost totally unknown, he became the star of the evening.

After midnight the performers were taken to dinner at a restaurant on the Kurfurstendam. Dambudzo Marechera tried to pay for cigarettes with English money and was much offended that Queen Elizabeth's head was not accepted. He was then taken off to the Hotel am Zoo.

Dambudzo Marechera quickly annoyed the other writers. He, Nuruddin Farah and I shared a cab on the way to the reading at the Kunstlerhaus-Bethanien on the second evening. Nuruddin Farah, exasperated by his victim's act, told him he was lucky to get in without papers. He said sharply to him, 'This time last night I did not know you existed.'

Dambudzo Marechera's visit extended into a second and then a third week. For me, back in London, he was out of the way. Then I was cabled the date of his return. I knew that, yet again, I would have to put aside all my work on other people's books. I talked to the Immigration Advisory Service. A sympathetic but practical adviser assessed the probabilities. She said, 'He may have to spend a few days in detention, but we should be able to get him out fairly soon.' She rang the direct line on my desk in the late afternoon to say that he had landed at Heathrow at about midday. She sounded calmly confident that matters were in hand but then, minutes later, rang me to say that the situation was very serious. The immigration officers had just got hold of his Cardiff prison sentence and it was the conviction for possession of cannabis that had changed their whole attitude. She gave me the telephone number of Joan Lestor, MP and gave me a whole list of other people to contact. Margaret Thatcher had just got into Downing Street; the adviser said in the few weeks since the election the immigration services were already becoming much tougher. She said they would get a solicitor on to the case. The other phone on my desk rang while she was still telling me what to do. It was a man from the immigration service. He told me, what I knew only too well, that Mr Marechera had a conviction at Cardiff. He solemnly listed each of the three convictions.

My heart sank with every count. Then he said, 'I have given Mr Marechera ten days to get his papers in order. Would you like to speak to Mr Marechera?' When he came on he was screaming at me: 'Get me out of here. Get me a lawyer. You got me into this mess. You got me invited to Berlin. You got me to Berlin.' When I could get him to listen to me I asked him what he had been told. I did not want to tell him that he was being let back into Britain and to find the unbelievable news I had just been told was not true. I managed to get through all his hysterical shouting and tell him to put the immigration officer back on to the phone. I asked him whether he had told Mr Marechera what he had decided, and he replied: 'No. I thought you might like to tell him the good news.' Marechera had confounded the immigration officers in two countries – and cast them as villains in his play.

My major concern continued to be to get a publishable first novel. During the autumn of 1979 there was detailed consideration of the manuscript of the fourth script, *Black Sunlight* (AWS 237). John Wyllie was enthusiastic. I tried it on Pantheon in New York, who had published the American edition of *The House of Hunger,* but their reader reported in October:

> We are left with an experience of chaos and fragmentation, detached from meaning, and while the book may intend to be precisely about this explosion of meaning, roots and connections, its evocation is not achieved by replication of the process. As a result of this, and in contrast to *The House of Hunger*, characters are not fully developed. We are sealed inside the narrator's mind for the most part …

Tom Engelhardt, calling it 'self-indulgent and overwrought', said: 'To tell you the truth, James, I think the problem that confronts Marechera in this manuscript is one inherent in almost all exile literature – the increasing loss of a context within which the writing is done.' Simon Gikandi in Nairobi (report November 1979), while admiring the way in which Marechera used language without inhibitions 'in a way rivalled only by Wole Soyinka', could not bring himself to encourage publication. However, I wrote to Tom Engelhardt:

> I have decided that we ought to accept *Black Sunlight* and have got it formally approved. This is because I hope that it will remove a psychological block and that he will get down to finishing the Zimbabwean novel. We can afford to try *Black Sunlight* out in the African Writers Series (JC to Tom Engelhardt 12 December 1979)

John Wyllie was sent the manuscript for copy-editing and said:

> I have worked through it three times and now feel I need to go away into the nice quiet Irish countryside (south of the border) and have a nervous breakdown. (John Wyllie to JC 24 January 1980)

I was annoyed that *The Guardian* had not reviewed *The House of Hunger*. I had sent a copy of the book to Doris Lessing. In June 1979, six months after publication, her review in which she reflected on the word 'genius' was published in *Books and Bookmen*:

> The book is an explosion, writer and book are both in the nature of miracles. Hard for anyone to become a writer, but to do it against such handicaps? ... It is no good pretending this book is an easy or a pleasant read. More like overhearing a scream. (*Books and Bookmen* June 1979)

I sent a copy of the review to Bill Webb, the literary editor of *The Guardian,* and asked whether he might have it reviewed even so long after publication. On 21 June 1979 he published a review by Angela Carter, in which she said, 'It is rare to find a writer for whom imaginative fiction is such a passionate and intimate process of engagement with the world ... The writer's awareness of himself as a witness, a prophet is part of his immense, cruel seriousness.' Bill Webb rang me at home in the early autumn to say that I might not be surprised to hear that the judges had decided to share *The Guardian* fiction prize between two first collections of stories, the one by Dambudzo Marechera and the other by a young Irish writer and film-maker, Neil Jordan. The prize aimed to pick 'works of originality and promise' and had great prestige at that time in spite of only giving £250 to each of these writers.

The Guardian award ceremony was grand opera. It was held in the upper foyer of the Theatre Royal off Drury Lane in London. Two great staircases swept one up in carpeted silence. Candelabra dripped showers of light. Mirrors stretched from floor to ceiling. Neil Jordan had arrived but not, to Bill Webb's and my concern, Dambudzo Marechera. Worried, I went out to Drury Lane to look for him. He was instantly visible. He had dressed for the part in slouch hat and Basuto blanket and was holding a vast Faber paperback of Ezra Pound's *Cantos*. His biting speech played up the part he had planned. It spiked the accepted ritual. Livia Gollancz, daughter of the renowned left-wing publisher Victor Gollancz who stood beside her, airily said to me, 'We have seen these sort of young men coming up, you know; for a short while they are a bright spark and then they go away.' Her jaundiced prejudice was rapidly borne out when Dambudzo Marechera started throwing plates at the mirrors. I deserted the stage with Neil Jordan, who was later to make *Mona Lisa* and several other dramatic films. He said to me as we started to descend one of the great staircases, 'Why does he have to do it, why? He can make his statements with his writing. His writing is so good.' Meanwhile down the opposite staircase, which was grand enough for the grandest opera, the doormen were strong-arming Dambudzo Marechera.

His drama moved from play to film. Chris Austin, a South African born film director, managed to raise money from Channel 4 Television in London to make a film about his reactions to returning to independent Zimbabwe after eight years of exile. The documentary sections about Dambudzo Marechera would be interspersed with dramatized scenes from his fiction. He negotiated a return ticket for the five weeks of filming. He had expected to feel alienated. He felt that he wanted to be free to come back to Britain. Yet again he had done nothing about his passport and in the end left on a one-way travel document in February 1982. Penny Butler, my deputy at Heinemann, was on one of her many flights to work with Zimbabwe Publishing House. She found that, to her horror, she was but a few seats behind Dambudzo Marechera. Stoked up with duty-free, he occasionally shouted out during the night that they were about to be attacked by Rhodesian fighters.

They were heady years in Zimbabwe; once again one felt the exhilarating atmosphere of years of independence in the rest of Africa. Everything was possible. David Martin and Phyllis Johnson, founders of the Zimbabwe Publishing House, took over the organisation of the Zimbabwe International Book Fair. In 1982 there was a writers' workshop with a distinguished attendance of writers mostly from southern Africa. Nadine Gordimer recalled that at the writers' workshop at the 1982 Zimbabwe International Book Fair Dambudzo Marechera 'always made an entrance like an actress, very late, with that big red scarf flying'. At one session he attacked publicly Eddison Zvogbo, a minister who had published poetry. Dambudzo Marechera was protesting that the returned soldiers had no jobs. This was to become the issue which led in the late 1990s to the farm invasions. Nadine Gordimer remarked on his bravery:

> I found, getting to know him a little better during the next few days, there was strange contradiction in his character. On the surface he was a self-obsessed person, very much preoccupied with the presentation of his own personality. This comes out in his writing as well: obsessed with his own feelings, with his own anger. But there was the contrast that among all of us he was the one who took up a burning social issue so that he stepped out of the self-obsession and turned all this anger and concern away from himself to others. (Nadine Gordimer *The Herald* 15 August 1988, cited in Veit-Wild, p. 331)

Flora Veit-Wild observes:

> When Marechera returned to Zimbabwe, he tried to adopt ZPH as his 'Family' as he had done with James Currey in London. Though Martin kept the demanding author at a distance, Johnson was always there to listen to him. ZPH gave him small royalty advances when he was broke, or copies of his book which he sold

> in bars. The ZPH premises were always open for him; he was welcome to share lunch with the staff, store his belongings when he was homeless, change clothes or have a bath. He would spend hours with Charles Mungoshi – then a ZPH editor – reading, talking or helping him empty a bottle of vodka. (Flora Veit-Wild p. 338)

They were far more hospitable than I ever was. But of course he overstrained that hospitality. He withdrew the manuscript of *Mindblast*. Stanley Nyamfukudza, his old Oxford contemporary who had become an editor at College Press, published it at the time of the Zimbabwe Book Fair in August 1984. In his last years he could not get any of the very active Zimbabwean publishers to accept his work. In 1986, my Wadham contemporary the writer David Caute did his best to help him by going through my manuscript cupboard at Heinemann and sending manuscripts to Tom Engelhardt at Pantheon. David Caute was to publish an extraordinary account of how Dambudzo Marechera provoked the Zimbabwean Special Branch to beat him up in a hotel toilet.

In 1987 Dambudzo Marechera died of pneumonia which had probably been allowed to advance by Aids. Lewis Nkosi had recorded in *The Herald* in Harare in September 1983 that Dambudzo Marechera had once said:

> I told [the police] the only relatives I have are my publishers. But imagine being buried by Heinemann.

CONCLUSION *Is there still a role for the African Writers Series?*

This book is about the first quarter-century of the African Writers Series from 1962 to 1988 when Keith Sambrook left Heinemann. Initially the Series was conceived as a textbook series for students in secondary schools and universities in Africa. It was consequently launched and developed by an educational publisher, Heinemann Educational Books. The Series gained the support of teachers, academics and examination boards in the late 1950s wishing to introduce some writing by Africans into secondary-school and university courses within Africa. Anthologies of poetry, prose extracts and short stories were put together but this literature also required the reprinting of complete works, first published by hardback houses, in a cheap paperback format.

In the mid-1960s Chinua Achebe and Keith Sambrook quickly ran out of suitable titles to reprint in the paperback series. This was because so few African writers, unlike those from the Caribbean, were being published by general-market literary publishers in London. Alan Hill and Keith Sambrook were sure that there were other writers of the quality of Chinua Achebe and Ngũgĩ. Out of necessity Heinemann Educational Books therefore took on the first-time publication in hardback of new writers and these were mostly sold in Britain. However, it was the paperback African Writers Series which was increasingly read and noticed in literary circles inside Africa as well as used in literature courses in Africa and worldwide wherever there were African studies courses.

This book shows how, with Chinua Achebe's encouragement, the Series gave people in Africa the idea that they could get published, that they really could write back. Africans then bought back the books in such numbers that new writers could be encouraged. The collapse of the African market into debt in 1982, and the beginning of the African book famine, meant that Heinemann Educational Books had to depend upon sales in Britain, Europe and the rest of the rich world where it was impossible to make the enormous textbook sales which the Heinemann accountants had come to take for granted. The closing of the Nigerian foreign exchanges and the consequent debt meant that their crude logic was that the African Writers Series should reprint only bestselling titles, put slow-selling books out of print and no longer underwrite new publishing.

In 1983 Tilling, the owners of the Heinemann Group, had been taken over in a dawn raid on the London Stock Exchange by British Tyre and Rubber (BTR).

In September 1984 the new managing director told me that, whereas in that year there were 17 new African Writers Series titles in the catalogue, in future years I would only be able to publish one or two new titles by established writers and a couple of volumes such as the *UNESCO General History of Africa*. I argued successfully that the firm no longer had a job for me and therefore that I should be made redundant and paid off. I had already decided that there was no future for me under the new owners of Heinemann and had made plans to set up James Currey Publishers to publish academic paperbacks on Africa.

While working out my contractual notice there was an unexpected development. David Godwin, the editorial director at William Heinemann, rang in October 1984 to say that he was distressed to hear that Heinemann Educational Books was dropping out of publishing new authors in the African Writers Series. He had recently joined the firm and felt that the father firm William Heinemann ought to continue the Heinemann reputation for publishing new writing from Africa which had started with *Things Fall Apart* in 1958 and taken off with the African Writers Series. He was proposing the complementary role that, back in the 1960s, Alan Hill and Keith Sambrook had expected that William Heinemann would take up (p. 12). David Godwin got it agreed at William Heinemann that I should become a consultant to advise him on possible new authors from Africa, on the sale of US rights and the sale of foreign-language rights. It was planned that I should go with the rights director on her next visit to publishers in New York to introduce her to the editors in US publishers who had a good track record of trying out new writers from Africa. At the 1985 Frankfurt Book Fair I would introduce her to the rights people in European publishing houses who had been publishing translations of African books in increasing numbers since the Frankfurt Africa Year of 1980.

David Godwin and I planned to publish three ways: William Heinemann would publish in hardback and would reserve educational paperback rights for the African Writers Series, but would also set out to sell to the new upmarket trade paperback houses who published in the new larger 'B' format. One of the most enterprising imprints was Picador, which had been started by Pan. Keith Sambrook and I strongly felt that the best of the authors, by being confined to the African Writers Series, were missing out on the serious general paperback market where bookshop buyers could discover that interesting work was coming from the continent. The millions of sales of Chinua Achebe's *Things Fall Apart* were mostly in the orange covers of the African Writers Series. Colleagues at Heinemann Educational Books feared that these phenomenal sales, which had mostly been through educational outlets in Africa, would have been put in peril if the book had also appeared in the orange covers of Penguin books. It does now appear in the Penguin Classics as well as in the African Writers Series and Picador issued the classic first two novels in a single volume.

During the autumn of 1984 I showed several manuscripts to David Godwin for consideration for hardback publication by William Heinemann. Among them was *Search Sweet Country,* a first novel by an unknown Ghanaian writer called B. Kojo Laing (p. 78). I attached a report by Robert Fraser, who was so excited that later he was to describe the novel in the journal *Kunapipi* as 'the finest novel ever to be written in Africa'. On publication in hardback by William Heinemann other reviewers were to share his enthusiasm, if not his over-statement. David Godwin successfully sold trade paperback rights to Picador; sadly in that tense period Heinemann Educational Books was not able to secure educational rights for the African Writers Series. He also wanted to publish poetry from Africa. Heinemann Educational Books had in 1971 published Christopher Okigbo's *Labyrinths* with *Path of Thunder* in hardback as well as in the Series paperback. David Godwin decided to publish in 1986 a hardback edition of the *Collected Poems* of Christopher Okigbo, with a preface by Paul Theroux. He was also interested in the poetry of Kofi Awoonor, whom Keith Sambrook had first known as George Awoonor-Williams in Ghana in the 1950s. He was one of the poets whose first books of poetry had been published by Mbari in the mid-1960s. Further collections were published in the US in the 1970s and Heinemann and Doubleday published a novel (p. 76). I was delighted, in those difficult times, to get his collected poetry accepted; it was listed in the African Writers Series catalogue of 1984 for publication in 1985 under the title *Until the Morning After* as AWS 260. Delays mounted as the new management forced Vicky Unwin, the editor who had been put in charge of the African Writers Series, to slow down the publication of new titles that Aig Higo, Henry Chakava and I had agreed to take on. Vicky Unwin was doing her best to keep the contracted titles coming out. But Kofi Awoonor, for instance, finally insisted that he must withdraw his manuscript, in spite of Vicky Unwin telling him on 13 February 1986 that William Heinemann was strongly considering issuing a general-market hardback.

At last it had seemed that William Heinemann would take an active role in the publication of writers from Africa. Keith Sambrook's and my hopes did not have to survive long. David Godwin soon left William Heinemann for the far more prestigious literary publisher, Jonathan Cape. He got them to publish Ben Okri's magical mystery novel, *The Famished Road*, which was the first novel by a writer from West Africa to win the Booker Prize in London. He then set up his own literary agency which had singular success in helping writers, often from India and Africa, to publication and to prizes.

So what was to happen in those straitened times? 'The outlook for the African Writers Series is not healthy,' wrote Keith Sambrook on 13 November 1985 in a prophetic policy memo to John Watson at Heinemann Inc in the US, with copies to the team in Africa. A further 15 to 20 titles had been put out of print by the new management, which was setting out to reduce the size of the Heinemann Educational Books list, which the accountants considered self-indulgent. The market had changed and Keith Sambrook was being realistic. Also it could well be viewed that the Series had done more than its job in encouraging new writing. It was over to the publishers in Africa and the publishers in New York and London to find and publish new writing. Keith Sambrook argued:

> The Series, however, is really no longer the right place for a *new* book by an *established* writer. If it ever was! It's certainly not the *only* place for a book by an established writer.

> An established writer, say Ngũgĩ, needs (1) a UK hardback (2) a UK paperback (3) a UK educational edition (4) a US hardback (5) a UK educational edition (6) a local school edition in Kenya and possibly Nigeria and Zimbabwe (7) translations. ... For such a writer HEB(UK) cannot be the right originating publisher. It does not have the marketing or rights-selling clout and know-how. (KS to John Watson 13 November 1985)

His prediction was that the Series could continue to originate some titles by new authors or by middle-ranking established authors. Print runs to cover the first two or three years would be some 3,000 to 5,000 copies (which is certainly a better start than many home-grown authors could hope for). Some titles would reprint but in the reduced market far more of the new titles would have to go out of print after the first impression.

Vicky Unwin managed, with the support of John Watson in the US (p. xxiv), to persuade a doubtful new management that a flow of new books should keep appearing. John Watson liked to quote an American publishing sage – probably the wry Tom Seavey – as saying, 'You can't keep a backlist without fresheners.' Vicky Unwin did her best to relaunch the Series in the British market with a new 'B' format and full-colour art covers by British artists. Her committed team at one time or another included Caroline Avens, Charlotte Svensson and Becky Ayebia Clarke.

She used Adewale Maja-Pearce and then Abdulrazak Gurnah, both of whom worked in Britain, as editorial advisers at different times. Henry Chakava felt that she had abandoned the triangular system of consultation and that she 'chose to work with a host of new readers and advisers, completely ignoring the earlier arrangements ... I can say for myself that my services or advice were never sought' (*Issues in Book Publishing in Nigeria* Heinemann Nigeria 2005, p. 19). South Africa and the other countries of southern Africa accounted for over 70 per cent of the sales of the African Writers Series to Africa from Britain in 1987 and so that was the market where Vicky Unwin directed her very considerable energies. The celebration of the thirtieth anniversary in 1992 was marked by a party at Dillons bookshop in London which was well publicised in the British press and in South Africa. The World Bank and the IMF prescribed structural adjustment for the African countries in the 1990s which made foreign currency available once again, although at a cost which drove up the price of books. Becky Ayebia Clarke managed to sell the Series in Africa again, especially in her native Ghana.

Another prophecy by Keith Sambrook in his 1985 memo was that new writing by top-ranking, internationally recognised writers would be originated by publishers in their own countries (including Heinemann companies) or by UK or US fiction houses. He could already see this was happening in Zimbabwe. Rights for new Ngũgĩ novels now came from Henry Chakava's company in Nairobi who published the Gikuyu language original. These national editions could be produced in bigger quantities and sold at lower prices than the imported titles in the Series.

Keith Sambrook said that the Series would buy international educational rights from fiction publishers. In other words, the African Writers Series could continue to provide international accessibility to a useful body of established work, but the titles would mostly be originated by other publishers, as had been intended in Alan Hill's original plans in the 1960s. Keith Sambrook pointed out in this same memo that in the successful Caribbean Writers Series, which he and I had started in 1968, our educational editions revived out-of-print books and kept books available for a wide range of uses. The BBC programme 'Caribbean Voices' and British literary hardback publishers had given writers the idea that they could get published. Heinemann originated very few new titles by Caribbean writers because there were plenty of published titles to choose from to reprint in that Series.

At the end of 2002 extraordinary amounts of money were lavished on marking the fortieth anniversary of the African Writers Series. It had ambitiously been decided that the celebration should be international, in contrast to the London-based thirtieth anniversary. Ngũgĩ performed the honours in San Diego, California. Aig Higo and Henry Chakava were at the occasion held at the Nigeria International Book Fair in Abuja in 2002, but felt that Becky Ayebia Clarke did not convince them that there was a continuing commitment by the management.

In 2003 Robert Sulley, the International Director, tried to arrange that the Heinemann office in Johannesburg should be given the right to initiate new publishing. He asked me what I thought might be the feeling in Ibadan and Nairobi. I said: 'At least publishing will be on the African continent. And surely you could bring in Nairobi and Ibadan? After all they already do a lot of their own publishing.' Six weeks later he was out of a job with some thirty other members of the international department.

In 2003 the owners of the Heinemann imprint issued a confusing statement that no new work was to be added to the African Writers Series. They managed to give the impression that the African Writers Series was being closed. Nana yaa Mensah said in *The New Statesman* (24 February 2003): 'At one fell swoop, another of the few British outlets for African writing has been blocked off, one that has played a central part in establishing the continent's literature in the public imagination.' The 2007 catalogue in fact still listed 64 lucrative titles. By the standards of most publishers that is quite a substantial body of work. All the firm needed to do was to buy in a few 'fresheners' from other hardback houses and national publishers in Africa to keep interest in the Series alive. Unfortunately one of the prophecies in Keith Sambrook's 1985 memo had been completely realised: 'Gradually the Series will be reduced to a rump of established titles by well-known writers, reprinting annually.'

In recent years British and American publishers have shown a new interest in work from the continent or by writers who have their origins in Africa. All Heinemann had to do was to give confidence and cash to a new editor to acquire educational rights in the best of the new publishing and they would have shown a continuing commitment to representing a selection of new work from Africa. In the early years of the new century the African Writers Series could have at last become, as in its original conception, a paperback reprint Series representing the best of writers from the continent and making them available throughout the African continent and the rest of the English-speaking world.

1962–2003
African Writers Series by year of publication

Please note that this list is by year of publication in the paperback African Writers Series only; earlier hardback publication has not been recorded. The list was kindly supplied by N.B. Bejjit, a postgraduate from Morocco at the Open University, who is working on the African Writers Series. It is based on the one orginally compiled by Proquest, who are building up an electronic edition of the whole Series of some 350 titles. Heinemann International also kindly supplied information. John Watson, formerly President of HEB Inc, supplied the information on publishers of titles from the African Writers Series in the USA.

African Writers Series titles selected by the jury of the Zimbabwe International Book Fair (ZIBF) for their list of 'Africa's 100 Best Books of the 20th century' have been been indicated.

Year	Number, Author & Title US publishers	Country	Genre
1962	1 Achebe, Chinua, *Things Fall Apart* Astor-Honor Fawcett pb Anchor pb HEB Inc 80s –1995 Classics in Context (HEB Inc) 1997 ZIBF Africa's 100 Best Books (Cited as one of best 12)	Nigeria	Novel
	2 Ekwensi, Cyprian, *Burning Grass*	Nigeria	Novel
	4 Kaunda, Kenneth, *Zambia Shall be Free*	Zambia	Politics
1963	3 Achebe, Chinua, *No Longer at Ease* Astor-Honor Fawcett pb Anchor pb HEB Inc 80s –1995	Nigeria	Novel
	5 Ekwensi, Cyprian, *People of the City*	Nigeria	Novel
	6 Abrahams, Peter, *Mine Boy*	S.Africa	Novel
1964	7 Ngũgĩ, *Weep Not, Child*	Kenya	Novel
	8 Reed, J. and Wake, Clive (eds), *A Book of African Verse*		Poetry
	9 Rive, Richard (ed.), *Modern African Prose*		Prose
	12 Conton, William, *The African*	Gambia	Novel
	13 Beti, Mongo, *Mission to Kala*	Cameroun	Novel
1965	11 Aluko, T. M., *One Man, One Matchet*	Nigeria	Novel
	14 Rive, Richard (ed.), *Quartet*	S.Africa	Stories
	15 Cook, David (ed.), *Origin East Africa*		Prose&Poetry
	16 Achebe, Chinua, *Arrow of God* John Day Anchor pb ZIBF Africa's 100 Best Books	Nigeria	Novel
	17 Ngũgĩ, *The River Between*	Kenya	Novel

Year	No.	Author, Title	Country	Genre
1966	18	Ijimere, O. [Duro Ladipo & Ulli Beier] *The Imprisonment of Obatala and Other Plays*	Nigeria	Plays
	19	Ekwensi, Cyprian, *Lokotown*	Nigeria	Stories
	20	Gatheru, Mugo, *Child of Two Worlds*	Kenya	Autobio
	21	Munonye, John, *The Only Son*	Nigeria	Novel
	22	Peters, Lenrie, *The Second Round*	Gambia	Novel
	23	Beier, Ulli (ed.), *The Origin of Life and Death*		Stories
	24	Kachingwe, Aubrey, *No Easy Task*	Malawi	Novel
	25	Amadi, Elechi, *The Concubine*	Nigeria	Novel
	26	Nwapa, Flora, *Efuru*	Nigeria ⋆	Novel
	29	Oyono, Ferdinand, *Houseboy*	Cameroun	Novel
	31	Achebe, Chinua, *A Man of the People* John Day Anchor pb	Nigeria	Novel
1967	10	Equiano, Olaudah, *Equiano's Travels,*	Nigeria	Autobio
	27	Selormey, Francis, *The Narrow Path*	Ghana	Novel
	30	Aluko, T. M., *One Man, One Wife*	Nigeria	Novel
	32	Aluko, T. M., *Kinsman and Foreman*	Nigeria	Novel
	33	Samkange, Stanlake, *On Trial for My Country*	Zimbabwe	Novel
	35	La Guma, Alex, *A Walk in the Night* Northwestern University Press	S.Africa	Stories
	36	Ngũgĩ, *A Grain of Wheat* ZIBF Africa's 100 Best Books	Kenya	Novel
	37	Peters, Lenrie, *Satellites*	Gambia	Poetry
	38	Odinga, Oginga, *Not Yet Uhuru*	Kenya	Politics
	40	Konadu, Asare, *A Woman in her Prime*	Ghana	Novel
1968	34	Pieterse, Cosmo (ed.), *Ten One-Act Plays*		Plays
	41	Djoleto, Amu, *The Strange Man*	Ghana	Novel
	46	Brutus, Dennis, *Letters to Martha*	S.Africa	Poetry
	48	Gbadamosi, B. & U. Beier, *Not Even God Is Ripe Enough*		Oral
	49	Nkrumah, K., *Neo-Colonialism: The Last Stage of Imperialism* (announced but dropped from catalogue)	Ghana	Political
	50	Clark, J.P., *America, Their America* Africana Publishing	Nigeria	Autobio
	51	Ngũgĩ, *The Black Hermit*	Kenya	Drama
1969	39	Oyono, Ferdinand, *The Old Man and the Medal* ZIBF Africa's 100 Best Books	Cameroun	Novel
	43	Armah, Ayi Kwei, *The Beautyful Ones Are Not Yet Born* Houghton Mifflin HEB Inc 1979 ZIBF Africa's 100 Best Books	Ghana	Novel
	45	Munonye, John, *Obi*	Nigeria	Novel
	47	Salih, Tayeb, *The Wedding of Zein*	Sudan	Stories
	52	Sellassie, Sahle, *The Afersata*	Ethiopia	Novel
	53	Palangyo, Peter K., *Dying in the Sun*	Tanzania	Novel
	55	Konadu, Samuel Asare, *Ordained by the Oracle*	Ghana	Novel
	57	Dipoko, Mbella Sonne, *Because of Women*	Cameroun	Novel
	58	Beier, Ulli (ed.), *Political Spider*		Stories
	60	Honwana L.B. *We Killed Mangy-Dog and other stories* ZIBF Africa's 100 Best Books	Mozambique	Stories

Year	No.	Author, Title	Country	Genre
	61	Umeasiegbu, R. N, *The Way We Lived: Ibo Customs*	Nigeria	Oral
	66	Salih, Tayeb, *Season of Migration to the North* ZIBF Africa's 100 Best Books	Sudan	Novel
	69	Taban lo Liyong, *Fixions*	Uganda/Sudan	Stories
	71	Senghor, L. S., *Nocturnes*	Senegal	Poetry
1970	28	Cook, D. & Miles Lee (eds), *Short E. A. Plays in English*		Plays
	42	Awoonor, Kofi & G. Adali-Mortty (eds), *Messages*	Ghana	Poetry
	44	Amadi, Elechi, *The Great Ponds*	Nigeria	Novel
	54	Serumaga, Robert, *Return to the Shadows*	Uganda	Novel
	56	Nwapa, Flora, *Idu*	Nigeria ★	Novel
	59	Asare, Bediako, *Rebel*	Ghana	Novel
	63	Sembene Ousmane, *God's Bits of Wood* ZIBF Africa's 100 Best Books	Senegal	Novel
	67	Nwankwo, Nkem, *Danda*	Nigeria	Novel
	68	Okara, Gabriel, *The Voice* Africana Publishing	Nigeria	Novel
	70	Aluko, T. M., *Chief the Honourable Minister*	Nigeria	Novel
	72	Tam'si, Tchicaya U, *Selected Poems*	Congo-Brazz	Poetry
	73	Ortzen, Len (ed. and trans.), *North African Writing*		Prose
	74	Taban lo Liyong, *Eating Chiefs*	Uganda/Sudan	Oral
	75	Knappert, Jan, *Myths and Legends of the Swahili*		Oral
	76	Soyinka, Wole, *The Interpreters*	Nigeria	Novel
	77	Beti, Mongo, *King Lazarus*	Cameroun	Novel
	80	Farah, Nuruddin, *From a Crooked Rib* Graywolf pb Penguin pb	Somalia	Novel
	81	Mboya, Tom, *The Challenge of Nationhood*	Kenya	Politics
	82	Dipoko, Mbella Sonne, *A Few Nights and Days*	Cameroun	Novel
1971	62	Okigbo, Christopher, *Labyrinths* with *Path of Thunder* Africana Publishing ZIBF Africa's 100 Best Books	Nigeria	Poetry
	64	Pieterse, C.(ed.), *Seven South African Poets*	S.Africa	Poetry
	83	Knappert, Jan, *Myths and Legends of the Congo*		Oral
	84	Ekwensi, Cyprian, *Beautiful Feathers*	Nigeria	Novel
	85	Nzekwu, Onuora, *Wand of Noble Wood*	Nigeria	Novel
	86	Bebey, Francis, *Agatha Moudio's Son* Lawrence Hill	Cameroun	Novel
	87	Dadié, Bernard B., *Climbié* Africana Publishing ZIBF Africa's 100 Best Books	C. d'Ivoire	Novel
	88	Beti, Mongo, *The Poor Christ of Bomba* ZIBF Africa's 100 Best Books	Cameroun	Novel
	89	Maddy, Yulisa Amadu, *Obasai*	Sierra Leone	Plays
	90	Taban lo Liyong, *Frantz Fanon's Uneven Ribs*	Uganda/Sudan	Poetry
	94	Munonye, John, *Oil Man of Obange*	Nigeria	Novel
	95	Ibrahim, Sonallah, *The Smell of It*	Egypt	Stories
	96	Cook, D. & Rubadiri, D. (eds), *Poems from East Africa*		Poetry
	97	Mazrui, Ali A., *The Trial of Christopher Okigbo*	Kenya	Novel
	98	Mulaisho, Dominic, *The Tongue of the Dumb*	Zambia	Novel
	99	Ouologuem, Yambo, *Bound to Violence*	Mali	Novel
	102	Omotoso, Kole, *The Edifice*	Nigeria	Novel

Year	No.	Author, Title	Country	Genre
	103	Peters, Lenrie, *Katchikali*	Gambia	Poetry
	105	Lubega, Bonnie, *The Outcasts*	Uganda	Novel
1972	78	Pieterse, Cosmo (ed.), *Short African Plays*		Plays
	79	Chraïbi, Driss, *Heirs to the Past*	Morocco	Novel
	91	Nzekwu, Onuora, *Blade among the Boys*	Nigeria	Novel
	92	Sembene O., *The Money-Order with White Genesis*	Senegal	Novel
	93	Knappert, Jan (ed. and trans.), *A Choice of Flowers*		Poetry
	100	Achebe, Chinua, *Girls at War and Other Stories* Doubleday Anchor pb	Nigeria	Stories
	101	Head, Bessie, *Maru*	S.Africa ⋆	Novel
	104	Themba, Can, *The Will to Die*	S.Africa	Stories
	106	Reed, J & Wake, C. (ed. and trans.), *French African Verse*		Poetry
	107	Dipoko, Mbella Sonne, *Black and White in Love*	Cameroun	Poetry
	108	Awoonor, Kofi, *This Earth, My Brother*	Ghana	Novel
	109	Obiechina, E.N. (ed.), *Onitsha Market Literature*	Nigeria	Study
	110	La Guma, Alex, *In the Fog of the Seasons' End*	S.Africa	Novel
	111	Angira, Jared, *Silent Voices*	Kenya	Poetry
	112	Vambe, Lawrence, *An Ill-Fated People* University of Pittsburg Press	Zimbabwe	Autobio
	113	Mezu, S. Okechukwu, *Behind the Rising Sun*	Nigeria	Novel
	114	Pieterse, Cosmo (ed.), *Five African Plays*		Poetry
	116	Taban lo Liyong, *Another Nigger Dead*	Uganda	Poetry
	118	Amadu, Malum, *Amadu's Bundle*	Nigeria	Novel
	119	Kane, Cheikh Hamidou, *Ambiguous Adventure* ZIBF Africa's 100 Best Books	Senegal	Novel
	120	Achebe, Chinua, *Beware, Soul-Brother* Doubleday-Anchor *Christmas in Biafra* HEB Inc	Nigeria	Poetry
	122	Omotoso, Kole, *The Combat*	Nigeria	Novel
1973	115	Brutus, Dennis, *A Simple Lust* Hill & Wang HEB Inc 1979	S.Africa	Poetry
	117	al-Hakim, Tewfik, *Fate of a Cockroach*	Egypt	Plays
	121	Munonye, John, *A Wreath for the Maidens*	Nigeria	Novel
	123	Mandela, Nelson, *No Easy Walk to Freedom*	S.Africa	Politics
	124	Dikobe, Modikwe, *The Marabi Dance*	S.Africa	Novel
	125	Worku, Daniachew, *The Thirteenth Sun*	Ethiopia	Novel
	126	Cheney-Coker, Syl, *Concerto for an Exile*	Sierra Leone	Poetry
	127	Henderson, G. & C. Pieterse (eds), *Nine African Plays for Radio*		Plays
	128	Zwelonke, D. M., *Robben Island*	S.Africa	Novel
	129	Egudu, R. & D. Nwoga (trans.), *Igbo Trad. Verse*	Nigeria	Poetry
	130	Aluko, T. M., *His Worshipful Majesty*	Nigeria	Novel
	131	Lessing, Doris, *The Grass is Singing* Popular Library	Zimbabwe ⋆	Novel
	132	Bown, Lalage (ed.), *Two Centuries of African English*		Prose
	134	Henderson, Gwynneth (ed.), *African Theatre*		Plays
	135	Maran, René, *Batouala*	Martinique	Novel
	137	Maddy, Pat Amadu, *No Past, No Present, No Future*	Sierra Leone	Novel
	138	Owusu, Martin, *The Sudden Return*	Ghana	Plays
	139	Ruheni, Mwangi, *The Future Leaders*	Kenya	Novel
	140	Amadi, Elechi, *Sunset in Biafra*	Nigeria	Autobio
	141	Nortje, Arthur, *Dead Roots*	S.Africa	Poetry

Year	No.	Author, Title	Country	Genre
	143	Mwangi, Meja, *Kill Me Quick*	Kenya	Novel
	144	Fall, Malick, *The Wound*	Senegal	Novel
1974	136	Sekyi, Kobina, *The Blinkards*	Ghana	Play
	142	Sembene Ousmane, *Tribal Scars*	Senegal	Stories
	145	Mwangi, Meja, *Carcase for Hounds*	Kenya	Novel
	147	Okot p'Bitek, *Horn of My Love*	Uganda	Poetry
	148	Aniebo, I. N. C., *The Anonymity of Sacrifice*	Nigeria	Novel
	149	Head, Bessie, *A Question of Power*	S.Africa ★	Novel
		ZIBF Africa's 100 Best Books		
	152	La Guma, Alex, *The Stone Country*	S.Africa	Novel
	154	Armah, Ayi Kwei, *Fragments*	Ghana	Novel
		Houghton Mifflin Collier-Macmillan pb		
	155	Armah, Ayi Kwei, *Why Are We So Blest?*	Ghana	Novel
		Doubleday		
	158	Kahiga, Samuel, *The Girl from Abroad*	Kenya	Novel
	162	Kayira, Legson, *The Detainee*	Malawi	Novel
	163	Sellassie, Sahle, *Warrior King*	Ethiopia	Novel
	164	Royston, Robert (ed.), *Black Poets in South Africa*	S.Africa	Poetry
1975	133	Mukasa, Ham, *Sir Apolo Kagwa Discovers Britain*	Uganda	Autobio
	146	Ekwensi, Cyprian, *Jagua Nana*	Nigeria	Novel
	150	Ngũgĩ, *Secret Lives*	Kenya	Stories
		Lawrence Hill		
	151	Mahfouz, Naguib, *Midaq Alley*	Egypt	Novel
	153	Munonye, John, *A Dancer of Fortune*	Nigeria	Novel
	156	Ruheni, Mwangi, *The Minister's Daughter*	Kenya	Novel
	157	Kayper-Mensah, A. W., *The Drummer in Our Time*	Ghana	Poetry
	159	Mvungi, Martha, *Three Solid Stones*	Tanzania ★	Oral
	160	Mwase, George Simeon, *Strike a Blow and Die*	Malawi	Autobio
		Harvard University Press		
	161	Djoleto, Amu, *Money Galore*	Ghana	Novel
	165	Etherton, Michael (ed.), *African Plays for Playing*		Plays
	166	de Graft, Joe, *Beneath the Jazz and Brass: Poems*	Ghana	Poetry
	167	Rabéarivelo, Jean-Joseph, *Translations from the Night*	Madagascar	Poetry
	169	Samkange, Stanlake, *The Mourned One*	Zimbabwe	Novel
	170	Mungoshi, Charles, *Waiting For the Rain*	Zimbabwe	Novel
	171	Soyinka, Wole, (ed.) *Poems of Black Africa*		Poetry
		Hill & Wang		
	172	Ekwensi, C. *Restless City & Christmas Gold*	Nigeria	Stories
	173	Nwankwo, Nkem, *My Mercedes is Bigger Than Yours*	Nigeria	Novel
	174	Diop, David Mandessi, *Hammer Blows*	Senegal	Poetry
1976	168	Echewa, T. Obinkaram, *The Land's Lord*	Nigeria	Novel
	175	Sembene Ousmane, *Xala*	Senegal	Novel
	176	Mwangi, Meja, *Going Down River Road*	Kenya	Novel
	177	Gordimer, Nadine, *Some Monday for Sure*	S.Africa ★	Stories
	178	Peteni, R. L., *Hill of Fools*	S.Africa	Novel
	179	Etherton, M., (ed.), *African Plays for Playing 2*		Plays
	180	Senghor, L. S., *Prose and Poetry*	Senegal	Poetry
	184	Farah, Nuruddin, *A Naked Needle*	Somalia	Novel
		HEB Inc Rights withdrawn late 80s Penguin pb		
	185	Ekwensi, Cyprian, *Survive the Peace*	Nigeria	Novel

Year	No.	Author, Title	Country	Genre
	189	Iroh, Eddie, *Forty-Eight Guns for the General*	Nigeria	Novel
1977	182	Head, Bessie, *The Collector of Treasures*	S.Africa ★	Stories
	186	Boateng, Yaw M., *The Return* Pantheon	Ghana	Novel
	187	Rugyendo, Mukotani, *The Barbed Wire*	Tanzania	Plays
	188	Ngũgĩ, *Petals of Blood* Dutton	Kenya	Novel
	191	Ngũgĩ & Mĩcere Mũgo ★, *The Trial of Dedan Kimathi*	Kenya	Play
	192	Jahadhmy, Ali. A. (ed.), *Anthology of Swahili Poetry*	Kenya	Poetry
	264	de Graft, Joe, *Muntu*	Ghana	Play
1978	181	Beti, Mongo, *Perpetua and the Habit of Unhappiness*	Cameroun	Novel
	183	Okara, Gabriel, *The Fisherman's Invocation*	Nigeria	Poetry
	190	Samkange, Stanlake, *Year of the Uprising*	Zimbabwe	Novel
	193	Okot p'Bitek, *Hare and Hornbill*	Uganda	Poetry
	195	Munonye, John, *Bridge to a Wedding*	Nigeria	Novel
	196	Johnson-Davies, Denys (ed. and trans.), *Egyptian Short Stories* Three Continents Press		Stories
	197	Mahfouz, Naguib, *Miramar* Three Continents Press	Egypt	Novel
	201	Plaatje, Sol T., *Mhudi* Three Continents Press	S.Africa	Novel
	202	Vieira, J. Luandino, *The Real Life of Domingos Xavier*	Angola	Novel
	203	Njau, Rebeka, *Ripples in the Pool*	Kenya ★	Novel
	205	Bebey, Francis, *The Ashanti Doll* Lawrence Hill	Cameroun	Novel
	206	Aniebo, I. N. C., *The Journey Within*	Nigeria	Novel
	207	Marechera, Dambudzo, *The House of Hunger* ZIBF Africa's 100 Best Books	Zimbabwe	Fiction
	208	Brutus, Dennis, *Stubborn Hope* Three Continents Press HEB Inc 1993	S.Africa	Poetry
	209	Idris, Yusuf, *The Cheapest Nights* Three Continents Press	Egypt	Stories
	210	Amadi, Elechi, *The Slave*	Nigeria	Novel
1979	194	Armah, Ayi Kwei, *The Healers*	Ghana	Novel
	204	Mulaisho, Dominic, *The Smoke that Thunders*	Zambia	Novel
	211	Kunene, Mazisi, *Emperor Shaka the Great*	S.Africa	Poetry
	212	La Guma, Alex, *Time of the Butcherbird*	S.Africa	Novel
	213	Iroh, Eddie, *Toads of War*	Nigeria	Novel
	215	Wolfers, Michael (ed. and trans.), *Poems from Angola*	Angola	Poetry
	217	Biko, Steve, *I Write What I Like* Harper & Row	S.Africa	Politics
	218	Armah, Ayi Kwei, *Two Thousand Seasons* Third World Press (Chicago)	Ghana	Novel
	219	Kenyatta, Jomo, *Facing Mount Kenya* Random House ZIBF Africa's 100 Best Books	Kenya	Anthropology
	227	Emecheta, Buchi, *The Joys of Motherhood* Braziller HEB Inc 1992 ZIBF Africa's 100 Best Books	Nigeria ★	Novel

Year	No.	Entry	Country	Genre
1980	198	Cabral, A., *Unity and Struggle: Speeches and Writings* Monthly Review Press ZIBF Africa's 100 Best Books	Guinea-Bissau	Politics
	199	Sassine, Williams, *Wirriyamu*	Guinée	Novel
	214	Beti, Mongo, *Remember Ruben* Three Continents Press	Cameroun	Novel
	216	Yirenkyi, Asiedu, *Kivuli*	Ghana	Plays
	221	Cheney-C., Syl *The Graveyard Also Has Teeth*	Sierra Leone	Poetry
	222	Vieira, J. Luandino, *Luuanda*	Angola	Stories
	223	Ghanem, Fathy, *The Man Who Lost his Shadow*	Egypt	Novel
	226	Farah, Nuruddin, *Sweet and Sour Milk* HEB Inc Graywolf pb Penguin pb	Somalia	Novel
	230	Feinberg, Barry (ed.), *Poets to the People*	S.Africa	Poems
	231	Jumbam, Kenjo, *The White Man of God*	Cameroun	Novel
	233	Nyamfukudza, S., *The Non-Believer's Journey*	Zimbabwe	Novel
	237	Marechera, Dambudzo, *Black Sunlight*	Zimbabwe	Novel
1981	220	Head, Bessie, *Serowe: Village of the Rain Wind*	S.Africa ★	Historical
	224	Kente, Gibson, *South African People's Plays*	S.Africa	Plays
	225	Mahfouz, Naguib, *Children of Gebelawi*	Egypt	Novel
	228	Hussein, Taha, *An Egyptian Childhood*	Egypt	Autobio
	229	Mofolo, Thomas, *Chaka* ZIBF Africa's 100 Best Books	Lesotho	Novel
	232	Johnson-Davies, Denys (ed.), *Egyptian One-Act Plays* Three Continents Press		Plays
	234	Kunene, Mazisi, *Anthem of the Decades*	S.Africa	Poetry
	236	Mapanje, Jack, *Of Chameleons and Gods*	Malawi	Poetry
	238	Peters, Lenrie, *Selected Poetry*	Gambia	Poetry
	239	Kourouma, Ahmadou, *The Suns of Independence* Africana Publishing ZIBF Africa's 100 Best Books	C. d'Ivoire	Novel
	240	Ngũgĩ, *Detained: A Writer's Prison Diary*	Kenya	Autobio
	241	Akare, Thomas, *The Slums*	Kenya	Novel
	243	Mutloatse, M., (ed.), *Africa South: Contemporary Writing*	S.Africa	Prose
	248	Bâ, Mariama, *So Long a Letter* ZIBF Africa's 100 Best Books (Cited as one of best 12)	Senegal ★	Novel
	249	Obasanjo, General Olusegun, *My Command*	Nigeria	Autobio
	251	Lewin, Hugh, *Bandiet: Seven Years in a S.A. Prison*	S.Africa	Autobio
1982	200	Ngũgĩ, *Devil on the Cross* ZIBF Africa's 100 Best Books	Kenya	Novel
	235	Kunene, Mazisi, *The Ancestors and the Sacred Mountain*	S.Africa	Poetry
	242	Aluko, T. M., *Wrong Ones in the Dock*	Nigeria	Novel
	244	Ya-Otto, John, *Battlefront Namibia: An Autobiography* Lawrence Hill	Namibia	Autobio
	246	Ngũgĩ & Ngũgĩ, *I Will Marry When I Want*	Kenya	Play
	252	Farah, Nuruddin, *Sardines* Graywolf Press pb	Somalia	Novel
	255	Iroh, Eddie, *The Siren in the Night*	Nigeria	Novel
1983	250	Sembene Ousmane, *The Last of the Empire*	Senegal	Novel
	253	Aniebo, I. N. C., *Of Wives, Talismans and the Dead*	Nigeria	Stories
	254	Scanlon, Paul A. (ed.), *Stories from Central & Southern Africa*		Stories

Year	No.	Author, Title	Country	Genre
	256	Bruner, Charlotte (ed.), *Unwinding Threads*		Stories ★
	257	Calder, A., Mapanje, J. & Pieterse (eds), *Summer Fires*		Poetry
	263	Serote, Mongane Wally, *To Every Birth Its Blood*	S.Africa	Novel
	269	Pepetela [Artur Pestana], *Mayombe*	Angola	Novel
1984	261	Anyidoho, Kofi, *A Harvest of Our Dreams*	Ghana	Poetry
	266	Okot p'Bitek, *Song of Lawino* and *Song of Ocol*	Uganda	Poetry
		ZIBF Africa's 100 Best Books		
	267	Idris, Yusuf, *Rings of Burnished Brass*		
		Three Continents Press	Egypt	Stories
	268	Sepamla, Sipho, *A Ride on the Whirlwind*	S.Africa	Novel
1985	258	Pheto, Molefe, *And Night Fell*	S.Africa	Autobio
	270	Achebe, Chinua & C. L. Innes (eds), *African Short Stories*		Stories
		Rifaat, Alifa, *Distant View of a Minaret*	Egypt ★	Stories
1986	262	Nagenda, John, *The Seasons of Thomas Tebo*	Uganda	Novel
		Amadi, Elechi, *Estrangement*	Nigeria	Novel
		Echewa, T. Obinkaram, *The Crippled Dancer*	Nigeria	Novel
1987		Lopes, Henri, *Tribaliks*	Congo-Brazz	Novel
	247	Head, Bessie, *When Rain Clouds Gather*	S.Africa ★	Novel
		Sembene Ousmane, *Black Docker*	Senegal	Novel
		Rive, Richard, *Buckingham Palace*	S.Africa	Novel
		Tambo, Oliver, *Preparing for Power*	S.Africa	Politics
1988		Achebe, Chinua, *Anthills of the Savannah*	Nigeria	Novel
		Karodia, Farida, *Coming Home and Other Stories*	S.Africa ★	Stories
1989		Anyidoho, K., P. Porter & M. Zimunya (eds), *The Fate of Vultures*		Poetry
		Laing, Kojo B., *Godhorse*	Ghana	Poetry
		Mahjoub, Jamal, *Navigation of a Rainmaker*	Sudan	Novel
		Mungoshi, C. *The Setting Sun and the Rolling World*	Zimbabwe	Stories
		Ngũgĩ, *Matigari*	Kenya	Novel
		Vassanji, M. G., *Gunny Sack*	Kenya	Novel
		Wangusa, Timothy, *Upon This Mountain*	Uganda	Novel
1990		Cheney-Coker, Syl, *Last Harmattan of Alusine Dunbar*	Sierra Leone	Novel
		ZIBF Africa's 100 Best Books		
		Cheney-Coker, Syl, *The Blood in the Desert's Eyes*	Sierra Leone	Poetry
		Chinodya, Shimmer, *Harvest of Thorns*	Zimbabwe	Novel
		Couto, Mia, *Voices Made Night*	Mozambique	Stories
		Gool, Réshard, *Cape Town Coolie*	S.Africa	Novel
		Head, Bessie, *A Woman Alone*	S.Africa ★	Autobio
		Head, Bessie, *Tales of Tenderness and Power*	S.Africa ★	Stories
		Hove, Chenjerai, *Bones*	Zimbabwe	Novel
		ZIBF Africa's 100 Best Books		
		Maja-Pearce, A. *The Heinemann Book of African Poetry in English*		Poetry
1991		Akwanya, Amechi, *Orimili*	Nigeria	Novel
		Chipasula, Frank M., *Whispers in the Wings*	Malawi	Poetry
		Gordimer, Nadine, *Crimes of Conscience*	S.Africa ★	Stories
		Ojaide, Tanure, *Blood of Peace*	Nigeria	Poetry

Year	Author, Title	Country	Genre
1992	Achebe, C. & C.L. Innes, *Book of Contemporary African Short Stories*		Stories
	Bandele-Thomas, Biyi, *The Man Who Came In from the Back of Beyond*	Nigeria	Novel
	Hove, Chenjerai, *Shadows*	Zimbabwe	Novel
	Laing, Kojo B., *Major Gentl & the Achimota Wars*	Ghana	Novel
	Mwangi, Meja, *Striving for the Wind*	Kenya	Novel
	Sembene Ousmane, *Niiwam* and *Taaw*	Senegal	Novel
	Zeleza, Paul Tiyambe, *Smouldering Charcoal*	Zimbabwe	Novel
1993	Bandele-Thomas, Biyi, *The Sympathetic Undertaker & Other Dreams*	Nigeria	Novel
	Botha, W. P. B., *Reluctant Playwright*	S.Africa	Novel
	Bruner, Charlotte (ed.), *The Heinemann Book of African Women's Writing*		Prose *
	Jacobs, Steve, *Under the Lion*	S.Africa	Novel
	Karodia, Farida, *A Shattering of Silence*	S.Africa *	Novel
	Mapanje, Jack *The Chattering Wagtails of Mikuyu Prison*	Malawi	Poetry
	Tuma, Hama, *The Case of the Socialist Witchdoctor*	Ethiopia	Stories
	Vassanji, Moyez G., *Uhuru Street*	Kenya	Stories
1994	Chimombo, Steve, *Napolo and the Python*	Malawi	Poetry
	Couto, Mia, *Every Man Is a Race*	Mozambique	Stories
	Emecheta, Buchi, *Head Above Water*	Nigeria *	Autobio
	Emecheta, Buchi, *Destination Biafra*	Nigeria *	Novel
	Emecheta, Buchi, *Gwendolen*	Nigeria *	Novel
	Emecheta, Buchi, *In the Ditch*	Nigeria *	Novel
	Emecheta, Buchi, *Kehinde*	Nigeria *	Novel
	Emecheta, Buchi, *Second Class Citizen*	Nigeria *	Novel
	Hirson, D., *The Heinemann Book of S. A. Short Stories*	S.Africa	Stories
	Mahjoub, Jamal, *Wings of Dust*	Sudan	Novel
	Sam, Agnes, *Jesus is Indian*	S.Africa	Stories
1995	Beyala, Calixthe, *Loukoum*	Cameroun *	Novel
	Botha, W. P. B., *Wantok*	S.Africa	Novel
	Chipasula, Stella & Frank Chipasula (eds), *The Heinemann Book of African Women's Poetry*	Malawi	Poetry *
	Collen, Lindsey, *The Rape of Sita*	S.Africa *	Novel
	Darko, Amma, *Beyond the Horizon*	Ghana *	Novel
	Emecheta, Buchi, *Slave Girl*	Nigeria *	Novel
	Emecheta, Buchi, *The Bride Price*	Nigeria *	Novel
	Head, Bessie, *The Cardinals with Meditations*	S.Africa *	Stories
	Jacobs, Steve, *The Enemy Within*	S.Africa	Novel
	Sobott-Mogwe, Gaele, *Colour Me Blue*	S.Africa	Stories
	Tansi, Sony L., *The Seven Solitudes of Lorsa Lopez*	Congo	Novel
1996	Accad, Evelyne, *Wounding Words: A Woman's Journal*	Tunisia *	Novel
	Beyala, Calixthe, *Your Name Shall be Tanga*	Cameroun *	Novel
	Beyala, Calixthe, *Sun Hath Looked Upon Me*	Cameroun *	Novel
	Mahjoub, Jamal, *In the Hour of Signs*	Sudan	Novel
	Pepetela [Artur Pestana], *Yaka*	Angola	Novel
	Jacobs, Rayda, *Eyes of the Sky*	S.Africa *	Novel
1997	Botha, W. P. B., *A Duty of Memory*	S.Africa	Novel
1998	Darko, Amma, *The Housemaid*	Ghana *	Novel

	Kanengoni, Alexander, *Echoing Silences*	Zimbabwe	Novel
	King-Aribisala, Karen, *Kicking Tongues*	Guyana	Stories
	Kwakye, Benjamin, *The Clothes of Nakedness*	Ghana	Novel
1999	Vera, Yvonne (ed.), *Opening Spaces*	Zimbabwe ⋆	Prose
2000	Emecheta, Buchi, *The New Tribe*	Nigeria ⋆	Novel
	Ndibe, Okey, *Arrows of Rain*	Nigeria	Novel
	Oguine, Ike, *A Squatter's Tale*	Nigeria	Novel
	Sinyangwe, Binwell, *A Cowrie of Hope*	Zambia	Novel
2001	Aboulela, Leila, *The Translator*	Sudan ⋆	Novel
	Andreas, Neshani, *The Purple Violet of Oshaantu*	Namibia ⋆	Novel
	Chinodya, Shimmer, *Dew in the Morning*	Zimbabwe	Novel
	Chinodya, Shimmer, *Can We Talk*	Zimbabwe	Stories
	Momplé, Lilia, *Neighbours: The Story of a Murder*	Mozambique ⋆	Novel
	Tadjo, Véronique, *As the Crow Flies*	C. d'Ivoire ⋆	Novel
2002	Aidoo, Ama Ata, *The Girl Who Can*	Ghana ⋆	Stories
	Mapanje, Jack (ed.), *Gathering Seaweed*	Malawi	Prose
	Pepetela, *Return of the Water Spirit*	Angola	Novel
	Tadjo, Véronique, *The Shadow of Imana*	C. d'Ivoire ⋆	Novel
2003	Aidoo, Ama Ata, *Changes: A Love Story*	Ghana ⋆	Novel
	Mengara, Daniel, *Mema*	Gabon	Novel

259 Chipasula (editor) *This is the Time* advertised as a prose collection, was numbered 259, but never published. (See Heinemann AWS Catalogue 1983).

260 Awoonor, Kofi, *Until the Morning After: Collected Poems 1963–1985*, 1987 [Note: this title was advertised as AWS number 260, but never published] (See Heinemann AWS Catalogue 1983).

⋆ Women writers. Pages 309 and 310 show, that as the years went on, women gained the confidence that they might also get published. In the early years there are lamentably few books by women. This was not for want of looking. Ros de Lanerolle, later Managing Director of The Women's Press, was always on the look out for promising scripts. The all-woman editorial team in the years 1994–2003 achieved balance.

Index

(Illustrations are shown as italic page numbers)